FORENSIC PSYCHOLOGY, CRIME AND POLICING

Key Concepts and Practical Debates

Edited by

Karen Corteen, Rachael Steele, Noel Cross and
Michelle McManus

D1556696

P

First published in Great Britain in 2023 by

Policy Press, an imprint of
Bristol University Press
University of Bristol
1–9 Old Park Hill
Bristol
BS2 8BB
UK
t: +44 (0)117 374 6645
e: bup-info@bristol.ac.uk

Details of international sales and distribution partners are available at
policy.bristoluniversitypress.co.uk

© Bristol University Press 2023

British Library Cataloguing in Publication Data
A catalogue record for this book is available from the British Library

ISBN 978-1-4473-5938-8 hardcover
ISBN 978-1-4473-5939-5 paperback
ISBN 978-1-4473-5940-1 ePub
ISBN 978-1-4473-5941-8 ePdf

The right of Karen Corteen, Rachael Steele, Noel Cross and Michelle McManus to be
identified as editors of this work has been asserted by them in accordance with the Copyright,
Designs and Patents Act 1988.

Cover design: Nicky Borowiec
Front cover image: adobestock/kurkalukas
Bristol University Press and Policy Press use environmentally responsible
print partners.
Printed and bound in Great Britain by CPI Group (UK) Ltd, Croydon, CR0 4YY

FSC
www.fsc.org
MIX
Paper | Supporting
responsible forestry
FSC® C013604

Contents

Contents

Contents

Contents

Contents

Contents

List of abbreviations

AA	appropriate adult
ACEs	adverse childhood experiences
ASPD	anti-social personality disorder
BAI	behavioural analysis interview
BPS	British Psychological Society
CAADA	Co-ordinated Action Against Domestic Abuse
CCRC	Criminal Case Review Commission
CI	cognitive interview
CJJI	Criminal Justice Joint Inspection
CJS	criminal justice system
CoP	College of Policing
CPS	Crown Prosecution Service
CSEW	Crime Survey for England and Wales
DAT	defensive attribution theory
DPH	directors of public health
DSM	Diagnostic and Statistical Manual of Mental Disorders
DT	dark triad
DTC	District Training Centre (six districts across England and Wales, North East/North West/Midlands/South East/South West/Wales)
EBP	evidence-based policing
FCAMHS	Forensic Child and Adolescent Mental Health Service
FMHS	Forensic Mental Health Services
FMIT	Force Major Investigation Teams
FPN	fixed penalty notice
FSS	Forensic Science Service
HCPC	Health and Care Professions Council
HE	higher education
HEIs	higher education institutions
HMICFRS	HM Inspectorate of Constabulary (and) Fire and Rescue Services
IACP	International Association of Chiefs of Police
ICMHP	Independent Commission on Mental Health and Policing
ICVA	Independent Custody Visiting Association
ICVS	Independent Custody Visiting Scheme
IDVA	independent domestic violence advisor
ILP	intelligence-led policing
IOPC	Independent Office for Police Conduct
IPLDP	Initial Police Learning and Development Programme (pre-PEQF)
ISO	International Organization for Standardization

JWB	just world beliefs
KBP	knowledge-based policing
KIRAT	Kent Internet Risk Assessment Tool
LRFs	Local Resilience Forums
MAPPAs	multi-agency public protection arrangements
MARACs	Multi-Agency Risk Assessment Conferences
MASHs	Multi-Agency Safeguarding Hubs
MCIS	Major Crime Investigative Support
ME	micro expressions
MHA	Mental Health Act
MHT	mental health tribunal
MMPI	Minnesota Multiphasic Personality Inventory
MO	modus operandi
MOJ	Ministry of Justice
MOSOVO	management of sexual or violent offenders
MPV	Mapping Police Violence
NCA	National Crime Agency
NDM	national decision model
NGRI	not guilty by reason of insanity
NHS	National Health Service
NLP	neurolinguistic programming
NPCC	National Police Chiefs' Council
NPOIU	National Public Order Intelligence Unit
NVC	non-verbal communication
OBPs	offending behaviour programmes
ONS	Office for National Statistics
OPD	offender personality disorder
PACA	Police and Crime Act
PACE	Police and Criminal Evidence Act
PCC	police and crime commissioner
PCP	Police and Crime Panel
PD	personality disorder
PEACE	Preparation and Planning, Engage and Explain, Account and Clarification, Closure and Evaluation
PEQF	Police Education Qualifications Framework
PIP	Professionalising Investigation Programme
PIPEs	psychologically informed planned environments
PME	post-mortem examination
PPUs	Public Protection Units
PTSD	post-traumatic stress disorder
RNR	risk-need-responsivity
RSU	Regional Secure Unit
SARA	Scanning, Analysis, Response and Assessment
SCAS	Serious Crime Analysis Section

SDS	Special Demonstration Squad
SIDS	self-inflicted deaths
SIO	senior investigating officer
SMI	serious mental illness
SOTP	Sex Offenders Treatment Programme
SPJ	structured professional judgement
SSRIs	selective serotonin reuptake inhibitors
SUE	Strategic Use of Evidence
SVA	Statement Validity Analysis
TC	Therapeutic Community
TCSEW	Telephone-Operated Crime Survey for England and Wales
UCPI	Undercover Policing Inquiry
UN	United Nations
VA	Verifiability Approach
ViCLAS	Violent Crime Linkage Analysis System
VRUs	Violence Reduction Units
YJB	Youth Justice Board

Glossary

Actus reus	The term (literally meaning 'guilty act') used to describe the external behaviour, circumstances, omission or state of being which is prohibited by a criminal offence forming part of English criminal law.
Bedlam	Nickname for the famous Bethlem Mental Health Hospital.
Behavioural investigative advisor	An advisor, usually a psychologist, who gives specific investigative advice on criminal behaviour.
Behavioural profiling	Form of profiling which draws on psychological knowledge such as research on personality theory and use this insight and, where appropriate, experience of working with previous forensic cases, to make predictions as to the offender's nature and future behaviour.
Case formulation	Process of evaluating predisposing, precipitating, perpetuating and protective factors to assist in understanding why the person offended.
Case linkage	Where two or more previously unrelated cases can be linked together based on similarities such as those seen at the crime scene, behavioural indicators and distinctiveness.
Cognition	The mental processes involved in acquiring knowledge and understanding through the senses, thought and experience.
Cognitive interview	A toolkit of techniques used (for example, by the police) to help the interviewee mentally reinstate the memory to improve accuracy and number of details recalled.
Complainant	Individual bringing their case to court.
Confirmation bias	The searching or favouring of evidence that fits an investigator's preconceived set of theories, values or beliefs.
Cross-examination	The process of evidence-giving in an adversarial criminal trial where a witness is questioned by the opposing legal counsel, with the aim of revealing inconsistencies, weaknesses or a lack of credibility in relation to the witness's evidence.
CSI effect	Where the portrayal of forensic science in television shows such as *CSI* can influence public perception, including that of offenders.

Dangerousness	An older term which was used to describe a person's propensity to cause serious physical injury or lasting psychological harm.
Dark triad	Three distinct yet overlapping personality traits: narcissism, Machiavellianism and psychopathy.
Defendant	Individual who is accused and is defending their innocence at court.
Desistance	Process of moving away from offending, usually characterised by a graduated and complex process, rather than a linear change.
Displaced aggression	Aggression towards an innocent victim not responsible for any provocation.
Equivocal deaths	Where a manner of death is ambiguous and could equally be attributed to a homicide, suicide or accident.
Examination-in-chief	The process of evidence-giving in an adversarial criminal trial where a witness is questioned by the legal counsel representing the party for whom the witness is appearing.
Extroversion	Measure of personality referring to someone who is outgoing, social and enjoys being with people rather than being alone. Scale opposite to introversion.
Eyewitness testimony	Evidence given in court, or in a police interview, by a witness of a crime.
Forensic awareness	Where an offender is knowledgeable enough about forensic science to avoid leaving evidence behind that could link them to the crime.
Globalisation	The impact of the increasing homogeneity of global economies on national politics and culture.
Green crime	Crimes which harm the environment and can include such diverse activities as trade in endangered species, illegal fishing and illegal disposal of toxic waste.
Health and Care Professions Council (HCPC)	HCPC oversees the professional practice of practice-based psychologists and other health professionals.
Heuristics	The mental shortcuts that humans use to make decisions quickly and generally efficiently, which can lead to inaccurate or biased decision making and judgment errors called cognitive biases.
Human rights	Human rights are based on values such as dignity, fairness, equality, respect and independence. They are the fundamental rights and freedoms that belong to every individual globally. Although human rights are defined and protected by law, they can in some instances be restricted.

Introversion	Measure of personality referring to someone who is inward facing, shy or prefer the inner life rather than external stimulation. Scale opposite for extroversion.
Managerialism	The reduction of the role of the state and public expenditure and the increase in managerial techniques and practices. Regarding criminal justice and other public sector services there is a belief that changes in management and management techniques would increase efficiency, lower costs and improve performance.
Mens rea	The term (literally meaning 'guilty mind') used to describe the internal mindset which, when combined with *actus reus*, is prohibited by some criminal offences forming part of English criminal law (including intention, recklessness or negligence, or none, depending on the offence).
Miscarriage of justice	An unfair judicial outcome secondary to flaws in legal proceedings resulting in an innocent person being convicted of a crime.
Modus operandi	The method of carrying out a crime.
Multi-Agency Safeguarding Hubs (MASH)	MASH representatives from a range of services, which may include the police, probation services, social services and more, gather to discuss serious cases and plan to support victims.
Narcissism	Personality trait represented by persons who exhibit behaviour that is selfish and boastful, and who have low empathy, are very sensitive to criticism and have a general entitled nature.
Naturalistic decision making	A group of theories which examine how people (particularly experts) make decisions in real-world situations defined by ill-structured problems, in uncertain, time-pressured and dynamic environments with shifting or competing goals and high stakes.
Neoliberalism	A political approach which favours competition, deregulation and reduced government spending.
Non-fatal violence	Crimes whereby the individuals involved are injured, but the injuries are not fatal.
Nudge approach	Using psychology to influence the behaviour of offenders and potential victims into behaving more pro-socially.
Offending behaviour programme (OBP)	Programme of intervention designed to alter or address offending behaviours.

Pains of imprisonment	The 'pains of imprisonment' was coined by Gresham Sykes (in 1958) to encapsulate the inherent deprivations of prison life for men in prison. The five fundamental deprivations that Sykes contended characterised daily prison life were the loss of liberty, desirable goods and services, heterosexual relationships, autonomy and security. Contemporarily these 'pains' have been added to and it has been acknowledged that women experience additional pains because of their gender.
Parole	Process for discussing and possibly granting early release of a prisoner based on good behaviour or positive change.
PEACE	Police model for interviewing to ensure good practice and avoid false confession and so on. It stands for Preparation and Planning, Engage and Explain, Account and Clarification, Closure and Evaluation.
Plural policing	The policing role being fragmented and being conducted by other private actors.
Post-traumatic stress disorder (PTSD)	Mental health disorder caused by a traumatic experience that can be extremely distressing and debilitating.
Psychometric test	A test based on research evidence designed to assess an attitude, belief and so on at that point in time.
Psychopath	A psychological construct that can be defined by manipulation, shallowness, lying and a total lack of empathy and conscience.
Recidivism	The tendency towards reoffending of a convicted criminal.
Rehabilitation	Process of restoring a former offender to the community, to good citizenship or to normal life.
Restricted patient	Hospital patient, usually in a special hospital, subject to specific controls by the Ministry of Justice.
Risk	A complex construct with numerous possible definitions. The ISO 31000 defines it as the effect of uncertainty on objectives and emphasises that risk can be both positive and negative.
Risk assessment	A process for identifying and evaluating risk and protective factors to inform risk-management planning.
Risk management	Identifying and managing potential risks to minimise potential negative impact. This may be through meaningful, coordinated activities, interventions or procedures which support the minimisation of harm and reduction of negative risk(s).

Risk-need-responsivity (RNR) model	A model of delivery of services which asserts that to be effective an intervention should match the person's risk (level of service/intervention should match the person's level of risk of reoffending), need (assess risk-related needs and target these in the treatment) and responsivity (provide treatment that is tailored to the individual needs of the person).
Self-selection policing	An approach by which police can identify active, serious offenders from the minor offences they commit.
Signature behaviour	Acts carried out by the offender during the commission of a crime that are not required to complete the crime, but are done to meet an intrinsic, psychological need.
Special hospitals	Also known as secure hospitals, these facilities are dedicated to treating and housing those who have committed offences and are suffering from mental disorders that mean they are not suitable for inclusion within the general prison population.
Statistical profiling	A mathematical technique to establish linked behaviours within different crimes.
Therapeutic Community	A lengthy intervention, overseen by a psychologist, where offenders can access therapy to help address those factors that contributed to risk of offending and other problems within a supportive group.
Threatened egotism	Potential response of a narcissist when positive views of themselves are questioned, challenged, mocked and so on; they may respond aggressively, particularly against the source of the threat.
Triage	The prioritisation of cases. It entails the sorting and allocation of cases based on an assessment of the degree of urgency. In medical cases or in disaster situations this means assigning treatment to individuals based on their injuries, wounds or illnesses. Street triage comprises prioritising emergency and non-emergency cases.
Victim typologies	A way to categorise victims based on commonalities across a range of characteristics including demographics, social, psychological, psychiatric and biological features.
Voir dire	A hearing within a criminal trial to determine whether evidence can be admitted as part of the trial, or to determine the reliability of a witness or juror in the trial.

| Witness testimony | The account a bystander or victim provides to the police or court, describing what they observed during a specific incident. |
| Wrongdoing | Refers to inappropriate and harmful behaviour and behaviour that is potentially illegal. |

Notes on contributors

Davut Akca has a PhD in forensic psychology and an MA in criminology. He is a research officer in the Centre for Forensic Behavioural Science and Justice Studies at the University of Saskatchewan. Dr Akca's research interests fall within the domains of investigative interviewing, gangs, programme evaluation, radicalisation and hate crimes. Before his graduate studies, he served as a ranked police officer and crime analyst at the Anti-Organized Crimes Department of the Turkish National Police for five years. He has published works on investigative interviewing, police personality, crime mapping, hate crimes, radicalisation and technical reports on programme evaluations within the criminal justice system (CJS).

Cherie Armour is Professor of Psychological Trauma and Mental Health at Queens University Belfast. Cherie is the Director of the Research Centre for Stress, Trauma and Related Conditions. Her publication profile is centred on the psychological consequences of traumatic life experiences, particularly those of an interpersonal nature such as childhood maltreatment and intimate partner violence. Her work also focuses on those who experience trauma as part of their occupation, for example, those in the military or police, or healthcare workers. Cherie is past President of the UK Psychological Trauma Society and Associate Editor of the *European Journal of Psychotraumatology*.

Charlotte Barlow is Reader in Criminal Justice and Policing at the University of Central Lancashire. Her areas of research expertise are domestic and sexual violence, policing and, more broadly, violence against women and girls. She has led various externally funded research projects and published widely in these fields. Impact is central to her research. Charlotte's work on domestic abuse has been used to inform policy developments and professional practice and she regularly collaborates with practitioners and professionals through her research.

Kate Bates is Senior Lecturer in Criminal Justice in the School of Justice Studies at Liverpool John Moores University (LJMU). She has extensive experience of criminal justice, having served as both a police officer and a civilian caseworker investigating police complaints. She has also served as a panel member for Children's Hearings Scotland. Her teaching expertise and research interests include policing, victimology and the history of crime and criminal justice.

Sean Bell is an experienced former police inspector who acted as an advocate for officers with physical and mental health issues. He is a lecturer in policing organisation and practice in the Faculty of Business and Law at the Open University, UK. His research and publications cover police culture and attitudes to mental ill health in policing.

Mike Berry is Professor in the Psychology Department at LJMU. He is also a consultant chartered clinical forensic psychologist and an associate fellow of the British Psychological Society (BPS). Formerly an NHS Consultant Clinical Psychologist, Senior Lecturer in Forensic Psychology at Manchester Metropolitan University, Visiting Professor of Forensic Psychology at Dublin Business School, Honorary Senior Lecturer at the Royal College of Surgeons of Ireland and a Visiting Professor at Birmingham City University, he has over thirty years' clinical experience and has published widely (see Researchgate). He has appeared in magistrates courts through to the Court of Appeal.

Victoria Blinkhorn is Lecturer in Forensic Psychology at LJMU and a principal research consultant for the NHS and National Probation Service. Her research interests include the understanding of criminal behaviour, personality disorders, mental illnesses, anti-social behaviour, criminal profiling and offender management. Victoria has many publications in journals such as *Personality and Individual Differences*, *Social Psychology*, *European Journal of Probation* and *Deviant Behaviour*.

Laura Boulton is Senior Lecturer in Policing Studies in the School of Justice Studies at LJMU. Her research and publications cover a range of policing-related topics, including firearms, missing from home, serious organised crime and police demand, as well as decision making and expertise. Her specific interest lies in providing an evidence base upon which policing practice can be informed. Her current research focuses on police enforcement of COVID-19 powers in the UK.

Lol Burke is Professor in Criminal Justice at LJMU and specialises in the areas of probation research, policy and practice. He has a particular interest in the impact of marketisation upon service delivery and the way that occupational culture acts out in probation settings as well resettlement provision for released prisoners. He has published extensively on probation-related issues and rehabilitation in general and is co-author of *Redemption, Rehabilitation and Risk Management* (Routledge, 2012), *Delivering Rehabilitation: The Politics, Governance and Control of Probation* (Routledge, 2015) and *Reimagining Rehabilitation: Beyond the Individual* (Routledge, 2019).

Ellena Cooke is Principal Psychologist at HMYOI Feltham, a young offenders' institute which houses male young people/adults aged between 15 and 21, based just outside London. She has worked with children and young people who have had contact with or are at risk of contact with the CJS in both community and custodial settings, and she is interested in the traumatising effects of the CJS.

Karen Corteen is Senior Lecturer in Criminal Justice at Liverpool John Moores University. Her research and publications cover critical criminology, victimology, crime, harm and victimisation. This includes an interest in state-corporate crime, particularly in relation to professional wrestling and sports entertainment. Her current research focuses on professional wrestling and COVID-19. Karen has many publications and is co-editor of four books in the Companions in Criminology and Criminal Justice series (Policy Press, 2014–17).

Noel Cross is Programme Leader in Law and Criminal Justice at Liverpool John Moores University. He became a programme leader in 2011. He has worked at LJMU since 2002 and holds degrees in law and criminology from Oxford and Swansea universities. His research interests include the links between criminalisation, criminal law and criminal justice, youth justice, zemiology, crime and power. He is the author of *Criminal Law and Criminal Justice* (Sage, 2010), *Law Express: Criminology* (Pearson, 2012) and, most recently, *Criminal Law for Criminologists* (Routledge, 2020).

Stephanie Davies has over 15 years' experience as a coroner's officer, where she has investigated over 5000 deaths on behalf of the police and the coroner. She has degrees in psychology, forensic behavioural science and forensic science, and she is researching a PhD in equivocal death investigation at the University of Liverpool. She has also completed training in the US in bloodstain pattern analysis, advanced homicide investigation, investigating staged crime scenes and psychological autopsy investigation. Her aim is to establish a fully holistic approach towards death investigation, utilising a number of different disciplines.

Ava Green is a chartered psychologist and Lecturer in Forensic Psychology at City University of London. Her research interests include gender differences in personality disorders and traits, criminal behaviour, assessment, clinical diagnosis and treatment. Her current research focuses particularly on female narcissism and offending behaviours. Ava's research has been published in peer-reviewed journals, such as *Personality and Individual Differences* (2020) and *Open Sage* (2019), and in media outlets, including 'PsyPost' (2020) and 'The Conversation' (2019).

Paul V. Greenall is a registered forensic psychologist and a fellow of the UK Higher Education Academy. Dr Greenall works clinically within an NHS forensic mental health service, where he specialises in the assessment and formulation of violent crime, with a particular focus on sexual violence. Dr Greenall's areas of interest include mental disorder and crime, violence risk assessment, sexual offending involving strangers, index offence analysis and the application of forensic psychology to criminal investigations. He has several publications in these areas and periodically delivers lectures on these topics to postgraduate forensic psychology students.

Eric Halford is Assistant Professor in Policing and Security Studies at Rabdan Academy in the United Arab Emirates. He is on five-year career break from his service as a detective chief inspector within the UK Police Service, where his role was Head of Vulnerability and Investigation within a provincial policing area. As an academic he has conducted research publications into topics including the risk and response of repeat missing children, the use of innovative learning methods within policing, and the impact of COVID-19 and crime.

Robert Hesketh is Lecturer in Criminal Justice at LJMU; in addition he has taught at the University of Chester and Edge Hill University. His research interests are multidisciplinary, focusing on areas of critical criminology, forensic psychology and criminal justice. Robert has published widely in academia and in the mainstream media on street gang membership, the topic that formed the basis for his PhD and his forthcoming monograph.

Amy Hughes–Stanley is Lecturer in Criminal Justice at LJMU. Amy's research interests include women's imprisonment, practices of prison body searching, sexual violence and state crime and harm. Amy's PhD research, undertaken at the University of Liverpool, investigates women's experiences of body searching in prisons in England and Wales from a feminist critical criminological perspective. Importantly, Amy's research pioneers the study of body-searching technologies for women and explores the contribution of prison body searching to the gendered pains of imprisonment and state-inflicted sexual violence.

Vesa Huotari is a senior researcher at the Police University College of Finland. Generally, his research interests are around questions of methodology, administration, management, leadership and education. He believes in joint learning, built upon feedback and the open exchange of ideas, experiences and insights, across fields and borders of all kinds.

Adrian James is Reader in Police Studies at the Liverpool Centre for Advanced Policing Studies, LJMU. A former police detective, Adrian principally researches and publishes on the subjects of criminal investigation and criminal intelligence. Adrian has led research projects sponsored by the College of Policing (CoP), the National Police Chiefs' Council (NPCC) and the Home Office. His publications cover European police cooperation, intelligence-led policing, police reform and criminal intelligence. His current research focuses on the proportionality and the necessity tests applied to the police's use of informers.

Nick Kealey is an advanced practitioner fellow at LJMU. He is an experienced former Merseyside police sergeant who led the police team at North Liverpool Community Justice Centre from 2010 to 2014. Here he worked closely with a variety of agencies, including Mersey Care NHS, as part of a multi-agency partnership to identify and improve the support available to service users and those with mental ill health who found themselves in the CJS as offender, victim or witness.

Tim Kelly is Lecturer at LJMU. Following a thirty-year career in the police, Tim has worked on the policing programmes since 2016. He is a member of the CoP Initial Policing Education Board as an academic advisor. Tim is currently researching the ongoing professionalisation of the police; his other research interests include safeguarding children and adults, policing mental health and multi-agency team working. Previously he has contributed to the review of the Troubled Families Programme and, more recently, the direct entry of detectives into the police.

Stephanie Kewley is Reader in Forensic Psychology at LJMU. The central focus of her research and publications is to advocate and promote the safe and healthy functioning of marginalised and highly stigmatised populations involved and/or incarcerated by criminal justice structures and systems. Her research explores the unique lived experiences of these 'hidden' populations, for example, people with sexually violent criminal histories, victims of sexual abuse, people in recovery from addiction, refugees in the Middle East and incarcerated women in sub-Saharan Africa.

Tammy Landau is Associate Professor in the Department of Criminology at Ryerson University, Toronto. She has been a consultant to federal, provincial and local governments on a wide range of criminological issues. Her current research and publishing interests include police accountability and governance, critical criminology and victimology.

Gary Macpherson is a consultant forensic clinical psychologist in the NHS who practises independently as an expert witness. He is Professor of Forensic and Legal Psychology in the Netherlands. He has presented expert evidence in the UK and Europe and was cited as the 'leading forensic psychologist' by the President of the Supreme Courts. His clinical interests and research publications involve clinical risk assessment and expert evidence. He was awarded a fellowship of the BPS in recognition of over 20 years of expert psychological evidence to the courts.

Margaret S. Malloch is Professor of Criminology at the University of Stirling and Associate Director of the Scottish Centre for Crime and Justice Research. Her work aims to challenge carceral and punitive responses to 'crime' and to work towards collective action for change. She has published on topics that include gender and justice, crime, critique and utopia, communities of recovery and state responses to human trafficking.

Michelle McManus is Professor of Safeguarding and Violence Prevention at Manchester Metropolitan University, with research expertise in child criminal exploitation, children safeguarding, domestic abuse, multi-agency working and, more specifically, county lines exploitation and serious youth violence risk. Michelle is the Western Europe Research Lead for 'Envisaging the Future of

Policing and Public Health Globally' as part of the Centre for Law Enforcement and Public Health. Previously, Michelle was the National Research Lead for Public Health and Policing at Public Health Wales, leading the Police and Adverse Childhood Experiences evaluation. Michelle's PhD co-created the Kent Internet Risk Assessment Tool (KIRAT), an intelligence tool used by law enforcement in prioritising indecent-image offenders most likely to be contact sexually abusing, now used across 24 EU countries as well as Canada, New Zealand and Australia.

Monique Moffa is Associate Lecturer in Criminology and Justice Studies at Royal Melbourne Institute of Technology (RMIT) University and Monique is the Assistant Manager of the Bridge of Hope initiative at the same university. Monique's research interests focus on wrongful conviction, parole and the reintegration of individuals who have experienced a miscarriage of justice. Monique is also a PhD student at Monash University focusing on defendant experiences of plea negotiations.

Jennifer Murray is Associate Professor at Edinburgh Napier University and an associate fellow of and chartered member of the BPS. She is an active researcher in the areas of forensic psychology and applied health research, with an overarching theme of decision science pulling these two areas together. She is passionate about developing useful, theoretically sound interventions and outputs from her research. In her forensic psychology work, Jennifer's main research interests lie in practitioner decision making in risk assessment, and, most recently, she has been active in research across the law enforcement and public health intersect.

Sue Palmer-Conn recently retired from a 45-year, award-winning career in academia. Her interest in forensic psychology led her to work with applied psychology, policing, criminal justice and criminology departments in a number of universities around the UK. Sue's knowledge of false memory is now being put to good use with some of her clients in her new career as a divorce coach.

Elizabeth-Jane Peatfield is Senior Lecturer in Policing at LJMU. Her research looks at the issue of racial identity and the effect of policy in the presentation of risk within the counterterrorism narrative. Her current research explores the experiences of Black and Asian police officers focusing on master status shifts. Her research interests include counterterrorism policy, race, radicalisation, identity, victimology and harm. Her latest co-authored journal article is concerned with policy-based evidence making in relation to assembling and deconstructing radicalisation in PREVENT (Critical Social Policy, 2017).

Nicoletta Policek is Professor in Policing and Criminology and Head of Social Policy, Sociology and Criminology at the University of Salford, UK. Her scholarly interests and her many publications are in the broad field of critical criminology, victimology, penology, gender and sexuality studies, migration and criminal and social justice. More specifically, she is concerned with the policing and the criminalisation of migration and the criminalisation of statelessness. Currently she is engaged on the following research endeavours ethics in policing, enforced mobility and abortion rights, victimisation of migrant women in prison settings, criminalisation of stateless children and women.

Andy Rhodes is the former Chief Constable of Lancashire Constabulary and for ten years he was the NPCC lead for wellbeing, staff engagement and organisational development. His policing background was in uniform and specialist operations disciplines including Counter Terrorism Firearms Command. He was awarded the Queen's Police Medal in 2016 and has an MBA. Andy has worked with experts from across policing and academia setting up the National Police Wellbeing Service – Oscar Kilo www.oscarkilo.org.uk, which serves 200,000 law enforcement professionals. Andy is now Service Director for the National Police Wellbeing Service.

Jason Roach is Professor of Psychology and Policing and Director of the Applied Criminology and Policing Centre, at the University of Huddersfield. He is also Editor-in-Chief for the *Police Journal* and a chartered psychologist. Jason has co-authored four books, including *Self-Selection Policing* and *Decision Making in Police Inquiries and Critical Incidents: What Really Works?* (Palgrave Macmillan, 2019). Jason has written over forty research papers and book chapters covering a wide range of crime and policing topics. He previously worked for the UK Home Office, Manchester University, the Open University and different psychiatric and mental health services in the North of England.

Shona Robinson–Edwards is a teaching fellow in criminology at the University of Warwick. Shona's research and publications are centred on race, rehabilitation, religion and desistance. This includes the exploration of the role of religion in the lives of individuals convicted of violent offences. Shona's current research focuses on rehabilitative practices and trajectories of desistance, specifically looking at examining prisoner experiences of rehabilitative practices such as equine-assisted psychotherapy, the arts and religious identity.

Helen Selby–Fell is Senior Lecturer in the Faculty of Business and Law at the Open University, UK. Her research interests and publications cover various areas of policing and forensic psychology, including 'evidence-based policing' (EBP), decision making and police–academic partnerships. This includes an interest in the challenges associated with embedding EBP in the police service. Her current research focuses on senior decision making (in the police service) in the context of the COVID-19 pandemic. Prior to her appointment as senior lecturer, Helen has almost 15 years' experience in the police service, where she held various senior police staff roles.

David Sheldon is a teaching associate at the University of Bristol. David's research interests include prison sociology, prison violence, sexual offenders and questions of legitimacy in prisons and in the police service. David has some notable publications on the sexual offender hierarchy in *Criminology & Criminal Justice* (2019) and an article discussing the problems of policing a pandemic published in the *King's Law Journal* (2021).

Rachael Steele is Programme Leader for the BSc in Forensic Psychology and Criminal Justice at LJMU. A chartered psychologist, Rachael spent over 15 years within the Probation Service working with staff and offenders in various capacities, carrying out applied research into subjects as diverse as desistance and impact of cognitive behavioural interventions of reoffending. Rachael teaches forensic psychology at undergraduate level and also leads on the undergraduate dissertation module. She is currently working on a book around decision-making theory and crime, and she has published on a range of related areas.

Greg Stratton is Lecturer in Justice and Legal Studies at RMIT University and also Manager of the Bridge of Hope Innocence Initiative at the same university. Stratton's research interests focus on wrongful conviction, state crime, media and crime and identity in the digital age. In pursuing these interests under a broader social justice agenda, he has conducted research across a range of interdisciplinary fields including criminology, sociology, marketing and education.

Ruth J. Tully is a consultant forensic psychologist and clinical lead of Tully Forensic Psychology Ltd, where she and her team of expert forensic and clinical psychologists work throughout the UK in the provision of psychological assessment, treatment/therapy, consultancy and training. Dr Tully's wider experience includes working with adults and young people in secure healthcare, social care, prison and community settings. She has an active research, publication and public-speaking profile. Dr Tully is considered a leading authority on violence and sex offender risk assessment in relation to research, clinical work and training professionals.

Jo Turner is Associate Professor of Criminology and Head of Department for Criminology, Policing and Forensic Science at Staffordshire University, UK. Her research and publications are in the broad field of the history of crime and punishment, principally around female offending in the past and reactions to that offending. Jo is currently researching disability and the modern prison system supported by the British Academy. Jo is co-editor for the Companions in Criminology and Criminal Justice series published by Policy Press and lead editor for *A Companion to the History of Crime and Criminal Justice* (Policy Press, 2017).

Clea Wright is Senior Lecturer in Forensic Psychology at the University of Chester. Her research and publications are related mainly to investigative psychology, in particular deception and detection of deception, and investigative interviewing. Current projects include investigating deception in police suspect interviews, understanding of the police caution, aspects of effective investigative interviewing and disclosure of evidence, the use of summaries in police interviews and how deception is detected across different channels of communication. Clea has published in various journals including the *Journal of Investigative Psychology and Offender Profiling* (2017) and the *Personality and Social Psychology Bulletin* (2018).

Acknowledgements

The editors would like to extend their thanks to Rebecca Tomlinson, Becky Taylor and Freya Trand, together with the production editor and team and all the staff at Policy Press, for their interest and continued support for this edited collection. Thanks also to the reviewers, commissioned by Policy Press, for their generous insights. The reviewers' comments and the comments from the publishing committee at Policy Press have helped to make this edited collection what it is – a unique and original contribution to the areas of forensic psychology, crime and policing.

Thanks are also extended to the authors, who between them have produced 55 chapters. Working with national and international colleagues, new and experienced, from a variety of backgrounds has been a rewarding experience. Many of the authors occupy a range of positions and collectively these include academics, centre directors, research officers and consultants, former police officers and inspectors and former and practising psychologists, to name a few.

Finally, thanks to students, colleagues inside and outside of academia and family and friends who have expressed an interest in and their support for this edited collection. That means so much.

Preface

Forensic Psychology, Crime and Policing: Key Concepts and Practical Debates was a response to the formation of a new School of Justice Studies at Liverpool John Moores University. It was also a response to the increasing popularity and growth of forensic psychology, crime and policing inside and outside of academia, and within and without the UK. This is evidenced by increasing media and social media representations of these areas. Such interest, for better or worse, is continually stoked by media representations that include documentaries, films, TV dramas, TV soaps, the true crime genre and the news, online or otherwise. This is also or even more so the case regarding forensic psychology. There is a growth of media representations that depict gruesome and violent crimes including homicide, crime scene investigations, forensic evidence gathering, offender profiling and witness testimonies. Often these representations comprise misrepresentations. Therefore, many of these areas are addressed in the edited collection. Simultaneously, within academia a growth of academic programmes, modules and journals related to forensic psychology, crime and policing has been witnessed in England and Wales and further afield.

The edited collection thus comprises a valuable, original and unique resource for students, educators, trainers, researchers and practitioners interested in forensic psychology, crime and policing and related concepts and practice debates. It reflects the distinctiveness of the areas together with the simultaneous overlap and convergence of these areas inside and outside of academia. It also reflects the diversity of individuals occupying these spaces, including those who have contributed to this edited collection. The authors occupy a range of positions and collectively these include academics, centre directors, research officers and consultants, former police officers and inspectors and former and practising psychologists to name a few.

Forensic Psychology, Crime and Policing: Key Concepts and Practical Debates provides an edited collection that is a pedagogically and scholarly robust reflection of contemporary topics, concepts and practical debates related to forensic psychology, crime and policing. The aim of this edited collection is to bring together the popular and growing areas of forensic psychology, crime and policing. It provides a selection of 55 chapters that are pivotal to key concepts and practice debates regarding forensic psychology, forensic psychology and crime, and forensic psychology, policing and policing studies. Each chapter provides a succinct definition of the topic/concept together with a description and overview of it, an evaluation of the topic/concept and a summary of the chapter. Relevant chapters from within the edited collection and key readings are provided to guide the reader to other key sources from inside and outside academia.

Forensic Psychology, Crime and Policing: Key Concepts and Practical Debates is made up of four parts. Part I includes chapters related to forensic psychology and forensic psychology and crime, victims, and branches and processes of the criminal justice system. The final two chapters explore forensic psychology past and present and the future directions of forensic psychology. Part II is dedicated to crime and criminal justice. It includes chapters that explore crime, crime and youth justice, crimes of the powerful, risk and vulnerability, criminal injustices and criminal justice and punishment. In keeping with Part I, Part II provides two final chapters on crime and criminal justice past and present and the future directions of criminal justice. Part III comprises chapters related to police and policing. This includes key areas and debates such as police and policing models, police accountability and legitimacy, police and victims, controversial areas in policing such as undercover policing and police abolitionism. Mirroring Parts I and II, this section ends with two chapters which examine policing past and present and policing futures. The penultimate section of this edited collection is Part IV. This provides insights into criminal false confessions, false allegations and wrongful convictions, crime scene investigations, detecting deception, expert evidence and witness testimony. Finally, Part V concludes with an overview of contemporary and future concepts and debates in the areas of forensic psychology, crime and policing.

In essence, *Forensic Psychology, Crime and Policing: Key Concepts and Practical Debates* brings something truly unique to this area. Rather than being a traditional theoretical textbook or an introductory guide this edited collection stands alone in not only bringing together the different disciplines in the study of forensic psychology, crime and policing, but also in that its content is themed, accessible, comprehensive and contemporary. Where the fields of forensic psychology, crime and policing are distinct and where they overlap and converge can be discerned in the edited collection. Furthermore, in order to bridge the gap between academics, policy makers and practitioners the chapters are underpinned by academic research including psychological, criminal justice, criminological and policing research. Finally, what sets this edited collection apart is its breadth, depth, brevity and the themed integration of the chapters. This will be invaluable to students, educators, trainers, scholars and practitioners within any of the covered areas who would like to learn more about the wider themed and integrated topic areas.

Karen Corteen, Rachael Steele, Noel Cross and Michelle McManus
Liverpool, 2023

PART I

Forensic psychology

1

Forensic psychology

Rachael Steele

Forensic psychology is a relatively new branch of psychology, first being recognised as a specialist division in its own right by the British Psychological Society (BPS) in 1999 (Howitt, 2018). Originally pertaining only to the study of the courts and related matters, the definition has now widened to include matters of psychology related to any area of crime, the criminal or those who work in the field (Gavin, 2018). Psychologists working in this area may have roles as varied as giving expert witness statements in court, working in secure hospitals or working with the police, prisons or even in private practice (Davis, 2021). Psychologists with an interest in crime are involved at all stages of the criminal justice process, from investigation and convicting a crime, to assessing risk of harm and dangerousness, sentence planning and mental health treatment (Howitt, 2018).

Widening the remit

That is not to say that the reasons that individuals commit crime has not been an area of interest prior to the defining of the field of forensic psychology. Understanding why people commit crime, and how to stop them, has been a concern of philosophy, law and criminology scholars for a long time (Davis, 2021). Forensic psychology, as a relatively newly defined discipline, borrows from these and many other disciplines to create a body of knowledge. Despite the modern expansion of forensic psychology, the roots can be traced as far back as the late 1800s when academics such as Albert von Schrenk-Nortzing began to investigate the effects of memory on the validity of eyewitness testimony. Schrenk-Nortzing testified at a murder trial, basing his testimony on the latest research about memory at the time, that witnesses confuse real-life experiences with what they have read in the press. His argument was unpersuasive, but this assertion, and the fact that witness confidence often bears no relationship to witness accuracy, is still demonstrated in modern eyewitness testimony research (Howitt, 2018). Another early trailblazer in the world of forensic psychology, Hugo Münsterberg, was also interested in the application of psychology to the courtroom. In 1908, Münsterberg published his book *On the Witness Stand* in which he advocated the use of psychology in legal matters; he believed psychology had applications across various topics such as witness memory, crime investigation and prevention as well as the reasons behind false confession (Davis, 2021).

The role of the psychologist in court

The involvement of psychologists within the courtroom grew, though their position as experts was still seen as inferior to medical professionals. However, things began to change throughout the 1940s, when the demand for clinical psychologists and their expertise grew exponentially. The demand for expert psychological treatment after World War II established psychology as an essential and expert profession in its own right (Howitt, 2018). The need for psychological expertise within the court and legal system was cemented in the case of the *People* v *Hawthorne* (Michigan, 1940), in which the defendant, Hawthorne, had been accused of murder. The court refused to accept the credentials of a highly experienced psychologist, a decision which was criticised by the Supreme Court, which determined that it was the level of experience that was important in an expert witness and not the possession of a medical degree (Wiener and Otto, 2013).

Later, another pivotal case, *Jenkins* v *United States* in 1962 (Howitt, 2018) saw the Court of Appeal for the district of Columbia rule that a psychologist could act as an expert witness in regard to the mental health of the defendant at the time of the crime. This decision helped cement the role of the psychologist in matters related to crime and behaviour in the US (Howitt, 2018).

Though the UK had yet to catch up with these developments, nevertheless important psychological research related to crime and criminal behaviour was being undertaken from the 1970s onwards. Developments in the field led to the establishment of the division of psychology and law within the American Psychological Association in 1981 and the establishment of the Division of Criminological and Legal Psychology within the BPS, which later became the Division of Forensic Psychology in 1977 (Howitt, 2018).

The ability to determine whether an individual's mental health was an issue at the time of their offence is a key role for many forensic psychologists, and the over-representation of mental illness within the criminal justice system (CJS) means that these skills are in demand (Davis, 2021). For an individual to stand trial for their alleged offences they must be deemed as having capacity and this is where the expertise of the forensic psychologist will be necessary (Wiener and Otto, 2013). Being found as lacking in capacity does not mean a case is dropped – it may instead mean forcible detainment in a secure hospital or medical facility for an indeterminate amount of time – perhaps in some cases far longer than the original sentence may have been (Gavin, 2018).

Multiple influences

Taking the scope of forensic psychology away from the courtroom and into the reasons why an individual may offend sees the discipline draw on many different aspects of the psychological tradition. For example, forensic psychology was also expanded in scope and reach by developments in the field such as Hans Eysenck's theory of personality. The resulting introversion/extraversion and neurotic/stable scales were employed to try and explain crime at an individual level. Levels of impulsiveness, aggressiveness and low mood can all be linked to propensity for criminal behaviour (Gavin, 2018). Personality factors can be explored in terms of the neurobiology of the brain, with research (for example) showing that violent offenders have different levels of damage in the brain (Williams et al, 2015) and in terms of social factors such as how these behavioural traits are reinforced in the environment (Gavin, 2018).

Bandura's work in the area of social learning demonstrating how unwanted and anti-social behaviours could be learned by observation formed a core explanation of the development of criminal behaviour (see Bandura, 1983). Likewise, Bowlby's work in how the security of a child's attachment to a parent figure can affect their behaviour in later life was influential in understanding criminal behaviour in both children and adults (Bowlby, 1944), and later research into attachment and offending has led to developments of specific interventions to change criminal behaviour.

Profiling, investigation and interviewing are other areas where forensic psychology lends expertise and development. Profiling involves generating hypotheses about the perpetrator of an offence based on clinical and statistical knowledge and is an area still in its relative infancy, though is developing rigour using the established scientific methodologies used within psychology (Davis, 2021). The development of the 'cognitive interview', a collection of tools and techniques used to improve accuracy and depth of recall, has been influential in police work and is rooted in research on memory and cognitive processing (see Memon et al, 1994).

As a discipline, forensic psychology borrows from the whole range of psychological disciplines – from cognitive psychology (such as how memory can affect eyewitness testimony) through developmental and biological psychology (at what age can a child be held criminally responsible?) and organisational psychology (how does police culture affect its members?) (Howitt, 2018).

From the understanding of why an individual may commit a particular offence, to what happens in the courtroom, to how to best work with those convicted of an offence, forensic psychology has a wide remit and a fascinating range. This wide remit makes the study of forensic psychology both challenging and highly varied. As the understanding and definition of criminal behaviour develops, forensic psychologists engage in an ever-developing remit of work. For example, the recognition of stalking as an offence in its own right has seen a burgeoning research base establishing knowledge with which to support the justice system in tackling this behaviour.

Within the UK, the roles of forensic psychologists include work within courts, secure medical facilities, prisons, academia and more. The impact of forensic psychology within the CJS in the UK and worldwide is significant. One of the ways in which this psychological expertise has directly influenced work with those who have committed offences is the body of work that comes under the 'What Works' movement. This body of work is concerned with using expertise to develop interventions and ways of working with offending individuals that are based on psychological principles and effectively promote changes in behaviour and reductions in recidivism (Wiener and Otto, 2013). Perhaps the best examples of these interventions are what are known as 'accredited programmes'. These programmes or interventions consist of a set number of sessions and are designed to engage individuals in work that is focused on changing behaviour; they are based on proven theoretically driven models that have been approved by an expert panel and are backed up with research. Many of these interventions are rooted in cognitive behavioural theory and carefully match the risk, responsivity and needs of the offending individual. These programmes can be for specific offence types (such as domestic abuse), specific problems (such as anger management) or general issues (for example, focusing on thinking styles and decision making) (for a fuller review see Redondo et al, 2002). However, ongoing research suggests that perhaps these programmes are not as effective as first thought (see Chapter 5 for more details).

Risk assessment

The fingerprint of forensic psychological research can be found in all areas of the post-sentence journey. Indeed, the very sentence a court delivers will probably be influenced by an assessment of the likelihood of future harm, the likelihood of future reoffending and where the individual's personal needs are related to their criminal behaviour. These tools are all based on extensive research (Davis, 2021). Forensic psychologists have worked to develop both actuarial and clinical risk assessments across a whole range of behaviours, from sex offences, through anger management to terrorism. These interventions and risk assessment tools are used across the CJS in England and Wales, both within custody and the community, and of course within secure forensic hospitals. Qualified forensic psychologists may find themselves working directly within HM Prison and Probation Service, but equally they may work within a range of related fields, such as social services, private or public specialist mental health providers, the wider National Health Service, within the police, or indeed within education and research (BPS, 2021).

Studying and working in forensic psychology

Within the UK, to be able to practise as an accredited forensic psychologist, you must achieve Health and Care Professions Council (HCPC) registration. In order to achieve this, you will usually complete a psychology undergraduate degree (see the BPS website for details of accredited courses) followed by a master's programme that is approved by the HCPC. This will be followed by either a period of supervised forensic practice or an HCPC-approved doctoral programme which also includes practice placements in a forensic setting.

As with most branches of psychology, forensic psychologists are researcher practitioners. Forensic psychologists not only apply existing knowledge, but are generators of it (Howitt, 2018), and the many journals and conferences within the area are testament to this growing area of psychological expertise. The concept of 'evidence-based practice' is key across the whole remit of the work of the forensic psychologist, with knowledge constantly being generated, critiqued and developed. This continues to develop both the more established areas of work – eyewitness testimony, interviewing and profiling of offenders, risk assessment, treatment of mental illness and many more besides – but also new and rapidly developing areas such as stalking, as mentioned earlier, and also areas such as terrorism, hate crime and even environmental crime.

As a discipline, forensic psychology has deep roots, and although its establishment as a distinct discipline in and of itself is relatively new, the field is certainly now well established. From the original focus of working within the courts, to the wider fields of human behaviour, offender rehabilitation, risk assessment and mental health treatment, there is no doubt that this discipline is expanding in both scope and influence.

References

Bandura, A. (1983) 'Psychological mechanisms of aggression', in R.G. Green and C.I. Donnerstein (eds) *Aggression, Theoretical and Empirical Reviews, Vol. 1: Theoretical and Methodological Issues*, New York: Academic Press, pp 1–40.

Bowlby, J. (1944) 'Forty-four juvenile thieves: their characteristics and home-life', *International Journal of Psychoanalysis*, 25: 19–53.

BPS (British Psychological Society) (2021) 'Division of Forensic Psychology', [online] Available from: https://www.bps.org.uk/member-microsites/division-forensic-psychology/careers [Accessed 14 April 2021].

Davis, T. (2021) *Forensic Psychology: Fact and Fiction*, London: Red Globe.

Gavin, H. (2018) *Criminological and Forensic Psychology* (2nd edn), London: SAGE.

Howitt, D. (2018) *Introduction to Forensic and Criminal Psychology* (6th edn), Harlow: Pearson Education.

Memon, A., Holley, A., Milne, R., Koehnken, G. and Bull, R. (1994) 'Towards understanding the effects of interviewer training in evaluating the cognitive interview', *Applied Cognitive Psychology*, 8: 641–59.

People v *Hawthorne* (1940) 'Supreme Court of Michigan', [online] Available from: https://casetext.com/case/people-v-hawthorne-36#:~:text=In%20People%20v%20Hawthorne%2C%20293,within%20the%20study%20%20of%20medicine [Accessed 6 June 2022].

Redondo, S., Luque, E. and Funes, J. (2002) 'Social beliefs about recidivism in crime', in G. Davies, S. Lloyd-Bostock, M. McMurran and C. Wilson (eds) *Psychology, Law and Criminal Justice: International Developments in Research and Practice*, Berlin: Walter de Gruyter, pp 394–400.

Wiener, I. and Otto I. (2013) *The Handbook of Forensic Psychology* (4th edn), Hoboken, NJ: Wiley & Sons.

Williams, W.H., McAuliffe, K.A., Cohen, M.H., Parsonage, M. and Ramsbotham, D.J. (2015) 'Traumatic brain injury and juvenile offending: complex causal links offer multiple targets to reduce crime', *Head Trauma Rehabilitation*, 30(2): 69–74.

2

Forensic psychology and criminal justice

Rachael Steele

Forensic psychology is often thought to be mainly concentrated around one of two areas: work within the courtroom, wherein forensic psychologists may act as expert witnesses, or alternatively in crime investigation, where they are involved in profiling and behavioural analysis in order to help apprehend an offender. In actual fact, the work of forensic psychology is impactful at each stage of the criminal justice process (Scott-Snyder, 2017) from investigation, through interviewing and prosecution, through sentencing right through to the execution of that sentence. This overview will give a brief introduction to how forensic psychology has impacted the everyday running of the criminal justice system (CJS) and the processes that it depends on.

Crime investigation and profiling

The impact of forensic psychology on the investigation of crime is perhaps the best-known facet of the field, as it is the primary focus of popular TV and fiction (Herndon, 2007). The term profiling is often generally linked to two different activities, that of crime linkage (using patterns to link offences to a single offender) and behavioural profiling (deducing aspects of the offender by observing crime scene behaviour) (see Canter, 2004; Goodwill et al, 2010). Crime linkage (or statistical profiling) uses mathematical techniques to establish linked behaviours within different crimes and can be applied to a wide range of offending from arson offences to fraud (Alison and Rainbow, 2011). Behavioural profiling is more commonly used for violent or interpersonal offences, and as it is resource intensive it tends to be used when dealing with more serious incidents (Howitt, 2018). Behavioural profiling draws on psychological knowledge, such as research on personality theory, and uses this insight and, where appropriate, experience of working with previous forensic cases, to make predictions as to the offender's nature and future behaviour (Davies and Beech, 2018).

Police work

Forensic psychology has also had a significant impact on the day-to-day procedures and practices of the police. One of the most significant impacts is from the research on interviewing. Conducting an effective interview is at the root of good police practice, whether this is with a suspect, a witness or a victim, with the aim of ensuring that this process is fair, unbiased and obtains the best information possible.

In the UK, this is incorporated into the PEACE model of interviewing (Preparation and Planning, Engage and Explain, Account and Clarification, Closure and Evaluation), which is designed to seek truth and avoid false confessions and so on (Gudjonnson and Pearse, 2011). Psychological research around memory and communication comes together into a range of techniques collectively known as the cognitive interview (Fisher and Geiselman, 1992). These techniques are used by trained interviewers to improve the accuracy and level of detail of recall for the interviewee (Memon et al, 1994). The first technique, based on research around memory, suggests that if one method of recall fails another pathway to accessing the memory may work. Therefore, interviewees are prompted to probe their memory via various methods, perhaps by reporting what was heard as well as seen, by repeating the events in reverse chronological order or focusing on other senses (Memon et al, 1997). Interviewees are encouraged to report all details they recall even if they seem trivial or unimportant – these details may actually be important to the case or trigger further memories. The effort to mentally reinstate the event is encouraged; this involves the individual recalling their internal state at the time of the event (how were they feeling, what were they thinking about beforehand) as well as the external events (the sound of building works, the smell of a nearby bakery, the feeling of the wind or rain). In doing so, the memories of the event may be enhanced and forgotten detail recalled (Memon et al, 2010).

The behaviour of the interviewer is also important. Communication psychology reports suggest that a nervous, uncomfortable or defensive interviewee will not report accurate information, so interviewers are trained in how to use body language to put the interviewee at ease as well as in how to build effective rapport. It is crucial not to ask nested or leading questions and to pause long enough to give the respondent time to speak; this is especially important with young or vulnerable interviewees (Goodman and Melinder, 2010). In doing so, the correct psychological conditions can be established to maximise accuracy and level of recall. When used correctly, by trained officers, there is evidence that using this range of techniques does increase the number of details recalled, though research also suggests that some elements, such as recalling events from different perspectives, are less effective and are also less frequently used in actual practice (Dando et al, 2011).

Hostage negotiation

The psychology of communication has also directly impacted the work of hostage negotiation. Hostage negotiators, usually the police, work in high stress situations which often carry a high level of risk. Psychological research has directly influenced the training for hostage negotiators and focuses on skills such as assessment of the motivation of the hostage taker and on active listening

(Howitt, 2018). Active listening helps the negotiator understand the other party's point of view, and it involves techniques such as mirroring, using personal statements and clear communication back to the hostage maker about what has been understood (Noesner and Webster, 1997). A hostage taker may be extremely agitated or aggressive and may be motivated by personal, criminal or ideological reasons. Assessment of this will affect the techniques used for negotiation. Likewise, if the hostage taker is thought to be suffering from a severe mental disorder this will also demand a change in technique, making this a very challenging process (Davis, 2021). The techniques rooted in psychological knowledge of communication, mental health and personality theory are clearly important in this area of work.

Courtroom testimony and expert witnesses

The original remit of forensic psychology is within the courtroom, and this is clearly demonstrated by the level of research and expertise eyewitness testimony and memory. Much psychological research in the area of memory has improved the general understanding of how an eyewitness may store, recall and report their memories of an incident (see Loftus and Palmer, 1974, for a classic study). A witness testimony is powerful evidence in court, but research has shown that a number of things, such as post-event misinformation, stress, or poor interviewing can affect the recall of an event (Griffiths and Milne, 2006). Management of line-ups wherein a witness is asked to identify a suspect from a selection of individuals is another element of practice that has been impacted by forensic psychology. Ensuring that the foils in a line-up represent the witness description and do not make the suspect stand out is important to ensure a fair process. Ensuring a double-blind procedure wherein neither the officer nor the witness know which person is the suspect also improves the fairness and accuracy of line-ups (Davis, 2021). Following proper procedures in the management of eyewitnesses is essential to ensure that evidence given to the court is as accurate as possible.

Forensic psychologists may also be called on as expert witnesses within the courtroom. Measuring fitness to plead is one of the most common reasons a forensic psychologist will be called to speak in court (Davis, 2021), but they could also be called to provide context and information on any area in which they have particular expertise (Davies and Beech, 2018). Determining a defendant's fitness to plead involves making a judgement about whether the individual has the mental capacity to comprehend the proceedings of the trial, understand the evidence presented and instruct a legal counsel (Grubin, 1996). Such assessments are usually based on an interview with the defendant and a review of their case notes, and in some cases a discussion with any members of the individual's medical or psychology care team. The forensic psychologist may comment not only on the current mental state of the defendant but can also make a judgement of the level of cognitive impairment or emotional distress present at the time of the offence, or of the impact of any previously diagnosed mental disorder (Davies and Beech, 2018). Various tools have been developed for assessment of fitness to plead in these circumstances, such as the Evaluation of Competency to Stand Trial, which is interview based and also screens for feigned competency issues (see Anderson et al, 2022).

Risk assessment

Established assessment tools are also used to try and establish any risks posed by the defendant and how these may be managed. Before being sentenced, many defendants will meet with the Probation Service in order for them to present a report to the court on the risks and needs particular to the individual. Risk assessment is an area of practice that is directly based on research by forensic psychologists, who bring together large datasets to predict future behaviour based on individual characteristics (Howitt, 2018). These risk assessments can be based on statistical models and will predict the likelihood of future criminal behaviour using static factors such as age at first offence, gender and so on (Scott-Snyder, 2017). A more detailed risk assessment can be completed based on individuals' needs and risks that are subject to change, across a wide remit from financial management through thinking and attitudes, to relationships and emotional management. These offending-related needs are known as criminogenic needs and interventions will likely be based on the individual's particular needs profile (see Andrews et al, 1990). These risk assessment tools are varied, but all are standardised and are based on psychological research into criminal behaviour. Specialist risk assessments are available for domestic abuse (for example, SARA – Scanning, Analysis, Response and Assessment) and sexual offending (for example, RM2000/OASys Sexual Reoffending Predictor – OSP), and these are specifically designed to help criminal justice practitioners work with individuals who have committed these specific offences. The level of risk calculated, and the needs identified will inform the sentencing process significantly. The risk assessment may help indicate a custodial sentence, or it could guide the particular requirements given to someone as part of a community order.

This work on risk assessment, and guiding sentencing, therefore leads to the next way in which forensic psychology has directly impacted the CJS. A range of approved interventions, known as accredited programmes, have been developed for a huge range of offending behaviours, from domestic abuse to driving offences. Programmes can be thought of as fitting into an ABC model, with some rehabilitation programmes focusing on affective issues (A) such as anger management, focusing on changing emotion and managing feelings. Other interventions will have behavioural theory at their core (B) and focus on changing unwanted behaviour. The final category is cognitive (C) and it focuses on attitudes and beliefs (Jennings and Deming, 2013). Many programmes will combine cognitive and behavioural approaches, rooted in psychological research on the link between thinking, feeling and behaviour, and are matched to the particular criminogenic needs, as well as offending behaviour, of the individual.

Working with offending behaviour

Both risk assessment and delivery of interventions are present in custodial settings as well as in the community and prisons/prisoners are a particular focus for forensic psychologists. There are a significant number of individuals in prisons who have severe and medium-level mental health issues (Davies and Beech, 2018) and who need support and treatment from psychology services. As well as working with those in prison to assess and treat serious mental health issues, many forensic psychologists will work within special hospitals. These special hospitals, or secure hospitals, are specifically dedicated to treating and housing those who have committed offences and are suffering from mental disorders that mean they are not suitable for inclusion within the general prison population, or whose illness has not responded to treatment and cannot be managed within the community. The demand for psychological services for the care of mentally disordered offenders is growing and the rate of suicide within prisons is a cause for serious concern (Fazel and Benning, 2006).

After a review of the ways in which forensic psychology has impacted the CJS it would be reasonable to assume that all the work in the field is focused on the offenders' behaviour, but forensic victimology is also an area of work that impacts the work of the CJS. Forensic victimology seeks to examine the characteristics of victims of crime in order to inform legal procedures or to support investigations (Davis, 2021). This work looks at groupings of victim characteristics based on empirical research and creates typologies which may predict the types of crimes that people with particular victim characteristics might experience in the future (Petherick and Ferguson, 2012).

Summary

Forensic psychology – its research and practice – is interwoven throughout the whole of the CJS from investigation to sentence and at each stage in between. Many areas of influence are well established, for example research around eyewitness testimony and interviewing, and yet more are emerging and growing, such as profiling and forensic victimology, with more work to be done in these areas. There is no doubt that the evidence-based impact of forensic psychology has enabled CJS to improve its work with offenders and has supported those who do this work within the various facets of the system, from risk assessment in custody or the community, delivery of interventions, police training or courtroom practice. As knowledge of new offences develops there is a clear role for forensic psychology to continue to support and develop the CJS. For example, a range of work around the detection, treatment and impact of stalking is one new area of investigation; likewise, an increased focus on terrorist activity and hate crime have also posed new directions for forensic psychology research. It is clear that the impact of forensic psychology within the CJS and beyond will continue to influence policy and practice.

References

Alison, L. and Rainbow, L. (2011) *Professionalizing Offender Profiling: Forensic and Investigative Psychology in Practice*, Oxford: Routledge.

Alison, L., Goodwill, A., Almond, L., van den Heuvel, C. and Winter, J. (2010) 'Pragmatic solutions to offender profiling and behavioural investigative advice', *Legal and Criminological Psychology*, 15: 115–32.

Anderson, J.L., Plantz, J., Glocker, S. and Zapf, P. (2022) 'The MacCAT-CA and the ECST-R in competency to stand trial evaluations: a critical review and practical implications', *Journal of Personality Assessment*, 104(2): 281–8, DOI: https://doi.org/10.1080/00223891.2021.2006671.

Andrews, D.A., Bonta, J. and Hoge, R.D. (1990) 'Classification for effective rehabilitation: rediscovering psychology', *Criminal Justice and Behavior*, 17: 19–52.

Canter, D.V. (2004) 'Offender profiling and investigative psychology', *Journal of Investigative Psychology and Offender Profiling*, 1: 1–15.

Dando, C.J., Ormerod, T.C., Wilcock, R. and Milne, R. (2011) 'When help becomes hindrance: unexpected errors of omission and commission in eyewitness memory resulting from change temporal order at retrieval?' *Cognition*, 121(3): 416–21.

Davies, G.M. and Beech, A.R. (2018) *Forensic Psychology: Crime, Justice, Law, Interventions* (3rd edn), Chichester: John Wiley & Sons.

Davis, T. (2021) *Forensic Psychology: Fact and Fiction*, London: Red Globe.

Fazel, S. and Benning, R. (2006) 'Natural deaths in male prisoners: a 20-year mortality study', *European Journal of Public Health*, 16: 441–4.

Fisher, R.P. and Geiselman, R.W. (1992) *Memory Enhancing Techniques for Investigative Interviewing: The Cognitive Interview*, Springfield, IL: Charles C. Thomas.

Goodman, G.S. and Melinder, A. (2010) 'Child witness research and forensic interviews of young children: a review', *Legal and Criminological Psychology*, 12(1): 1–19.

Griffiths, A. and Milne, R. (2006) 'Will it all end in tiers? Police interviews with suspects in Britain', in T. Williamson (ed) *Investigative Interviewing: Rights, Research and Regulation*, London: Routledge, pp 167–89

Grubin, D. (1996) *Fitness to Plead*, Hove: Psychology Press.

Gudjonsson, G.H. and Pearse, J. (2011) 'Suspect interviews and false confessions', *Current Directions in Psychological Science*, 20(1): 33–7.

Herndon, J.S. (2007) 'The image of profiling: media treatment and general impressions' in R.N. Kocsis (ed) *Criminal Profiling: International Theory, Research and Practice*, Totowa, NJ: Humana Press, pp 303–26.

Howitt, D. (2018) *Introduction to Forensic and Criminal Psychology* (6th edn), Harlow: Pearson Education.

Jennings, J.L. and Deming, A. (2013) 'Effectively utilizing the "behavioral" in cognitive-behavioral group therapy of sex offenders', *International Journal of Behavioral Consultation and Therapy*, 8(2): 7–13.

Loftus, E. and Palmer, J.C. (1974) 'Reconstructions of automobile destruction: an example of the interaction between language and memory', *Journal of Verbal Learning and Verbal Behavior*, 13: 585–9.

Memon, A., Meissner, C.A. and Fraser, J. (2010) 'The cognitive interview: a meta– analytic review and study space analysis of the past 25 years', *Psychology, Public Policy and Law*, 16(4): 340–72.

Memon, A., Holley, A., Milne, R., Koehnken, G. and Bull, R. (1994) 'Towards understanding the effects of interviewer training in evaluating the cognitive interview', *Applied Cognitive Psychology*, 8: 641–59.

Memon, A., Wark, L., Holley, A., Koehnken, G. and Bull, R. (1997) 'Context effects and event memory: how powerful are the effects?', in D. Payne and F. Conrad (eds) *Intersections in Basic and Applied Memory Research*, Mahwah, NJ: Lawrence Erlbaum, pp 175–91.

Noesner, G.W. and Webster, M. (1997) 'Crisis intervention: using active listening skills in negotiations', *FBI Law Enforcement Bulletin*, [online] Available from: http://www.wshna.com/yahoo_site_admin/assets/docs/Active_Listening_Skills__Webster__Noesner_.307125550.pdf [Accessed 3 June 2022].

Petherick, W. and Ferguson, C. (2012) 'Understanding victim behaviour through offender behaviour typologies', in G. Coventry and M. Shircore, *Proceedings of the 5th Annual Australian and New Zealand Critical Criminology Conference*, Queensland: James Cook University Press, pp 100–11.

Scott-Snyder, S. (2017) *Introduction to Forensic Psychology: Essentials for Law Enforcement*, New York: CRC Press.

3

Forensic psychology and policing

Jason Roach and Helen Selby-Fell

Introduction

Ask a member of the UK public what a forensic psychologist does for the police and the most likely response will be 'offender profiling'. Although academics have yet to agree on an exact definition of what offender profiling is, generally it is accepted as being an approach by which inferences are drawn about an unidentified offender from their behaviour at the crime scene (for example, personality and criminal characteristics).

In the last century, films such as *Silence of the Lambs*, television drama series such as *Cracker* (*Fitz* in the US version) and crime fiction novels such as *Wire in the Blood* have portrayed psychologists as mystical beings with the power to read the minds of others (such as criminals) from the crime scenes they leave behind. The investigative utility of their 'profiles' take the form of valuable clues and psychological evidence with which to identify serious criminals (often serial murderers) as yet undetected by conventional police investigations. In the US, this perception of psychologists as profilers has been propagated by autobiographical accounts of ex-FBI agents, such as Robert Ressler, and in the UK similar accounts of 'profiler' contributions to serious crime investigations have been provided by psychologists including David Canter and Paul Britton. That is not to say that offender profiling has, or has ever had, a homogenous approach, as profilers come from different disciplines and even different areas of psychology, such as clinical psychology, psychiatry (including non-forensic) and personality psychology, to name but a few. Offender profiling was not and is still not simply the province of those who call themselves 'forensic psychologists'.

Any heyday of offender profiling in the UK lasted little more than a decade (the 1990s), as advances in forensic science and other new investigative tools were added to the police armoury (for example, mobile phone data and social media footprints), helping the police to identify serious criminals more quickly, thereby reducing the demand for offender profilers. Contrastingly, the remit of psychologists working in policing in the UK since around 2010 has broadened to provide wider investigative advice on the behaviour of serious offenders, such as how an unidentified serial rapist is likely to respond to investigative decisions made by police or whether a series of crimes should be linked to the same offender or multiple offenders. This is reflected by many in the UK

16

now preferring to use the title of 'behavioural investigative advisor' rather than 'offender profiler'.

What is forensic psychology?

Interestingly, in the UK, contributions to policing have increasingly come from those who would not necessarily identify themselves as being forensic psychologists. The main explanation for this is that forensic psychology has become more defined since the start of the 1900s, probably driven by what forensic psychologists appear to do most – reforming or rehabilitating convicted criminals in prison and probation (parole) settings. Although few would disagree with the view that working as a psychologist with police is indeed working in a 'forensic setting', being called a 'forensic psychologist' has become virtually synonymous in the UK with being a 'prison psychologist'. It is therefore unsurprising that a large proportion of forensic psychology graduates graduating in the UK in recent years will go on to be employees of HM Prison Service.

Curiously, although what constitutes a forensic psychologist in the UK has narrowed, 'forensic psychology' as a discipline has not. The representative body for psychologists in the UK – the British Psychological Society (BPS), for example, still describes forensic psychology in broader terms than the application of psychology to reform and rehabilitate convicted criminals. The BPS states that forensic psychology is the application of psychology within the legal system to create safer communities and to assist people to find pathways away from criminal behaviour.

Psychology and policing

This may leave some psychologists who work routinely with police without the title of forensic psychologist (they are now probably better described as 'psychologists who work with police'). Although the work they do is often very much still within the realms of forensic psychology itself, it can be much wider than helping the police to better understand criminal behaviour. For example, helping police make better decisions in criminal investigations and or how they can better communicate in appeals for information from the general public. Although the need for UK police to call on the services of offender profilers may have decreased since around 2010, the contribution of psychologists to other aspects of policing and criminal investigation has remained high.

It is not uncommon for psychologists who engage with police work to be asked for their assistance in determining whether a series of crimes should be attributed to the same offender or to multiple offenders. For example, in the absence of forensics or evidence from witnesses, in an approach commonly referred to as 'crime linking', psychologists will analyse a series of crimes for 'behavioural consistency' (such as whether and how an offender speaks to his/her victims), with high behavioural consistency being more indicative of the same offender being present than where low consistency is found (for example, Bennell et al, 2021). Although far from perfect, the work of academic psychologists in this area has shown that discerning whether a series of crimes has been committed by the same person or by multiple (different) individuals is vitally important to criminal investigators and the investigative decisions they make. This can include whether to split investigative resources to look for numerous different offenders or to concentrate resources on looking for just the one.

Interviewing witnesses and suspects

Another significant contribution made by psychologists to UK policing is in the advancement of the interviewing of suspects and witnesses. Up until the late 1980s, most criminal convictions for serious crimes were secured by confession, many of which were later found to be false, with a large percentage obtained under duress. A review of police training at this time identified existing interview techniques to be generally inappropriate and inadequate and therefore an area where psychological research could be employed to help to improve investigator skills. Psychologists, for example, have helped to inform the development of 'investigative interviewing', including the PEACE training package, which is a five-step process within which to structure interviews in criminal investigations. Although less common than in previous decades, some UK psychologists are still on occasion called by police to assist with the interviewing of particular suspects.

Research conducted since the 1990s by forensic psychologists (for example see Bull et al, 2009) has also seen the development of ways to assist witnesses to recall as much as information as possible about the crimes they have observed. One such technique, known as the 'cognitive interview', utilises theories from cognitive psychology (such as how human memory works) and social psychology (for example, how to build rapport and good communication skills) to help witnesses to reinstate key aspects of the context of the crime in their minds and 'trigger' other aspects which hitherto might not have been retrieved.

Lying and deception

Another area of the criminal investigation process where prominent psychologists (for example, see Granhag et al, 2015) continue to make an important contribution to policing is in the detection of lying and deception in police–suspect interview scenarios. Two common misperceptions exist about the detection of lying and deception which have major implications for key police interviewers: (1) humans are not as good at spotting liars and lies as they think they are; and (2) many of the subjective indicators that people typically use to judge whether someone is telling the truth or not are unreliable (for example, a suspect avoids eye contact so must be lying). Interestingly, police have been found to perform no better (or marginally better) than non-police participants in lie/truth detection studies. Although in the US police commonly employ lie-detection equipment in interview scenarios, such as the polygraph test, a vast majority of UK police forces do not.

Investigative decision making

Investigative decision making has increasingly become an important focus for psychologists and is used to inform UK police practice and training. This research generally comes from two directions: (1) top down, for example whereby knowledge obtained from *traditional* psychological research and experimentation in a non-police setting is imported and applied in a policing context (see Kahneman, 2011, on cognitive decision making and cognitive bias); and (2) from more *naturalistic* research whereby police are observed making decisions in real-world encounters (this can include what makes them more suspicious of some people than others when they are out on patrol). Both have contributed much to the understanding and enhancement of police decision making in a host of different police contexts and situations, including police decision making in time-poor, split-second contexts such as whether to shoot a suspect who is endangering the lives of others. Roach and Pease's (2016) *Self-Selection Policing* is an example of how the application of forensic psychology research can be used by police to identify active serious offenders from the minor offences they commit.

Identifying common cognitive bias such as tunnel vision, confirmation bias and heuristics (mental short-cuts) has become important to identifying how both unconscious and conscious bias can have a negative influence on the decision making and conduct of police in criminal investigations (for example, see Rossmo, 2009). For example, psychological research has identified how some police will make biased assumptions about victims when investigating sexual offences, such as if a victim does not appear to look or sound like they believe a genuine victim would. These assumptions are often referred to as 'rape myths'.

Furthermore, the negative effects of different types of cognitive bias leading to 'investigative failure' has been identified by psychologists, for example when investigators move too prematurely from the identification of a prime suspect to the building of an evidential case against a suspect, exemplified in the late 1970s where a 'hoaxer' was believed erroneously by police investigators to be the actual 'Yorkshire Ripper' – Peter Sutcliffe, a serial murderer of at least 13 women. Or in the initial police investigation into the practice of Dr Harold Shipman, where an inexperienced police investigator thought it unlikely that a doctor would harm their patients. It was later found that he had murdered hundreds of his patients (see Roach and Pease, 2016). At the beginning of his 2009 book *Criminal Investigative Failures*, Kim Rossmo gives a masterful account of how cognitive bias can 'derail' criminal investigations.

Preventing crime

A popular area of policing for psychologists to be involved with but which does not fall easily within the boundaries of forensic psychology is the 'prevention of crime'. Traditionally perhaps, crime prevention has been perceived as simply 'target hardening', such as fitting locks and bolts to make it harder to steal cars or break into houses. Since the early 1990s, this simplistic view of preventing crime has given way to a plethora of psychological and criminological research aimed at influencing the decision making not just of potential offenders but also that of victims and potential victims of crime. In UK policing it is common for psychologists to advise or help police to reduce specific crime problems in 'hot-spot' areas, for example by reducing student burglary victimisation or by influencing criminal behaviour by making the potential offenders feel that the risk of being caught is high. 'Nudge' is a psychological approach becoming more commonly used by psychologists and police in crime prevention scenarios, to influence the decision making of offenders and potential victims of crime towards making more 'pro-social' decisions, such as putting up posters displaying human eyes next to bicycle shelters to deter bike thieves.

Another related area where psychologists have made an impact on policing is by helping police look more systematically at local crime and disorder problems. One example is the SARA (Scanning, Analysis, Response and Assessment) model, which provides a framework within which police are encouraged to address specific crime problems, such as the vandalism of bus shelters, in bespoke ways based on a firm understanding of the underlying mechanisms involved.

Although the definition of what constitutes a forensic psychologist in the UK has narrowed, many psychologists continue to make significant contributions to UK policing in areas such as investigative decision making, interviewing suspects and witnesses, crime prevention, and in the solving of crime and disorder problems.

References

Bennell, C., Mugford, R., Woodhams, J. Beauregard, E. and Blaskovits, B. (2021) 'Linking serial sex offences using standard, iterative, and multiple classification trees', *Journal of Police and Criminal Psychology*, 36(4): 691–705.

Bull, R., Valentine, T. and Williamson, T. (2009) *Handbook of Psychology of Investigative Interviewing: Current Developments and Future Directions*, Chichester: John Wiley & Sons.

Granhag, P.A., Vrij, A. and B. Verschuere (eds) (2015) *Detecting Deception: Common Challenges and Cognitive Approaches*, Chichester: John Wiley & Sons.

Kahneman, D. (2011) *Thinking Fast and Slow*, New York: Penguin Books.

Roach, J. and Pease, K. (2016) *Self-Selection Policing: Theory, Research and Practice*, Basingstoke: Palgrave Macmillan.

Rossmo, D.K. (2009) *Criminal Investigative Failures*, Boca Raton, FL: CRC Press.

4

Forensic psychology and court processes

Ruth J. Tully

Introduction

Forensic psychologists are practitioner psychologists registered with the Health and Care Professions Council (HCPC) and have to follow HCPC standards of conduct, performance and ethics (HCPC, 2016). Forensic psychologists typically work with people who have offended or who are at risk of offending. Therefore, it is easy to assume that the settings in which they work are limited. However, this is not the case, although, as most readers might imagine, a key arena in which forensic psychologists work is the court. This can include various contexts including criminal court, family court, immigration tribunal, mental health tribunal and other court settings. This chapter will focus on forensic psychology involvement in criminal and family court processes.

Criminal court work

The main input forensic psychologists have in criminal court relates to the expert assessment of defendants, complainants or witnesses. The purpose of these assessments is not only to inform the court but is often to inform the services working with the court, for example probation, police and witness services. This can happen at various stages and can include the following, although this is not exhaustive:

- Assessment of a *complainant before the case comes to court/trial*, assessing issues such as mental health, cognitive ability, how they might best give a statement/ evidence, what support might be needed to achieve best evidence before and in court. This most often would be commissioned by the police or the Crown Prosecution Service (CPS) and typically considers any pre-existing psychological presentation and mental health. This type of assessment needs to consider the trauma that may have been experienced by the person during the index incident and how best to work with them to support the course of justice while avoiding re-traumatisation.
- Assessment of the *defendant before trial* in respect of potential learning disability and whether an intermediary might be needed to support fair engagement with trial. Outcomes might also affect decisions about a person's fitness to stand trial.

- Assessment of the *defendant before or sometimes mid-trial*, considering any relevant diagnoses or symptoms that may affect participation in the trial and also issues associated with their alleged offending behaviour such as mental health conditions, learning disability, autism, 'personality disorder', psychopathy.
- *Pre-sentence case formulation assessment* of the perpetrator of the offence, in relation to understanding the contributory factors to offending. This is often referred to as a 'case formulation', whereby predisposing, precipitating, perpetuating and protective factors are considered to assist in understanding why the person offended. Instructions might focus on, for example, 'what is the likely impact of the defendant's autism on their thinking and behaviour within the offence?' Or there might be a question the court would like to know more about such as further analysis of sexual deviance (see Tully, 2019, for a case study example).
- *Pre-sentence psychological risk assessment*, which would usually include the case formulation analysis of offending as described in the earlier point, but also includes a formal assessment of risk, usually based on a structured professional judgement approach to forensic risk assessment.
- Within any post-conviction pre-sentence report of the person who has committed the offence(s), of interest to the court is the psychologist's *assessment of what treatment or risk reduction strategies are needed to reduce risk of reoffending.* This requires consideration of options in prison and the community so that the judge is aware of all the options and of the psychologist's opinion on how these might meet the offender's risk-related needs, or indeed how they might not meet those needs. This aids the judge when they are considering the appropriate sentence and any other mandated requirements or 'conditions' to which the person will have to adhere.
- Some assessments of complainants and defendants can be a *'second opinion' assessment*, whereby a psychologist may have been instructed by the defence that the CPS/police want a second opinion or vice versa.

Assessment of people for court

The process of assessing the person for criminal court will typically involve clinical interview, psychometric testing, discussion with professionals and/ or family members or carers (where appropriate) and writing a report. The psychologist may then be needed in court to speak of their report and answer a range of questions.

There is a lot of skill and planning involved in all stages of this process. This begins from the planning of the interview session, which in many cases has to take place in a prison where the visiting facilities may not be optimal for a psychological assessment. Issues in such a setting that could potentially impact on the assessment include being in a loud busy area, windows around the room being distracting for the person being assessed, the room not being soundproof and the person being assessed being understandably concerned about privacy, and in some cases the need to have a second professional present due to risks posed by the person being assessed to the assessor. In complainant assessments, often the police station is an appropriate venue if they have a vulnerable witness suite, as a standard interview room may negatively impact the complainant's engagement. This is because the complainant may feel that they are being blamed for what has happened to them and the environment may not be conducive to the psychologist forming a positive rapport in a situation where the complainant may be highly traumatised or otherwise vulnerable.

As mentioned earlier, psychometric testing is often used in criminal court assessments. Psychometric tests can involve self-reporting, such as the person rating symptoms they have experienced or rating attitudes they hold. Or tests may be 'performance' measures, such as specially designed memory tasks which aim to assess memory functioning. The psychologist has to select and use appropriate tests that measure the phenomenon of interest (for example, IQ, personality, depression), are well validated and are appropriate to use with the specific person being assessed (such as in relation to age-related norms or other subpopulation identification such as a person with learning disability) among other responsivity considerations. This requires up-to-date knowledge of the literature in the field, such as why one measure of a condition (for example, anxiety) might be better to use in a given case compared to another available measure of the same condition, and the psychologist also needs to have up-to-date practice experience and knowledge. It is a mixture of clinical and academic expertise that assists the psychologist in this regard. Importantly, the psychologist needs to use clinical expertise to know if the tests conducted are valid, to identify any limitations of the test and its administration and to be able to communicate this clearly in the report.

Psychometric testing alone may not provide the 'objective truth' in terms of assessment of what are often abstract concepts. Forensic psychologists may make a mental health diagnosis, for example personality disorder or learning disability, but psychometric tests alone would not be used to 'make' the diagnosis, or indeed to draw other non-diagnostic conclusions. Psychometric test results are combined with the assessor's careful analysis of all the information available in the case, including a careful review of the available documentation, clinical interview and the person's self-report, as well as information from other people such as professionals and family members, to aid the psychologist's conclusions. If making a diagnosis, the information would be considered against a diagnostic classification system such as DSM-5 (APA, 2013). Malingering (meaning to fake or exaggerate symptoms) is a real issue of concern to the court; for some defendants it might be of benefit to feign mental illness. Psychologists have to consider this issue clinically from their observations of the person being assessed and they might also supplement their psychometric tests with symptom validity tests or other measures of malingering. Conversely, when it comes to attitudes and risk assessment, it may serve a defendant to 'fake good', meaning that they minimise or deny having problems in their attitudes or functioning.

This type of deception can be usefully framed as 'impression management'. This is something all people do, for instance, it can be considered natural to want to present at one's best for a job interview. However, in forensic psychology assessment of someone alleged or proven to have committed an offence or pose risks to themselves or others, impression management can affect the information provided during interview. Where risk is concerned, those involved in the case will benefit from knowing that impression management could be affecting the person's engagement with services (see Tully and Bailey, 2017); this emphasises the importance of triangulation of information where possible and consideration of 'real-world' behaviour rather than over-reliance on self-reporting.

When writing up a report to be used in criminal court, the court context has to be given careful consideration. The psychologist's duty is to the court, regardless of who has instructed the assessment, yet a range of stakeholders need to be considered in relation to clarity and language used for example. Several people often need to understand and take key messages from the report, such as the judge, the jury of laypeople, solicitors and barristers, other clinicians in the future and, importantly, the person being assessed. Court reports can include a diagnosis in some cases, and it is therefore important that the condition is explained and the person being assessed is signposted to appropriate resources and services, regardless of whether they receive a conviction. Given this range of stakeholder interest, the report has to be clear and concise, with technical terms explained in a way laypeople can understand, yet there needs to be a balance, with the report showing that the appropriate tests were used and explanation of diagnostic criteria where relevant. This way of writing can differ greatly from, for example, reports that might be used within a psychiatric service and refining the skills involved in this style of writing is hugely important in determining how useful the psychologist's report is in any given case.

Court skills

Other considerations for the work of forensic psychologists in court includes the psychologist's ability to form a rapport with the person being assessed in what is often a time-limited assessment session/situation and in stressful circumstances for that person, whether they are the defendant, complainant or a witness. A non-judgemental, empathic approach is needed. Forensic psychologists often come across people who have committed acts of extreme violence and sexual violence against others. Many people may perhaps understandably struggle to demonstrate empathy towards a perpetrator of such violence, yet this is an important aspect of the role and can affect whether a perpetrator decides to engage in risk reduction treatment. The demonstration of empathy towards marginalised groups, including those convicted of murder, has been studied (see Batson et al, 1997) but there is still a lot of room for improving knowledge in this area and applying this to the practice of forensic psychology.

Court assessment also involves giving oral evidence. This requires skills in public speaking, thinking on one's feet, and also comprehensive knowledge of the case and their own assessment, and the relevant literature in that specific area of practice. Flexibility is needed, as new evidence or information may be provided at a late stage, or indeed in court, which may affect the psychologist's opinions and recommendations, and this will need careful consideration. The process of giving evidence in court can be considered stressful as the court might feel like a public platform given the number of people who might be present, including press. Research has demonstrated that psychiatric expert witnesses fear making errors (Grøndahl et al, 2013) which may contribute to stress; therefore, a good ability to manage stress is required.

Family court work

In the family court work of a forensic psychologist, some of the processes discussed earlier in relation to criminal court work are similar and equally important, such as the ability to write reports that are concise and accessible and the ability to give good oral evidence. However, the family court procedure rules differ to criminal court practice rules and the psychologist needs to have a good understanding of these. The purpose of a forensic psychologist's assessment in family court is often to inform the court about risk issues associated with parenting. This might include more subtle issues associated with poor or 'not good enough' parenting, or more obvious risk issues such as a parent having sexual offence convictions, a parent failing to protect the child from abuse or other harm or a parent physically abusing their child. These cases involve considering all of the information, just like in criminal court, but also can involve assessment of multiple people from the same family, such as a mother, father and several children. As such, these can be big assessments, yet the reporting still needs to be concise in order to help the court.

The focus of a family court assessment is often on the parents' psychological needs and/or diagnoses, insight and ability to mentalise and provide safe parenting. Assessments also focus on the needs of the children and how these can be met. As with criminal court cases, the family court will decide what will happen in the case/outcomes and the psychologist's conclusions and recommendations are designed to inform this process. Psychologists need to be familiar with the wider systems involved in family court cases, such as the structure of social care and support that has been, or can be, provided to the family, and they also need to be alert to the fact that professionals involved in a case may disagree as to what is best for the children/family.

Conclusions

As in all court cases, and indeed in any case the psychologist is involved in, the forensic psychologist needs to be as objective as possible in family court cases.

Achieving this aim is aided by them recognising that the specifics of the case, which might involve evidence about the abuse of children, can have an emotional impact on them which they need to work through. Psychologists are encouraged to have supervision no matter what their level of experience for reasons such as this, so that they are supported and also so that they recognise factors which can affect judgement. They should also be familiar with relevant guidance from professional bodies on being an expert witness in general (for example, BPS, 2017), or specific to aspects of the case they are working on (such as BPS, 2009), and they should keep up to date with continued professional development (HCPC, 2018).

The role of the forensic psychologist in court is very specialist; most psychologists work in services such as those within prisons or forensic psychiatric settings and not all engage in court work; this is a common misconception about forensic psychology. Psychologists need to be appropriately qualified and experienced any area in which they work and the same applies to the court setting, otherwise they could cause harm. Relevant to this point, not all forensic psychologists would want to complete court work, which, as described within this chapter, differs from standard client work that might involve risk reduction therapy and consultancy to services working with victims and offenders. Court work is considered by many forensic psychologists to be a challenging area of work. However, many forensic psychologists refine their skills over time and have the qualities needed to engage people involved in court systems effectively and to provide good written and oral evidence for the court. Their input can be invaluable to aid the course of justice and other important processes, such as the safe and nurturing care of children.

References

APA (American Psychiatric Association) (2013) *Diagnostic and Statistical Manual of Mental Disorders* (5th edn), Arlington, VA: American Psychiatric Association.

Batson, C.D., Polycarpou, M.P., Harmon-Jones, E., Imhoff, H.J., Mitchener, E.C., Bednar, L.L., Klein, T.R. and Highberger, L. (1997) 'Empathy and attitudes: can feeling for a member of a stigmatized group improve feelings toward the group?', *Journal of Personality and Social Psychology*, 72(1): 105–18, DOI: https://doi.org/10.1037/0022-3514.72.1.105.

BPS (British Psychological Society) (2009) *Assessment of Effort in Clinical Testing of Cognitive Functioning for Adults*, Leicester: British Psychological Society.

BPS (British Psychological Society) (2017) *Psychologists as Expert Witnesses: Guidelines and Procedure* (4th edn), Leicester: British Psychological Society.

Grøndahl, P., Stridbeck, U. and Grønnerød, C. (2013) 'The truth and nothing but the truth: court-appointed forensic experts' experience with testifying and their perceptions of legal actors in criminal courts', *Journal of Forensic Psychiatry & Psychology*, 24(2): 192–204, DOI: https://doi.org/10.1080/14789 949.2013.771278.

HCPC (Health and Care Professions Council) (2016) *Standards of Conduct, Performance and Ethics*, London: Health and Care Professions Council.

HCPC (Health and Care Professions Council) (2018) *Standards of Continued Professional Development*, London: Health and Care Professions Council.

Tully, R.J. (2019) 'Sexual deviancy: assessment for court', in R.J. Tully and J. Bamford (eds) *Case Studies in Forensic Psychology: Clinical Assessment and Treatment*, London: Routledge, pp 25–47.

Tully, R.J. and Bailey, T. (2017) 'Validation of the Paulhus Deception Scales (PDS) in the UK and examination of the links between PDS and personality', *Journal of Criminological Research, Policy and Practice*, 3(1): 38–50.

5

Forensic psychology and prisons

Ruth J. Tully

Forensic psychology most often involves working with perpetrators or 'offenders'. This is exemplified within prisons, which is where the subdiscipline of psychology that is known as 'forensic psychology' began to develop. It is unsurprising that an outside assumption would be that the work of a forensic psychologist in prison is just about 'offenders'. However, it is about so much more. The role involves working with prison staff, modifying and evaluating the environment itself (including for optimal rehabilitation support) and, of course, working with prisoners. The latter is, however, multifaceted; prisoners often do not just fall into the category of 'offender' as they also fit the category of 'victim' (of various traumas experienced inside and outside of prison), 'patient' (in relation to mental health, learning disability, neurodevelopmental, brain injury and personality diagnoses), as well as 'family member' or 'parent'. Therefore, the work of a psychologist in a prison can vary; this chapter provides an overview of some of the key areas of work but is in no way exhaustive.

Risk reduction

The chapter will begin with a discussion of risk reduction and offending behaviour programmes (OBPs). Risk reduction is a key area of work for a prison psychologist. This can take many forms and one activity that psychologists are involved in is the management and delivery of OBPs. OBPs are, in essence, manualised interventions that are mostly delivered in a group-based, cognitive behaviour therapy-informed manner. They are often based on the risk-need-responsivity (RNR) model of offender treatment, which is a model first formalised in 1990 (Andrews et al, 1990) and later elaborated upon by others in relation to personality and cognitive and social learning theories of criminal behaviour (Andrews and Bonta, 2006). The core principles of the RNR model are: risk (level of service/intervention should match the person's level of risk of reoffending), need (assess risk-related needs and target these in the treatment) and responsivity (provide treatment that is tailored to the individual needs of the person). OBPs cover risk reduction needs such as general thinking skills; for example the Thinking Skills Programme (MoJ, 2008) aims to help participants develop social, relationship, problem-solving and other skills. Other examples include RESOLVE (MoJ, 2013), which is a moderate intensity programme that is primarily targeted at developing awareness of, and skills related to, anger and emotion management associated with a person's offences, as well as programmes such as sex offender treatment programmes, partner violence programmes and other similar interventions. Psychologists working in prisons are often involved in the development, oversight and delivery of such programmes. Sessions are often delivered several times per week over several months. Other professions have typically also been involved in delivery such as prison officers and non-psychology facilitators. This brings differing backgrounds and experiences to intervention sessions. An issue to consider with OBPs is that with these being manual based (meaning that the sessions and content are manualised to enable standardised delivery, but with there being some scope for responsivity), sometimes they are not appropriate in specific cases. Additionally, they sometimes do not enable change for a variety of reasons which can relate to the prisoner and internal processes, their circumstances or possibly problems with the design or delivery of the programmes. For example, evaluation of the previous version of the prison-based sex offender treatment programmes was disappointing and controversial, suggesting that these programmes were ineffective at reducing risk and, in some cases, may have led to increased recidivism (Mews et al, 2017). However, OBPs are not the only psychological approach to risk reduction in prisons.

A 'pathway' of available services aimed to facilitate risk reduction in prisons (and beyond when prisoners are released into the community), and which has expanded greatly in recent years with significant psychologist involvement, is referred to as the offender personality disorder (OPD) pathway (see Craissati et al, 2020). OPD services have had massive investment in recent years and are designed to support and address factors that are associated with a diagnosis of 'personality disorder' (PD). These services are often designed, evaluated and delivered by psychologists, although a multidisciplinary approach is taken which includes other prison staff, healthcare staff and probation officers. A key role of prison psychologists in these settings is to 'upskill' other prison staff to work with the specific client group. Despite the name of the pathway, diagnosis is not a requirement for entry to services; evidence of potential personality 'difficulties' or recurring interpersonal problems is often enough for a person to be eligible for these services. One important psychological principle applied in prisons and beyond in the field of forensic psychology is that to attempt to understand risk of reoffending there is a need to try to understand why the previous offending happened. The label of PD may describe the person's presentation but it does not help practitioners understand what happened in the person's life, both in the past (predisposing factors) and in the lead-up to the offending (precipitating factors). Questions and answers relating to 'what happened in your life/to you' can reasonably be seen as providing more qualitative and risk-relevant information than a diagnosis alone (Johnstone and Boyle, 2018). On this basis, many OPD services operate from a therapeutic psychological perspective, for example, one of the most intense therapeutic interventions offered is a democratic Therapeutic Community, often referred to as a 'TC', which prison psychologists oversee and deliver. This is a lengthy treatment modality (often 18 months in duration) offered to prisoners to aim to provide therapy to help address those factors that contributed to risk of offending and other problems, which may include self-harm, substance misuse, vulnerability to being victimised themselves and other harm-related matters.

Importantly, the role of a prison psychologist involves identifying those factors and what contributed to the decision to offend, in order to assess what sort of intervention is needed to reduce risk. Other OPD support methods involve psychologists but operate less directly as therapy, for example, the consultation model involves a psychologist providing reflection and case consultation advice to the staff members (prison and community-based probation officers) working with the prisoner now or in the future. Other OPD interventions which provide a model delivered largely by prison officers with supervision and support from a psychologist include prison-based PIPEs (psychologically informed planned environments). At such sites, prisoners undergo 'key work' with specially trained officers and engage in peer groups and other activities which aim to provide a platform for consolidation of learning/development and also to help prepare prisoners for release into the community. Psychologists are often central in the delivery of these models of support.

There are many other risk reduction interventions that psychologists are involved in within prisons, such as substance misuse treatment, violence reduction interventions for prisoners who have bullied or been violent to others in prison (such as interventions not just aimed at targeting the offences the person was sentenced for), self-harm and suicide-monitoring risk reduction interventions and assessment, trauma therapy delivery, and also reintegration interventions aimed at those whose behaviour or violence risk is so high or harmful in prison that they have to reside in segregation. There are many excellent examples of such practice in the prisons within the UK and beyond which I have seen first-hand. The forensic psychologist's role in these services again often involves direct delivery of psychological interventions but also can involve supporting other prison staff through providing consultancy on the case or through providing support/supervision to help staff cope with their challenging roles. Prison psychologists are often also involved in the design of such interventions and evaluation or research into their effectiveness.

Parole risk assessment

The chapter will now turn to risk assessment and parole. Forensic psychology in prisons commonly involves formal risk assessment of a prisoner's risk of reoffending, whether that might relate to general physical violence to others, violence to a specific group (such as intimate partners), sexual offending, extremism/ideology-related offending, deliberate fire setting, stalking or general offending. These are just a few examples, as prisoners' offences are diverse. Risk assessment is important in prisons for a myriad of reasons, such as protecting those at risk, knowing what might be needed to reduce risk, planning for release and assessing those on parole-type sentences to make recommendations to the

Parole Board as to whether the individual can safely be managed in a less secure setting or what risk reduction intervention is required. This often involves the psychologist assessing the risk and progress of a prisoner in a closed (Category A–C) prison to consider if they might be safely manageable in an open (Category D) prison or the community. The most common types of sentences of those prisoners assessed by psychologists as part of the parole process are mandatory life sentences, discretionary life sentences and indeterminate sentences for public protection; prisoners may include those who have been released via parole or automatically and who have been 'recalled' back to closed prison for breaching their community licence in some way.

Psychological assessment for parole typically involves reading information relating to the prisoner's past and recent behaviour, interviewing the prisoner (where they consent) and speaking to other people involved in the case. This is to assist the psychologist in completing a detailed review of the prisoner's offending history and all areas of their life, for example childhood, relationships, employment, mental health, substance use and so on. The assessment will often involve the application of a formal risk assessment tool such as the HCR-20v3 (Webster et al, 2013), which is the most commonly used violence risk assessment tool in the world (Singh et al, 2011). 'Structured professional judgement' tools like these enable the psychologist to apply an empirically informed framework to risk assessment while allowing for clinical judgement in relation to dynamic risk factors such as problems with insight, mental health, treatment/supervision and violent ideation. These tools guide risk analysis while allowing the assessor the flexibility to make appropriate recommendations for risk management, based on possible future risk scenarios and a detailed case formulation (case formulation being a way of understanding which risk factors may have come together to result in offending). The psychologist most often will use a tool like this to inform their opinions on risk and whether closed prison, open prison or the community is the least restrictive safe environment for risk management, with the focus being on public protection when considering this question.

The earlier description of forensic psychological risk assessment is, however, an oversimplification of a complex process. For example, the quality of information available can affect the psychologist's judgements. Prisoners may 'impression manage' during interview; they might present the way they think the assessor might want them to in order to try to demonstrate reduced risk. Information may be conflicting. Some prisoners can show great insight into risk but have problems putting this into practice to effect behaviour change. Therefore, a parole risk assessment is complex, uncertain and can often require other clinical or diagnostic assessments to fully understand the case, such as diagnostic assessment of autism, personality assessment, cognitive functioning and other tests. This can become even more complicated as the allocated psychologist for the parole assessment may not be an expert in the additional type of clinical assessment that is required and so a different psychologist may need to become involved. For example, an autism diagnostic assessment can be hard to source in prison (Ashworth, 2016). Assessments involve staff time and therefore cost services valuable resources and money, so decision makers have to decide if further psychological assessments are essential or 'just' desirable. External and independent psychologists often also become involved, for example in complex cases or to provide a second opinion on risk or other clinical issues. There can additionally be disagreements about risk in a case between several psychologists and/or between the psychologist and another key stakeholder in the parole risk assessment process, such as the prison-based or community probation officer.

Ultimately, the independent Parole Board will make a decision about whether the prisoner's risk can be safely managed in less secure conditions, based on their own analysis of the information and the available range of opinions. This involves not only a risk assessment report being provided by the psychologist but also the psychologist giving formal live verbal evidence at the prisoner's oral parole hearing. The psychologist has to draw on their knowledge of the case and skills in giving oral evidence to speak about their assessment and opinions in order to assist the panel. This goes beyond technical knowledge and typical skills used to work with prisoners; a specific skill set in relation to communicating with non-psychology colleagues, thinking on the spot and explaining clearly the basis of and any limitations to their opinion is needed. Challenge is important to ensure evidence is tested and the view is well rounded and based on all relevant considerations.

Conclusions

To summarise, the role of a psychologist in a prison is much more diverse than is able to be explored in this chapter. In addition to the earlier discussion, important and varied work goes on behind those closed gates, such as helping train officers as hostage negotiators, advising on policy, evaluating interventions, undertaking research and, importantly, supporting colleagues. An area for ongoing review and development is the assessment of the efficacy of OBPs, which typically have been evaluated internally but which, like most evaluations, would benefit from independent analysis, such as by external organisations. Additionally, the practice of forensic psychology in prisons does not only rely on those registered as 'forensic psychologists'; people from other disciplines of psychology also work in prisons, such as clinical psychologists or counselling psychologists. Psychologists' work is, however, often hidden by the nature of the secure environment.

References
Andrews, D.A. and Bonta, J. (2006) *The Psychology of Criminal Conduct* (4th edn), Newark, NJ: LexisNexis.
Andrews, D.A., Bonta, J. and Hoge, R.D. (1990) 'Classification for effective rehabilitation: rediscovering psychology', *Criminal Justice and Behavior*, 17: 19–52.

Ashworth, S. (2016) 'Autism is underdiagnosed in prisoners', *British Medical Journal*, 353, [online] Available from: https://www.bmj.com/content/353/bmj.i3028 [Accessed 27 May 2021].

Craissati, J., Joseph, N. and Skett, S. (eds) (2020) *Practitioner Guide: Working with People in the Criminal Justice System Showing Personality Difficulties* (3rd edn), HM Prison and Probation Services and NHS England, [online] Available from: https://assets.publishing.service.gov.uk/government/uploads/system/uploads/attachment_data/file/869843/6.5151_HMPPS_Working_with_Offenders_with_Personality_Disorder_v17_WEB.pdf [Accessed 27 May 2021].

Johnstone, L. and Boyle, M. (with Cromby, J., Dillon, J., Harper, D., Kinderman, P., Longden, E., Pilgrim, D. and Read, J.) (2018) *The Power Threat Meaning Framework: Towards the Identification of the Patterns in Emotional Distress, Unusual Experiences and Troubled or Troubling Behaviour, as an Alternative to Functional Psychiatric Diagnosis*, Leicester: British Psychological Society.

Mews, A., Di Bella, L. and Purver, M. (2017) *Impact Evaluation of the Prison-Based Core Sex Offender Treatment Programme* (Ministry of Justice Analytical Series), London: Ministry of Justice.

MoJ (Ministry of Justice) (2008) *Thinking Skills Programme Theory Manual*, London: Ministry of Justice.

MoJ (Ministry of Justice) (2013) *Theory Manual RESOLVE Programme*, London: Ministry of Justice.

Singh, J.P., Grann, M. and Fazel, S. (2011) 'A comparative study of risk assessment tools: a systematic review and metaregression analysis of 68 studies involving 25,980 participants', *Clinical Psychology Review*, 31(3): 499–513.

Webster, C.D., Douglas, K.S., Eaves, D. and Hart, S.D. (2013) *HCR-20: Assessing Risk for Violence Version 3*, British Columbia: Mental Health, Law and Policy Institute, Simon Fraser University.

6

Forensic psychology and victims of crime

Cherie Armour

Forensic psychology is devoted to the application of psychological theory and knowledge to improving an understanding of crime, offenders, victims and legal and justice systems (for example, criminal investigations, psychological problems associated with criminal behaviour, the treatment of criminals, policing practices such as investigative interviewing, the psychological impact of criminal victimisation, risk assessment and restorative justice to name only a few). Consequently, forensic psychology, as a subdiscipline of psychology, often overlaps with disciplines such as law, criminology and sociology.

Forensic psychology

Forensic psychology has largely been focused on the study of crime and criminals, asking why people offend, how often, in what way, and how professionals can assess and manage risk with a view to encouraging crime desistence. However, a significant proportion of forensic psychology also focuses on the study of victims of crime. Scholars attempt to understand the characteristics of a victim and their lifestyle in an objective and impartial manner to explain how someone came to be a victim of crime and what, if any, was the relationship with an offender. Moreover, scholars aim to understand the impact of crime upon a victim regarding a range of social, psychological and economic outcomes, particularly to aid victims and those who work within the criminal justice system and within victim support agencies. This subfield is termed forensic victimology and is the objective and scientific study of victims of crime (Turvey, 2014; Brotto et al, 2017).

The origins and study of victimology

The field of victimology gained prominence in the 1940s when a range of scholars moved their focus on the offender towards a renewed interest in the victim and offender relationship. The goal was to improve understanding of the victim's role in a crime, particularly concerning whether the victim had in some way contributed to their own victimisation. This led to the study of victim typologies, whereby scholars aimed to categorise victims based on commonalities across a range of characteristics, including demographics and social, psychological, psychiatric and biological features.

Several prominent typologies emerged which varied quite considerably in their definitions of victim types. Hans von Hentig's victim typology described 13 victim types characterised by age, gender, race, cognitive capabilities, promiscuity, loneliness and brokenness to name a few; notably these categories could not therefore be mutually exclusive. Benjamin Mendelsohn, often referred to as a father figure of victimology, took a different approach by creating a typology based on situational factors rather than personal characteristics. Mendelsohn's victim typology focused on a victim's level of culpability; in other words, how responsible a victim was for their own victimisation. In a similar manner, Stephen Shafer developed a seven-part typology which again categorised victims based on their level of responsibility for their own victimisation (Brotto et al, 2017).

Contemporary research studying typologies of victims tends to focus on victim experiences rather than on sociodemographic characteristics or ascribed levels of culpability. For example, there is a growing and burgeoning field of research focused on poly-victimisation and re-victimisation, which refers to evidence that when people are victimised this often occurs across multiple types of experiences and increases the risk for further victimisation in the future. Scholars are interested in both types of experiences that co-occur within a typology and the various demographic, social and psychological predictors of membership within typologies (Finkelhor et al, 2007a, 2007b; McLafferty et al, 2019).

The concept of attributing responsibility of victimisation of crime to the victim is termed 'victim precipitation'; this is further subcategorised into passive and active victim precipitation. The former is when a victim unknowingly shares responsibility for the crime through perhaps inadvertently inciting rage or jealousy in the attacker. The latter is thought to result from a deliberate act on the part of the victim which results in the attacker feeling threatened and retaliating. This can include a situation where someone throws the first punch in a pre-emptive strike, or someone verbally abuses an attacker who in turn physically retaliates. The concept of victim precipitation is, however, problematic given that attributing part of the responsibility of the crime to the victim is synonymous with victim blaming. Victim blaming, by its very definition, is the process by which the blame is transferred from the perpetrator to the victim. In turn, victim precipitation is further problematic as it is more often applied to specific types of crimes, such as being the victim of interpersonal violence, in the form of assault, rape, stalking and violence, which occurs in intimate relationships.

The belief that one will be blamed by others for one's victimisation is a powerful predictor of non-disclosures of crimes. This has been frequently reported in the context of sexual offences, whereby victims have stated they do not, or have not, disclosed their experience as they believe that others would blame them for the events; this in turn can have short- and long-term impacts on psychological well-being. Justifications from others as to why a sexual assault has occurred have included statements such as the victim was intoxicated, the victim did not fight back or the victim was promiscuous or seductive (Whatley, 2005). However, it is important to recognise that no matter the characteristics or lifestyle choices of a victim, a victim is never responsible for the actions of a perpetrator of crime; particularly that of sexual violence (Turvey, 2011).

Psychological theories of victim blaming

Several explanations, based on psychological theory, have been put forth as to why people blame victims for their own victimisation. The most prominent of these are the defensive attribution theory (DAT) and just world beliefs (JWB). DAT proposes that people have an innate need to protect their view that they are not vulnerable to victimisation. Strongly held beliefs are that terrible events that occur to other people are avoidable. Therefore, when faced with a victim, they attribute a cause for the victimisation directly to the victim. This increased attribution of responsibility to the victim is a cognitive coping strategy which maintains the view that people have control over events that happen to them, which in turn provides a sense of predictability and security. Ultimately, the perceived threat to oneself is minimised, irrespective of potential errors or biases in the attribution of cause.

Shaver reported that the key components in how much responsibility was attributed to a victim by others were related to how similar/dissimilar people perceived themselves to be to a person involved and how likely they believed that they could find themselves in a similar situation in the future. Indeed, a study by Grubb and Harrower (2009) focused on attribution of blame in cases of rape. The authors surveyed 160 undergraduate students (105 women and 55 men) from a university in the UK. Participants were asked to read one of three rape scenarios and then respond to a series of questions related to their own perceived similarity to both the male perpetrator and the female victim. They concluded that when participants perceived themselves to be highly similar to the victim they attributed less blame to the victim. Shaver (1970) refers to this as judgemental leniency. This is a process explained within the field of forensic psychology as one where people employ self-protective defence mechanisms, for example harm avoidance and blame avoidance. The former refers to a refusal to accept that random misfortune may happen to them and the latter to a need to believe that should they experience a similar event they will not be held responsible (blamed) for that event.

The concept of JWB proposes that individuals have a need to believe that they live in a world where people get what they deserve. The belief that the world is 'JUST' enables individuals to perceive the world as being stable and orderly. In other words, if people get what they deserve and they are 'good' people then bad things will not happen to them. Without such a belief it would be difficult for individuals to commit to long-range goals. Therefore, a belief in a just world serves an important adaptive function for the individual; indeed, any evidence to the contrary which suggests that the world is not just can be psychologically troublesome to the person and their overall sense of safety within the world. Prior research has concluded that JWB may predict victim blaming, with stronger JWB being associated with a higher propensity of victim blaming (Strömwall et al, 2012; Hayes et al, 2013). In other words, the more a person believes that people get what they deserve, the more likely they are to blame victims for their own victimisation. Sleath and Woodhams (2014) reported that the JWB literature has been relatively consistent in concluding that higher JWB relates to increased victim blaming, but that when specifically looking at this relationship for the offence of rape the picture is less clear. For example, in assessing university students regarding ratings of blame and responsibility for a sexualised crime, Rye et al (2006) reported that belief in a just world was not a significant predictor of ratings.

The trauma of criminal victimisation

Unfortunately, being potentially blamed for one's own victimisation is not the only adverse consequence that victims of crime experience. Indeed, there is a myriad of potential adverse social and psychological outcomes which have been reported. One core perspective relates to the fact that many occurrences of crime can also be defined as traumatic life events for the victim (for example, rape, sexual assault, physical assault). The Diagnostic and Statistical Manual of Mental Disorders (DSM-5) defines a traumatic life experience as 'exposure to actual or threatened death, serious injury, or sexual violence in one or more of the following ways: direct experience, witnessing, or learning about, repeated or extreme exposure to aversive details.' Crimes against one's person, such as physical assault, rape and childhood maltreatment therefore clearly constitute a traumatic life event. Trauma is known to likely impact adversely on psychological well-being.

One outcome of traumatic life experiences, including crimes against the person, is post-traumatic stress disorder (PTSD), which is therefore an issue of concern in forensic psychology. PTSD is a psychological reaction that results from exposure to a traumatic life event which is characterised by 20 symptoms grouped into four separate symptom clusters. The clusters are termed Intrusion (also referred to as Re-experiencing [five symptoms]), Avoidance (two symptoms), Negative Alterations in Cognition and Mood (seven symptoms) and Alterations in Arousal and Reactivity (six symptoms). Symptoms include nightmares, flashbacks, avoidance of reminders of the trauma, memory and concentration problems and irritability and anger (Armour et al, 2016). PTSD is a debilitating disorder which can significantly impact a person's ability to function in both their private and occupational lives. Moreover, despite PTSD being the most studied of trauma outcomes, it is perfectly normal for PTSD to be experienced co-morbidly with other psychological disorders such as substance use disorders, depressive disorders and anxiety disorders (Breslau et al, 2009).

It is of course important to acknowledge that not all crime victims experience PTSD. Indeed, some may experience a range of alternative adverse psychological outcomes after victimisation including depression. Many studies have established a link between crimes against the person, such as intimate partner violence and childhood maltreatment, and depressive symptomatology (Lamothe et al, 2019). However, many victims of crime may also be regarded as resilient to the potential adverse psychological outcomes and may experience little to no impact on their well-being because of their criminal victimisation.

Of note is that a potential consequence of criminal victimisation is re-victimisation. Indeed, a known reliable predictor of victimisation is past victimisation and a growing body of literature has demonstrated the cumulative impacts of the experience of trauma on overall psychological well-being. Armour and Sleath (2014) assessed retrospective reports of victimisations and uncovered homogenous groups of individuals who reported victimisations in childhood, adolescence and again in adulthood. It is also well established in the childhood maltreatment literature that children rarely experience a single stand-alone event of maltreatment; rather, it is the case that multiple victimisations often co-occur. Thus, victimisations can occur both concurrently and longitudinally (Burns et al, 2016). Re-victimisation of criminal events has been reported frequently in the literature on intimate partner violence (see Kuijpers et al, 2012) and childhood sexual abuse (see Classen et al, 2005; McLafferty et al, 2018), and this co-occurring and cumulative nature of victimisation is known to impact adversely on a wide range of social and psychological outcomes which impact an individual's ability to function occupationally and within personal relationships (Contractor et al, 2018; McLafferty et al, 2018).

The far-reaching consequences of criminal victimisation

Another important consideration in the study of forensic psychology, as focused on victims, is that crime victimisation can be far-reaching beyond the person who has been directly victimised. Indeed, there are many secondary victims, including those within the immediate family of the victim and those in the victim's wider social and occupational networks, their occupational organisations and wider society (the latter through lost productivity due to absenteeism and presenteeism and economical costs related to the aftermath of the crime). A clear example of the deleterious impact on relatives of victims of crime is the impact on non-offending caregivers in cases of childhood maltreatment disclosures and responses.

Non-offending caregivers are known to experience significant psychological distress and mental health difficulties which can last for many years post disclosures (Elliott and Cairns, 2001). On top of this, they may also face rejection from prior support networks such as other family members and friends (particularly if the support networks are shared with the perpetrator of the abuse) and, similarly, if the perpetrator was their intimate partner or spouse the separation can also impact on financial stability. Non-offending caregivers have reported experiences of criticism over their parenting and their corresponding ability to protect the child, accusations of supporting or encouraging false allegations, being denied access to support and services, and experiencing a lack of sensitivity towards them and the situation from professionals. It has been reported that the need for support for non-offending caregivers is often synonymous with the need for support of the maltreated child but that these needs may not be in tandem and that professionals should bear this in mind (Elliott and Cairns, 2001).

Conclusion

This chapter has introduced the reader to forensic psychology and the historical developments of forensic victimology, which is the objective and scientific study of victims of crime (Turvey, 2014; Brotto et al, 2017). The chapter presented information on early victim typologies and more contemporary research into the study of poly-victimisation categories and predictors. This led to a discussion of the forensic psychological concepts of victim precipitation and victim blaming and two theoretical perspectives within forensic psychology explaining why this occurs: DAT and JWB. Subsequently, the traumatic nature of criminal victimisation was discussed, leading into an overview of a possible psychological consequence of trauma exposure, namely PTSD. The chapter acknowledged that re-victimisation could occur concurrently and longitudinally and that a predictor of victimisation is past victimisation. To conclude, the chapter presented information within the field of forensic psychology on how the impact of crime extends far beyond the direct victim.

References

Armour, C. and Sleath, E. (2014) 'Assessing the co-occurrence of intimate partner violence domains across the life-course: relating typologies to mental health', *European Journal of Psychotraumatology*, 5(1): 24620.

Armour C., Műllerová, J. and Elhai, J.D. (2016) 'A systematic literature review of PTSD's latent structure in the Diagnostic and Statistical Manual of Mental Disorders: DSM-IV to DSM-5', *Clinical Psychology Review*, 44: 60–74.

Breslau, J., Miller, E., Breslau, N., Bohnert, K., Lucia, V. and Schweitzer, J. (2009) 'The impact of early behavior disturbances on academic achievement in high school', *Pediatrics*, 123(6): 1472–6.

Brotto, G.L.M., Sinnamon, G. and Petherick, W. (2017) 'Victimology and predicting victims of personal violence', in W. Petherick and G. Sinnamon (eds) *Psychology of Criminal and Antisocial Behavior*, Cambridge, MA: Academic Press, pp 70–144.

Burns, C.R., Lagdon, S., Boyda, D. and Armour, C. (2016) 'Interpersonal polyvictimization and mental health in males', *Journal of Anxiety Disorders*, 40: 75–82.

Classen, C.C., Palesh, O.G. and Aggarwal, R. (2005) 'Sexual revictimization: a review of the empirical literature', *Trauma, Violence, and Abuse*, 6(2): 103–29.

Contractor, A.A., Caldas, S., Fletcher, S., Shea, M.T. and Armour, C. (2018) 'Empirically derived lifespan polytraumatization typologies: a systematic review', *Journal of Clinical Psychology*, 74(7): 1137–59.

Elliott, A.N. and Carnes, C.N. (2001) 'Reactions of nonoffending parents to the sexual abuse of their child: a review of the literature', *Child Maltreatment*, 6(4): 314331.

Finkelhor, D., Ormrod, R.K. and Turner, H.A. (2007a) 'Poly-victimization: a neglected component in child victimization', *Child Abuse & Neglect*, 31(1): 7–26.

Finkelhor, D., Ormrod, R.K. and Turner, H.A. (2007b) 'Polyvictimization and trauma in a national longitudinal cohort', *Development and Psychopathology*, 19(1): 149–66.

Grubb, A.R. and Harrower, J. (2009) 'Understanding attribution of blame in cases of rape: an analysis of participant gender, type of rape and perceived similarity to the victim', *Journal of Sexual Aggression*, 15(1): 63–81.

Hayes, R.M., Lorenz, K. and Bell, K.A. (2013) 'Victim blaming others: rape myth acceptance and the just world belief', *Feminist Criminology*, 8(3): 202–20.

Kuijpers, K.F., Van der Knaap, L.M. and Winkel, F.W. (2012) 'Victims' influence on intimate partner violence revictimization: an empirical test of dynamic victim-related risk factors', *Journal of Interpersonal Violence*, 27(9): 1716–42.

Lamothe, J., Fortin, C., Fortin, M., Lapierre, S. and Guay, S. (2019) 'Identifying crime victims vulnerable to persistent depressive symptoms: results from a secondary analysis', *Journal of Affective Disorders*, 255: 23–6.

McLafferty, M., O'Neill, S., Murphy, S., Armour, C. and Bunting, B. (2018) 'Population attributable fractions of psychopathology and suicidal behaviour associated with childhood adversities in Northern Ireland', *Child Abuse & Neglect*, 77: 35–45.

McLafferty, M., Ross, J., Waterhouse-Bradley, B. and Armour, C. (2019) 'Childhood adversities and psychopathology among military veterans in the US: the mediating role of social networks', *Journal of Anxiety Disorders*, 65: 47–55.

Rye, B.J., Greatrix, S.A. and Enright, C.S. (2006) 'The case of the guilty victim: the effects of gender of victim and gender of perpetrator on attributions of blame and responsibility', *Sex Roles*, 54: 639–49.

Shaver, K.G. (1970) 'Defensive attribution: effects of severity and relevance of the responsibility assigned for an accident', *Journal of Personality and Social Psychology*, 1492: 101–13, DOI: http://dx.doi.org/10.1037/h0028777.

Sleath, E. and Woodhams, J. (2014) 'Expectations about victim and offender behaviour during stranger rape' *Psychology, Crime & Law*, 20(8): 798–820.

Strömwall, L.A., Alfredsson, H. and Landström, S. (2012) 'Blame attributions and rape: effects of belief in a just world and relationship level', *Legal and Criminological Psychology*, 18(2): 254–61.

Turvey, B.E. (2011) 'Forensic victimology in cases of sexual assault', in J.O. Savino and B.E. Turvey (eds) *Rape Investigation Handbook* (2nd edn), San Diego, CA: Elsevier Science, pp 209–29.

Turvey, B.E. (2014) *Forensic Victimology: Examining Violent Crime Victims in Investigative and Legal Contexts*, Cambridge, MA: Academic Press.

Walster, E. (1966) 'Assignment of responsibility for an accident', *Journal of Personality and Social Psychology*, 3(1): 73–9.

Whatley, M.A. and Valdosta State University (2005) 'The effect of participant sex, victim dress, and traditional attitudes on causal judgments for marital rape victims', *Journal of Family Violence*, 20(3): 191–200.

7

Forensic psychology and perpetrators of crime: the dark triad and narcissism

Victoria Blinkhorn

Introduction

Individuals who are labelled 'perpetrators of crime' are those who have committed a criminal offence and have been subsequently convicted. Despite the Office for National Statistics releasing frequent reports including figures of crime rates and victim information within the UK, little is ever published concerning the characteristics of the perpetrators. So which individuals are more likely to commit an offence? Psychological theories of crime have become quite influential within forensic psychology and much research has been conducted in this area to support the significant links between personality traits and offending behaviour. This chapter will focus on one of the dark triad (DT) personalities, narcissism, and its relationship with different types of criminal behaviour.

The DT refers to three distinct but yet overlapping personality traits: narcissism, Machiavellianism and psychopathy. Narcissism originates from the Greek myth of Narcissus who was a hunter and son of the river god Cephissus. He was a physically beautiful young man and fell in love with his own reflection in a pool of water. After realising that his love could not be reciprocated, he lost his will to live and committed suicide. This Greek myth is significant with regard to how narcissism can be described as today. Narcissistic individuals are typically selfish, boastful, have low empathy, are very sensitive to criticism and have an entitled nature. Narcissism, as a subclinical personality construct, has attracted the attention of social and personality psychologists worldwide. Studies have found a significant rise in mean narcissism scores between 1979 to the present from the Narcissistic Personality Inventory (Raskin and Hall, 1979), one of the most popular measures of narcissism within the literature. As a result, research on subclinical narcissism has increased dramatically in recent years.

Narcissism and aggression

Over the years, narcissism has been linked to a large number of offensive behaviours, ranging from minor to very severe. It is well known that narcissists are prone to break social etiquette norms (for example, Bockler et al, 2017).

Narcissists display lower generosity and higher retaliation in everyday life, they are more likely to use offensive language to attract attention and they engage in truancy (Adams et al, 2014). They are also more likely to believe everyday transgressing is acceptable and they report more willingness to engage in behaviour that could trouble others (Daddis and Brunell, 2015; Wallace et al, 2016). Aggressive behaviour has frequently been linked with narcissism, and numerous theories, or explanations, exist as to why that is. One of the most accepted and empirically supported explanations as to why narcissists may engage in aggressive behaviour is based around the ego. Due to narcissists having very high self-esteem, if they experience an ego threat, for example, if the positive views of themselves are questioned, challenged, mocked and so on, they may respond aggressively, particularly against the source of the threat. Bushman and Baumeister (1998) referred to this as 'threatened egotism' and empirically demonstrated this through a number of experimental studies. Since then, many studies have found that narcissism is significantly related to direct aggression following negative feedback or insult (for example, Barry et al, 2006; Bushman et al, 2009; Vaillancourt, 2013) and to displaced aggression following an ego threat (see Martinez et al, 2008).

One particular type of negative feedback which can provoke narcissists to react aggressively is social exclusion. It has been found that narcissists are more aggressive after experiencing social exclusion (Twenge and Campbell, 2003). This aggression is more likely directed towards the individual who excluded them; however, they can also display aggression against an innocent third party who was not involved. In contrast, narcissism can also be linked with unprovoked aggression (for example, Centifanti et al, 2013), while others suggest that narcissism can be related to both provoked and unprovoked aggression (Barry et al, 2007). Some research has found a relationship between narcissism and displaced aggression towards an innocent victim not responsible for any provocation (Bushman and Baumeister, 1998). As such, this suggests that 'threatened egotism' is not necessarily always the reason for narcissists to behave aggressively and instead, narcissism can be associated with provoked and unprovoked aggression and the aggression can also be directed to a completely uninvolved individual, such as a stranger. Another, more recently suggested explanation as to why narcissists are prone to aggression is the notion that they have low levels of self-control (Vaughn, et al, 2007). Narcissism has been linked with low self-control and, independently, both narcissism and low self-control have been associated with a range of anti-social behaviours (for example, Vazire and Funder, 2006). However, less research has been conducted to investigate whether low self-control is actually a predictor, or explanation, of anti-social behaviour in narcissists. The few studies that have investigated this have found that individuals with high levels of narcissistic traits and deficiencies in self-control were much more likely to engage in violence (for example, Larson et al, 2015). As such, despite a large amount of research focusing on 'threatened egotism', there may be other explanations as to why narcissists are likely to behave aggressively.

Narcissism and sexual aggression

A particular type of aggressive behaviour which narcissism has been linked to is sexual aggression. Baumeister et al (2002) suggested two main explanations as to why narcissists may engage in sexualised aggression. Firstly, they are more likely to perceive an individual they desire as being interested and sexually available to them, when in reality, this may not be the case. As such, narcissists believe that sexual contact is what the individual wants and aggression is an incidental means by which the end is achieved. Narcissists' recollections of sexual activity would most likely concern consenting encounters with little or no memory of resistance and rejection. Secondly, aggression towards an individual is more likely to be sexualised if narcissists perceive themselves to have been offended as a result of their sexual advances being rejected. By reacting in a sexually aggressive way, the narcissist intends to sexually humiliate the individual as a form of payback due to feeling that way themselves when rejected.

Baumeister et al (2002) develop this idea in their 'narcissistic reactance theory of rape', which generally suggests that narcissists will desire sex more when it is refused. This creates an increased risk of sexualised aggression as the narcissist pursues sex, with the immediate goal of rape being to affirm their entitlement to have sex with any individual they choose. Intercourse is desired as a symbolic act of claiming another individual rather than sexual satisfaction and, as such, the primary goal is egotistical rather than physical. This theory has been empirically tested a number of times by Bushman et al (2003) and the findings are generally conclusive. Narcissism relates to higher levels of rape myth acceptance and lower levels of empathy towards rape victims. Narcissists also respond more favourably towards some scenes shown on a videotape depicting rape and they rate those scenes as more entertaining, enjoyable and more sexually arousing. Further, narcissistic males reacted more negatively and punitively towards a female confederate who refused the sexual stimulation the participant expected (Bushman et al, 2003). Findings such as these support the 'narcissistic reactance theory of rape' and also the theory that narcissistic males feel less empathy towards females who may have been a victim of sexual coercion or aggression.

A number of studies have found relationships between specific facets of narcissism and types of aggression, particularly sexual aggression. A common finding is that this type of behaviour is related to the entitlement/exploitative facet of narcissism. This particular facet is deemed as being maladaptive and socially toxic compared to other facets such as leadership/authority and grandiose exhibitionism. Some research has focused on couples and asked them about their partner's aggression. The findings typically show that for females this facet of narcissism is significantly correlated with both their own perpetrated sexual coercion and also their reported partner's sexual coercion. For males, it is correlated with perpetrated physical assault and their reported partner's sexual coercion (Simmons et al, 2005). Other research has found that maladaptive narcissism in a male clinical sample is positively correlated with sexual violence including rape (Russell and King, 2017). These findings suggest that this may be a defensive reaction in which the males overestimate their partner's sexual coercion in order to justify their own coercive behaviour.

Narcissism in women

Similar to the discussions around gender bias and domestic violence, the majority of research on narcissism and offending behaviour has focused on aggression, sexual aggression, interpersonal violence and domestic violence, specifically in males. Up until quite recently, only a few select studies had been conducted on narcissism and offending behaviour in women. Using a clinical sample, one study found that incarcerated women who had committed violent crimes, including murder, had much higher levels of narcissism than average (Warren et al, 2002). Another used a female adolescent sample and found relationships between narcissism and crime severity, conduct disorder, violent crimes and alcohol and drug use (Pechorro et al, 2017). There is also the research conducted by Simmons et al (2005), as mentioned earlier, which focused on couples and reported aggression.

More recently, the work of Blinkhorn et al (2015, 2016, 2019) has expanded what is currently know about narcissism and offending behaviour in women. The first study focused on sexually coercive behaviours including four types: sexual arousal, emotional manipulation, exploitation of the intoxicated and physical force, threats and harm. It was found that women who scored highly on the entitlement/exploitative facet of narcissism were significantly more likely to have engaged in all four types of sexually coercive behaviour compared to men. The second study investigated attitudes towards violence covering four themes: war, corporal punishment of children, penal code violence and intimate violence. Again, women who scored highly on this particular facet of narcissism had more accepting attitudes towards violence concerning war, penal code and intimate violence. Interestingly, attitudes towards the corporal punishment of children did not change regardless of how narcissistic they scored. This could perhaps be due to the arguably natural (whether conscious or unconscious) maternal instinct certain theorists state women have.

The third study focused on a wide range of offending behaviours including general violence, drug taking, interpersonal violence, criminal damage and theft. Women who scored highly on the same facet, entitlement/exploitative, reported engaging in more overall criminal behaviour (a combination of all the types computed together) and also having engaged in general violence within the last 12 months, thus demonstrating that they were arguably criminally active at the time of the research (Blinkhorn et al, 2019). Further, a later study by Blinkhorn et al (2021) investigated the same attitudes towards violence as per the previous (Blinkhorn et al, 2016), but by provoking social exclusion via a custom-made game beforehand. Narcissism was correlated with less boredom and stronger feelings of rejection when excluded from the game and the entitlement/ exploitativeness facet of narcissism was correlated with higher acceptance of violence in the exclusion condition.

A quite recent study by Green et al (2019) used a very novel approach to investigating female narcissism and intimate partner violence by interviewing male ex-partners in order to gain an insight into their perceptions and experiences. The findings illuminated that perceived expressions of female narcissists depicted presentations of narcissistic vulnerability. The ways in which the females were obtaining their positions of power and control over their partners was by using gender-related norms and adopting a 'victim status', playing the 'mother card' and taking advantage of legal and societal benefits. This research demonstrates that female narcissists engage in offending behaviour in a different way than males do. The traditional presentation of a narcissistic person is to be overt and grandiose, but perhaps women behave in more strategic and manipulative ways. Of course, much more research is required in this field in order to elucidate gender differences in narcissistic offenders.

Conclusion

In summary, this chapter has demonstrated why psychological theories of crime have become rather influential within forensic psychology by focusing on one of the personalities within the DT, that being narcissism. A large number of perpetrators of aggression, general violence, domestic violence and sexual abuse are likely to have some type of narcissistic personality traits according to the theories and research discussed in this chapter, which of course is not exhaustive. Only recently has research investigated the gender differences in narcissistic offenders and, to date, it seems there is a significant contrast in presentation between men and women.

References
Adams, J.M., Florell, D., Burton, K.A. and Hart, W. (2014) 'Why do narcissists disregard social-etiquette norms? A test of two explanations for why narcissism relates to offensive-language use', *Personality and Individual Differences*, 58: 26–30.
Barry, C.T., Chaplin, W.F. and Grafeman, S.J. (2006) 'Aggression following performance feedback: the influences of narcissism, feedback valence, and comparative standard', *Personality and Individual Differences*, 41: 177–87.
Barry, T.D., Thompson, A., Barry, C.T., Lochman, J.E., Adler, K. and Hill, K. (2007) 'The importance of narcissism in predicting proactive and reactive aggression in moderately to highly aggressive children', *Aggressive Behavior*, 33: 185–97.
Baumeister, R.F., Catanese, K.R. and Wallace, H.M. (2002) 'Conquest by force: a narcissistic reactance theory of rape and sexual coercion', *Review of General Psychology*, 6: 92–135.

Blinkhorn, V., Lyons, M. and Almond, L. (2015) 'The ultimate femme fatale? Narcissism predicts serious and aggressive sexually coercive behaviour in females', *Personality and Individual Differences*, 87: 219–23.

Blinkhorn, V., Lyons, M. and Almond, L. (2016) 'Drop the bad attitude! Narcissism predicts acceptance of violent behaviour', *Personality and Individual Differences*, 98: 157–61.

Blinkhorn, V., Lyons, M. and Almond, L. (2019) 'Criminal minds: narcissism predicts offending behavior in a non-forensic sample', *Deviant Behavior*, 40(3): 353–60.

Blinkhorn, V., Lyons, M., Collier, E.S. and Almond, L. (2021) 'The relationship between narcissism and acceptance of violence revealed through a game designed to induce social ostracism', *Journal of Social Psychology*, 161(3): 261–71.

Bockler, A., Sharifi, M., Kanske, P. and Singer, T. (2017) 'Social decision making in narcissism: reduced generosity and increased retaliation are driven by alterations in perspective-taking and anger', *Personality and Individual Differences*, 104: 1–7.

Bushman, B.J. and Baumeister, R.F. (1998) 'Threatened egotism, narcissism, self-esteem, and direct and displaced aggression: does self-love or self-hate lead to violence?' *Journal of Personality and Social Psychology*, 75: 219–29.

Bushman, B.J., Bonacci, A.M., Baumeister, R.F. and van Dijk, M. (2003) 'Narcissism, sexual refusal, and aggression: testing a narcissistic reactance model of sexual coercion', *Personality Processes and Individual Differences*, 84: 1027–40.

Bushman, B. J., Baumeister, R.F., Thomaes, S., Ryu, E., Begeer, S. and West, S.G. (2009) 'Looking again, and harder, for a link between low self-esteem and aggression', *Journal of Personality*, 77: 427–46.

Centifanti, L.C., Kimonis, E.R., Frick, P.J. and Aucoin, K.J. (2013) 'Emotional reactivity and the association between psychopathy-linked narcissism and aggression in detained adolescent boys', *Development and Psychopathology*, 25: 473–85.

Daddis, C. and Brunell, A.B. (2015). 'Entitlement, exploitativeness, and reasoning about everyday transgressions: a social domain analysis', *Journal of Research in Personality*, 58: 115–26.

Green, A., Charles, K. and MacLean, R. (2019) 'Perceptions of female narcissism in intimate partner violence: a thematic analysis', *Qualitative Methods in Psychology Bulletin*, 28: 13–27.

Larson, M., Vaughn, M.G., Salas-Wright, C.P. and Delisi, M. (2015) 'Narcissism, low self-control, and violence among a nationally representative sample', *Criminal Justice and Behaviour*, 42: 644–61.

Martinez, M.A., Zeichner, A., Reidy, D.E. and Miller, J.D. (2008) 'Narcissism and displaced aggression: effects of positive, negative, and delayed feedback', *Personality and Individual Differences*, 44(1): 140–9.

Pechorro, P., Maroco, J., Ray, J.V., Goncalves, R.A. and Nunes, C. (2017) 'A brief measure of narcissism among female juvenile delinquents and community youths', *International Journal of Offender Therapy and Comparative Criminology*, 62(8), DOI: https://doi.org/10.1177/0306624X17700855.

Raskin, R.N. and Hall, C.S. (1979) 'A Narcissistic Personality Inventory', *Psychological Reports*, 45: 590.

Russell, T.D. and King, A.R. (2017) 'Distrustful, conventional, entitled, and dysregulated: PID-5 personality facets predict hostile masculinity and sexual violence in community men', *Journal of Interpersonal Violence*, 35(3–4), DOI: https://doi.org/10.1177/0886260517689887.

Simmons, C.A., Lehmann, P., Cobb, N. and Fowler, C.R. (2005) 'Personality profiles of women and men arrested for domestic violence: an analysis of similarities and differences', *Journal of Offender Rehabilitation*, 41: 63–81.

Twenge, J.M. and Campbell, W.K. (2003). '"Isn't it fun to get the respect that we're going to deserve?" Narcissism, social rejection, and aggression', *Personality and Social Psychology Bulletin*, 29: 261–72.

Vaillancourt, T. (2013) 'Students aggress against professors in reaction to receiving poor grades: an effect moderated by student narcissism and self-esteem', *Aggressive Behavior*, 39: 71–84.

Vaughn, M.G., DeLisi, M., Beaver, K.M., Wright, J.P. and Howard, M.O. (2007) 'Toward a psychopathology of self-control theory: the importance of narcissistic traits', *Behavioral Sciences & the Law*, 25: 803–21.

Vazire, S. and Funder, D.C. (2006) 'Impulsivity and the self-defeating behavior of narcissists', *Personality and Social Psychology Review*, 10: 154–65.

Wallace, H.M., Scheiner, B.R.M. and Grotzinger, A. (2016) 'Grandiose narcissism predicts willingness to behave badly without proportional tolerance for others' bad behaviour', *Current Psychology*, 35: 234–43.

Warren, J.I., Burnette, M., South, S.C., Chauhan, P., Bale, R. and Friend, R. (2002) 'Personality disorders and violence among female prison inmates', *Journal of the American Academy of Psychiatry and the Law*, 30: 502–9.

8

Forensic psychology and rehabilitation

Shona Robinson-Edwards and Stephanie Kewley

Rehabilitation is multifaceted in terms of its role, implementation and purpose. In its simplest form rehabilitation is the result of planned intervention/action that restores and returns the person to a *state* prior to offending by incorporating various psycho-social programmes. Employed either alongside or after punishment, rehabilitation has invariably been perceived as a *type* of punishment; rarely is it promoted as an alternative, despite the Probation Service's lengthy history. Over recent decades, both the concept and application of rehabilitation have been challenged, from claims of 'nothing works' to criticisms of systemic discrimination due to coercive programme design, psychological/individualistic focus and correctional policy that targets the most disadvantaged in society (Burke and Collett, 2016). Indeed, with record incarceration rates, reoffending levels stubbornly high and collapsed policies designed to *transform rehabilitation* and offer a *rehabilitation revolution* the notion of rehabilitation has become a somewhat unattractive blot on the criminal justice landscape.

Despite the proliferation of punitive social, welfare and judicial policy, added to a consistent rhetoric of the irredeemability of the 'criminal', nearly all those criminally sanctioned will return to the community at some point. While incapacitation is a common punishment in that it removes or restricts movement (for example, electronic monitoring or imprisonment) of people in society, it is a temporary solution. In essence, incapacitation in and of itself does not deal with the root causes of crime, rather it shifts and delays the consequences of crime from one place to the next (McNeill, 2019). Although orthodox responses to crime focus on punitive controls, management and risk aversion, there are increasing models 'of practice and criminological theory in which the principles of strength-based approaches are in existence and indeed, thriving' (Kewley, 2017, p 13; Kewley and Brereton, 2022).

Four forms of rehabilitation

McNeill (2012) proposes that effective rehabilitation can only be addressed by considering the *four forms of rehabilitation*. This concept serves as an excellent framework in which the interdisciplinary nature of rehabilitation and reintegration consider at least the four key domains: psychological, moral, legal and social. While rehabilitation approaches have historically approached treatment or restoration strategies mainly from an individual and psychological stance, there are important known external factors related to crime and criminal behaviour. While the role of the psychological process for the individual is key to understanding any rehabilitation process, of equal importance is a need to explore and engage with the moral, legal and social aspects of reintegration and desistance from crime. McNeill (2012) calls for greater diversity in rehabilitation approaches, as to provide psychological interventions in isolation will only partially support an effective process of rehabilitation.

Firstly, McNeill argues that the psychological dimension remains crucial in any effective rehabilitation approach as personal and psychological factors contribute to the desistance trajectory and any process of individual change. Indeed, identity theory or cognitive transformation posits that in order for a person to desist from crime, a new non-offending identity needs to be established first; that is, the person must make internal shifts in the sense of self to such a degree that they are open to alternative, non-criminal life choices (Maruna, 2001; Maruna et al, 2004). As such, and without internal shifts, McNeill articulates that rehabilitation cannot be done to a person, rather, the process is mutual: rehabilitation can only be carried out 'with' the person. In order for a person to effectively engage in such a process they have to have some 'will' or internal capacity to do so; indeed, without a cognitive transformation or a shift in identity desistance from crime is difficult. There are, however, barriers to cognitive transformation, therefore many people will encounter difficulties with this process, in that they may lack the capability, opportunity or capacity to change (Giordano, 2016). With this in mind, support and assistance may be needed to aid the person to develop their capacity to change, perhaps by developing existing psychological skills and abilities or learning and practising new skills. To achieve this, 'appropriate' and 'accessible' means of support will be essential to any process of psychological rehabilitation; these might include cognitive behavioural support such as thinking or problem-solving skills or the development of emotional regulation, overcoming trauma or tackling addiction (Carter and Mann, 2016). However, all of these require professional assessment and support.

A shift in identity and a new construct of the sense of self are transforming factors by which a person moves away from offending to a new identity rooted in non-offending. Rehabilitation approaches that focus on providing hope for the future and the construction of an identity centred on a positive affiliation are essential to the process of cognitive transformation (Gålnander, 2020). While the process requires an internal change, this can only be achieved when the person has a sense of authentic hope; when they have the confidence that they can live a life free from crime and are optimistic that they will be accepted into society as their transformed non-offending self. One of the ways in which a sense of hope can be nurtured is by providing people with greater senses of autonomy, choice and responsibility. Cognitive transformation is likely to take place when rehabilitation is done 'with' the person rather than 'to' them. Cultivating a greater sense of autonomy helps centre the control back to the individual, fostering a belief in personal growth and change.

McNeill's second form is the moral dimension of rehabilitation and is concerned with the concept of 'justice'. Within academic literature the question of what constitutes 'justice' is consistently debated. Embedded in this discussion is the notion of rehabilitation and the role it plays in people's concept and perception of 'justice'. While an understanding of punishment is quite clear, the extent to which mechanisms of punishment provide opportunities for moral redress (for both victim and perpetrator of crime) through engagement with the person and the community who has been harmed is unclear (Maruna, 2016). The effectiveness of prison as a form of punishment or rehabilitation, for example, in terms of how it helps people desist from crime, is contentious, particularly given high reoffending rates. In addition, the current system fails to offer moral redress and reform, instead, with punishment as a priority of justice, victims' voices are silenced and accounts between the person and the community who have been harmed are ignored. Appreciating the needs of the person criminally convicted is important to a collective understanding; nevertheless, there has to be a balance. In order to move forward and attempt to repair the harm caused through moral redress, engaging with victims, the communities they live in and the person criminally convicted are essential (Maruna, 2011). Not considering all parts and the unique needs of this trio is detrimental to an effective rehabilitation process.

Thirdly, the legal dimension and role of the judicial system to return citizens from an 'offender' back to a citizen are fundamental. McNeill (2012) challenges the lack of support and gateways in which people criminally convicted are able to 'return' to their communities as 'reformed citizens'. Rather, current legal processes support the continued stigmatisation of people with convictions, alongside their community and family members, long beyond periods of offending and after the end of their prison or community sentence. Indeed, the construction of such stigmatised labels and a criminal identity are continuous features in their lives. To move away from criminal and legal labelling is particularly challenging and McNeill (2012) argues that legal processes play a direct role in the formation and continued stigmatisation inflicted on the person, community and family members. Indeed, symbols of punishment and in particular imprisonment are highly problematic when considering their impact on the rehabilitation process. The prospect of returning home for some who have been convicted of a crime is a challenge; without a legal lens of rehabilitation that mirrors and counters the harms caused by the rituals of prosecution, incarceration and labelling many are unable to navigate the reintegration process effectively (Henley, 2018). Thus, from a legal perspective, how symbolic gestures, processes or procedures can be used when individuals embark upon their process of re-entry must be considered. The role of the legal system in supporting those released from prison and those who attempt to reintegrate back into the community is failing. These limitations impact the person's desistance process; the stigmatisation and criminalisation of those attempting to build a 'good life' is caused by a legal system which operates in a social and political vacuum, one that is individualistic, punitive and reductivist

(Cavadino et al, 2013). Legal constructions and assumptions must be challenged by effective rehabilitation systems that include opportunities for moral redress and reform.

Fourthly, McNeill's (2012) requirement for social rehabilitation resonates with a nested ecological system in which humans exist and function within interconnected layers of social structures (Kewley, 2017). The social aspect of rehabilitation is concerned with the reciprocal process of the re-socialisation of citizens, the nature of society/community and the connections people have with each other. Simply put, connections with communities and the state play vital roles in this process (Weaver, 2015). Social relationships are important predictors of the desistance process. Weaver and McNeill (2015) explored the narratives of desisters who endorsed the importance of meaningful relationships which helped support the process of 'successful' reintegration. Central to this are connections and reconnections with family ties, getting married or starting a family. For people attempting to desist but without informal ties, meaningful formal relationships with probation or social workers can be effective sources of developing social capital. This thus helps to strengthen wider community interactions in which community bonds can help reconnect and repair relationships. The development of such formal social relationships and bonds is reciprocal and provides exposure to opportunities in which desisters can have their needs met, but they too can develop insight and awareness of the needs of their community and how they can contribute to it.

Criminal justice systems (CJSs) tend to centre on the notion of punishment, often in the form of imprisonment, with limited opportunity for people to repair and engage in moral redress. Yet the desistance literature indicates that giving people with convictions the opportunity to 'give back' and make amends helps foster a process of desistance. Despite a rising prison and community-sentenced population, along with the social and economic costs that are required to resource such a system, it is surprising greater opportunities that foster a climate which promotes the process of desistance are not embraced. Fundamental changes are needed to radically overhaul rehabilitation and sentencing practices. McNeill's (2012) four forms of rehabilitation provide a platform for such reform to be built upon. Like offending behaviour, rehabilitation and desistance from crime are complex and multifaceted, thus any response to crime must take an interdisciplinary approach that tackles the psychological, moral, legal and social factors that support people, their families and the communities in which they live throughout a process of desistance and reintegration.

However, while the current system continues to tackle these issues from an individual and reductivism position, harm and reoffending rates persist. Reform is needed, but reform that moves beyond the siloed contributions of criminologists, psychologists, practitioners and legal representatives. Kewley (2017, p 16) calls for a 'true interdisciplinary approach' in which those impacted by the CJS (people with convictions and/or victims of crime), policy makers, academics from all disciplines, health and social work practitioners, education, community groups/members, businesspeople and so forth must contribute to future solutions. While criminal justice agents must continue to play a role in supporting effective rehabilitation strategies, they must do so nested within a much broader network of stakeholders and indeed, all must consider McNeill's (2012) four forms.

References

Burke, L. and Collett, S. (2016) 'Transforming rehabilitation: organizational bifurcation and the end of probation as we knew it?' *Probation Journal*, 63(2): 120–35, DOI: https://doi.org/10.1177/0264550516648400.

Carter, A.J. and Mann, R.E. (2017) 'Organizing principles for an integrated model of change for the treatment of sexual offending', in D.P. Boer (ed) *The Wiley Handbook on the Theories, Assessment and Treatment of Sexual Offending*, Chichester: Wiley & Sons, pp 359–81.

Cavadino, M., Dignan, J. and Mair, G. (2013) *The Penal System: An Introduction* (5th edn), London: SAGE.

Gålnander, R. (2020) 'Desistance from crime—to what? Exploring future aspirations and their implications for processes of desistance', *Feminist Criminology*, 15(3): 255–77.

Giordano, P.C. (2016) 'Mechanisms underlying the desistance process: reflections on "A theory of cognitive transformation"', in J. Shapland, D. Farrington and A. Bottoms (eds) *Global Perspectives on Desistance*, London: Routledge, pp 27–43.

Henley, A. (2018) 'Mind the gap: sentencing, rehabilitation and civic purgatory', *Probation Journal*, 65(3): 285–301.

Kewley, S. (2017) 'Strength based approaches and protective factors from a criminological perspective', *Aggression and Violent Behavior*, 32: 11–18.

Kewley, S. and Brereton, S. (2022) 'Public protection: examining the impact of strengthened public protection policy on probation practice', in L. Burke, N. Carr, E. Cluley, S. Collett and F. McNeill (eds) *Reimagining Probation Practice: Re-forming Rehabilitation in an Age of Penal Excess*, London: Routledge, pp 112–31.

Maruna, S. (2001) *Making Good: How Ex-offenders Reform and Reclaim their Lives*, Washington, DC: American Psychological Association.

Maruna, S. (2011) 'Reentry as a rite of passage', *Punishment & Society*, 13(1): 3–28, DOI: https://doi.org/10.1177/1462474510385641.

Maruna, S. (2016) 'Desistance and restorative justice: it's now or never', *Restorative Justice an International Journal*, 4(3): 289–301.

Maruna, S., Lebel, T., Mitchell, N. and Naples, M. (2004) 'Pygmalion in the reintegration process: desistance from crime through the looking glass', *Psychology, Crime & Law*, 10(3): 271–81.

McNeill, F. (2012) 'Four forms of "offender" rehabilitation: towards an interdisciplinary perspective', *Legal and Criminological Psychology*, 17(1): 18–36.

McNeill, F. (2019) *Pervasive Punishment: Making Sense of Mass Supervision*, London: Emerald Group Publishing.

Weaver, B. (2015) *Offending and Desistance: The Importance of Social Relations*, London: Routledge.

Weaver, B. and McNeill, F. (2015) 'Lifelines: desistance, social relations, and reciprocity', *Criminal Justice and Behavior*, 42(1): 95–107.

9

Forensic psychology and desistance

Stephanie Kewley and Lol Burke

The chapter will begin with a discussion of desistance. The desistance paradigm helps to understand how and why people cease criminal behaviour; however, defining desistance is not without debate. Desistance denotes the cessation of criminal behaviour, not as a distinct one-off event but as a process characterised by both distinguishable and graduated phases (Laub and Sampson, 2001; Maruna, 2001). This process is also not linear, people 'zig and zag' in and out of offending for periods of time, often long before permanent cessation occurs (Nugent and Schnizel, 2016). Desistance involves primary, secondary and, as has been explored more recently, tertiary phases (Weaver, 2019). The primary phase is understood as the period in which crime ceases whereas the secondary phase involves the transformation of the person's sense of self from one of 'offender' to that of a 'non-offender'; here crime stops, plus the person makes internal shifts in their perception of self. A tertiary phase occurs when the person is 'de-labelled' by others recognising and validating behaviour change. Phases of desistance are likely to feature periods of intermittency, indecisiveness, ambivalence, lapse and even relapse. Thus, desisting from crime is complex; people will likely experience barriers that not only prevent desistance but will derail and inhibit transformation (Patton and Farrall, 2021). Understanding this process of desistance is crucial, as effective desistance impacts all those involved in the criminal justice system (CJS). Not only does it help break the offending cycle, and therefore reduce recidivism and prevent future harm, but it also serves to help (re)build relationships, provide reparation and help desisters develop the strengths and resources needed to live a life free from crime (Burke et al, 2019). A summary of the key desistance domains is provided here: they include individual/agentic theory, social and structural theories, interactionist theory and situational theory.

Key desistance theories

Individual/agentic theories draw on ontogenetic explanations (maturation theory) and agentic explanations (cognitive processes) to explain why people desist from crime. Maturation theory claims people age out of crime because they simply grow up, becoming biologically and physically less able and motivated to commit crime (Laub and Sampson, 2001). While individual/agentic theories are useful, there are methodological and value-laden problems (Weaver, 2019). Firstly, rational choice theory (Cornish and Clarke, 1987) assumes all human choice is equal and free, yet inequalities such as barriers and the constraints of marginalised communities across CJSs and wider global communities can be observed. Secondly, it is debatable whether an individual level of analysis can equate to aggregate levels as these fail to recognise the idiosyncratic nature of individuals. Thirdly, specific crime types appear to have differing trajectories (for example, sexual offending and white-collar crime); thus the operationalisation of the desistance process is more complex than individual/agentic theories first propose.

Social and structural theories involve factors external to the actor (sociogenic). Social control theorists argue that where informal social and institutional bonds are weak or broken or values/beliefs/norms are not shared, people deviate away from these norms (Gottfredson and Hirschi, 1990). Young people are caught between the bonds of youth (peer groups) and informal social ties of adulthood such as marriage, employment, family, education and so forth (Hirschi, 1969). However, the process of desistance through social learning, like that of offending behaviour, can be (re)learned. Laub and Sampson (2001) found desistance occurs when informal bonds are repaired through affiliation with pro-social peers, groups and communities, exposure to rewarding and meaningful activities and employment, and the development of healthy intimate relationships. While these theories begin to inform an ecological application to desistance, they fail to respond to cultural, structural and historical nuances experienced by many people (Weaver, 2019). Much of the desistance research draws on dated male, heteronormative populations and ideologies, with little known of the experiences of women, non-heterosexuals and people from diverse religious backgrounds for example. While sociogenic factors are clearly important in the process of desistance, it is not yet fully understood how these structures shape people's decisions to desist, or how these are experienced by different populations nested within varying social ecologies.

Interactionist approaches consider the interplay and dependency of both agency and structure in the process of desistance; debate regarding whether one precedes the other, or if the two work together and are interconnected, continues (see Weaver, 2019, for a more detailed review of this debate). In Maruna's (2001) seminal *Making Good* study, he observed that those engaged in a process of desistance generated new or renewed self-identities; they did this as a reflection of their own shifting contexts and realities, making sense of internal transformations and changing behaviours. Giordano et al (2002) brought into focus the interaction between agency and structure. They observed that for desistance to occur external triggers are required and document key stages of the process – the person must be: (a) open to change; (b) exposed to opportunities or 'hooks for change'; (c) begin to see themselves as a new self, begin to replace old descriptions of themselves with new ones; and (d) distance themselves from old behaviours, seeing the old self negatively.

Like the previous two domains, interactionist theories remain highly individualised. While they take account of external contexts, they do this in the sense of the impact these external factors have on the actor's sense of self; they do not fully explore or explain the complexity of relationships within the mesosystem (mesosystems are structures and institutions that influence human development across the life course, such as school, peer groups, the workplace, church and so on) or how these are experienced by the desister. Greater understanding of the networked systems people exist in is needed (Fox, 2022), not only to understand the impact of these networks (friendship groups or families) on the process of desistance but to also understand how the desistance process is helped or hampered by relational, cultural and/or social systems and networks.

Situational theorists highlight the importance of situation for people moving away from crime (Farrall et al, 2014; Flynn, 2017). Routine in people's daily lives and activities take people to specific places and geographies (Flynn, 2017). The nature of these spaces influence how people perceive themselves in the world and, thus, determine the nature of activities and choices they make and inform their identity and sense of purpose. Unsurprisingly, desisters are more likely to engage in daily routines such as work, education or family life; interacting in particular social and geographical spaces and places. Spaces and places can, however, be harmful and impede desistance; for example, people recovering from substance abuse are often encouraged not to frequent places where substance use may occur, to avoid old haunts to prevent relapse, as the place itself (sounds, smells, and visual cues) can rouse memories and emotions linked to abuse. Place, space and time all play important but significantly underexplored roles in both the persistence and desistance of crime (Weaver, 2019). This is likely a result of the individualistic approach to tackling crime. If solutions to crime remain with the individual, policy makers and practitioners will not look to wider environmental and situational factors to address the causes of and the solutions to support desistance.

As the discussion has highlighted, the desistance paradigm consists of several models, theories and approaches, each of which draw on different explanations of crime at varying ecological levels. At the individual level, desistance is often about discovering new purposes, achievements and forms of recognition, which may be facilitated through involvement in generative activities, and practitioners can undoubtedly have a positive role to play in supporting and encouraging this process. Forensic and criminal justice practitioners are, however, somewhat restricted by current criminal justice regimes; the rehabilitation agenda for example, unintentionally labels individuals as central to the problem and not part of wider social and environmental contexts. The desistance literature highlights that if anything it is that achieving a non-offending identity, and crucially being seen by others as such, is neither easy nor straightforward. Solely focusing on the individual and their supposed deficits might assist in building human capital (for example, in terms of improving reasoning and decision-making skills, reinforcing pro-social behaviour and providing practical assistance and guidance) but it cannot generate the social capital which resides in the relationships through which participation, inclusion and, ultimately, desistance are facilitated. In conclusion, tackling crime and the problems of crime ought not to be addressed through a forensic, criminal justice or policing lens only, but instead through multifaceted and interdisciplinary approaches.

References

Burke, L., Collett, S. and McNeill, F. (2019) *Reimagining Rehabilitation: Beyond the Individual*, London: Routledge.

Cornish, D.B. and Clarke, R.V. (1987) 'Understanding crime displacement: an application of rational choice theory', *Criminology*, 25(4): 933–48.

Farrall, S., Hunter, B., Sharpe, G. and Calverley, A. (2014). *Criminal Careers in Transition: The Social Context of Desistance from Crime*, Oxford: Oxford University Press.

Flynn, N. (2017) *Criminal Behaviour in Context: Space, Place and Desistance from Crime*, Abingdon: Taylor & Francis.

Fox, K.J. (2022) 'Desistance frameworks', *Aggression and Violent Behavior*, 63: 101684.

Giordano, P.C., Cernkovich, S.A. and Rudolph, J.L. (2002) 'Gender, crime, and desistance: toward a theory of cognitive transformation', *American Journal of Sociology*, 107: 990–1064.

Gottfredson, M. and Hirschi, T. (1990) *A General Theory of Crime*, Stanford, CA: Stanford University Press.

Hirschi, T. (1969). *Causes of Delinquency*, Berkeley: University of California Press.

Laub, J.H. and Sampson, R.J. (2001) 'Understanding desistance from crime', *Crime and Justice*, 28: 1–69.

Maruna, S. (2001) *Making Good: How Ex-offenders Reform and Reclaim their Lives*, Washington, DC: American Psychological Association.

Nugent, B. and Schinkel, M. (2016) 'The pains of desistance', *Criminology & Criminal Justice*, 16(5): 568–84.

Patton, D. and Farrall, S. (2021) 'Desistance: a utopian perspective, *The Howard Journal of Crime and Justice*, 60(2): 209–31.

Weaver, B. (2019) 'Understanding desistance: a critical review of theories of Desistance', *Psychology, Crime & Law*, 25: 641–58.

10

Forensic psychology and mental disorder

Paul V. Greenall

On 15 May 1800 in London's Drury Lane Theatre, military veteran James Hadfield fired a pistol at King George III, missing him by inches. At his subsequent trial for high treason, Hadfield was found to be experiencing delusions relating to head injuries sustained in battle several years earlier which were underpinning his desire to shoot the king. Consequently, Hadfield was found not guilty by reason of insanity (NGRI). A not guilty verdict meant Hadfield could not legally be imprisoned. However, reluctant to release a lunatic who tried to kill the king, Parliament hastily and retrospectively enacted the Criminal Lunatics Act 1800. Under this Act, offenders found NGRI could legally be detained indefinitely and Hadfield spent the rest of his life in Bethlem Royal Hospital, the infamous 'Bedlam' (Moran, 1985). The events of 1800 not only led to a new legal framework for dealing with criminal lunatics, but set in motion an important chain of events. These events included the more famous case of Daniel McNaughton in 1843, the opening of Broadmoor criminal lunatic asylum in 1864 and eventually led to our current Forensic Mental Health Services (FMHS).

FMHS

Today's FMHS specialise in the assessment, treatment and management of offenders with a mental disorder who have previously or are currently involved in criminal proceedings or under sentence. FMHS are typically multidisciplinary, having input from psychiatry, psychology, nursing, social work and occupational therapy, and operate within prisons (such as mental health in-reach teams), community settings (for example, probation) and secure hospitals.

Secure hospitals exist at three security levels: high, medium and low. Offenders can be admitted to any security level depending on the circumstances of their case and the level of risk they are considered to present. The notion of risk has been traditionally associated with dangerousness. Indeed, only those offenders who need to be detained under conditions of special security on account of their dangerous, violent or criminal propensities are admitted to the high secure hospitals (section 4, National Health Service Act 1977). The assessment of risk (or dangerousness) is therefore a key feature of modern forensic practice and essentially involves assessing an individual's capacity to be violent in future and under what circumstances this may happen, in order that their risk (or level of dangerousness) can be managed (Douglas et al, 2013).

Legal detention in hospital

Under the Mental Health Act 1983, courts can detain offenders with a mental disorder in a secure hospital while on remand and/or after being found guilty of an offence. Prisoners can also be transferred to a secure hospital if they develop a mental disorder during their sentence. Under the Criminal Procedure (Insanity) Act 1964,[1] courts can detain offenders with a mental disorder in a secure hospital if they are found unfit to plead or NGRI. Offenders sent to a secure hospital from court or prison are generally referred to as 'restricted patients' as they are subjected to special controls by the Ministry of Justice. A small number of people are detained in secure hospitals under civil sections of the Mental Health Act (for example, they do not have an index offence) due to presenting a risk of harm to themselves or others. Regardless of their pathway into a secure hospital, once there patients move from admission to treatment to pre-discharge wards. During this process, periods of therapeutic leave from the hospital may be granted and discharge may be into the community, back to prison or to a lower secure hospital. However, patients can be transferred to a higher secure hospital if their behaviour means they cannot be safely managed in their current level of security. In all cases, security relates to more than high walls and locked doors, as 'see think act' guidelines highlight the importance of knowledge and understanding of the patients and of the environment. The number of people detained in secure hospitals has been rising in recent years and in 2011 was reported to be between 7,000 and 8,000 patients, with most of them detained in medium and low secure services and with less than 1,000 in high secure services (Centre for Mental Health, 2011).

Patients in secure hospitals

Mental disorder is a clinical and legal concept which encompasses a range of problematic psychological conditions. Within FMHS, mental illness (for example, schizophrenia) is the most common disorder, with other common disorders including personality disorder (PD) and substance misuse disorders. FMHS patients are mostly single males with poor educational histories and from a White ethnic background. With around a quarter of patients coming from ethnic minority backgrounds, these people are over-represented within FMHS. Around half of FMHS patients were admitted to hospital from prison, with others coming from other secure hospitals and community settings. Lengths of stay within secure hospitals range from five to 30 years, with an average duration of nine years. A key feature of FMHS patients is their complex and challenging nature, as illustrated by the fact that most have histories of self-harm or suicide attempts, present with two or more co-morbid mental disorders (for example, they have a mental illness and a PD) and large numbers have diverse criminal histories (see Kasmi et al, 2020).

Mental disorder and offending

Does a link exist between mental disorder and offending? To answer this question, two factors need to be considered, namely the levels of criminality among the mentally disordered and levels of mental disorder among offenders. Research into the level of mental disorders among adults in the general population suggests the rates of such disorders are low. For example, a 2014 survey into mental health and well-being in England (McManus et al, 2016) found less than 1 per cent of adults had a psychotic disorder, 13.7 per cent screened positive for any PD and 3.1 per cent showed signs of dependence on illicit substances. With a UK population of around 66 million one can tentatively extrapolate there being around 600,000 people with a psychotic illness, 9 million people with a PD and 2 million people dependent on illicit substances. If these estimates are correct then, notwithstanding the 'dark figure' of unreported crime, it can be reasonably concluded that the vast majority of people with these disorders are not offenders. Therefore, the link between mental disorder and criminality arguably appears weak.

However, research on the level of mental disorder among adult offenders paints a different picture. Using the same three key mental disorders, a 1998 survey of psychiatric morbidity among prisoners in England and Wales (Singleton et al, 1998) found the level of psychotic disorders among prisoners ranged from 7–14 per cent, the level of any PD ranged from 50–78 per cent, while the percentage of prisoners who reported being drug dependent in the year before coming into prison ranged from 41–54 per cent. The range represents differences found between male sentenced prisoners, male remand prisoners and female prisoners. What these figures tell us, therefore, is that levels of mental disorder among known offenders are significantly higher than in the general population. So, while the link between mental disorder and criminality may be weak when viewed in general terms, when focusing on offender samples mental disorder appears to be an important consideration.

Functional link

How might a mental disorder contribute to offending? Psychologists working in secure hospitals often encounter patients who have been violent to a family member, a neighbour or a stranger. Initially, this may appear a random motiveless assault. However, a forensic assessment may reveal it was related to the positive symptoms of psychosis, such as hallucinations or delusions. The patient may, for example, have been convinced their victim was spreading malicious rumours about them or were out to get them as part of a conspiracy or had stolen something valuable from them. In such cases, violence was aimed at addressing these subjectively unpleasant situations. Alternatively, violence may be related to the patient's belief that it was necessary to save the world or may have been in accordance with voices in their head instructing them to assault their victim.

In the realm of sexual violence, an individual may be similarly driven to sexually offend by the positive symptoms of their illness or be disinhibited by their illness and sexually assault someone whom they find attractive, even a complete stranger (Lewis and Dwyer, 2018).

Psychologists working in secure hospitals also encounter people whose offending is related to aspects of their personality. This may include factors such as holding pro-offending attitudes/beliefs, having a lack of empathy for others, holding feelings of entitlement, feeling a sense of superiority is threatened, impulsivity, perceiving others as threatening, an inability to form relationships with age-appropriate peers or having a fear of abandonment. In such cases, offending is not the behaviour of an individual with a deluded mind, but a purposeful and goal-directed act aimed at satisfying various subjective needs. For some offenders, these needs may be of a sexual nature and evidence one or more paraphilic (sexual) disorders, such as a sexual interest in children (for example, paedophilic disorder), a desire to expose one's genitals to strangers (such as exhibitionistic disorder) or a sadistic sexual appetite (for example, sexual sadism disorder). Even an innocuous desire to cross-dress (such as transvestic disorder) may lead some people into extreme acts of sexual violence, as illustrated by the case of Colonel D. Russell Williams in Canada in 2010 (see Brankley et al, 2014). In some or all of these cases, the offender's ability to deal with challenging situations and to formulate pro-social responses may have been further impaired by intoxication by alcohol or drugs or their intellectual disability. Indeed, in some cases, the presence of two or more mental disorders (for example, sexual deviancy, a PD and intoxication) can enhance the risk posed by an offender (see Schug and Fradella, 2015; Craissati et al, 2020).

Conclusion

While the majority of people with a mental disorder do not offend, levels of mental disorder among offenders are significantly higher than in the general population. This finding has implications for forensic practice, where determining the presence/relevance of various mental disorders is an important consideration when assessing an offender's history and future risk of violence (for example, see www.hcr-20.com). Similarly, criminal investigations may be aided by consideration of the possible presence/relevance of a mental disorder following what appears to be a random motiveless act of violence.

Having its origins in the attempted assassination of a king, today's FMHS operate throughout the country within the public and independent sectors and within institutional and community settings. FMHS specialise in the assessment, treatment and management of offenders with a range of mental disorders, and various therapeutic interventions are provided by staff with specialist forensic training. These interventions are not only aimed at addressing a patient's mental disorder, but their offending behaviour and future risk. In 2009/10 secure FMHS were costing the NHS around £1.2 billion a year, or about a fifth of all public expenditure on adult mental health (Centre for Mental Health, 2011). Like any area of the criminal justice system (CJS) in the UK, FMHS have periodically encountered serious difficulties which have led to public inquiries (for example, Fallon at Ashworth), some patients have famously escaped (for example, Robert Mone and Thomas McCulloch from Carstairs) and reoffended after discharge (for example, Graham Young after leaving Broadmoor). Despite this, the task of assessing and working with some of the most dangerous and challenging offenders in the UK ensures FMHS remain a valuable part of the CJS in this country.

Note
1   These Acts apply to England and Wales only, Scotland and Northern Ireland have separate legislation.

References

Brankley, A.E., Goodwill, A.M. and Reale, K.S. (2014) 'Escalation from fetish burglaries to sexual violence: a retrospective case study of former Col., D. Russell Williams', *Journal of Investigative Psychology and Offender Profiling*, 11(2): 115–35, DOI: https://doi.org/10.1002/jip.1406.

Centre for Mental Health (2011) *Pathways to Unlocking Secure Mental Health Care*, London: Centre for Mental Health, National Mental Health Development Unit, [online] Available from: https://www.centreformentalhealth.org.uk/sites/default/files/2018-09/Pathways_to_unlocking_secure_mental_health_care.pdf [Accessed 31 March 2021].

Craissati, J., Joseph, N. and Skett, S. (eds) (2020) *Practitioner Guide: Working with People in the Criminal Justice System showing Personality Difficulties* (3rd edn), London: HM Prison & Probation Service/National Health Service, [online] Available from: https://www.gov.uk/government/publications/working-with-offenders-with-personality-disorder-a-practitioners-guide [Accessed 31 March 2021].

Douglas, K.S., Blanchard, A.J.E. and Hendry, M.C. (2013) 'Violence risk assessment and management: Putting structured professional judgment into practice', in C. Logan and L. Johnstone (eds) *Managing Clinical Risk: A Guide to Effective Practice*, Abingdon: Routledge, pp 29–55.

Kasmi, Y., Duggan, C. and Völlm, B. (2020) 'A comparison of long-term medium secure patients within NHS and private and charitable sector units in England', *Criminal Behaviour and Mental Health*, 30(1): 38–49, DOI: https://doi.org/10.1002/cbm.2141.

Lewis, E.T. and Dwyer, R.G. (2018), 'Psychosis and sexual offending: a review of current literature', *International Journal of Offender Therapy and Comparative Criminology*, 62(11): 3372–84, DOI: 10.1177/0306624X17740016.

McManus, S., Bebbington, P., Jenkins, R. and Brugha, T. (2016) *Mental Health and Wellbeing in England: Adult Psychiatric Morbidity Survey 2014*, Leeds: NHS Digital.

Moran, R. (1985) 'The origin of insanity as a special verdict: the trial for treason of James Hadfield (1800)', *Law & Society Review*, 19(3): 487–519, DOI: http://dx.doi.org/10.2307/3053574.

Schug, R.A. and Fradella, H.F. (2015) *Mental Illness and Crime*, Thousand Oaks, CA: SAGE.

Singleton, N., Meltzer, H., Gatward, R., Coid, J. and Deasy, D. (1998) *Psychiatric Morbidity among Prisoners in England and Wales*, London: The Stationery Office.

11

Forensic psychology and psychopathy

Robert Hesketh

Psychopathy has become one of the most studied psychological constructs in forensic psychology. It is a term that has become synonymous with evil, mainly as a result of considerable media attention. Hare (1999, p xi) has described individuals who suffer from psychopathy as 'social predators who charm, manipulate, and ruthlessly plough their way through life leaving a broad trail of broken hearts, shattered expectations and empty wallets'. Hare's definition focuses on two key components: firstly, aspects of personality which include manipulation, shallowness, lying and what is probably two of the most cited psychopathic traits, a total lack of empathy and conscience. Secondly, there are aspects of behaviour that can start early on in life and can include cruelty to animals, pyromania and uresis (bedwetting). Other behavioural features noted by Hare involve impulsivity (risk taking) and boredom.

Historical overview

One of the first accounts of psychopathy was documented by French psychiatrist and founding father of psychiatry, Philippe Pinel in the 19th century (cited in Hare, 1999). Pinel observed a pattern of completely remorseless behaviour that lacked any form of hallucination or delusion. He subsequently diagnosed this as 'insanity without delirium' (cited in Hare, 1999, p 25). The modern history of psychopathy in the 20th century can be traced back to the 1941 seminal work of Cleckley, *The Mask of Sanity* (Cleckley, 2015). Cleckley examined a series of case studies involving incarcerated prisoners whom he described as 'psychopaths'. In discussing this condition, Cleckley noted the power of natural manipulation which some individuals used to negotiate their way from prison to an easier hospital setting. The book's title is in reference to the mask of normality psychopaths wear to conceal the disorder. This highlights Pinel's key observation (cited in Hare, 1999) that unlike most mainstream forms of psychotic mental distress which involve a distortion of reality (usually a key sign of some form of abnormality) or other distinctive, abnormal behavioural symptoms, the psychopathic condition allows sufferers to maintain a veil of rationality and complete control of their behaviour. In the early part of the 20th century, the use of the term psychopathy was quite liberal, extending beyond those who not only lacked a conscience to individuals with milder psychological disorders such as depression (Haycock, 2019).

In recent times the term 'psychopath' has been refined and used either alongside or interchangeably with 'sociopath'. This, has, in turn, begged the question of what exactly is the difference? The simple answer is one of individual viewpoint. If belief is rooted in the idea of an environmental cause, the preference will be sociopath. In contrast, those who argue for a more biologically deterministic reason will use psychopath (Hare, 1999), although there is now strong evidence that points towards the condition having both environmental and biological roots.

Debates, theories and research: psychopathy and emotional processing

Research surrounding psychopathy has been driven by neuropsychological underpinnings that have concentrated on cortical dysfunctions of the brain. These have further intensified as technology has developed. In recent years, studies into psychopathy have increased considerably, which turn has resulted in the emergence of many key debates. These have centred around what has become known as the 'dark triad' or three malevolent personality constructs which have become interrelated: narcissism, Machiavellianism and psychopathy (Paulhus and Williams, 2002). One of the most common debates to emerge in psychopathy is the impairment of emotional processing. In investigating this aspect, Casey et al (2013, p 541) have commented that 'emotional processing in psychopathy is an important area of study because the associated deficits are functionally linked to violent offending and can be a target for treatment'. An early theory by Hare (1970), for instance, has suggested that psychopathy can be linked to low arousal, that, unlike most people, psychopathic individuals suffer from long-term lack of stimulus and require more intense sensory inputs to sustain attention. Thus, psychopaths will not be affected by stressful or fearful situations that others would naturally react to and run from. In contrast to neurological dysfunction, social learning theory has highlighted a link between learning and the psychopathic personality. Here, the focus has been on autonomic response to rewards and punishments between incarcerated psychopaths and a control group of non-psychopaths involving a passive avoidance task. Passive avoidance involves side-stepping an unpleasant stimulus as a result of a conscious or unconscious restraint known as inhibition. In many cases, psychopathic offenders have been shown to be unresponsive to unpleasant stimulus such as punishment when compared to the non-psychopathic control group. Moreover, moral reasoning has also come under the spotlight – specifically deficits within the moral reasoning of psychopathic individuals. Most studies examining moral reasoning and psychopathy have concentrated on judgements regarding physical harm caused to others, but this has been challenged by the assertion that such inconsistency is because physical harm is an alternative for the psychopath's emotional distress.

Diagnosis and treatment

Since a formal diagnosis of psychopathy cannot be made, the fifth edition of the American Psychiatric Association's Diagnostic Statistical Manual Revised (DSM-5) instead includes a new term which acts as a synonym: anti-social personality disorder (ASPD). ASPD, like sociopathy, initially caused some confusion with psychopathy. While DSM-5 does highlight some similarity in symptoms with individuals who are diagnosed with ASPD, such as interpersonal functioning and disinhibition, for reasons associated with the immense stigmatising power of the term 'psychopath' ASPD focuses considerably less on personality traits such as lack of guilt, lack of empathy, shallowness, recklessness and manipulation (in particular, gaslighting) that would point towards a more specific conclusion of psychopathy.

While an individual cannot be diagnosed as a psychopath, the condition can be identified using the Psychopathy Checklist-Revised (formally the Hare Psychopathy Checklist-Revised). The list is split into two factors, Factor 1, affective – that is, personality traits such as coldness and callous manipulation – and Factor 2, lifestyle behaviours that are risky and impulsive. A Likert scale of 1–3 is used to examine 20 symptoms. If the clinician arrives at a score of 30 or close to this (the highest possible score is 40), a diagnosis of psychopathy is then made. A second test is also available and is often used in penal institutions. Called the Minnesota Multiphasic Personality Inventory (MMPI), the test, which is one of the most frequently used assessments to examine abnormal behaviour, aims to assess personality traits and psychopathology as part of one of ten clinical subscales. The MMPI, which can only be administered by a trained psychologist, comes in two distinct forms: the MMPI-2, which consists of 567 statements, and the MMPI-2-RF, containing 338 statements, all of which are answered by either true or false responses. Of the two, it is the MMPI-2 which includes assessment for psychopathy.

Treating psychopathy can be complex, like many other psychotic conditions, and there are no medications aimed at specifically attempting to cure, although drug treatment such as anti-psychotics and anti-depressants can help manage episodes. Undoubtedly by far the most effective treatments are multi-modal approaches that combine medication with behavioural therapies that include individual and family- focused methods. While the former can be utilised with people of all ages, the latter is aimed more specifically towards children and young people. However, critics of treating psychopathy have argued that therapy simply does not work.

In recent years there have been grave concerns about the notion of psychopathy in terms of how individuals are judged to have psychopathic traits. In particular, for example from a criminal justice perspective, defending individuals who are seen as psychopathic can be problematic since in Scotland and England any defence of insanity has excluded the condition on the basis of moral understanding of criminal responsibility. That is, defendants are judged to be able to distinguish right from wrong. However, there is the contention that an individual who lacks empathy will also lack the ability to understand and care about the emotions of other people and, as such, the capacity of knowing right from wrong in the commission of repeated violent criminal acts is lacking, thus providing solid grounds for a plea of insanity.

Conclusion

In conclusion, psychopathy has a long history of research with studies dating back to the early 19th century. It is a condition that has no limitations where race, religion and gender is concerned, and while the debate over definitions of psychopathy and the official use of the term and its true origins will continue it is now possible to identify its most prevalent symptoms: lack of empathy and conscience combined with low arousal, allowing reckless behaviour without fear of punishment. Such dangerous traits, regardless of origin, inevitably will increase the risk that many sufferers will become involved in violence and criminality. Conversely, while the condition does increase the risk of criminal involvement, many individuals with this condition will only go on to commit minor offences such as theft, fraud or coercion. However, an estimated 4 per cent of people in the general population suffer from undetected mental health issues that include the same psychopathic traits. Treating the condition can be complex and often fraught with potential failure, which is the reason why there is a need for further research covering risk factors and causes.

References

Casey, H., Rodgers, R., Burns, T. and Yiend, J. (2013) 'Emotion regulation in psychopathy', *Biological Psychology*, 92: 541–8.

Cleckley, H. (2015) *Mask of Sanity*, Mansfield, CT: Martino Publishing.

Hare, R. (1970) *Psychopathy: Theory and Research*, New York: Wiley.

Hare, R. (1999) *Without Conscience*, New York: Guilford Press.

Haycock. D.A. (2019) 'Psychopathic, sociopathic, or antisocial personality? Psychopathy is often the first trait people think of when they think of tyrants', *Psychology Today*, [online] 2 July, Available from: https://www.psychologyto day.com/gb/blog/tyrannical-minds/201907/psychopathic-sociopathic-or-antisocial-personality [Accessed 3 April 2021].

Paulhus, D.L. and Williams, K.M. (2002) 'The dark triad of personality: narcissism, Machiavellianism and psychopathy', *Journal of Research in Personality*, 36(6): 556–63, DOI: https://doi.org/10.1016/S0092-6566(02)00505-6.

12

Forensic psychology and non-fatal violence

Victoria Blinkhorn

Introduction

Non-fatal violence can occur within a number of different crimes whereby the individuals involved are injured but the injuries are not fatal. Some examples of non-fatal violence include assault and battery, assault occasioning actual bodily harm, wounding and inflicting grievous bodily harm, administering poison and offences related to explosive substances and corrosive fluids (including offences related to 'acid attacks'). Of course, non-fatal violence occurs much more often than other fatal types of violence and, as such, it is important to understand how and why it occurs.

This chapter will focus on a particular crime which is becoming more prevalent – domestic violence. While domestic violence can result in fatalities, much of what constitutes domestic violence is non-fatal. The terminology around domestic violence can differ quite a lot, sometimes it is termed as 'intimate partner abuse' or 'partner abuse', for example, but essentially, they are all the same concept. Domestic violence is defined within the Domestic Violence, Crime and Victims Act 2004 as any incident of controlling, coercive or threatening behaviour, violence or abuse between those aged 16 or over who are or have been intimate partners or family members, regardless of their gender or sexuality. It can include honour-based violence, female genital mutilation and even forced marriage.

Types of domestic violence

The non-fatal nature of most domestic violence is due to the wide range of offences related to it. Offences can encompass psychological, emotional, physical and sexual abuse that can differ extensively in severity. Psychological abuse involves purposely attempting to frighten, control or isolate a person. This can be in the form of verbal threats, stalking or defamation. Similar to this is emotional abuse, which can often involve comparable behaviour as with psychological types of abuse; however, it is usually conducted in a much more subtle way. A good example of both emotional and sometimes psychological abuse is gaslighting. This involves making an individual doubt their own thoughts, feelings and sanity by manipulating the truth. Physical abuse involves the use of physical force on a person such as hitting, pushing, strangling and biting. In short, any sort of force which does not result in fatality. Finally, sexual abuse involves forcing a person to participate in unwanted sexual activity. This can include unwanted fondling, forcing sex in ways that hurt, forcing a person to have sex with others and rape.

According to the Crime Survey for England and Wales, between March 2021 and 2022 an estimated 5 per cent of adults aged 16 to 74 years (2.4 million) experienced domestic abuse. The police recorded a total of 1,500,369 domestic abuse-related incidents and, of these, 910,980 were recorded as domestic abuse-related crimes, an increase of 7.7 per cent from the previous year. It can be suggested that these figures have increased due to COVID-19 pandemic. The reason for this is because, for many, the home is not a safe place, and when lockdown measures were announced these put many individuals at further danger from their partners and subsequently exposed them to more frequent abuse (see Mazza et al, 2020).

Why does domestic violence happen?

Forensic psychology can help to understand non-fatal violence through a number of perspectives. Empathy deficits have long been linked to many types of offending, significantly those violent or sexual in nature. The causes of general, group or person-specific empathy deficits can be varied, depending on the offender in question, and they can be conceptualised as 'blocks' by looking at the processes involved in empathy and how they link to offending. It is acknowledged that there are five main empathy processes and, as such, each can be looked at in terms of how a deficit may appear in particular offenders (Seidel et al, 2013). The first refers to the ability to take on the perspective of others and imagine how an experience would feel. Most individuals are able to do this and also use this simple activity to guide their behaviour. However, some offenders have a limited ability to do this based on a simple deficit in this area and, as such, do not have this element of empathy to appropriately guide their behaviour. The second process is having a view of others that is respectful and compassionate. Some offenders instead have a hostile and aggressive view of others and a general lack of concern for other individuals' experiences. The third process is having the capacity to produce an emotional response to another person or situation. It has been found that some offenders are unable to experience or even feel emotion, and therefore are unable to present this response externally. The fourth process refers to the ability to manage personal distress. If an individual has difficulty with emotion, the management of it becomes challenging, often due to them becoming consumed with their own feelings. As a result, this refocuses their attention on themselves rather than the other person in question. Finally, the fifth process concerns applying the other four processes to any given person or situation. This is particularly important as the difficulty that individuals with empathy deficits have can be dramatically increased if other specific factors are involved, such as stressful experiences, mood–altering medication or alcohol and drug use.

The links between alcohol use and non-fatal violence such as domestic offences are well established in research; it has been found repeatedly that alcohol is a significant contributing cause in domestic violence. As with the empathy deficit perspective, intoxication does not completely excuse aggressive or violent behaviour, however, it encourages deficits in empathy and therefore increases the likelihood of domestic violence. Interestingly, it is also well established that intoxication in the victim is often viewed as an excuse for the perpetrator's behaviour (Dent and Arias, 1990), thus demonstrating that mutual alcohol use in relationships can sometimes be unhealthy. A number of reviews have argued that alcohol interventions are crucial in reducing intoxication and aggressive behaviour, not just within the rehabilitation of offenders but in young individuals presenting an element of risk. The argument here is that an intervention could prevent future violent offending completely in young individuals who are presenting aggressive behaviour and are known to be abusing alcohol (see Leonard, 2001).

A particular theory that helps understand regularly occurring non-fatal violence and how alcohol use can exacerbate it is the routine activities perspective (Cohen and Felson, 1979). This explains that offenders do not go out of their way to manufacture a criminal opportunity and this is simply because they have no need to. Opportunities present themselves on a daily basis and as long as the 'basic chemistry' is present then crime will occur. Cohen and Felson (1979) state that the 'basic chemistry' consists of three elements: a motivated offender, suitable target and the absence of a capable guardian. When applying these three elements to domestic violence, it becomes apparent that much non-fatal offending behaviour that occurs can easily become 'routine'. Of course, when within the home the victim is unlikely to have a capable guardian and naturally become the easiest target for the offender to be violent towards. This is why the majority of domestic violence occurs in a private environment, usually within the home. In relation to alcohol use, again, this can become 'routine' for many reasons; however, it is easy for a pattern to occur in acting violently if alcohol exacerbates the offender's aggression. The routine activities perspective aids understanding in terms of why, over the COVID-19 pandemic, domestic abuse-related crimes increased, simply because people were forced to spend more time in the home. Due to the lack of witnesses in this environment, it means that a large proportion of non-fatal violence is not reported. As the popular saying goes, 'you never know what goes on behind closed doors'.

Conclusion

In summary, non-fatal violence accounts for a significant proportion of crime, especially within domestic abuse-related crimes. This chapter has discussed how non-fatal violence can occur within domestic abuse incidents and the different forms this can take. Recent statistics show that it is even more important to attempt to understand non-fatal domestic violence in the hope that interventions can be refined and introduced earlier to act as preventative measures. Certain perspectives within forensic psychology – such as the empathy deficit and routine activities perspectives – can help to elucidate why some people commit types of non-fatal violence. Further, alcohol abuse has a strong relationship with these types of violence and links to both empathy deficit and routine activities regarding exacerbating the likelihood of domestic violence occurring. It is suggested that after the COVID-19 pandemic is completely over more will be learnt about non-fatal violence due to the unusual situations that lockdown measures imposed on individuals' lives.

References

Cohen, L.E. and Felson, M. (1979) 'Social change and crime rate trends: a routine activity approach', *American Sociological Review*, 44: 588–608.

Dent, D. and Arias, I. (1990) 'Effects of alcohol, gender and role of spouses on attributions and evaluations of mental violence scenarios', *Violence and Victims*, 5: 185–93.

Leonard, K. (2001) 'Domestic violence and alcohol: what is known and what do we need to know to encourage environmental interventions?' *Journal of Substance Use*, 6(4): 235–47.

Mazza, M., Marano, G., Lai, C., Janiri, L. and Sani, G. (2020) 'Danger in danger: interpersonal violence during COVID-19 quarantine', *Psychiatry Research*, 289: 113046.

Seidel, E.M., Pfabigan, D.M., Keckeis, K., Wucherer, A.M., Jahn, T., Lamm, C. and Derntl, B. (2013) 'Empathic competencies in violent offenders', *Psychiatry Research*, 210(3): 1168–75.

13

Forensic psychology and homicide

Paul V. Greenall

Introduction

Homicide is the killing of one person by another. Although some homicides are lawful (for example, judicial executions, soldiers in combat and so forth) the focus of this chapter is unlawful homicide. These killings generally result from an interaction between two or more people, during which violence and/ or weapons are used, resulting in the death of one or more persons. In England and Wales, the two main homicide offences are murder and manslaughter (CPS, 2019). While both crimes have a common *actus reus* or guilty act (such as unlawful killing), the difference between them relates to the killer's state of mind or *mens rea* at the material time. With murder the *mens rea* involves 'malice aforethought', which relates to an intention to kill or to cause grievous bodily harm. Although manslaughter involves the same *mens rea*, the killer's culpability is reduced due to various mitigating circumstances, such as diminished responsibility (Homicide Act 1957 – as amended by the Coroners and Justice Act 2009) or a loss of control (Coroners and Justice Act 2009). Unlawful homicides can involve single, double or triple killings that occur in one event and in one location. In more serious cases, unlawful homicides can involve mass killings that occur in one event and in one location (for example, school shootings), spree killings that occur in one event but in different locations (for example, Derrick Bird in Cumbria in 2010) and serial killings that occur in different events, different locations and with a cooling off period in between (for example, the Yorkshire Ripper, Peter Sutcliffe, in the 1980s) (Fox and Levin, 2015).

Prevalence of homicide

Official statistics for England and Wales show that in the year ending March 2020 there were 695 recorded homicides, which equates to 11.7 homicides per million. Homicide offenders were mostly (93 per cent) males, with over 65 per cent aged 16–34 and 67 per cent coming from a White ethnic background. Victim profiles were similar, as most (73 per cent) were male, with just under 73 per cent aged 16–54 and just under two-thirds coming from a White ethnic background. Males were more likely to be killed by friends/acquaintances or strangers while females were more likely to be killed by a current or ex-partner or family member. Almost half of females were victims of domestic homicide while only 7 per cent of males were killed in such circumstances. The most common method of killing for males and females was by a sharp instrument (for example, a knife). Hitting or kicking was the second most common method of killing for males while for females it was strangulation/asphyxiation. Around half of all homicides resulted from a quarrel, a revenge attack or a loss of temper. Females were more likely to be killed in or around a house or dwelling. This was also a frequent location for male homicides, as was the street, a footpath or alleyway. Finally, almost a third of offenders and victims were under the influence of alcohol or drugs at the material time.

Understanding homicide

Police officers, forensic psychologists and other criminal justice professionals may be required to investigate homicides and/or assess homicide offenders. Therefore, an understanding of the context and circumstances in which homicides occur, plus the psychological processes that may underpin them, is crucial. One way of understanding homicide is to consider whether the level of violence used was of an instrumental or expressive nature. The instrumental expressive classification is based on the goal(s) or reward(s) the offender anticipates from their violent attack. Instrumental violence seeks to achieve non-aggressive goals and involves hitting the victim in order to accomplish them. Examples include acquisitive offending where only sufficient force is used to steal from an unwilling victim, or homicides in which the violence is limited to that needed to kill the victim. By contrast, expressive violence seeks to cause injury to the victim and the aim is not simply to hit them but to hurt them. Examples include assaults with high levels of violence resulting in serious injury or homicides in which the violence exceeds that required to cause death (Adjorlolo and Chan, 2017). Within this classification the hypotheses could be that instrumental violence is an impulsive reaction to a negative situation, while expressive violence is premeditated and accompanied by negative emotional states, such as anger and/or negative views of the victim.

Another important consideration involves exploring the various factors that can motivate or drive homicide. Here the work of Schlesinger (2004) is useful as his motivational spectrum suggests homicides can be driven by various motivational factors:

- Environmental homicides occur in and are influenced by social context, for example, atrocities or mass killings of civilians during wars, gang violence and the acts of professional killers.
- Situational homicides are behavioural reactions to stressful circumstances, for example, domestic homicides and killings during other crimes.
- Impulsive homicides are usually unplanned and carried out by unpredictable individuals who lead a generally anti-social lifestyle.
- Catathymic homicides are underpinned by emotionally charged inner conflicts. Acute types are unprovoked and triggered by deep emotional conflict that

suddenly erupts into violence, often against a stranger. Chronic types result from a build-up of tension, the solution to which is a planned assault of someone known to the killer, who they may have ruminated over or stalked.

- Compulsive homicides are driven by a compelling internal sexual need and have a high likelihood of repetition. Offence-related fantasies may precede the homicides and planning helps the offender to elude capture and become a serial killer.

A key feature about these motivational factors is that a negative correlation exists between the external and internal drives which underpin them. So, homicides driven by external factors have low levels of internal drive and vice versa. For example, environmental homicides have the highest level of external drive and the lowest level of internal drive, while compulsive homicides have the highest level of internal drive and the lowest level of external drive.

Interpersonal dynamics of homicide

Given that many homicides result from a quarrel, a revenge attack or loss of temper, one can hypothesise that they are of a situational and/or impulsive nature. To understand how such killings may occur, Brookman (2005) has illustrated the interpersonal dynamics that may underpin them. In relation to male-on-male homicides, these killings are hypothesised as resulting from one of two scenarios. Firstly, confrontational homicides involve spontaneous face-to-face violence. The offender and victim become involved a dispute that escalates into homicidal violence. Given the prevalence of intoxicants in cases of homicide, one can hypothesise that many confrontational homicides occur in the context of alcohol or drugs. These substances act as a disinhibitor and help to facilitate the violent encounter and its escalation towards a lethal ending, either through hitting or kicking or by the usage of a weapon.

It can further be hypothesised that homicides which involve intoxicants will occur in a social setting (such as in or around a pub or club and so forth) where these substances are obtained and consumed and where males are likely to be among friends/acquaintances or strangers. Secondly, revenge homicides are premeditated attacks in which the offender intends to kill their victim to avenge a perceived wrongdoing against themselves or another person. Weapons are often involved and the offender and victim often have a history of conflict between them. Given that sharp instruments are a common means of killing, one can hypothesis that knives will be involved in many cases and that they would have been brought to the crime scene by the offender with the intention of facilitating the act of vengeance.

Although most homicides are male-on-male encounters, men also kill women. In most cases their victims are current or ex-partners or family members. Brookman (2005) has illustrated the interpersonal dynamics that may underpin such killings, which again are hypothesised as resulting from one of two scenarios.

Firstly, possessiveness/control homicides occur in the context of a problematic intimate relationship. This may involve the woman threatening to leave the relationship or when she is believed to have been unfaithful. Both situations present a threat to the existing relationship and, perhaps feeling overwhelmed by jealousy or the prospect of pending loss, the man responds with homicidal violence. Brookman (2005) suggests that in relationships of long duration the violence is often a premeditated response to the woman's behaviour. In relationships of shorter duration the violence is often an impulsive attempt to control the woman's behaviour. Secondly, sudden rage homicides are spontaneous killings with no evidence of premeditation. Brookman (2005) suggests these killings often occur in the context of one or both parties being intoxicated and some type of dispute or disagreement existing between them, which the man decides to resolve through violence. Although the dynamics between these two scenarios differ, Brookman (2005) highlights the fact that both involve a man's attempt to exercise control over his female partner.

Along with killing women whom they know, some men kill women who they do not know. Brookman (2005) suggests most of these stranger killings occur in the context of other crimes. Examples include acquisitive offences like robbery or burglary, plus other offences such as arson and sexual assault. That idea that sexual assault can accompany a homicide is supported by a growing body of research into the phenomenon of sexual homicide (see Proulx et al, 2018). Although sexual homicides are rare events, they do occur from time to time and therefore police officers, forensic psychologists and other criminal justice professionals need to understand some of the basic features of these killings in order to: (a) recognise that a killing may have been sexual; and (b) understand the dynamics that may underpin them. Like other types of interpersonal violence, sexual homicides can occur between strangers and between people who know each other. Some sexual homicides may include overt sexual behaviours (for example, rape), while in others the sexual dynamics may be inferred from other crime scene evidence (for example, the victim found partially naked). In still others, evidence of a sexual element may be absent and may only be unearthed during post-conviction clinical sessions with the offender. As for the motivational dynamics that underpin sexual homicides, research suggests these include anger, sexual sadism and wanting to silence a potential accuser after a sexual assault (Kerr et al, 2013).

Conclusion

Homicide is an extreme and statistically rare form of interpersonal violence, with prevalence rates equating to around 11.7 homicides per million. Although most cases involve male-on-male confrontations, men also kill women and in some rare instances women are the killers (of, for example, their abusive male partner [situational] or their children [catathymic] – Brookman, 2005). Indeed, on some notable occasions women have joined their male partners in murder (for example, Rose and Fred West) and on some very rare occasions (such as

Joanna Dennehy), they have become serial killers (Fox and Levin, 2015). Despite the differing manifestations of unlawful homicide, consideration of some key features can help police officers, forensic psychologists and other criminal justice professionals to understand how and why a particular homicide occurred. The instrumental/expressive classification of homicide helps to understand the role and function of violence and the subjective needs that were satisfied by the usage of violence. Schlesinger's (2004) motivational spectrum aids in considering whether environmental, situational or psychological factors drove the homicide, while the work of Brookman (2005) is useful for understanding the interpersonal dynamics between the offender and victim. Finally, in some very rare instances, a homicide may be sexual. Once again, research can help in understanding whether such killings were satisfying emotional or sexual needs, or whether the killing was simply a means of silencing a chief witness to a sexual assault and thereby aimed at assisting a sexual offender to evade justice.

Although the research summarised in this chapter can aid an understanding of homicide, it should be recognised that individuals and their behaviours may not always fit nicely into one particular category. There is no clear boundary, for example, between instrumental and expressive homicides, and sexual homicides can be catathymic and not just compulsive. Despite these minor shortcomings, when faced with a homicide to investigate or a homicide offender to assess and work with, criminal justice professionals will be able to draw upon research, such as that summarised in this chapter, to build evidence-based hypotheses about how and why the killing(s) occurred.

References

Adjorlolo, S. and Chan, H.C. (2017) 'The nature of instrumentality and expressiveness of homicide crime scene behaviors: a review', *Trauma, Violence, & Abuse*, 18(2): 119–33, DOI: https://doi.org/10.1177/1524838015596528.

Brookman, F. (2005) *Understanding Homicide*, London: SAGE.

Fox, J.A. and Levin, J. (2015) *Extreme Killing: Understanding Serial and Mass Murder*, Thousand Oaks, CA: SAGE.

Kerr, K.J., Beech, A.R. and Murphy, D. (2013) 'Sexual homicide: definition, motivation and comparison with other forms of sexual offending', *Aggression and Violent Behavior*, 18(1): 1–10, DOI: https://doi.org/10.1016/j.avb.2012.05.006.

Proulx, J., Beauregard, E., Carter, A., Mokros, A., Darjee, R. and James, J. (eds) (2018) *Routledge International Handbook of Sexual Homicide Studies*, Abingdon: Routledge.

Schlesinger, L.B. (2004) 'Classification of antisocial behavior for prognostic purposes: study the motivation, not the crime', *Journal of Psychiatry & Law*, 32(2): 191–219, DOI: https://doi.org/10.1177/009318530403200204.

14

Forensic psychology and sexual offences

Robert Hesketh

Although there is no universally agreed definition of what constitutes a sexual offence, generally it is accepted that it can involve any individual who knowingly engages another individual in a sexual act by force or threat. Sexual offences can include a wide variety of criminal acts against victims from all walks of life. Presently, according to the England and Wales Sexual Offences Act 2003, sexual offences fall into several categories that include rape, sexual assault, child sexual abuse, extreme pornography, indecent images of minors and the more recently accepted form of revenge porn or the disclosing of private images without consent. Of note is the Sexual Offences Act 1967, which decriminalised some male homosexual activity (but significantly increased the penalty for some homosexual acts) and the fact that in 1997 changes were made to criminalise male rape.

History

Historically, sexual violence dates back to biblical times, with more focused observations surrounding sex offending emerging in the late 19th century, earliest references being cited in 1889 with the publication of *Psychopathia Sexualis* by Richard von Krafft-Ebing (2011). It wasn't until the 1880s, however, that sexual offences started to become embedded within public discourse. The catalyst came in the East End of London in 1888 with the Whitechapel Murders, five of which pointed towards one suspect, who was given the now notorious nickname of 'Jack the Ripper'. The Ripper case gave way to a plethora of media reports that focused on sexual violence and that also began to include children as victims (Jenkins, 1998). The reasons why sex offences appeared to emerge at this point in time, it was suggested, was a result of the impact of the Industrial Revolution: the population had more leisure time and sex had become a central point of interest (Wilson, 1990). In more recent times, the evolution of the internet over the last two decades (2000–22) with the advent of broadband allowing greater accessibility has rightly caused increased concern about the proliferation of new and evolving forms of sex crimes facilitated by the World Wide Web. Internet sexual offending can include a broad range of crimes, from possession or distribution of child pornography to the production of child pornography and grooming leading to actual child molestation (Seto et al, 2011).

Theories

From an aetiological perspective, sexual offending has proven complex to the extent that understanding about motivation is still quite equivocal. For instance, offences may not necessarily be sexually motivated or, for that matter, involve violence; however, the one assumption that can be made is that they will include a perpetrator, a victim and a social context with the main focus on the question of consent or lack thereof.

Theories surrounding offending are generally placed into either the single or multiple factor category. Single factor theories point to a specific reason offenders are drawn towards sexual abuse. That is as a result of solitary underlying causes, these include factors embedded within biological determinism (hormonal [Bain et al, 1987], mental retardation [Day, 1994], frontal lobe abnormality [Cummings, 1999], evolutionary psychology (courtship disorder [Freund, 1990], sexual coercion [Baily, 1988]) and personality (parent–child attachment theory [Bowlby, 1988], intimacy and loneliness [Ward et al, 1995]). Multiple factor theories focus on more composite reasons, they involve precondition theory (Ward and Hudson, 2001), quadripartite theory (Hall and Hirschman, 1991) and integrated theories of sexual offending (Ward and Beech, 2016).

Reporting and sentencing of sex offenders

There are a variety of sources, including individual reports, that record sexual offences in the UK; the most common currently are Multi-Agency Safeguarding Hubs and child protection conferences. Sadly, the 2018 Crime Survey for England and Wales (CSEW) has noted that under-reporting of sexual offences to the police has become a regular feature. In many cases, incidents of sexual offences, particularly rape, can go unreported, mainly due to fear of being not believed, having to relive the situation for the second time in a court, or simply a lack of faith in the justice system and distress at the possible prospect that the perpetrator may still be able to walk free. Nonetheless, in recent years the number of sexual offences recorded by police in the UK has increased considerably compared to the past. This has been partially attributed to improvements in the police recording process of sexual offences, which sees crimes placed into two main categories – rape and other sexual offences. Other reasons are a dramatic change in culture as well as the number of survivors who take the brave decision to make an official complaint. The CSEW has estimated that 700,000 people aged 16 to 59 were victims of sexual assault in 2018 (This was equivalent to 2.1 per cent prior to CSEW interviews being carried out, with the majority of victims observed to be women).

To date, in the UK, the definitive guidelines for the sentencing of sexual offences involve over 50 types of offence that include rape and assault, offences involving minors, including the uploading and circulation of indecent images of children, exploitation and offences that involve victims with mental health issues as well as other offences such as exposure, voyeurism and trespass with intent to commit a sexual act.

Like the reporting process, the management of sexual or violent offenders in the UK involves a multi-agency approach. Three of the main agencies include HM Inspectorate of Constabulary, HM Prison and Probation Service and the Independent Office for Police Conduct. In 2013, the Ministry of Justice (MoJ) noted that serious violent and sexual offenders spend more time in prison than any other criminal perpetrator groups, with an average of 32 months compared with an average of ten months for other offences. In 2003, the Home Office introduced the Sexual Offences Act, which requires all individuals released from custody and who have signed the sex offenders register to provide the police with personal details, including their name, date of birth and current residential address (if they are living with minors under the age of 18) as well as their national insurance number and, since 2012, all foreign travel and bank account details. Importantly, the law covering sexual offending can and often does change, so what can be regarded as a sexual offence one day can become legal the next or vice versa.

Interventions/treatment

Where sex offender interventions are concerned, these are predominantly psychological. Since 1993, this had focused around a 46-week Sex Offenders Treatment Programme (SOTP), which was offered through secure units to individuals who have to be detained under the Mental Health Act (1983), have a history of sexual offending and are deemed to be at risk of further acts of sex offending. SOTP took a cognitive behavioural therapy approach, with the aim of getting offenders to reflect on their past actions and behaviour patterns and, through discussion, develop strategies to reduce the risk of potential reoffending and provide a basis for living a healthy lifestyle. However, in March 2017, the MoJ replaced the SOTP with two new treatment programmes: Kaizen (for high-risk, high-need and high-priority offenders) and Horizon (aimed at medium-risk offenders). While the former is based around a multidimensional/holistic approach that is biological, social and psychological, the latter is focused on criminogenic needs, for instance, problems examining relationships, problem-solving skills and self-restraint (McCartan and Prescott, 2017). In cases where offenders possess very strong deviant sexual desires or urges that can sometimes override psychological approaches, additional medical treatment can be offered voluntarily, although there is no guarantee that reoffending will cease. Should the offender choose to take this added route, two types of medication can be considered. Firstly, selective serotonin reuptake inhibitors (SSRIs), which are normally prescribed in cases of depression. SSRIs concentrate on increasing levels of a neurotransmitter in the brain called serotonin which can affect an individual's mood and, in the case of sexual offenders, their impulsivity around sexual behaviour. With SSRIs, the aim is to help provide the offender with greater control over intense sexual urges and, as a result, maintain a focus on healthy living. Secondly, there is antilibidinal medication which aims to considerably reduce testosterone levels and subsequent interest in sex. Offenders who volunteer to have medication must show issues that include sexual preoccupation, hypersexual arousal or the presence of deviant sexual fantasies psychological therapy has failed to subdue.

While treating those who wish to cease sex offending can be complex, research into sex offender desistance can be equally multifaceted. Although there have been a considerable number of studies that have addressed desistance from mainstream criminality, research examining sex offending has been relatively scarce. In attempting to structure sexual offending desistance research, such theoretical understandings have been placed into three key themes: natural desistence (age–sex curve), external desistance (informal social controls) and internal desistance (cognitive transformation and identity) (Harris, 2014).

Where sexual offender desistance and age are concerned there are parallels with mainstream criminal desistance. Just like the age–crime curve which highlights that crime is committed mainly by young people (teens and twenties) and decreases as offenders get older, there is an age–sex curve that appears to show a similar effect. In examining an array of informal social controls that included marriage, employment, having children and treatment, evidence suggests that employment is significant in diverting offenders away from further recidivism more so than marriage. In terms of cognitive transformation, rational choice can play a part – being a sexual offender can become too dangerous to the extent that the costs of long-term imprisonment will outweigh any intrinsic benefit of offending.

Conclusion

Sexual offending has had a long history, dating back to the biblical era, and over the years it has evolved in many different forms, some of which have eventually transcended into the realms of legitimacy. Although a relatively high proportion of sexual offending still remains unreported, there has been a major increase in reporting in recent times. This has largely been accredited to improved police recording of incidents and also a dramatic change in culture and the realisation of the long-term psychological harm sexual offences cause survivors and their families. The topics of definition, aetiology, management, treatment and desistence have become challenging and highly complex for both clinical and social science researchers, but only through further empirical scrutiny can greater understanding be achieved and effective policy formulated.

References
Bailey, R.C. (1988) 'The significance of hypergyny for understanding subsistence behavior among contemporary hunters and gatherers', in B.V. Kennedy and G.M. LeMoine (eds) *Diet and Subsistence: Current Archaeological Perspectives*, Calgary: University of Calgary Press, pp 57–65.

Bain, J., Langevin, R, Dickey, R. and Ben-Aron, M. (1987) 'Sex hormones in murderers and assaulters', *Behavioural Science and the Law*, 5(95): 101.

Bowlby, J. (1988) 'Developmental psychiatry comes of age', *American Journal of Psychiatry*, 145: 1–10.

Cummings, J.L. (1999) 'Neuropsychiatry of sexual deviations', in R. Osview (ed) *Neuropsychiatry and Mental Health Services*, Washington, DC: American Psychiatric Press, pp 363–84.

Day, K. (1994) 'Male mentally handicapped sex offenders', *British Journal of Psychiatry*, 165: 630–9.

Freund, K. (1990) 'Courtship disorder', in W.L. Marshall, D.R. Laws and H.E. Barbaree (eds) *Handbook of Sexual Assault: Issues, Theories, and Treatment of the Offender*, New York: Plenum Press, pp 195–207.

Hall, G.C. and Hirschmann, R. (1991) 'Towards a theory of aggression: a quadripartite model', *Journal of Consulting and Clinical Psychology*, 59: 662–9.

Harris, D.A. (2014) 'Desistance from sexual offending: findings from 21 life history narratives', *Journal of Interpersonal Violence*, 29(9): 1554–78.

Jenkins, P. (1998) *Moral Panic: Changing Concepts of the Child Molester in Modern America*, London: Yale University Press.

McCartan, K. and Prescott, D.S. (2017) Bring me the Horizon! (and Kaizen), [Blog] 29 June, [online] Available from https://www.blog.atsa.com/2017/06/bring-me-horizon-and-kaizen.html [Accessed 5 June 2021].

Seto, M.C., Hanson, R.K. and Babchishin, K.M. (2011) 'Contact sexual offending by men with online sexual offences', *Sexual Abuse: A Journal of Research and Treatment*, 23: 124–45.

Von Krafft-Ebing, R. (2011) *Psychopathia Sexualis*, New York: Arcade.

Ward, T. and Beech, A.R. (2016) 'The integrated theory of sexual offending revised: a multifield persective', in P. Boer (ed) *The Wiley Handbook on the Theories, Assessment and Treatment of Sexual Offending*, Chichester: Wiley & Sons, pp 123–37, DOI: https://doi.org/10.1002/9781118574003.wattso006.

Ward, T. and Hudson, S.M. (2001) 'Finkelhor's precondition model of child sexual abuse: a critique', *Psychology, Crime & Law*, 7(1–4): 291–307.

Ward, T., Hudson, S., Marshall, W. and Siegert, R. (1995) 'Attachment styles and intimacy deficits in sexual offenders: A theoretical Framework', *Sexual Abuse: A Journal of Research and Treatment*, 7(4): 317–35.

Wilson, C. (1990) *The Mammoth Book of True Crime 2*, London: Robson Publishing.

15

Forensic psychology and future directions

Rachael Steele and Michelle McManus

The role of the forensic psychologist has traditionally been tied to the work of the courtroom and to the expert assessment of those moving through the criminal justice system (CJS). The traditional role of the forensic psychologist within prisons has also been a clear career route for aspiring psychologist, with roles in risk assessment, parole hearings and mental health support forming the central provision (McGuire and Duff, 2018). HM Prison and Probation Service is the largest single employer of forensic psychologists in the UK, with over 500 psychologists employed (according to government figures in 2018).

However, the role of the forensic psychologist has now widened to include all types of crime in all aspects of the CJS. From crime prevention to crime analysis, from profiling to treatment, the role of the forensic psychologist has never been so in demand or so varied. As crime and the criminal develop in scope, expertise and remit, so must the role of the forensic psychologist expand to inform and enable the CJS to manage these new offences and offenders.

Routes to qualification

The changes and widening of the remit are reflected in the new route to qualification for the forensic psychologist in the UK as per the British Psychological Society (BPS). Previously, the BPS had offered a Stage 2 qualification, which could be completed after a qualifying master's degree as a two-year programme. This was replaced from July 2021, with a revised Stage 2 qualification taking four years, equivalent to a doctorate, suitable for those already working in a relevant role such as within a criminal justice or health setting. This increase in length and scope of the qualification aims to better prepare new forensic psychologists in a broader range of skills as both practitioners and researchers.

Changes such as this will prepare the profession for future areas of development and, as part of this, move the focus of the forensic psychologist outside of the hospitals, prisons and homes of offenders and victims and into cyberspace. The incredible rise in the scope and reach of the internet has seen a concurrent rise in crime committed in the relative anonymity of cyberspace. Such crime ranges from the creation and sharing of illegal images, fraud, identity theft and phishing, right through to the technological sabotage and hacking of secure systems, such as within the government or large business (Gavin, 2018). As new societal opportunities are created by global and digital developments, criminals also adapt and take advantages of those opportunities (Canter, 2017).

New types of crime

Forensic psychologists can offer much in the way of insight into these new and developing fields of crime. Of course, the psychology of the offender is still a primary concern for the forensic psychologist and, despite the crimes being online, the motivations, antecedents and mitigators of criminal behaviour still apply – after all, crimes in cyberspace are still committed by real people. However, there are particular challenges that need to be met to understand crimes of this nature. The feeling of anonymity on the internet not only encourages individuals and groups of people to say and do things that they may be inhibited from doing in real life, but also makes detection and prosecutions more challenging. Some of these offences still occur within the 'real world', but also now have a digital presence. Part of the challenge for forensic psychology is to understand the level of overlap of these offences and how closely they align. For example, the investigation into those individuals and groups who engage in the creation and sharing of indecent images of children has led to several developments in research and understanding. The sheer number of images that may be held by any one individual certainly poses a challenge, with these often easily in the millions, therefore overwhelming the resources that the police have available. There are ongoing debates about whether individuals who view indecent images of children will move on to contact offences in the future, are simultaneously committing contact sexual offences or if, for some people, this access to images will actually prevent a future contact offence, being enough to satisfy their needs (McManus et al, 2015). There is certainly evidence to suggest that for some individuals seeking actual contact with a child the use of online chatrooms and other social media give access to potential victims that they may not have had before; this distinct activity has been coined 'cyber exploitation' or online grooming (McGuire and Duff, 2018).

Internet offending

Research into the nature of contact and internet sex offenders does suggest that there are noted differences within their profiles (see McManus et al, 2015), with research indicating that indecent-image-only offenders tend to have a higher level of education and more secure adult relationships than contact offenders. However, due to the pace of advancement and use of technology, this research is continuing to develop and poses continuous challenges for forensic psychology (Howitt, 2018). Similarly, 'cyberstalking' is another area where offences in the physical and digital spaces overlap. Some research suggests that the internet simply provides more opportunities for stalkers to harass and intimidate their victims, whereas other work suggests that the accessibility and relative anonymity of the internet has spawned a whole new different set of stalkers (Howitt, 2018). Just as with internet-based sex offending, initial work suggests that there are some behavioural differences between internet and offline stalkers, with the internet offenders being more likely to make direct threats as well as being more likely to threaten suicide if caught. Victims of online stalking can be subject to all sorts of harassment, from threats of violence to delivery of unwanted goods ordered in their name, and yet are less likely than victims of offline stalking to report this to the police (Sheridan and Grant, 2007).

Subsequently, the challenge of understanding and working with people who offend on the internet pose distinct challenges for forensic psychology. As stated earlier, the sheer volume of offences make meaningful, timely analysis of materials and risk assessments very difficult. Justice systems and agencies can be overloaded with information and with crimes to investigate, but forensic psychology also has a role to play in analysis and synthesis of this data. Technology can be used to support the analysis and categorisation of millions of online indecent images and link this with details of known offenders to help risk assess and plan where resources are best used (for example, KIRAT: Kent Internet Risk Assessment Tool). Other technological developments can be based in the data analysis and research done by forensic psychologists, such as the 'Dragnet-K' software. This is a program that analyses thousands of items of data along with an understanding of criminal behaviour and motivations in order to deliver a map of potential crime locations (Canter, 2017). Developments such as this bring forensic psychology firmly into the area of crime prevention, an area that has more traditionally been informed by criminological and social theories (Canter, 2017).

Global and organised crime

Along with the increased work and knowledge required within cyberpsychology by forensic psychologists, the growth in global crime is another area that poses significant challenges to forensic psychology. Global crimes come with their own challenges. These complexities relate to geographic and legislative variations that exist within and across countries and that test levels of communication and cooperation between agencies, researchers and governments. Some of these crime types, such as hijacking and piracy, are age-old in nature, but have become more prevalent in recent years as criminals become more sophisticated. Hijacking, where criminals illegally take possession of an occupied ship or aeroplane, can be motivated in various ways – whether that be simply to transport the hijacker to a safe place, to extract a ransom for the cargo or crew (McGuire and Duff, 2018) or, of course, to commit a much bigger crime, such as in the terrorist hijacking of aeroplanes in the 9/11 attack in the US in 2011 (Gavin, 2018). This range of criminal motivations can be complex to understand. Globally, the drugs market and traffickers have extended their market due to COVID-19 and increased global movement of populations online. Recent statistics from the

United Nations Office on Drugs and Crime report on COVID-19 and drugs highlighted that drug markets on the dark web are now worth $315 million annually, utilising advances in contactless sales in their movement.

Green crime

Additional growth areas for forensic psychologists include the emerging field of green or environmental crime; this again is an area of criminal behaviour where impacts are felt globally. These crimes can involve such disparate behaviours as trade in endangered species, illegal fishing and illegal disposal of toxic waste (Durrant, 2018). Crimes of this nature not only have the complexity of covering multiple areas and legal jurisdictions, but usually involve organised crime groups. This, of course, adds to the complexity and dangers of research and work in this area and brings in aspects of organisational psychology, understanding of culture and the psychology of groups, all which are areas where forensic psychology has something to offer. Understanding how the individual is motivated and enabled to commit the crime is intertwined and affected by the understanding of the business, social and/or organisational processes that may support this behaviour. Crimes such as those relating to hijack, and environmental crime, will inevitably involve individuals at several levels of an organised process (Gavin, 2018). Another illustration of organised crime that crosses borders is human trafficking, an offence that has increased significantly in scope, with forced migration being known to be taking place in more than a hundred countries across the world. Human beings may be trafficked for a range of reasons. This may be to be used as slave labour, to be forced into sex work or begging, to become child soldiers or even for organ removal (Durrant, 2018). Once again, the complex nature of this crime demands a huge number of resources from lawmakers, legal systems, governments and, of course, forensic psychologists around the world. One of the complexities of crimes such as these, aside from the variety of reasons for trafficking, is the vast number of individuals and roles within the organisations that perpetrate these crimes. The motivations, reasoning and behaviours of those criminal individuals at the bottom of the organisational hierarchy may look different from those at the top, again posing a challenge for forensic psychologists intending to help identify, understand, respond and treat offenders of these crimes. The impact of these crimes is significant on the victims, with research suggesting that aside from physical injury, victims of trafficking can suffer ongoing and long-term poor mental health, depression and post-traumatic stress disorder, even if they are released from their exploitative situation (Durrant, 2018).

These developing areas of crime are rapidly changing the focus and research of the forensic psychology profession and, as such, offer many new and innovative opportunities to explore criminal motivations and antecedents. It is clear that crime, and the individuals that commit crime, are always evolving. Consequently, the justice system and the discipline of forensic psychology will also need to continually adapt and evolve. Whether crime is committed in the physical world or the digital world, and whether the impact is localised or global, crimes are still committed by people. The expertise and research of forensic psychologists is more necessary than ever to identify and assess the motivations of these perpetrators, the needs of the victims and the best way to support the CJS. The changing nature of crime ensures a fascinating and ever-expanding remit of influence for forensic psychology over the next few years, as new techniques and insights develop and keep forensic psychology relevant and at the cutting edge of research.

References

Canter, D. (2017) *Criminal Psychology*, London: Routledge.

Durrant, R. (2018) *An Introduction to Criminal Psychology*, London: Routledge

Gavin, H. (2018) *Criminological and Forensic Psychology* (2nd edn), London: SAGE.

Howitt, D. (2018) *Introduction to Forensic and Criminal Psychology* (6th edn), Harlow: Pearson Education.

McGuire, J. and Duff, S. (2018) *Forensic Psychology: Routes through the System*, London: Bloomsbury.

McManus, M.A., Long, M.L., Alison, L.J. and Almond, L.E. (2015) 'Factors associated with contact child sexual abuse in a sample of indecent image offenders', *Journal of Sexual Aggression*, 21(3): 368–84.

Sheridan, L.P. and Grant, T. (2007) 'Is cyberstalking different?' *Psychology, Crime and Law*, 13(6), 627–40.

PART II

Crime and criminal justice

16

Crime and criminal justice: past and present

Jo Turner and Karen Corteen

Introduction: the social construction of crime

The notion of 'crime' and consequent criminal justice responses have fluctuated throughout history and it is only by understanding the past that the present can be understood. First, though, a discussion defining crime and the social construction of crime is necessary. On first appearance, defining crime appears to be simple, however, this is not the case as the concept of 'crime' is contested and contextual. This means that social, economic, political and moral contexts impact on what is and what is not defined as 'crime'. 'Crime' is also temporal, spatial and cultural. Crime, therefore, 'has no ontological reality', is not fixed and there is no 'intrinsic quality of act which defines an event as a crime' (Hillyard and Tombs, 2006, p 7). Crime is, therefore, socially constructed.

This can be seen in that what constitutes crime changes over time, place and culture. For example, until the late 20th century, in England and Wales, suicide and homosexuality were against criminal law but rape within marriage was not. Also, in England and Wales until very recently acts which could be freely undertaken, such as driving and talking on a mobile phone and smoking in public places are now subject to legal restrictions. Same-sex relations are legal in England and Wales but in over seventy countries same-sex relations are criminalised. In England and Wales cultural practices such as female genital mutilation and forced marriage are criminal offences but in many places in the world they have not been criminalised. It can be evidenced, therefore, that time, place and culture influence what is and what is not socially constructed as crime.

In addition, in England and Wales in the social, political and media spheres there is an obsession with street crime and a neglect of 'crimes of the suites' and other crimes of the powerful (Tombs and Whyte, 2005/6, p 24). This means that the concept of 'crime' excludes many serious harms (Hillyard and Tombs, 2006), including 'the routine and large-scale killing of workers, passengers and consumers, to corporate fraud, to environmental devastation and so on' (Tombs and Whyte, 2005/6, p 24). This focus on the crimes of the most vulnerable and marginalised is reflected in the criminal justice system (CJS) and its responses to crime.

Changes in policing

As the entry point to the CJS, the police have immense influence over which crimes are taken forward for prosecution and thus which behaviour repressed, even once the Crown Prosecution Service (CPS) was established under the Prosecution of Offences Act 1985 and despite the continuing right people have to bring their own private prosecution. Therefore, the evolution of policing in England and Wales has had a direct impact on how criminal justice has changed. Initially, prior to the 19th century, men (and it was always men until 1915 when Edith Smith was appointed as the first female police officer in Grantham) working in a policing role were amateurs and semi-professionals organised on a parish system, controlled and paid by local councils rather than national government, a system that varied widely in quality across the country. Each parish had a constable and nightwatchmen. The constable was elected annually (some were regularly elected annually, making the role permanent) and essentially acted when called upon, following up on cases of theft, arresting and processing suspects and being reimbursed by the complainant in the case; nightwatchmen, paid from a tax on the wealthy residents of a parish, had powers of arrest and patrolled the streets of a parish at night. Both roles were open to corruption and were deemed ineffective in dealing with societal changes brought about by industrialisation.

However, starting with the Metropolitan Police Act 1829, 19th-century England and Wales saw new salaried, professional and uniformed police forces paid for by central government being founded across the country, initially running alongside the existing, older system of policing but gradually replacing it by the end of the century. Academic debates about this development range from it being a rational response to rising crime rates, to the middle classes needing to protect their newly earned property. The role of these salaried police, however, centred very much around public order and they made a virtue of their ability to prevent crime and to secure the streets from disorder (Churchill, 2017). Until the advent of police regulation of private motor vehicles in the early 20th century, this principally meant controlling public space and checking drunken disorder. The relationship between the police and the populace was a complex and ambiguous one with much regional and temporal variation and, while acceptance grew, there was considerable resistance. Even when tensions eased and this style of policing ostensibly became an accepted feature of modern criminal justice, the police and their role continued to face challenges and criticism in the 20th and 21st centuries stemming from major events such as, for example, women's activism for the vote, the two world wars and later political and industrial disturbances among others. Crime detection ran alongside the role of crime prevention and maintaining social order, originally the remit of the Bow Street Runners in the 18th century to becoming part of the role of the new salaried forces in the form of criminal investigation departments.

The new salaried police also helped victims of crime in their quest for justice by representing them in court. Victims in the past had the option of subjecting their transgressors to rough justice, informal, shaming, quick community-based punishments (effective in close-knit communities but deemed increasingly ineffective from the early 19th century) or paying to take them through the formal, expensive court system. As the police became established, and until the establishment of the CPS in 1985, they (rather than the victim of the crime) used the police courts and petty sessions to bring offenders to justice, so over time the victim was removed almost entirely from the prosecution process. Police discretion and control over which and how many offenders were prosecuted in court gave the police enormous influence over crime rates, which has led to present-day declining public confidence in criminal statistics.

Changes in the court system

The present-day complicated court system evolved over the past thousand years, resulting in different courts dealing with different types of cases. The period 1750–1950 saw the rise of the professional barrister, an adversarial trial process, more ceremony and a more solemn court atmosphere and an increased reliance of evidence. The notion of innocent until proven guilty did not arise until insisted upon by William Garrow, a barrister, in 1791. Thus, there has been a shift from a lively, contested, amateur court system where prosecution was initiated by the aggrieved party (at their own expense) to a more professional, orderly system where defendants are treated as innocent and the police (and CPS) are responsible for bringing most cases to court with the aid of full-time lawyers and judges.

Changes in punishment

Just as the detection and apprehension of offenders are clearly a part of policing, all societies must deal with the issue of what to do with their offenders. A long-term perspective suggests that society has been unable to make up its mind about the function and effectiveness of its punishment regime. Prior to the mid-19th century there were a number of formal punishments that ran alongside the traditional, informal, shaming, community ways of dealing with offenders: public execution, transportation (first to America then Australia), selective use of prisons (to detain people before a trial and debtors until they paid their debts), non-fatal mutilations such as branding or burning or even cutting off hands of thieves for example and whipping in public (Emsley, 2010). While in England and Wales the death penalty was not abolished until 1969 (finally in 1998), public executions had ended in 1868 along with transportation during the 1860s, and the number of offences carrying the death penalty had reduced from around two hundred in 1800 to just five by 1861. Thus, by the second half of the 19th century, as well as the continued use of financial penalties, imprisonment became the predominant method of dealing with offenders (Foucault, 1977). The rise and persistent use of imprisonment continues to be a hotly debated subject. Contemporary society has vastly overcrowded prisons, with debates abounding about whether the era of incarceration has failed to provide the solutions that its theoreticians, from Bentham onwards, propounded. There is now a hunt for cheaper alternatives such as improved community sanctions that can garner the confidence of the public and sentencers, modern shaming punishments and restorative justice.

Technological changes: impact on crime and criminal justice

Technological changes over time have had a direct impact on the nature of crime and the control of crime in society. Societal changes, such as the advent of regular, systematic collection of judicial statistics during the first half of the 19th century and the 21st-century proliferation of closed-circuit television, have had their impact on crime and criminal justice. Police work in combatting crime has obviously benefited from technological advances such as fingerprinting (in the late 19th century) to genetic profiling (in the late 20th century). The ability of the police to respond to incidents in progress has advanced, with the harnessing of telephone and radio technology. Crime prevention was arguably made more effective with the advent of the motor car, which allowed for a quicker response and a more extensive patrol area. Crime prevention is one area that has seen significant investment over recent years with the widespread and still growing application of other electronic surveillance devices. However, the growth of new technology has always changed the shape of crime itself: a wave of theft and larceny towards the end of the 18th century appeared because there were new high-value portable items to steal, while the 19th-century growing sophistication of the financial and banking sector and the advent of railways presented new opportunities for white-collar larceny in the form of fraud and the creation of the 'respectable' criminal. Some types of crime became organised and took advantage of economies of scale brought about by technological advances. In the 21st century, the internet is the most recent technological advance that has allowed crime and criminality to modernise, more so perhaps than the forces of law and order have in the fight against them.

Gender, crime and criminal justice

Crime and criminal justice have a distinctly gendered dimension. There are some crimes that are almost exclusively the preserve of one gender or another – the most obvious example being infanticide – but gender also has an important role to play in how people are treated by the CJS (Zedner, 1991). Perceptions of, and responses to, sex crimes are deeply rooted in patriarchal gender expectations. Those expectations are reinforced and reiterated in the media, which reports on court cases and creates opinion. For example, even the ways in which men and women found guilty of murder have been differentially treated have changed over time. Although not universally accepted, it has been suggested that women receive different treatment from the CJS than men (Ballinger, 2000). Certainly, society and the media have frequently tried to make male and female murder defendants fit into gender-specific stereotypes.

Gender has also influenced participation in criminal justice professions. It has only been since the Sex Disqualification (Removal) Act 1919, that women could become magistrates, barristers, solicitors and jurors; thus, for the majority of history, criminal justice has been a distinctly male province. It was only just over a hundred years later (in 2015) that there were as many women magistrates as there were men. The involvement of women in the police force has lagged significantly behind the involvement of men, with participation in the whole range of policing activities only possible with late 20th-century gender equality. In a change from the early 20th century, when women police officers were confined to dealing with the issues associated with women and children, women police officers should now expect the same range of career opportunities as their male counterparts.

A civilising society

The extent to which society has 'civilised' over the centuries is a debate that feeds into discussions around changing punishment regimes specifically and the nature of crime and criminal justice more generally (Pratt, 2002). On the one hand, increased levels of crime could be equated with increased lawlessness and a lesser civilised society but, on the other hand, the 19th and 20th centuries have seen increased levels of crime although they may be seen as more civilised. Likewise, more liberal punishment regimes could be considered a mark of a civilised society but, as Foucault (1977) warns, punishment regimes have changed from having a deterrent ethos to surveillance being predominant; rather than a civilising, humane change, it is a change that could be considered more intrusive and ominous, more brutal. Discussions about the death penalty are instructive, debates about what is the most effective and just punishment for those who take the life of another. Deterrence, retribution and justice are held up to be what is civilised but there is no one single standard – individual states of the US, for example, have different stances on the use of the death penalty which Garland (2012) has shown to be linked to US political and cultural institutions.

Conclusion

Present-day criminal justice faces many criticisms, from a police force that has been dubbed institutionally racist to prisons that fail to rehabilitate. What can be said with certainty is that 'crime' and the nature of criminal justice are historically and geographically specific and they differ across time, place and culture. What constitutes crime and criminal justice are in constant change, so these are interesting and dynamic phenomena.

References

Ballinger, A. (2000) *Dead Woman Walking: Executed Women in England and Wales, 1900–1950*, Abington: Routledge.

Churchill, D. (2017) *Crime Control and Everyday Life in the Victorian City*, Oxford: Oxford University Press.

Emsley, C. (2010) *Crime and Society in England, 1750–1900* (4th edn), Harlow: Pearson Longman.

Foucault, M. (1977) *Discipline and Punish: The Birth of the Prison*, New York: Pantheon Books.

Garland, D. (2012) *Peculiar Institution: America's Death Penalty in an Age of Abolition*, Cambridge, MA: Harvard University Press.

Hillyard, P. and Tombs, S. (2006) 'Beyond criminology', in D. Dorling, D. Gordon, P. Hillyard, C. Pantazis, S. Pemberton and S. Tombs (eds) *Criminal Obsessions: Why Harm Matters More Than Crime* (2nd edn), London: Centre for Crime and Justice Studies, pp 2–23, [online] Available from: https://www.crim eandjustice.org.uk/sites/crimeandjustice.org.uk/files/Criminal%20obsessions. pdf [Accessed 23 September 2019].

Pratt, J. (2002) *Punishment and Civilisation: Penal Tolerance and Intolerance in Modern Society*, Thousand Oaks, CA: SAGE.

Tombs, S. and Whyte, D. (2005/6) 'From the streets to the suites: researching corporate crime', *Criminal Justice Matters*, 62: 24–6, Available from: https:// www.crimeandjustice.org.uk/sites/crimeandjustice.org.uk/files/0962725050 8553096.pdf [Accessed 10 June 2022].

Zedner, L. (1991) *Women, Crime and Custody in Victorian England*, Oxford: Clarendon Press.

17

Crime

Noel Cross

Introduction

The concept of crime is a constant feature of public, media and political discourse in England and Wales. On its most basic level, crime can be defined as behaviour which is prohibited by criminal law and which can be punished by the criminal justice process. Yet crime is in fact a contested and divisive concept. Crime and its meaning can be viewed from a variety of different standpoints: classicist, positivist, constructionist, radical or hybrid. Such standpoints also speak to a range of different audiences for discourses on crime: the legal/professional, the public and the academic.

Classicist and positivist approaches to defining crime

Early ideas about the definition of crime come from writers on criminal law itself within the classicist tradition. The definition of crime at the beginning of this chapter was first put forward by Glanville Williams in the 1950s. Viewed like this, crime is simply whatever criminal law says it is. A freethinking individual has control over their actions and, as such, deserves to be held responsible for crime that they commit. Such a view did not always reflect definitions of crime. In criminal law in England and Wales, the idea of *mens rea*, or mental responsibility for crime, as part of the definition of criminal behaviour, only dates back as far as the 19th century. Before this, mental responsibility for crime was interpreted from the external behaviour (*actus reus* or guilty act) which formed the basis of the definition of what crime was and which could only be rebutted by evidence of good character in the court setting. It is no coincidence that the development of *mens rea* in criminal law's definition of crime emerged at the same time as the birth of psychology as a means of understanding behaviour through the processes of the mind (Norrie, 2014). Despite academic discourse around crime focusing to a greater or lesser extent on limitations over individual choice to commit crime, the classicist view of crime continues to drive criminal law's definition of crime, as well as being a key influence on macro-level criminal justice policy. This is true not only in England and Wales, but also in other countries influenced by a neo-conservative political economy, such as the US, Australia and South Africa – all of whom derive their criminal law frameworks from the one in England and Wales.

Such a consistently classicist approach contrasts with academic criminological discourse about crime and its causes in the first half of the 20th century. This academic discourse evolved from the view of crime as being committed by a discrete, biologically or psychologically distinct group of people to the ideas of the Chicago School, which attributed crime to the social disorganisation caused by living in the inner city (Shaw and McKay, 1942), and the Durkheim-influenced ideas of Robert Merton (1938), who pointed to the mismatch between individual ambition and societal opportunity for success as the source of crime. Psychological explanations for crime followed a similar path of emerging social awareness, developing from Freud's abstract psychoanalysis through John Bowlby's research into childhood development and onto B. F. Skinner's view of crime as an automatic behavioural response to external triggers (Blackburn, 1993). Although the classicist and positivist approaches take opposite views to defining crime and its causes they both locate criminal responsibility in individuals who represent a clearly identifiable social group.

Constructionist approaches to defining crime

The constructionist view of crime directly challenges the positivistic approach. Becker (1963), in his work on labelling theory, rejected the idea that there is a consensus on what is and should be seen as crime in society. As a result, what counts as crime can and does change and so who are considered criminals can also change. Constructionism, and more specifically labelling theory, as a part of criminological academic discourse, acknowledged how certain individuals and groups in society label particular types of behaviour as 'criminal' through a series of negotiations which may or may not result in behaviour being labelled as 'crime' in criminal law and criminal justice practice, depending on how successfully the label is applied. Such labelling could then cause further criminal behaviour (secondary deviation) if the labelled individual changed their self-image to fit in with the label imposed on them. On this view, there is a gap between the definition of a behaviour as a 'crime' in criminal law ('the law in the books') and the enforcement of that law in criminal justice practice ('the law in action'). The legal definition of a type of behaviour as a crime would have a very limited effect on society if criminal justice agencies (particularly the police) did not enforce the criminal law by taking action against those suspected of breaking that law. Yet this crucial aspect of criminalisation is necessarily shaped by police resources, strategic decisions about the use of those resources, legislation governing the extent and limits of police powers in England and Wales (primarily the Police and Criminal Evidence Act 1984), and the cultures and values driving police decision making in practice. All of these factors shape police decisions on recording reports of criminal behaviour reported to them, as well as police decisions on whether and whom to stop, search, arrest, interrogate and charge in connection with crime (Welsh, et al, 2021).

The constructionist approach does not in itself explain why some behaviours are labelled as criminal by society while others are not. It also fails to address the issue of power relations in society directly, in terms of making it clear who has the power to label behaviour as 'criminal' or 'deviant', who has the power to maintain the presence of labels and how this power operates.

Radical approaches to defining crime

Later, Marxist-influenced writers built on Ernest Becker's work by using a radical approach, focusing attention on who in society has the power to label others as criminal in this way and how that power might be used to promote a particular individual's or group's own interests (Box, 1983). In this way, it can be seen that how different agencies and groups (such as the government, Parliament and the judiciary) compete to use their power to shape the definition of crime. Radical approaches to defining crime share the constructionist view that what counts as crime can and does change according to time and place, but focuses particularly on the social, economic, political and moral conditions which drive criminalisation (Reiner, 2016). To give two well-known examples, homosexual activity between adult men was partially decriminalised in 1967 (under the Sexual Offences Act 1967) while the hunting of wild animals with dogs made the return criminalisation journey in 2004, following its criminalisation under the Hunting Act of that year. It would be wrong, however, to think that the decision to criminalise or legalise necessarily changed societal attitudes towards these types of behaviour or criminal justice regulation of them. Criminal justice convictions for gross indecency between men, an offence which survived the 1967 Sexual Offences Act's reforms, increased by over 300 per cent in the UK between 1966 and 1974 and there is evidence to suggest that hundreds of illegal hunts continue to take place despite the 2004 Act. The radical approach to crime not only interrogates the influence of power relations on the definition of crime, but also the effects of socioeconomic and other forms of inequality on the nature and extent of crime.

The radical approach has also been a key influence on the long-running academic debates over the relative importance of legislative rules on the one side and police culture and informal values on the other, in day-to-day police activity. These debates are of vital importance at a time when the evidence of racial discrimination in police activity is under such intense scrutiny following Black Lives Matter campaigns around the world. In the UK, those from a Black, Asian and minority ethnic background are over eight times more likely to be stopped and searched than White people, according to recent government data, and the Metropolitan Police in London were four times more likely to use force against Black people than White people in 2017–18 – in addition to the high-profile incidences of apparent police brutality during the arrest and detention process that result in death (such as the death of George Floyd as a result of police actions in the US on 25 May 2020).

These are vital issues, not just in terms of their challenges to the view of criminal justice as being fair and equal for all, but also in terms of society's understanding of what crime itself means. This is the case because police crime statistics, containing all crimes recorded by the police, are still widely accepted in media and public discourse as being an accurate representation of the nature and extent of crime. This acceptance persists despite the UK government's decision not to treat police crime statistics as being reliable enough to be treated as official statistics in 2014, despite the fact that the police do not record every incident of crime that is reported to them, despite the variation in crime recording practice across different police forces and despite the 'dark figure' of crime that is reported to crime surveys but not to the police. Of course, some forms of crime cannot be measured by crime surveys where the victim is asked about their own experiences – homicide being the obvious example. It is also true to say that crime surveys such as the Crime Survey for England and Wales (CSEW) cannot present a complete picture of crime, any more than police statistics can. They overlook such key issues as crimes by and against businesses, international crimes and cybercrime (Maguire and McVie, 2017). All of this means that current CSEW estimates of 10.4 million offences being committed in England and Wales in the year to December 2019 and police recording (excluding the Greater Manchester area) of 5.8 million offences over the same period cannot provide a true picture of crime, and that they convey as much about the methods of analysing crime data being used as they do about the nature and extent of crime itself.

Hybrid approaches to defining crime: moving beyond crime altogether?

Finally, hybrid criminological approaches have attempted to go beyond radical understandings of the state as a major cause of crime and a source of mystification and discrimination in terms of the response to crime. These approaches include (but are not limited to) a range of feminist criminologies that focus on the lived experience of women as perpetrators and victims of crime; left realism, which attempts to balance individual and structural causes of crime; zemiology, which sees crime as just one of a range of socially harmful behaviours; and ultra-realism, which focuses on the criminogenic nature of capitalism, its influence on psychological isolation and selfishness in terms of understanding crime and on the harm that results at all levels of society (Hall and Winlow, 2015). This is together with approaches which focus on the nature and extent of international, corporate and state crime, often grouped under the heading of crimes of the powerful. It is no surprise, given the critical and challenging view of the causes of crime taken by these approaches collectively, that they also provide a serious challenge to the limitations to understanding crime through criminal statistics discussed earlier. They seek to paint a truer picture of crime through local-level victimisation surveys, qualitative observation and interviewing on the criminal experience and international data providing comparison with crime in countries outside the UK. It is argued that these more nuanced and sophisticated approaches provide us with the best framework for understanding the causes, nature and extent of crime in the 21st century.

Conclusions

Crime is a contested and socially constructed concept, despite its central position in public, political and academic discourse. Official crime statistics, located as they are in the same classicist and individualistic understanding of criminal behaviour as is found in criminal law itself, can only give a partial understanding of the real causes, nature and extent of crime. To fill these gaps in an understanding of what crime means it is necessary to engage with the kind of critical academic discourse that tries to address the harm caused by behaviour which may or may not be officially labelled as 'crime', and that focuses both on the lived experience of individuals as the perpetrators and victims of crime and on the political, social and economic context in which such experiences are played out.

References
Becker, H. (1963) *Outsiders*, London: Macmillan.
Blackburn, R. (1993) *The Psychology of Criminal Conduct*, Chichester: Wiley.
Box, S. (1983) *Power, Crime and Mystification*, London: Tavistock.
Hall, S. and Winlow, S. (2015) *Revitalising Criminological Theory: Towards a New Ultra-Realism*, Abingdon: Routledge.
Maguire, M. and McVie, S. (2017) 'Crime data and criminal statistics: a critical reflection', in A. Liebling, S. Maruna and L. McAra (eds) *The Oxford Handbook of Criminology* (6th edn), Oxford: Oxford University Press, pp 163–89.
Merton, R.K. (1938), 'Social structure and anomie', *American Sociological Review*, 3: 672–82.
Norrie, A. (2014) *Crime, Reason and History*, Cambridge: Cambridge University Press.
Reiner, R. (2016) *Crime: The Mystery of the Common-Sense Concept*, Cambridge: Polity Press.
Shaw, C.R. and Mackay, H.D. (1942) *Juvenile Delinquency and Urban Areas*, Chicago: University of Chicago Press.
Welsh, L., Skinns, L. and Sanders, A. (2021) *Sanders and Young's Criminal Justice* (5th edn), Oxford: Oxford University Press.

18

Criminal justice systems

Mike Berry

Introduction

The criminal justice system (CJS) is a rather complex concept involving the application of the five main arms of the legal system with many differences across the UK. It starts with Parliament creating laws, the identification of potential offences committed in the community, police investigations of suspects, court proceedings, the imposition of custodial and non-custodial sentences, and detention in a secure environment through to review and sometimes assessment by the Parole Board and eventual release to the community following rehabilitation and reduction of the risk of reoffending. There are differences between the CJSs in the UK, for example, the prison system and Mental Health Acts (MHAs) of England and Wales, while Northern Ireland and Scotland have different legislation regarding a wide range of offences. In Scotland, the minimum age of criminal responsibility is 12 years old, compared to ten years old in England and Wales. Under Scottish law the 15-person jury have the option of finding the defendant guilty, not guilty or not proven.

Enforcing the changing law: the investigative stage

Where individuals or groups of individuals are perceived to have possibly committed an offence and the police consider it worthy of further investigation, officers will attempt to build up a case, using, where appropriate, the Forensic Science Service (FSS) to collect evidence which can help exclude some suspects and reinforce the case against others. The definition of crime which underpins the CJS and its enforcement of criminal law changes regularly as new statutory offences are added and old offences amended or replaced. However, offences that are not reported to either the police or a crime survey are a bigger issue than old offences – in any case, if the offences have fallen out of use, they would not be committed regularly.

In addition to the Constabulary Police, law enforcement includes Border Control, British Rail Police and the Civil Nuclear Constabulary, a specialised armed police force responsible for the protection of nuclear sites in the UK and the transportation of waste material worldwide. Individuals can be initially interviewed by the police as potential witnesses or as suspects for the offence. If the latter, they should be accompanied by a legal representative and an 'appropriate adult' if a vulnerable individual, as the issue of capacity and suggestibility to interrogation questions needs to be considered (see Gudjonsson, 2003). The police have up to 24 hours, with appropriate breaks for sleep, exercise and food, to interview a suspect while recording the interviews under PEACE (Preparation and Planning, Engage and Explain, Account and Clarification, Closure and Evaluation) regulations, with one copy for the police and the other for the defence team. If further time is required to gain information or present evidence, this can be extended by an independent senior officer. A magistrate can authorise detention up to a total of 96 hours, at which point the suspect must be charged or released, the exception being detention under the Terrorism Acts, which allows someone to be held for 14 days. Once charged, the suspect cannot be interviewed by the police and must appear in front of a magistrates' court, where, if necessary, the court can authorise detention in prison or bail to the community. Occasionally, the police may use the powers under section 136 of the Mental Health Act 1983 to take a person to a place of safety such as a hospital. Case files are sent to the Crown Prosecution Service (CPS), the Public Prosecution Service in Northern Ireland or the Scottish Procurator Fiscal Service where Justice of the Peace courts are equivalent to magistrates' courts.

The CPS stage

The CPS will review the case and decide if it is likely to be successful; that is, does it have at least a 51 per cent chance of a conviction. Sometimes the evidence is insufficient or based upon one person's report of another's behaviour and may not stand up to a barrister's robust cross-examination. Occasionally the prosecution may decide that the case is not in the public interest, especially when the accused is already serving a very long prison sentence.

The uses of science during criminal justice investigations

During the process of being on remand or on bail in the community, the FSS will be working on excluding and including evidence to provide details for presenting at trial. The FSS is currently privatised but it is the government's intention to renationalise it. The proposed Forensic Science Regulation Bill defines forensic science activities as those which occur within the criminal justice system. The FSS can link DNA samples from the scene of the crime where appropriate and extract samples from living and dead bodies as well as identifying paints, fibres, tyre, foot, finger and palm prints. McDermid (2014) also highlighted experts who can advise on the time a body was deposited at the disposal site by examining bugs, insects and plant life.

Since the 1980s, various UK police forces have engaged clinical or forensic psychologists to provide psychological offender profiles outlining the likely characteristics of the offenders of unusual crimes beyond the expertise of the senior investigating officer and their teams. However, this has to some extent been overtaken by advances in scientific techniques developed by the FSS.

The pre-sentence court stage

During the investigation, defence and CPS lawyers usually meet for a Plea and Trial Preparation Hearing to enable the trial judge to decide on a commencement date and an estimate of the trial length, from days to months, and schedule the diaries of all parties. Sometimes the prosecution will not accept a not guilty plea to a more serious offence but may accept a guilty plea to a lesser charge, such as manslaughter instead of murder.

The magistrate bench usually consists of three community-orientated non-legal volunteers supported by a legally trained clerk. Magistrates can sentence an offender to a fine, a community order or imprisonment up to six months. If a person has committed two or more offences the magistrate can sentence them for up to one year's imprisonment. Approximately 95 per cent of cases are heard in the magistrates courts. In England and Wales, cases which have a sentencing threshold of more than six months can be referred upwards to the Crown Court, where they will be heard by a 12-person jury. Anyone can observe a trial in the court's public gallery except when a security notice is issued or when children are involved in the Family Division. Defendants can plead guilty, where they will be referred for sentencing by the judge, or not guilty, where they will go to trial in front of a judge and jury. As with any aspect of the legal system there are rare occasions when other conditions are imposed, such as in Northern Ireland, which has approximately 1 per cent of judge-only trials; otherwise a 12-person jury is the norm. Pleading guilty saves the system considerable time and money and usually will, depending at the point of plea, result in a reduction in the initial sentence by the judge, subject to the sentencing guidelines.

Next to be discussed are expert witnesses. A material witness (usually a member of the public) can only report in court what they saw, heard or identified. They are not allowed to express an opinion about the case, unlike witnesses who are called as joint or sole experts by the defence team, the prosecution team or even in some cases by the judge to inform the court on matters considered to be beyond the expected knowledge of the jury. It is a requirement of experts to show that they have expertise in their field, be it weapons, drug usage, data analysis, treatment of sex offenders or individuals experiencing mental health issues. For many years, court experts were exposed to cross-examination by defence or prosecution barristers, sometimes lasting for days and often to the confusion of the jury. As a result of the time involved, Lord Chief Justice Woolf recommended that both experts meet beforehand and attempt to produce a joint report highlighting where they agree and where after discussion they cannot agree (Woolf, 1998). This saves a great deal of court time and often where experts may not agree on causation they may agree on outcome and possible risk factors. In the light of the COVID-19 regulations, Craig and Kock (2021) have provided advice for remote working as an expert.

Sentencing and punishment

The discussion will now turn to court disposal. Offenders can be disposed of by discharge to the community, imprisonment in a young offender institution if under 21 or a prison ranging from 'Category C' through to 'Category A' (maximum security). Offenders are rarely admitted directly to a 'Category D' (open prison). Alternatively, if the court decides that convicted offenders require treatment they can be sent to a local psychiatric hospital or a Regional Secure Unit (RSU). If maximum security is required they can be transferred to a special hospital (in England, Ashworth, Broadmoor or Rampton, or Carstairs in Scotland; there are none in Wales or Northern Ireland) where they are detained for treatment. While some patients stay in special hospitals for many years, McCullough et al (2020) reported the median length of stay at Broadmoor was 4.5 years (mean 6.3 years), median age 38 years (mean 39.5). Prisoners can be transferred from a prison to a special hospital or RSU if in need of treatment for mental health issues at any point during their sentence and then returned. However, the time spent in a special hospital is not taken into account in terms of the time served on their sentence and returning prisoners have to complete their sentence.

When a life sentence is imposed, the judge will fix a minimum tariff which must be served in prison before the prisoner can apply for parole. If the Parole Board recommend release, the prisoner is released on a life licence. They can be recalled to prison at any time if they are considered to be posing a risk to anyone, committing further crimes or breaching any of their licence conditions. The current Police, Crime, Sentencing and Courts Act (2022) has changed tariffs and some minimum terms of imprisonment have become more severe.

Besides containment, HM Prison and Probation Service has a responsibility to rehabilitate offenders before release. Most prisons (when not in a pandemic) offer training in various occupations such as bricklaying, motor maintenance, cooking and tailoring, as well as education classes in arts and social science and maths and English remedial classes, as many criminals lack such skills. Therapeutic interventions for general, sexual, domestic violence and offences such as terrorism and arson are offered on an individual and group basis, largely facilitated by psychologists and other trained staff.

It is important at this point to discuss the release process. Normally, prisoners can be considered for early release after serving a third of their sentence and will usually be automatically released after completing two thirds of their sentence. However, if the prisoner has been disruptive or breached certain prison regulations, s/he may appear in front of a judge-led adjudication hearing where they can be awarded a loss of remission, resulting in the prisoner spending longer in prison.

Parole Board panels can be comprised of one, two or three members, consisting of a combination of a judge, a psychiatrist or psychologist and an independent 'lay' member depending on the case. The prisoner's application is subjected to a paper-based review to ascertain the necessity for an oral hearing. If the case cannot be concluded on the case papers, an oral hearing will be held in a prison (or remotely by video) for the Parole Board to decide on the prisoner's further detention, transfer to a lower category prison or release to the community.

Increasingly, psychologists are required to provide written or oral opinions for lifer committees and mental health tribunals (MHTs), as well as second opinions from doctors and Parole Boards, often at the patient's or prisoner's request. Experts must be familiar with the structure and rituals of court appearances and be prepared for rigorous barrister cross-examination. Police officers, psychologists, probation officers and forensic scientists are required to have the skills to provide expert opinions.

Under various MHAs, there is a legal requirement for a detained patient (usually section 37/41 of the MHA [1983]) to be regularly reviewed regarding detention in a secure environment. A psychologist treating the patient is expected to submit a written report or attend the MHT in person. This will comprise a judge, psychiatrist and usually a lay member, who decide on the patient's detention.

In 2013, part of the National Probation Service became privatised, following failures and considerable criticisms. Currently, action is being taken to return the service to the public sector. The probation officer's role is to monitor, advise and review the released prisoner in the community and check the released person's compliance with the licence conditions. If concerned about the released person's behaviour they can initiate a return to prison. Some services are using polygraphs to assess sex offenders in the community to manage their risk levels, tagging where appropriate.

Appeals and miscarriages of justice

The final area to be discussed is that of the appeal. Occasionally a convicted prisoner can petition to challenge a conviction on the grounds of lack of evidence at the trial, inappropriate advice from the judge to the jury, the quality of the confession, which may have been compromised due to the suspect's vulnerability, which was not adequately catered for during the police interview, or some new evidence being presented, such as DNA, that casts doubts on the soundness of the conviction. Such cases are usually heard in the Court of Appeal but occasionally some are reviewed at the highest level by the Supreme Court, albeit with a low success rate.

Ethnic minority groups, individuals experiencing learning difficulties, those experiencing mental health issues, those whose English is poor or who speak English as second or third language and deaf people are all likely to be disadvantaged within CJSs. They are entitled to an intermediary to assist them in court proceedings. Although justice is meant to be equitable, many would argue that there is still some way to go to actually achieving this.

References

Craig, L.A. and Kock, H.C. (2021) 'Expert witness psychologists and remote working', *Expert Witness Journal*, [online] 6 April, Available from: https://www.expertwitness.co.uk/articles/journal/expert-witness-psychologists-and-remote-working [Accessed 30 April 2021].

Gudjonsson, G.H. (2003) *The Psychology of Interrogations and Confessions: A Handbook*, Chichester: Wiley.

McCullough, S., Stanley, C., Smith, H., Scott, M., Karia, M., Ndubuisi, B. Ross, C.C., Bates, R. and Davoren, M. (2020) 'Outcome measures of risk and recovery in Broadmoor High Secure Forensic Hospital', *BJPsych Open*, 6(4): 1–8.

McDermid, V. (2014) *Forensics: The Anatomy of Crime*, London: Profile Books.

Woolf, H. (1998) 'Lord Woolf's Reforms and Civil Procedure Rules', [online] Available from: https://www.mondaq.com/uk/civil-law/705694/lord-woolf 39s-reforms-and-civil- procedure-rules-1998 [Accessed 20 April 2021].

19

Criminal justice, *actus reus* and *mens rea*

Noel Cross

Introduction

Criminal justice is the primary vehicle through which criminal law is enforced. Without the mechanisms and state power used by the police, the Crown Prosecution Service (CPS), the criminal courts and criminal punishment agencies, criminal law would lose much of its authority, legitimacy and power. Yet, in enforcing criminal law, criminal justice must engage with its often-outdated discourse. This discourse includes various phrases and concepts dating back hundreds of years, the most important of which are the Latin phrases *actus reus* (literally translated as guilty act) and *mens rea* (literally translated as guilty mind). The two concepts were linked together in the writings of the jurist Sir Edward Coke (1552–1634) in his statement, when writing about homicide, that an act does not make a person criminally guilty unless their mind is also guilty (Hossain and Rahi, 2018). *Actus reus* and *mens rea* remain the foundation for criminal justice's ability to enforce the criminal law in England and Wales. However, the meanings of both *actus reus* and *mens rea* are not as straightforward as they appear, either in terms of their changing definitions in criminal law itself over time, or what is involved in terms of their enforcement in criminal justice practice.

The meanings of *actus reus* in criminal law

Focusing on *actus reus* first, the literal translation of *actus reus* as 'guilty act' clearly points to the need to prove some form of external conduct, as specified by individual criminal offences, to establish criminal guilt. For some criminal offences it seems easy to define the external criminal conduct needed – the unlawful killing required for homicide offences, for example, or the deliberate lying under oath in court required for perjury. However, many other criminal offences require more than just an 'act' for a conviction. For example, theft in England and Wales requires not only a taking (appropriation), but also the taking of property which belongs to someone else as part of its *actus reus* under the Theft Act 1968, and rape requires not only the act of sexual intercourse, but also the circumstance of sexual intercourse without the victim's consent, under the Sexual Offences Act 2003. Even homicide offences require not just unlawful killing, but also killing of another person in being (for example, not an unborn child) 'under the King's or Queen's peace' (for example, not during wartime). Also, an increasing number of criminal offences can be committed by omission, and another group of offences involve possession (of offensive weapons or controlled drugs, for example) rather than action. Nor does the phrase '*actus reus*' make it clear that only voluntary acts can form the basis of criminal behaviour, or that causation also needs to be proved for criminal offences where there is an outcome prohibited by criminal law (such as criminal assaults or homicide offences). It is therefore clear that the concept of '*actus reus*' involves more than just 'acts' (Cross, 2020). The usage of the phrase '*actus reus*' in the court setting is therefore likely to cause some confusion to laypeople, such as juries, whose job it is to decide on criminal guilt.

The historical development of *actus reus*

It is also significant that *actus reus* was not used in its current form of a general principle for criminalisation in criminal law until the first half of the 20th century. Earlier writers on criminal law, such as William Blackstone, defined criminal law through specific groups of criminal offences that involved wrongs against the public. Blackstone therefore organised his explanation of criminal law by using offence groups such as offences against religion, offences against the state, offences against property and offences against the person (Lacey and Zedner, 2017, p 61). This approach is not surprising considering that there were far fewer criminal offences in Blackstone's time than there are today. The expansion and diversification of criminal law offences happened because of societal processes of urbanisation and industrialisation, the extension of central government and the need to regulate a morally pluralised society (Norrie, 2014). Criminal justice underwent a process of modernisation and professionalisation over the same period, with the introduction of professional police forces, centralised legal education and formalised legal representation. The combined effect of these changes was a criminal law in need of a unifying principle and a criminal justice process looking to assert its authority, particularly in the light of rising crimes rates in the UK throughout the 20th century. This explains the increasing reliance on *actus reus* as a generalising, objective principle within criminal law and criminal justice processes.

Actus reus and criminal justice practice in England and Wales

Turning now to how criminal justice uses the concept of *actus reus* in practice, it is important to note that many criminal law-defined 'guilty acts' do not reach the criminal justice domain at all. Data for the year to June 2020 in England and Wales shows that of the 11.5 million offences recorded by the Telephone-Operated Crime Survey for England and Wales (TCSEW), only 48 per cent were recorded by the police, 15 per cent reached the court stage and only 8.5 per cent resulted in a court sentence. Some *actus reuses* – and there is no way of determining exactly how many – are not even reported to the TCSEW. It is therefore clear that the gap between criminal law and criminal justice understandings of '*actus reus*' looks more like a chasm. The police and the CPS play a key role in filtering out many *actus reuses* which cannot be matched up to a particular person or persons. It is also true to say that without the mass production of guilty pleas by these agencies and by the courts there would be even fewer 'matched up' criminal law and criminal justice *actus reuses* (Welsh et al, 2021). Over 90 per cent of defendants in the magistrates' court plead guilty each year.

The meanings of *mens rea* in criminal law

Just as with *actus reus*, the phrase '*mens rea*' disguises a range of different meanings relating to a person's state of mind at the time when an *actus reus* is committed. A small number of criminal offences – including murder and grievous bodily harm with intent – require intention as *mens rea* before an offence can be proved. Even here, the meaning of intent is not always clear. In most cases of this type, planning or desiring the occurrence of the *actus reus* is evidence of criminal intent, and so direct intent is proved. However, even where the *actus reus* is not the primary aim of the person accused of the crime, if that person foresaw the crime's *actus reus* as a virtually certain consequence of their actions, it is still open to the jury or magistrates to find the existence of criminal intent. Intent as a species of *mens rea* therefore has more than one meaning in criminal law. For most crimes, recklessness, or risk taking, in relation to the occurrence of an *actus reus* also counts as appropriate *mens rea* (in modern statutory law, the words 'knowledge' or 'belief' normally replace the concept of recklessness in *mens rea* term). Recklessness itself carries two possible meanings: subjective recklessness, where a defendant foresees a risk of a crime taking place but goes ahead with their actions anyway; and objective recklessness, where a defendant does not have to foresee any risk of the crime occurring if a hypothetical 'reasonable person' would have foreseen an obvious and serious risk of the crime taking place because of the defendant's actions. Discredited as unfair by the decision of the House of Lords (as it then was) in the case of *G and R* (2003), objective recklessness lives on as part of criminal justice *mens rea* discourse in the many cases where defendants fail to see the risks of their actions because they are intoxicated at the time of their offence.

Mens rea, negligence and strict liability

Mens rea can also denote negligence in an increasing number of statutorily defined offences – even serious ones, as shown by the definition of rape in the Sexual Offences Act 2003. There are also a growing number of statutory offences in which the historic relationship between *actus reus* and *mens rea* is split. These so-called strict liability offences only require proof of some or all elements of an offence's *actus reus* to establish liability. No proof of *mens rea* is required at all. Originally, strict liability developed in the 19th century as a criminal law and criminal justice response to the difficulties of regulating and enforcing the types of statutory offence (environmental pollution for example) which tended to be committed by people of the same kind of middle- or upper-class background as the magistrates who decided on guilt (Norrie, 2014). Strict liability's use has expanded far beyond health and safety offences. By the mid–1990s, 40 per cent of offences triable in the Crown Court were strict liability – and most of these offences carried maximum prison sentences of more than six months (Wells and Quick, 2010, p 103). Aside from raising questions about the fairness of using strict liability in this way, the phrase '*mens rea*' does not capture the reality of a criminal law which does not require any proof of a guilty mindset across a wide range of offences.

The historical development of *mens rea*

In terms of how criminal justice uses the concept of *mens rea*, it is no coincidence that the concept of *mens rea* in criminal law and criminal justice only emerged in the mid–19th century. Before that time, criminal guilt was presumed through *actus reus*, and capable of being disproved through evidence of good character presented in court (Lacey and Zedner, 2017). It was only with the emergence of psychology as a discipline capable of producing specialist knowledge about how the mind worked that criminal law began to use *mens rea* as a means of establishing responsibility and fault in relation to crime.

Mens rea and criminal justice practice in England and Wales

Even with the specialist knowledge that forensic psychology, psychiatry and medicine can bring to criminal justice investigation of *mens rea*, it is questionable whether investigation of *mens rea* can be conducted effectively in the current criminal justice system (CJS) in England and Wales. There are several possible reasons for this. Firstly, the English and Welsh system is adversarial and so courts are reliant on evidence presented by the parties to a criminal case. Secondly, considerations of time (a problem made worse by the extensive backlogs caused by the COVID-19 pandemic starting in 2020) and cost (an ongoing problem made worse by successive waves of government cutbacks in funding for the court system since 2010, resulting in widespread closure of Crown and magistrates' courts in England and Wales) limit the court's ability to investigate issues of *mens rea* (and indeed *actus reus*) in practice. Thirdly, more resources are available to the prosecution agencies than to the defence at the investigative stage. Finally, the inconsistency in judgements about the admissibility and reliability of evidence, from judges, magistrates and juries alike, introduce an element of chance into decisions on criminal responsibility, in terms of *actus reus* and *mens rea*, in court (Keane and McKeown, 2020, pp 2–3). As a result, and because of the continuing mistrust between legal experts and experts from other disciplines, such as forensic psychologists, *mens rea* is often proved or disproved in criminal justice practice through evidence which relates more to *actus reus* than to psychological understandings of how the mind and brain work. If it is agreed that in order to ensure a fair trial defendants are responsible citizens who are answerable before a court (Duff, 1998), then it is arguable that the criteria defining unfitness to stand trial (interpreted as inability to instruct legal representatives, inability to follow the course of court proceedings or the inability to give evidence), dating back over 180 years as they do (*Pritchard* [1836] 7 C and P 303), are too outdated and narrowly defined to reflect the extent and definitions of mental illness in the 21st century. A similar point could be made about the insanity defence, the principles of which again date back to the mid-19th century (*M'Naghten* [1843] 10 Cl and Fin 200). The outdated and ambiguous nature of the insanity defence – defined as a defect of reason caused by a disease of the mind, such that the defendant did not understand the consequences of their actions or did not understand that those actions were legally wrong – has led to such absurd results as hyperglycaemia, sleepwalking and epilepsy being classed as insanity (Horder, 2019, p 161). However, as Bows (2017, pp 96–8) shows, the majority of prisoners in England and Wales have a recognised mental illness. This demonstrates that most people who are mentally ill and convicted of a criminal offence are dealt with through criminal justice processes rather than the National Health Service. Criminal justice is not effective at identifying those who need hospital detention at the point of sentence (Peay, 2017, pp 648–9), despite the apparent protection the concept of *mens rea* appears to give to those who lack full responsibility for their crimes.

Conclusions

Criminal law and criminal justice present an objective image of proof of criminal responsibility through the concepts of *actus reus* and *mens rea* and the requirement of proof of guilt beyond reasonable doubt. However, *actus reus* and *mens rea* carry a variety of meanings in criminal law. In terms of how *actus reus* and *mens rea* are used by criminal justice, there are still many 'guilty acts' that are not dealt with by criminal justice at all. Various factors, such as the mass production of guilty pleas at various stages of the CJS, the limited time and resources available to the courts and the complexity of the law of evidence, mean that short cuts are often taken when proving *actus reus* and *mens rea* in criminal justice practice, in turn increasing the risk of miscarriages of justice.

References

Bows, H. (2017) 'Characteristics of offenders', in P. Davies, J. Harding and G. Mair (eds) *Criminal Justice in England and Wales: An Introduction*, London: SAGE, pp 85–105.

Cross, N. (2020) *Criminal Law for Criminologists*, Abingdon: Routledge.

Duff, R.A. (1998) 'Law, language and community: some preconditions of criminal liability', *Oxford Journal of Legal Studies*, 18(2): 189–206.

Horder, J. (2019) *Ashworth's Principles of Criminal Law* (9th edn), Oxford: Oxford University Press.

Hossain, M.B. and Rahi, S.T. (2018), 'Murder: a critical analysis of the common law definition', *Beijing Law Review*, 9(5): 460–80.

Keane, A. and McKeown, P. (2020) *The Modern Law of Evidence* (13th edn), Oxford: Oxford University Press.

Lacey, N. and Zedner, L. (2017) 'Criminalisation: historical, legal and criminological perspectives', in A. Liebling, S. Maruna and L. McAra (eds) *The Oxford Handbook of Criminology* (6th edn), Oxford: Oxford University Press, pp 57–76.

Norrie, A. (2014) *Crime, Reason and History*, Cambridge: Cambridge University Press.

Peay, J. (2017) 'Mental health, mental disabilities and crime', in A. Liebling, S. Maruna and L. McAra (eds) *The Oxford Handbook of Criminology* (6th edn), Oxford: Oxford University Press, pp 639–6.

Wells, C. and Quick, O. (2010), *Reconstructing Criminal Law* (4th edn), Cambridge: Cambridge University Press.

Welsh, L., Skinns, L. and Sanders, A. (2021) *Criminal Justice* (5th edn), Oxford: Oxford University Press.

20

Crime and youth justice

Ellena Cooke

Introduction

The very existence of the term 'youth justice' suggests an acknowledgement by the criminal justice system (CJS) that a different response is required when children are arrested for a criminal offence. Since 1998, in the UK the Youth Justice Board has provided guidance for agencies which support young people known to the CJS. Their vision is 'for a youth justice system that sees children as children, treats them fairly and helps them to build on their strengths so they can make a constructive contribution to society. This will prevent offending and create safer communities with fewer victims' (YJB/MoJ, 2020).

The separation of the judicial processes for children and adults is not a new notion; the Juvenile Offenders Act of 1847 provided the first legislation distinguishing between the two groups. Since that time, various Acts, governing bodies, policies and reports have provided guidance and recommendations for services working to support children at risk of and convicted of criminal offences. Over the decades, the direction of this guidance has changed, oscillating between attempts to reduce the amount of time children spend in custody and the imposition of more retributive measures. In 1908, the Children Act established a separate court specifically for children and young people accused of committing crime and abolished custodial sentences for children below 14 years of age. Almost 100 years later in 1993, legislation took a more punitive stance when the Criminal Justice Act (1993) provided the court with more power to impose longer sentences for children convicted of criminal offences. Then later, in 1994, the Criminal Justice and Public Order Act increased the range of offence types which could be referred to Crown Court, while also doubling the sentence length available to be imposed by the courts. Currently, the UK youth justice system purports to be committed to preventative as opposed to punitive measures. The introduction of detention and training orders in 2000, and their continued use, has, however, considerably increased the powers of the youth court to impose custodial sentences on children and young people.

The sway of public opinion

In the political landscape, the topic of youth justice in the UK can be a controversial one. The UK has the lowest age of criminal responsibility of any country in Europe. While in most of the UK children are considered criminally liable at ten years of age (in 2019 it was increased from eight to 12 years old in Scotland), in Germany and Italy only when a child reaches 14 are they considered culpable, whereas in Spain and Portugal it is later still, at 16 years of age. In February 2020, the UK Age of Criminal Responsibility Bill had its first reading in the House of Lords with the aim of raising the age of criminal responsibility in England and Wales to 12 years old; however, it made no further progress through Parliament. Professionals working in the UK youth justice system can often oppose wider public opinion, and the debate around age of criminal responsibility continues to be reignited whenever the media reports a child has been arrested for a serious crime. What follows can be trial by public opinion; the young person is reported as and subsequently considered only as a dangerous perpetrator and their identity and vulnerability are lost from the discourse. The outcome is that children are incarcerated for extended periods of time in punitive establishments with systems around them that do not meet their needs. This can leave professionals questioning how far services have come from times – as recently as the 1960s – when children were incarcerated with adult offenders.

Further disillusion creeps in when policy and governing are informed by public opinion; an often-cited example being the tragic killing of James Bulger in 1993, with subsequent legislation taking a distinctly punitive turn. Professionals working with children convicted of violent offences do not deny the importance of public protection or intensive support packages for the children convicted; however, when the ripple effect from individual cases impacts the justice system for decades it is as though the evidence upon which a separate judicial system was based has been forgotten. The onset of puberty signifies a period of immense change for children and adolescents. Physical development can often be mistaken for cognitive and emotional maturation, when in reality an adolescent's ability to apply logic, reason and empathy is neurobiologically immature. The central question faced through adolescence is 'Who am I?' This marks the shift from 'belonging' to parents to taking possession of oneself as an independent adult (Laufer and Laufer, 1975). In this process of identity development and increasing independence risk-taking behaviours increase, alongside experimentation with social groups, as the need to be accepted is acutely felt. A phrase commonly used to describe adolescence by those working with young people is 'a period of temporary insanity' and recognition of this can be found in the varied judicial processes for individuals under the age of 18. When legislation allows for the extended incarceration of children during this intense period of change, denying them the very social and educational structures which enable appropriate and 'normal' adolescent development, then the question which might be asked is how the UK judicial process represents a modern, preventative youth justice system?

The impact of incarceration

Aspects of the legal system for young people in the UK cannot only be considered archaic, but also, in the case of incarceration, ineffective, with 68 per cent of young people released from custody reoffending within a year (YJB/MoJ, 2020). Funding continues to be directed towards reactive measures rather than early intervention. In 2012, in an attempt to reduce the number of children held on remand in establishments, individual local authorities were made responsible for costs of placing children in custody. More children and young people are now appropriately directed away from custody towards community sentences. Those who continue to receive custodial sentences, however, can often get caught in the cycle of incarceration. This cycle can often reflect and intensify the chaos and trauma of their lives in the community. Up to half of children in custody have experience of the care system (Prison Reform Trust, 2016), and they are then housed in institutions where they are further traumatised by separation from family and community, physical restraints and witnessing and being involved in violence (Prison Reform Trust, 2019). Furthermore, nearly half of all children in custody are from various Black, Asian or other minority ethnic backgrounds.

Finally, children known to the CJS are three times more likely to experience difficulties with their emotional well-being and mental health (Centre for Mental Health, 2021). The evidence overwhelmingly indicates that the children more vulnerable to being incarcerated are those who have already experienced high levels of marginalisation and trauma, and yet the recognition of offending and subsequent incarceration as a social issue has not resulted in a welfare-based approach to youth justice. Funding continues to be poured into reactive measures – it costs £60,000 per year to house a child in a young offenders institute, while the cost to place a child in a secure children's home for one year is over £200,000. The redistribution of these funds to early intervention methods to support families or carers with children at risk of becoming involved with the CJS would likely provide better outcomes for both individuals and wider society.

Recent developments

In recent years, advances have been made regarding the treatment of children in the custodial estate. NHS England's Five Year Forward View for Mental Health (2016) identified a specialised health and justice strategy aimed to improve the experiences of young people known to the justice system in the community and also those accommodated in the secure estate. The introduction of the Forensic Child and Adolescent Mental Health Service (FCAMHS) signified the recognition that children engaging in risky and/or harmful behaviours have emotional well-being and social needs that mainstream health services often do not meet. Furthermore, the introduction of FCAMHS as a more flexible and responsive service is recognition that mainstream services are often inaccessible to the most vulnerable families in society, either because the children do not meet the threshold for mental health services or because the child's often chaotic family circumstances have resulted in appropriate support either being unknown or not sought. FCAMHS employs specialist clinicians who have experience of working within the CJS and with children who are considered 'high risk'. By providing consultation and expert advice to the services around the child and family, the aim is to intervene early enough to divert the child away from the CJS. For children in the secure estate, the introduction of the Framework for Integrated Care (Taylor et al, 2018) aims to intervene at a systems level rather than just an individual level. The stories of incarcerated children are thought about alongside their convictions, and intervention aims to be provided at every opportunity. Training is provided to prison staff to inform their interactions with children, and the intention is to create a shift in the culture of the youth estate towards a more trauma-informed way of working.

Forensic psychology in youth justice

The role of a forensic psychologist in the youth justice system is to attempt to understand, consult and support the services in place to enable children and young people to desist from offending. By holding the child in mind, while also considering the risk they may pose to both themselves and others, the hope is that services will become more attuned to and able to meet the needs of the vulnerable young people they serve to contain. Alongside this, providing care and support to children convicted of criminal offences, through recognising and responding to their 'story', is a core role for practitioners working within the youth justice system and is in line with the ultimate aims of crime prevention, rehabilitation and reintegration of young people. Supporting children's social care services, police and criminal justice agencies to better understand a child's strengths and experiences, and subsequently intervene at an earlier opportunity, not only offers the child an identity outside of that of just an 'offender', but also increases the chance of a reduction in criminal activity.

Conclusions

Youth justice is an area of the legal system which requires further consideration and development. Although systems have moved towards a more 'trauma-informed' way of working, these systems are primarily health-based services and not the earliest point of contact when a child has committed an offence, for example the police and courts. Children continue to receive long custodial sentences that separate them from their families and the services which are best placed to enable appropriate adolescent development. Professionals working in youth justice services today are united by an understanding of the impact of social inequality, trauma and exclusion of the young people they support. Services highlight the importance of communication between agencies to manage risk, but also utilise and develop strengths in the young people. Services need to continue to move towards a trauma-informed way of working which places the children's and young person's social and developmental needs at the centre of the intervention.

References

Centre for Mental Health (2021) 'Youth justice', [online] Available from: https://www.centreformentalhealth.org.uk/youth-justice [Accessed 22 April 2021].

Laufer, M. and Laufer, M.E. (1975) *Adolescence and Developmental Breakdown: A Psychoanalytic View*, New Haven, CT: Yale University Press.

Prison Reform Trust (2016) 'In care, out of trouble: how the life chances of children in care can be transformed by protecting them from unnecessary involvement in the criminal justice system', [Report] May, Available from: https://prisonreformtrust.org.uk/publication/in-care-out-of-trouble-how-the-life-chances-of-children-in-care-can-be-transformed-by-protecting-them-from-unnecessary-involvement-in-the-criminal-justice-system/ [Accessed 22 April 2021].

Prison Reform Trust (2019) 'Prison: the facts. Bromley briefings summer 2019', [online] Available from: https://prisonreformtrust.org.uk/publication/prison-the-facts-summer-2019/ [Accessed 22 April 2021].

Taylor, J., Shostak, L., Rogers, A. and Mitchell, P. (2018) 'Rethinking mental health provision in the secure estate for children and young people: a framework for integrated care (SECURE STAIRS)', *Safer Communities*, 17(4): 193–201.

YJB/MoJ (Youth Justice Board/Ministry of Justice) (2020) 'Youth justice statistics 2018/19: England and Wales', [online] Available from: https://assets.publishing.service.gov.uk/government/uploads/system/uploads/attachment_data/file/862078/youth-justice-statistics-bulletin-march-2019.pdf [Accessed 22 April 2021].

21

Crimes of the powerful

Amy Hughes-Stanley

Introduction: crimes of the powerful and the state's response to COVID-19

The term 'crimes of the powerful' is one which is routinely contested within criminological discourse. Historically, criminology has tended not to focus its lens upon crimes of the powerful, whether this be powerful individuals or institutions, and instead has generally focused upon crimes committed by those with little power, such as the 'street crimes' of the working classes (Rothe and Kauzlarich, 2016).

'Partygate' is emblematic of the influence that power has on how rule breakers are understood and responded to. During COVID-19 lockdowns in the UK, the police were given new powers to respond to coronavirus, including issuing fixed penalty notices (FPNs) to those found breaking COVID restrictions (Home Office, 2020). Between 27 March 2020 and 14 February 2021, across England and Wales, 68,952 FPNs were handed out to the public (NPCC, 2021a). Notable fines included 275 FPNs of £10,000 that were given to members of the public holding gatherings of more than thirty people (NPCC, 2021b). While members of the public were issued FPNs for gathering during lockdown, between May 2020 and April 2021, after information was leaked to the press, government officials (including Prime Minister Boris Johnson) were found to have been involved in a number of pre-planned 'gatherings' involving the 'excessive consumption of alcohol' (Cabinet Office, 2022b, p 7) while in breach of COVID regulations (Cabinet Office, 2022a). After investigation by the Metropolitan Police, 126 FPNs were handed out to 83 people involved in what has become colloquially known as the 'partygate' scandal, with only one of these fines given to Boris Johnson, who is known to have attended multiple gatherings (Stewart et al, 2022). The 'partygate' scandal is thus characteristic of how powerful individuals, institutions and the public experience disparate processes of regulation and criminalisation.

Conceptualising 'crimes of the powerful'

Until the mid-20th century, criminology generally had a 'downwards gaze', where theory and research into the causes of crime sought explanations in the individual pathology of offenders, as well as through exploring social and economic factors such as poverty and depravation (Croall, 2001). This, it is argued, may be due to a limited mainstream criminological definition and understanding of crime and criminal behaviour in which the actions of powerful individuals, institutions and states are excluded and the actions of those with little to no institutional power are prioritised (Friedrichs, 2015). Recognising these problems in criminological and legal definitions of crime, in 1949 Edwin Sutherland proposed 'that persons of the upper socio-economic class engage in much criminal behaviour; that this criminal behaviour differs from the criminal behaviour of the lower socio-economic class principally in the administrative procedures which are used in dealing with the offenders' (cited in Croall, 2001, p 3). What Sutherland drew attention to is the fact that those in a position of power and with high socioeconomic standing can and do commit crime. However, the type of lawbreaking they are involved in is unlike that of the working classes, and the way that it is responded to by the state is vastly different. Sutherland famously called such crimes committed by those 'of respectability and high social status in the course of his [sic] occupation' white-collar crimes. The concept of white-collar crimes has been advanced significantly since Sutherland's writings, and the development of the study of 'crimes of the powerful' (Pearce, cited in Friedrichs, 2015, p 44) has emerged.

Radical or critical criminologists, through the study of crimes of the powerful, have fundamentally critiqued the very definition of 'crime' itself. They argue that viewing crime through the state's legalist framework does not allow for a thorough analysis of harmful behaviours of the powerful. This is because it is the state which 'determines what behaviours are legal, which are illegal, and among those that are illegal, which will be nominated as serious crimes, which will be lesser offenses or minor infractions, and which will be treated as non-criminal administrative matters' (Michalowski, cited in Rothe and Kauzlarich, 2016, p 3). Some therefore advocate for a zemiological approach, whereby harm is studied rather than crime. This can allow for an analysis of the actions of the powerful which are not defined by law as criminal yet inflict harm upon society.

Crimes of the powerful can be split into two interrelated categories: occupational crime and organisational crime. The former are crimes that are committed by individuals within their occupation in order to advance their own self-interest (such as workplace theft) and the latter are crimes committed by individuals within their occupation to benefit, or advance, the organisation (such as manipulating audits to increase a company's stock price) (Rothe and Kauzlarich, 2014, 2016). Occupational offenders range from the relatively powerful, such as wealthy doctors and lawyers, to the relatively powerless, such as low-level employees (Friedrichs, 2015). Many debate the relevance of including occupational crimes under the umbrella of crimes of the powerful. However, as these crimes differ from 'conventional crime' or 'street crime' in that they are facilitated via the occupational status of an offender, they are broadly relevant to an understanding of crimes of the powerful (Croall, 2001). This is not to say that organisational crimes do not directly benefit an individual offender; however, a significant factor of organisational crime is that it fundamentally provides advantage for the organisation, not just the individual who commits the offence (Rothe and Kauzlarich, 2014). Organisational crimes can be broken down into four subtypes: corporate crime, state crime, state-corporate crime and crimes of globalisation.

Corporate crime

Corporate crimes are offences committed in the pursuit of business interests. Corporate crimes occur not only in large corporations, but also among small businesses and the self-employed. These offences can be undertaken by individuals within a corporation and by groups. Common forms of corporate crime include fraud, embezzlement, tax offences, bribery, manipulation of stocks, dumping of illegal waste, environmental damage and health and safety offences, just to name a few (Croall, 2001; Rothe and Kauzlarich, 2014, 2016).

The prioritisation of business goals, namely the accrual of profit, over human (and non-human) life, is central to many acts of corporate criminal behaviour (Croall, 2001; Friedrichs, 2015). A prime example of this is the case of the Ford Motor Company's Pinto. The Pinto was created by Ford in the late 1960s to compete in the small and affordable car market, which at the time was dominated by Volkswagen (Rothe and Kauzlarich, 2016). While putting the car through safety testing prior to its release, Ford found that there was a catastrophic issue with the design – if the car was involved in a collision from behind, the fuel tank easily ruptured, pouring out fuel. Despite this, senior executives at Ford decided that redesigning the vehicle would cost too much money (Croall, 2001). The Ford Pinto was therefore released to the public, and when rear-ended often burst into flames, killing and badly burning numerous drivers and passengers. After several successful civil lawsuits against Ford, it was discovered that prior to releasing the car to the public Ford in fact made a cost-benefit analysis of fixing the fuel tank issues. Through their calculations, Ford determined that it would cost less in insurance claims for deaths and injuries caused by the vehicle exploding (around 49 million dollars), than to fix the problem with the vehicles prior to their release (around 121 million dollars) (Rothe and Kauzlarich, 2016). Despite this, Ford was never held criminally accountable for the deaths and injuries caused (Croall, 2001; Rothe and Kauzlarich, 2016).

Other high-profile cases of corporate crime include the Bhopal disaster, where, in 1984, thirty tonnes of toxic gas was accidentally released from a pesticide plant; the Deepwater Horizon oil spill, which in 2010 killed 11 people and has done lasting damage to the ecosystem and local populations; and the Thalidomide tragedy, where expectant mothers were given a drug for morning sickness which caused severe birth defects (Croall, 2001; Rothe and Kauzlarich, 2016). Despite the capacity for corporations to cause significant harm to people and the planet, 'the criminal law is seen as costly and cumbersome, and ill adapted to deal with the problems of organizational offences' (Croall, 2001, p 150). While there are a range of laws and regulations concerned with corporate activity, these are poorly enforced. Moreover, when illegal activity is detected, there is significant difficulty in determining individual responsibility for crimes and harms which occur within large bureaucratic structures. Some have, therefore, described regulating corporate activity through criminal law as futile (Croall, 2001).

State crime

The state also has a significant role to play in crimes of the powerful. The work of William J. Chambliss in 1989 (cited in Friedrichs, 2015) can be attributed with turning criminology's attention to the crimes of the state. State crimes are illegal or harmful acts (as well as omissions and commissions) committed by an individual (or group(s)) within a legitimate institution of governance (Kauzlarich and Kramer, cited in Rothe and Kauzlarich, 2014). Importantly, motivation for state crime is generally 'tacitly or explicitly related to larger structural goals and objectives of government or its agencies' (Faust and Kauzlarich, cited in Rothe and Kauzlarich, 2016, p 100) and is not necessarily for the personal gain of individual offenders. Types of state crime are wide-ranging. Examples include the state's failure to address global warming, the commissioning of illegal wars, the use of torture, mass incarceration, genocide, human rights infractions, the abuse of whistle-blowers, the use of drones in warfare and state cybercrime (Rothe and Kauzlarich, 2014, 2016; Friedrichs, 2015).

Commissioned by the US and its allies (namely the UK), the wars in Iraq and Afghanistan have been considered state crimes by critical criminologists. Not only have the invasions of Iraq and Afghanistan been declared illegal, but the harms which resulted from the wars have had catastrophic environmental consequences (Rothe and Kauzlarich, 2016). The impacts of bombing and other military operations have left depleted uranium, trichloroethylene, benzene and perchlorate in the earth, and have drastically impacted upon water supplies, local wildlife and the health of Iraqi and Afghani populations (Eisenhower Study Group, cited in Rothe and Kauzlarich, 2016). Other forms of state crime, such as the genocides in Rwanda, Bosnia-Herzegovina, Germany and Cambodia, in which tens of millions of lives were taken (Rothe and Kauzlarich, 2014) demonstrate that the state is perhaps the most powerful (and criminal) actor of all (Friedrichs, 2015). Despite this, states are rarely held accountable for their actions due to their power to not only hide their criminal behaviours, but to define the very contours of the law itself. Furthermore, even when their criminal acts are exposed, states often engage in 'techniques of neutralisation' to legitimise their actions, or deny their responsibility altogether (Rothe and Kauzlarich, 2014, p 783).

State-corporate crime

The state and corporations also collude to conduct state-corporate offences. State-corporate crimes therefore occur when 'corporations and governments intersect to produce social harm' (Kramer et al, cited in Rothe and Kauzlarich, 2016, p 122) and/or engage in illegal behaviours. The close relationship between the state and corporations, in which boundaries between the private and public sector are often blurred, mean that state-corporate crime and harm are often difficult to detect or act against. An often-cited example of state-corporate crime is that of the 1986 Challenger space shuttle explosion. Bradshaw and Kramer (2014) note that at first glance, the Challenger explosion appeared to be an accident. However, upon further investigation, it was found that there had been a 'normalisation of deviant practices' between state organisations and private businesses which led to the incident (Vaughn, cited in Bradshaw and Kramer, 2014, p 5045). Risky decision making and unsafe working practices between the National Aeronautics Space Administration, a US government agency, and Morton Thiokol, Inc., a private corporation, led to budget concessions and pressure to launch the spacecraft, which ultimately led to the deaths of the seven people aboard (Bradshaw and Kramer, 2014).

Other examples of state-corporate crime include the 1991 fire at Imperial Food Products in North Carolina, US. The fire, which killed 25 workers and injured 56, was the result of 'privileging of business interests over labor' (Bradshaw and Kramer, 2014, p 5046), which meant that the state indirectly, through underfunding the Occupational Safety and Health Programme (by which businesses are regulated), created the conditions for a corporate crime to occur. Financial bailouts of private corporations by the state, state-corporate environmental crime, regulatory deficiencies of the pharmaceutical markets and many other forms of state-corporate crime have been examined within criminological literature (Rothe and Kauzlarich, 2016). While these instances of state-corporate crime may seem distinct and diverse from one another, Barak (cited in Rothe and Kauzlarich, 2016, pp 131–2) notes that society must not 'overlook large-scale patterns of collaborative state and corporate crime occurring across time and space', as to do so would overlook such patterns of state-corporate crime 'driven by neoliberal ideology' and 'powerful elite networks that are deeply embedded within government and business alike'.

Crimes of globalisation

Exploring further powerful elite networks, crimes of globalisation are a relatively new branch of study of crimes of the powerful and look to an understanding of the harms and crimes committed by international financial institutions, such as the World Bank and the International Monetary Fund. These crimes are unique in the sense that such financial institutions are neither state entities nor do they fall under the category of a corporation; they therefore exist within their own subcategory of crimes of the powerful (Friedrichs, 2015). Crimes of globalisation include acts such as the 'funding of capitalist expansion into less developed countries, which results in the marginalization of indigenous peoples, higher rates of income inequality, environmental disaster, health crises, and political corruption' (Rothe and Kauzlarich, 2014, p 780). It is important to note that while these harmful acts are not often legally defined as crimes by the state, utilising a critical criminological or zemiological approach provides a framework for including such acts within an understanding of crimes or harms of the powerful.

Conclusion

This chapter has illustrated the limitations of using a state-defined conception of crime in order to understand the harmful activities of those with significant institutional and social power. Perhaps, as argued by zemiologists, it is time to move away from the concept of 'crime' altogether, a term rooted in the social control of the powerless, and instead focus upon social harm?

References

Bradshaw, A. and Kramer, R. (2014) 'State-corporate crime', in G. Bruinsma and D. Weisburd (eds) *Encyclopaedia of Criminology and Criminal Justice*, New York: Springer, pp 5043–53.

Cabinet Office (2022a) 'Findings of second permanent secretary's investigation into alleged gatherings on government premises during COVID restrictions', [online] Available at: https://s3.documentcloud.org/documents/22036979/2022-05-25_final_findings_of_second_permanent_secretary_into_alleged_gatherings.pdf [Accessed 1 July 2022].

Cabinet Office (2022b) 'Investigation into alleged gatherings on government premises during COVID restrictions: update', [online] 31 January, Available at: https://s3.documentcloud.org/documents/21193251/investigation_into_alleged_gatherings_on_government_premises_during_covid_restrictions_-_update.pdf [Accessed 1 July 2022].

Croall, H. (2001) *Understanding White Collar Crime*, Buckingham: Open University.

Friedrichs, D.O. (2015) 'Crimes of the powerful and the definition of crime', in G. Barak (ed) *The Routledge International Handbook of the Crimes of the Powerful*, Abingdon: Routledge, pp 39–49.

Home Office (2020) 'Police given new powers and support to respond to coronavirus', [Press release] 26 March, Available at: https://www.gov.uk/government/news/police-given-new-powers-and-support-to-respond-to-coronavirus [Accessed 1 July 2022].

NPCC (National Police Chiefs' Council) (2021a) 'Fixed penalty notices issued under COVID-19 emergency health regulations by police forces in England and Wales', [online] Available at: https://cdn.prgloo.com/media/c1cd9d235 12643b28d36a2b5f0eabc3e.pdf [Accessed 24 June 2022].

NPCC (National Police Chiefs' Council) (2021b) 'Update on Coronavirus FPNs issued by police', [online] Available at: https://news.npcc.police.uk/releases/update-on-coronavirus-fpns-issued-by-police [Accessed 24 June 2022].

Rothe, D. and Kauzlarich, D. (2014) 'Crimes of the powerful', in G. Bruinsma and D. Weisburd (eds) *Encyclopaedia of Criminology and Criminal Justice*, New York: Springer, pp 778–86.

Rothe, D. and Kauzlarich, D. (2016) *Crimes of the Powerful: An Introduction*, Oxford: Routledge.

Stewart, H., Dodd, V., Walker, P. and Syal, R. (2022) 'Civil servants and No 10 advisers furious over single fine for Boris Johnson', *The Guardian*, [online] 19 May, Available at: https://www.theguardian.com/uk-news/2022/may/19/civil-servants-and-no-10-advisers-furious-over-single-fine-for-boris-johnson [Accessed 1 July 2022].

22

Criminal justice, marketisation and privatisation

David Sheldon

Introduction

Criminal justice has experienced a chequered history with privatisation and nationalisation through the centuries. The principal pillars of the criminal justice system (CJS), such as the police and prison services, have all been subject to different amounts of privatisation throughout their history. For example, in England, the police service only became a nationalised formal group in 1829 through the work of then Home Secretary Sir Robert Peel with the introduction of the Metropolitan Police Act 1829. Prior to this, there was no formalised national police force, with private bounty hunters, such as the Bow Street Runners in London, primarily responsible for policing local communities. Similarly, the prison service was only nationalised as recently as 1877 and, prior to this, local prisons were subject to local restrictions. Only in the latter part of the 19th century did public ownership of the CJS become the norm. In more recent times, a growing number of prisons have been entirely privatised but privatisation has not been a seamless success. For example, the deterioration in standards at the privately managed HMP Birmingham caused prisoners to riot in December 2016 and, after being listed as one of the ten worst prisons in England and Wales as a result, the prison was taken back into public sector control and the contract with G4S terminated.

Further, the Probation Service in England and Wales was only brought into full public ownership in 1948. That said, there has been an ill-fated attempt at partial privatisation within the Probation Service through the Offender Rehabilitation Act 2014, which sought to give complete control to private companies for the supervision of offenders after their release from prison. The attempt raised serious questions about the role of the private sector in the sphere of criminal justice, especially with the ultimate failure of the experiment and a renationalisation of the Probation Service (Tidmarsh, 2020).

Neoliberalism, the CJS and crime

The relationship between privatisation, marketisation and the CJS is far from simple. Firstly, the term privatisation can have two potential meanings. On the one hand, privatisation can mean the transfer of criminal justice infrastructure from the public to the private sector. On the other, it can denote a broad shift between the public and private sector (Bean, 2020, p 7). These two different definitions are not mutually exclusive and can be taken together to illustrate that broad shifts often bring about partial or complete transfers from the public to the private sector. Secondly, marketisation refers to the neoliberal ideology of a marketplace encouraging creativity, innovation and a race to the bottom in terms of cost. Neoliberal ideology therefore encourages the perception that public services are a commodity and can be auctioned off to the highest bidder with little regard for the social consequences. As such, the public sector is seen as 'overstaffed, uncreative, stifled by tradition and slow to change' (Raynor, 2020, p 25), with the consequence of this being the introduction of private companies into the CJS who have little, or no, experience within the sector. This is done due to a belief that they will be more effective, creative and able to deliver results at a lower cost. In a period where austerity has been pursued after the financial crash in 2007, it is perhaps unsurprising that there has been a shift towards greater privatisation of the public sector, but this has not been without consequence. As the failed privatisation of the Probation Service has shown, performing the same task for a lower cost does not always guarantee success.

The growth of neoliberalism across the globe has helped to establish an environment since the early 1980s where the marketplace, profiteering and commodification have become the key drivers of the political economy and everyday life (Hall et al, 2008; Hall and Winlow, 2015). As such, technological advances and the drive to exploit others for personal gain have become principal criminal concerns facilitating global drug and firearms markets, as well as the proliferation of human and sexual trafficking. Further, crime has mutated from taking place solely in the real-world domain to operating to an increasing extent in the virtual world either through the so-called dark web but also through legitimate internet channels such as social media and online marketplaces like eBay (Treadwell, 2012; Hall and Winlow, 2015; Bancroft, 2020).

Policing, privatisation and pluralisation

Inevitably, such a change in criminal activity has necessitated the CJS, and in particular the police, to begin developing a closer relationship with private companies to be able to access the necessary intelligence to combat this new virtual species of criminal activity. This has created its own problems, with a growing entanglement between private companies and the police service. Such private companies have become responsible for a wide array of technologies such as CCTV and facial recognition services, and have even provided the public police service with non-lethal weapons such as the Taser gun. The weapon was marketed to the police as being 'less than lethal' but it has had serious consequences on public confidence (Bowling et al, 2019, p 158). The weapons are frequently used against individuals suffering mental health crises (Dymond,

2017). Yet the neoliberal model of policing has moved the management of mental health issues into the realm of law and order and public safety (Bowling et al, 2019), further eroding the legitimacy of the public police force. Therefore, even though private companies are prohibited from carrying and using such weapons, they are still able to have a tangible effect on the public police service. Similar problems have been found with companies who provide police body cameras and the management of the data that they produce. Questions can be raised regarding the suitability of private companies being able to compile vast amounts of data on individuals and the use of that data, but these are yet to be explored (Button, 2019).

Policing in England and Wales is no longer something which is purely under the monopolised control of the state, as it has become increasingly fragmented since the 1960s onwards. Since this time there has been a rapid growth in the size, visibility and presence of the private sector, not only in providing security for wealthy individuals who are able and willing to pay, but also in their involvement in everyday police activities (Button, 2019). This has meant that the 'police are no longer the primary crime-deterrent presence in society' (Bayley and Shearing, 1996, p 588). Private policing can be defined as referring to 'the various lawful forms of organised for profit personnel services whose primary objectives include the control of crime, the protection of property and life and the maintenance of order' (Bowling et al, 2019, p 155). The growth in private policing has been termed as the 'pluralisation' of the police. Pluralisation generally refers to the increasing size of the private security sector, the growth and spread of new technologies such as CCTV and facial recognition programs, the enforcement of traffic regulations, the transportation and detention of prisoners and the patrolling of public areas such as new housing complexes (Crawford, 2012; Bowling et al, 2019).

Additionally, Loader (1999, pp 375–6) has noted that the concept of 'policing' has become increasingly commodified through the three separate mechanisms of consumerism, managerialism and promotionalism. The cumulative effect of these processes is to create a public police service which is more businesslike, and is able to satisfy consumer expectations and to promote the professional nature of policing as a product. All this has formed the foundations for private security companies, some of which previously had little or no experience in the security arena, to burrow their way into the public sphere of policing. The continued growth and acceptance of neoliberalism means that such a shift is unlikely to halt soon (Hall and Winlow, 2015). Rather, the future of policing is likely to be symbolised by an increasingly visible and broad range of providers beyond the public police force but with a similar overall aim of ensuring social order.

One of the challenges of an increasingly pluralised police force is that there comes a risk of seeing the police as a service aimed at achieving customer satisfaction (Bowling et al, 2019, pp 146–53). This creates several problems in terms of who comes to be defined as customers, whether it be the victims of crime or the wider public. Such connotations challenge the original conception of the police that it should be universal in its approach and not subject to satisfying individual complaints. However, in meeting the demands of victims and the wider public, the police will affirm their legitimacy and retain the widespread consent of the community. Nevertheless, the growing numbers of private police in the UK and across the globe have created an environment where customer satisfaction has become increasingly important and represents a key challenge to the traditional private/public divide.

However, even with the rise in private policing, there are still only three countries (Canada, the US and South Africa) where private police forces outnumber the public police force. The numbers are steadily rising across Western Europe and it is predicted that the private police numbers will soon exceed the public police force in the UK (Bowling et al, 2019, pp 146–53). This does raise questions about the function of the police as their 'policing' role can be easily co-opted by private actors. For example, levels of social order owe very little to the police per se, but rather the mass consensus of the public in generally obeying the law. Arguably, the main objectives of public and private policing are similar, but the means of producing them often differ. While the public police have recourse to the use of legitimate force and the powers given to them by the state through criminal law, private companies must enforce social order through private law mechanisms such as fines and injunctions. The accountability structures are therefore different, and as a result can impact on the perceived legitimacy of punishment by the public or private actors.

While the growth of the private sector within and alongside the police service can be viewed with trepidation, there remains a long history of the police working with secondary actors to achieve the goals of social order and the preservation of life and property. As such, rather than being viewed with unease, it should be celebrated as police forces will now have more time to focus their attention on crime reduction and investigation with the assistance of private companies. However, the price of privatisation has been a continued reduction in police numbers and funding. Therefore, any advantages which may have been produced through the increased police plurality are likely to be minimal. The growth of managerialism and the target-oriented practice of the police have also produced problems in combatting serious crime as it is costly and time consuming. As such, the programme of austerity and the continued political pursuit of the neoliberal model have created an environment where crime has been able to prosper due to the decreased likelihood of being detected, charged and convicted.

Conclusion

In conclusion, crime has mutated in recent years to become more virtual so as to take advantage of the neoliberal marketplace. At the same time, there has been a growing pluralisation of the police force, which started in the 1960s but has grown at an increasing pace since. The rationalisation of this has been for the private sector to assist the public police force in their activities to ensure the continued social control and the maintenance of social order. However, the intermingling of the private sector with the public is not without problems. Such problems include legitimacy, accountability and the appropriate role of the private sector in a public service, but the growth of technology has created new problems like the management and storage of data and who it can be used by and what for. Further, the pluralisation of the police force has increased the pressure on public sector police to provide value for money in a competitive marketplace continuing to blur the traditional distinction between the public and private sectors. The problems of privatisation, however, are not limited to their impact on the police. In the prisons system there has been a reduction in living standards and numbers of staff, as well as an increased focus on incapacitation as opposed to addressing offending behaviour. Further, privatisation of the Probation Service was an unmitigated disaster, with it being returned fully to the public sector in 2020. Privatisation is not without its risks and should not be seen as a direct replacement for the public sector in the CJS. Rather, if privatisation is to occur at all, it should work in tandem with the public sector.

References

Bancroft, A. (2020) *The Darknet and Smarter Crime: Methods for Investigating Criminal Entrepreneurs and the Illicit Drug Economy*, Cham: Palgrave Macmillan.

Bayley, D. and Shearing, C. (1996) 'The future of policing', *Law and Society Review*, 30(3): 585–606.

Bean, P. (2020) *Criminal Justice and Privatisation: Key Issues and Debates*, London: Routledge.

Bowling, B., Reiner, R. and Sheptycki, J. (2019) *The Politics of the Police* (5th edn), Oxford: Oxford University Press.

Button, M. (2019) 'The "new" private security industry, the private policing of cyberspace and the regulatory questions', *Journal of Contemporary Criminal Justice*, 36(1): 39–55.

Crawford, A. (2012) 'Plural policing in the UK: policing beyond the police', in T. Newburn (ed) *Handbook of Policing* (2nd edn), London: Routledge, pp 147–81.

Dymond, A. (2017) 'Taser! Taser! Exploring factors associated with police use of Taser in England and Wales', *Policing and Society*, 30(4): 396–411.

Hall, S. and Winlow, S. (2015) *Revitalising Criminological Theory: Towards a New Ultra-Realism*, London: Routledge.

Hall, S., Winlow, S. and Ancrum, C. (2008) *Criminal Identities and Consumer Culture: Crime, Exclusion and the New Culture of Narcissism*, Cullompton: Willan.

Loader, I. (1999) 'Consumer culture and the commodification of policing and security', *Sociology*, 33(2): 373–92.

Raynor, P. (2020) 'Probation for profit: neoliberalism, magical thinking and evidence Refusal', in P. Bean (ed) *Criminal Justice and Privatisation: Key Issues and Debates*, London: Routledge, pp 147–81.

Tidmarsh, M. (2020) 'The Probation Service in England and Wales: a decade of radical change of more of the same', *European Journal of Probation*, 12(2): 129–46.

Treadwell, J. (2012) 'From the car boot to booting it up? eBay, online counterfeit crime and the transformation of the criminal marketplace', *Criminology and Criminal Justice*, 12(2): 175–91.

23

Criminal justice and punishment

Karen Corteen and Jo Turner

Introduction

Punishment is never a random activity but always one that fits with the society of which it is a part. The *longue durée* of punishment shows that how societies deal formally and informally with their offenders has changed over time, and it is clear it will continue to change in the future. While still being relevant to the philosophical reasons for punishing people who offend against societal, moral and criminal codes, changes in formal punishment regimes often reflect contemporary societal and political understandings of the causes of crime and, therefore, what is considered at that time the most appropriate way or ways to respond to the offending. Although over time changes build and develop punishment regimes, there are aspects that are discarded but later reappear, becoming re-embedded as if new. There are also unfortunate, unintended consequences that transpire from changes to punishment regimes, such that punishment that may have been once thought to be a panacea in fact becomes dreadful and its outcomes contrary to those originally intended. This chapter will explore the concept and practice of punishment in relation to the criminal justice system (CJS) in England and Wales. It will pay particular attention to imprisonment as a form of punishment, as, in the UK and other places around the world, imprisonment is the most severe form of punishment. It is acknowledged that the 'pains of imprisonment' (see Sykes, 1958/2007) are more far-reaching than the person in prison. For example, it impacts on prisoners' families, including their children (Shammas, 2017; Condry and Mison, 2021). Prisoners' families are not punished in the legal sense, yet they are harmed as a result of a 'punishing experience' due to their relationship with a person in prison (Condry and Mison, 2021, p 541). However, when discussing imprisonment as method of punishment, people in prison will be the focus.

The purpose, type and degree of punishment

Punishment is usually conceived as containing different elements or purposes: retribution, deterrence, incapacitation and rehabilitation (Harrison, 2020). Retribution refers to the pain that is delivered to the person receiving the punishment. The message from the pain of the punishment is not necessarily for the offender themselves but the community, and it announces that the CJS delivers a just measure of pain to those who offend. Deterrence refers to the effect that the prospect of punishment has on those who might commit crimes, whether that be the offender, a prospective offender or an onlooking society. It assumes the punishment would be worse than the benefit of the offending and the individual being deterred a rational actor with an understanding of the CJS. Incapacitation refers to the extent that punishment prevents the offender committing more crimes in that society. The ultimate incapacitating punishments are banishment and the death penalty, but secure imprisonment also temporarily incapacitates. Rehabilitation is the process by which, during punishment, the offender is made to accept and reflect on their offending and adjust their behaviour so that reoffending is minimised. Rehabilitation is the primary objective of most contemporary formal punishments. It is important to note that alongside the formal criminal justice responses to wrongdoing on which this chapter focuses, there have always been informal responses such as ducking and rough music (Banks, 2014).

The type and degree of punishment inflicted on an offender also reflects the severity of the offence (Harrison, 2020). Up to the late 18th century in England and Wales, many found guilty of misdemeanours (or minor offences) were sentenced to non-capital punishments such as the pillory, whipping, branding, fines and providing sureties for good behaviour; sometimes people were sentenced to more than one punishment and usually such punishments were inflicted publicly to increase their deterrent effect. People found guilty of felonies (or more serious offences), such as murder and larceny, often faced the death penalty. The standard method of capital punishment was by hanging, often in the market square of a town, with all townspeople being expected to attend (Gatrell, 1994). In England and Wales in 1868, concern about public disorder at public executions led to their abolition and subsequent hangings were transferred away from the public gaze to inside the prison. Over the course of the 19th century, use of the death penalty was increasingly restricted to the most serious offences. By the 1840s, only those found guilty of the most serious offences, such as murder, wounding, violent theft, arson and sodomy, were sentenced to death, while later the Offences Against the Persons Act 1861 abolished the death penalty for all offences except for murder and high treason.

This growing reluctance to use the death penalty, except for the most serious of crimes, led to different punishments being used. Transportation to America began in 1717 with the Transportation Act as punishment for serious and sometimes capital offences but was ended with the American Declaration of Independence in 1776. Transportation to Australia began in 1787 following James Cook's discovery and claim of Australia for Britain in 1777. Penal transportation was more than just exile. While on a sentence of penal transportation, usually for seven years or life, convict labour was essential in British Empire building. Although it was thought that transportation would lead to the rehabilitation of the offender and was considered a deterrent, there was also a desire to simply remove serious offenders from society. However, many convicts transported to Australia returned to Britain; a few were re-convicted and transported again to Australia. Until the mid-19th century, a declining use of the death penalty and transportation to Australia were the predominant forms of punishment for serious offenders and some bodily punishments continued as punishment for non-capital offences. Growing opposition to transportation led to the Penal Servitude Act 1857, which effectively abolished the practice, leading to a subsequent growth in the use of imprisonment as a punishment in its own right (O'Donnell, 2016).

Prisons and imprisonment as a method of punishment

Pre-modern prisons, those in existence before the 19th-century reforms, were essentially holding places where debtors were kept until they could pay their debts, those not yet convicted were held while awaiting trial and those found guilty of serious offences were held prior to execution or transportation, with only a minority being imprisoned for punishment (O'Donnell, 2016). There was no segregation in these pre-modern prisons – male and women, children and adults, serious offenders and those awaiting trial were all held together, though debtors were held separately in debtors' prisons. Sex, alcohol and gambling were rife, those held there were expected to make their own arrangements for food and gaolers were open to inducement for better conditions. Such conditions led to John Howard's successful late 18th-century campaign for reform of prisons.

A growing desire to reform convicts, rather than just punish them, and the hiatus in transportation had led to the beginning of the development of imprisonment as a punishment for serious offences from the late 18th century, demonstrated by the passing of the Penitentiary Act in 1779 (Johnston, 2016). The traditionally open nature and poor conditions of pre-modern prisons were, over time, replaced by separate cells for prisoners and various combinations of experiments in 'silent' and 'solitary' prison regimes. Prisoners were put to hard labour and given religious instruction. In the late 1840s, for those sentenced to penal servitude (the most serious offenders), a progressive stage system was introduced, whereby prisoners started their sentences with solitary confinement at hard labour and then moved to a public works prison where they worked in quarries or on roads, before release on a prison licence (see Johnston, 2015). For all prisons, local and convict, the philosophies of *hard board, hard fare and hard work* was applied – prisons were never supposed to be pleasant places, but some offenders preferred conditions in prison to those in the workhouse. Although there have been many improvements in the conditions in prisons since the 19th century, such as separate prisons for men and women and for young people and adults, as well as a subsequent massive prison-building programme (between 1842 and 1877, 90 prisons were built or added to), the period 1770 to 1840 laid the foundations for the prison system and the prisons that exist today in England and Wales.

Scholars have tried to explain this move from pre-modern, harsh punishments (including transportation) to imprisonment as the main form of punishment for serious offending. Early accounts gave a largely positive impression, hailing the use of prison and imprisonment a success over an old corrupt and inefficient penal system; a success in which visionary humanitarians produced (what they considered) an efficient, modern and humane system. Later 20th-century scholars have challenged those positive accounts. The most famous and influential of these scholars is French philosopher Michel Foucault. In his classic work *Discipline and Punish: The Birth of the Prison*, first published in French 1975 and translated into English in 1977, he radically altered the history of the prison. Foucault argued that in the modern punishment system, power was far more ubiquitous and oppressive than it had previously been and that whole systems of science and technology were devoted to making the prisoner a totally controlled subject.

The changing face of punishment

Discipline and Punish begins with two contrasting pictures of the changing face of punishment. The first picture, intended to illustrate the pre-modern tendency to punish the body, is the shocking execution in 1757 of Robert-François Damiens, who was convicted of trying to kill the French king. Damiens was tortured, drawn and quartered, with his remaining torso burnt at the stake; it was a horrific death. The second picture is of the daily routine at a reformatory school for young offenders in 1837. The schedule is so detailed that every minute of every day is controlled and each inmate is under constant surveillance. The mind, not the body, was now being punished. Its purpose was to correct and reclaim, to remake the individual through constant observation, rules, penalties and repetitive work disciplines, thereby instilling habits of obedience and docility. Foucault argued that in bringing the body under close surveillance it becomes self-observing and self-regulating, using a more complete and subtle technique of power. Hence, for Foucault (1977, p 82), the overriding objective of prison was '[t]o punish better; to punish with an attenuated severity, perhaps, but in order to punish with more universality and necessity; to insert the power to punish more deeply into the social body'.

Foucault's work has been influential in shaping later scholars' thoughts on how power is wrought through punishment generally and prison specifically. Foucault's focus was how power operates rather than providing a historically accurate picture of the changes in punishment. His intention was to provide an account of changing intentions rather than describe actual changes. In particular, *Discipline and Punish* suggests the changes were seamless and that complex blueprints were created but not implemented due to financial constraints only. Thus, there have been several revisions since the publication of *Discipline and Punish* that provide more nuanced, empirically researched histories of the prison (see, for example, Johnston, 2008). Scholars have pointed out that modern prisons, though better than in pre-modern times, were still harsh places affecting the body, and Oscar Wilde's *Ballad of Reading Gaol* is a reminder that imprisonment had a serious impact on the psychological health of inmates. Nevertheless, the actual changes from punishment regimes that were mainly constituted of corporeal, bodily punishments to ones dominated by imprisonment, and Foucault's claim that

Western societies changed to punishing the mind rather than the body, remain generalised accepted truths of the development of the punishment system seen in the West today.

Contemporary prisons and imprisonment

However, today the prison system in England and Wales, and indeed globally, is still in an abject state despite a now accepted fact that the loss of liberty is the punishment being inflicted when people are sent to custody, not the conditions individuals are supposed to endure once incarcerated. Imprisonment continues to inflict harm on overwhelmingly poor and powerless incarcerated individuals, and it is argued here that prisons and imprisonment still punish *both* the mind *and* the body. Shammas (2017, p 1), drawing on the work of Sykes (1958/2007) and his concept of the 'pains of imprisonment, states:

> But while most modern states have traded in the branding iron for the jail cell, Syke's conceptual quintet remind social observers that although prison sentences may seem less immediately jarring or obviously pain-inducing than executions or torture, they do, in their way, nevertheless impose suffering.

For Scott and Flynn (2014, p 159) the '[t]hree "hot topics" in relation to prisoners' health are [one] mental health, [two] self-inflicted deaths, and [three] illicit substance misuse and the spread of infectious diseases'. As is the case in wider society, the most vulnerable people in prison are those who are suffering physically or mentally. In sum, '[p]eople with mental health problems are in pain' (Scott and Flynn, 2014, p 159) and those pains are not only psychological and emotional, they are physical – they manifest themselves in bodily ways. This can be seen in the manner in which prisoners' mental suffering presents itself, for example, 'neglect of personal hygiene, eating disorders and attempts to harm themselves' (Scott and Flynn, 2014, p 159). The chapter will now turn to the latter, self-inflicted deaths (SIDS). As Scott and Flynn (2014, p 161) starkly but truthfully comment, '[i]mprisonment is plagued by the death of prisoners'. Since the late 1980s there has been a dramatic rise in SIDS in prisons in England and Wales.

There are four main explanations of SIDS (Scott and Codd, cited in Scott and Flynn, 2014, 163).The first explanation comes under the umbrella of '[h]igh-risk inadequates, manipulators and attention seekers' – basically they comprise people who, due to being 'weak', would have taken their own life even if they had not been in prison (Scott and Flynn, 2014, p 163). The second explanation attributes SIDS to poor prison conditions. Prisons are and can become dangerous places. This is due to a lack of staffing, a lack of staff expertise, overcrowding, unhygienic conditions, dilapidated prisons and prisons not fit for purpose, having to share a cell made for one, a lack of nutritious food, food shortage, insecurity and fear for one's safety. The third explanation is 'People vulnerable to prison environment.' In a nutshell, Scott and Flynn (2014, pp 163–4) comment: '[p]risons are filled with large numbers of people with poor coping skills who are vulnerable to the unpredictability of prison life. SIDS arise from a combination of "risky prisoners", who may or may not be psychiatrically ill, and their inability to cope with confinement.' The fourth and final explanation comprises '[i]nherent harms and pains of imprisonment' (Scott and Flynn, 2014, p 164) – this is an experience that impacts on the majority, if not all, incarcerated individuals. This is because prison life is imbued with dehumanisation, hopelessness, isolation, despair and a brutal and toxic environment. In male prisons, toxic masculinity, insecurity and fear for one's safety permeates everything. The 'meaning of life' and 'constructions of the self' are damaged and destabilised (Scott and Flynn, 2014, p 164). It is also worth noting that vulnerability to suicide on release from prison has been evidenced, including SIDS in 'approved' accommodation.

Illicit substance misuse and transmitted infections are other bodily harms that are dominant in prisons. Drugs are available within prison, despite past and ongoing attempts on the part of the prison service to reduce and stop their availability. Drugs are regularly accessed in order to cope with the stresses, strains and boredom of prison life. While the drug of 'choice' in prison is predominately cannabis, other drugs such as heroin are available and are used. For up to one fifth of prisoners, the first time they used heroin was while they were in prison. One incentive to use heroin may be to avoid testing positive for illicit drug use, as heroin stays in the bloodstream for a much shorter time than cannabis. Up to two thirds or more of prisoners have used drugs in prison, most drug users are male, young (average age 23), of low socioeconomic background, are dependent and are polydrug users, they have failed treatments and they are in poor physical health and they have contracted infectious diseases (Scott and Flynn, 2014). One of the most significant transferrable infections that is spread in prison is HIV/AIDS. Sexually transmitted infections are another substantial problem in prison.

There are additional bodily pains and harms endured in prison. Numerous reports from HM Inspectorate of Prisons have highlighted overcrowding, violence and unsafe environments, dilapidated buildings and cells, including broken windows and broken heating systems, and poor hygiene and sanitary conditions (HM Inspectorate of Prisons, 2021). This means that prisoners can be too cold in winter and too hot in summer. Toilets often do not work, do not have seats or are filthy and unhygienic, and this can cause dysentery. Beds are hard, uncomfortable and often sweaty due to being covered in plastic. This can cause and exacerbate back problems and pain. Prison food lacks nutritional value and 'food' purchased via the canteen is high in sugar and carbohydrates; subsequently, many prisoners become overweight. Being overweight can result in various bodily health problems.

Due to overcrowding and unhygienic conditions prisoners are more at risk of COVID-19 than the general population. As a result of COVID-19, many of these bodily pains and harms were exacerbated and, moreover, additional pains and harms have resulted. The consequence of being locked up for 23 hours a day mean that prisoners have bedsores and muscle wastage. Also, there is a far higher incidence of a lack of physical activity among prisoners than the general population. This situation has worsened due to COVID-19. It has been established that, globally, physical inactivity plays a major role in rates of mortality. A study on restricted interaction, self-isolation and home confinement, and the subsequent inactive and sedentary behaviours during the pandemic, found that this physiological challenge resulted in serious health risks (Narici et al, 2021). The study found that muscle wasting can be detected within two days of the onset of inactivity, with a 6 per cent loss of muscle mass after ten days and 10 per cent after 30 days (Narici et al, p 628). One of the study's key findings is that 'just a few days of sedentary lifestyle are sufficient to induce muscle loss, neuromuscular junction damage and fibre denervation, insulin resistance, decreased aerobic capacity, fat deposition and low-grade systemic inflammation' (Narici et al, 2021, p 615). During the COVID lockdowns of 2020 and 2021, prisoners were locked down for 23 hours a day for 14 months (over 425 days).

Conclusion

In sum, the accumulation of punishment of the mind *and* the body while in prison results in a continuum of pains and harms from isolation, hopelessness and despair to suicidal ideation and death. Regular movement and light exercise, together with a nutritional diet, could alleviate and even solve this unacceptable and inhumane situation. Another more radical alternative would be to abolish imprisonment or to at least in practice (as opposed to in theory) preserve this punishment for the most serious and harmful forms of offending.

References
Banks, S. (2014) *Informal Justice in England and Wales, 1740–1914: The Courts of Popular Opinion*, Woodbridge: Boydell & Brewer.

Condry, R. and Minson, S. (2021) 'Conceptualising the effects of imprisonment on families: collateral consequences, secondary punishment, or symbiotic harms?' *Theoretical Criminology*, 25(4): 540–58, DOI: https://doi.org/10.1177/13624 80619897078.

Foucault, M. (1977) *Discipline and Punish: The Birth of the Prison*, Harmondsworth: Penguin.

Gatrell, V.A.C. (1994) *The Hanging Tree: Execution and the English People, 1770–1868*, Oxford: Oxford University Press.

Harrison, K. (2020) *Penology: Theory, Policy and Practice*, London: Red Globe Press.

HM Inspectorate of Prisons (2021) 'HM Chief Inspector of Prisons for England and Wales annual report 2020–21', [online] Available from: https://assets.publish ing.service.gov.uk/government/uploads/system/uploads/attachment_data/file/1003082/hmip-annual-report-accounts-2020-21.pdf [Accessed 25 May 2022].

Johnston, H. (ed) (2008) *Punishment and Control in Historical Perspective*, London: Palgrave Macmillan.

Johnston, H. (2015) *Crime in England 1815–1880: Experiencing the Criminal Justice System*, London: Routledge.

Johnston, H. (2016) 'Prison histories, 1770–1950s: continuities and contradictions', in Y. Jewkes, J. Bennett and B. Crewe (eds) *Handbook on Prisons* (2nd edn), London: Routledge, pp 24–38.

Narici, M., De Vito, G., Franchi, M., Paoli, A. (2021) 'Impact of sedentarism due to the COVID-19 home confinement on neuromuscular, cardiovascular and metabolic health: physiological and pathophysiological implications and recommendations for physical and nutritional countermeasures', *European Journal of Sport Science*, 21(4): 614–35, DOI: https://doi.org/10.1080/17461 391.2020.1761076.

O'Donnell, I. (2016) 'The aims of imprisonment', in Y. Jewkes, J. Bennett and B. Crewe (eds) *Handbook on Prisons* (2nd edn), London: Routledge, pp 39–54.

Scott, D. and Flynn, N. (2014) *Prisons and Punishment* (2nd edn), London: SAGE.

Shammas, V.L. (2017) 'Pains of imprisonment', in K. R. Kerley (ed) *The Encyclopedia of Corrections*, New York: John Wiley & Sons, pp 1–5, DOI: https://doi.org/10.1002/9781118845387.wbeoc020.

Sykes, G. (1958/2007) *A Society of Captive: A Study of a Maximum Security Prison*, Princeton, NJ: Princeton University Press.

24

Criminal justice and serious, violent and sexual offending

Stephanie Kewley and Charlotte Barlow

Introduction

When asked to think about serious violent and sexual crime, it is likely that individuals will recall high-profile cases reported in news or social media, or indeed those consumed through 'true crime' documentaries in which the motivation and investigation of perpetrators of crimes such as murder and rape are contemplated and dissected, often in a highly dramatic manner. Spectators of dramatised violence rightly respond to the abhorrent acts with shock and disgust. In an effort to make sense of perpetrators' behaviour, audience members, often led by media producers, conclude perpetrators of such serious violent sexual crimes must be *evil monsters*. However, violence and sexual violence is far from uncommon. Indeed, particular types of violence, such as acts against women and children, are 'mundane, ordinary, and an everyday occurrence' (Walklate and McCulloch, 2020, p 10). Yet, although acts of extreme violence (mass shootings, serial homicides) are very rare, these are often the cases that pique the interest of true crime producers and consumers; while routine, daily acts of murder, physical/sexual assault and psychological and emotional violence against women and children occur mostly without comment. This chapter aims to explore some of the key issues and debates surrounding violence and sexual violence. In particular, it examines some of the definitional challenges and problems with violence classification, noting the need for integrated theory to explain the complexity of violence, particularly when violence is gendered.

Consequences of violence

The consequences of violence (perhaps even legitimate violence) have far-reaching effects that impact not only individuals, but families, communities and society at large. The most obvious consequence of violence is the immediate physical injury experienced at the point of assault, and while many physical injuries repair over time, others can be life altering or life changing. In addition to physical injury, psychological and emotional damage can be equally detrimental. Victims of serious violence report changes in their mental health, with feelings of heightened fear, anxiety, depression, low self-esteem and poor confidence, to name a few (Rivara et al, 2019). These feelings can impact their ability to function across key domains in life, such as work, education, family/friendships and with intimate partners. Post-violence, victims' behaviours sometimes alter, particularly when violence is endured throughout adolescence: they might socially isolate themselves, engage in risky behaviours such as substance use, struggle to develop healthy interpersonal relationships and/or drop out of school. Broader socioeconomic costs of violence are further experienced, both in terms of the cost to criminal justice systems (CJSs) (investigating, prosecuting, managing and treating perpetrators of violence), but also longer-term economic costs to victims (Bindler and Ketel, 2021) including loss of earnings, rehousing costs, medical costs, welfare dependency and so forth (Soares, 2015). The prevalence and effects of violence, in particular sexual violence, disproportionally impacts women and children (ONS, 2021; UN Women, 2022), intersecting with Black and Asian populations, people with disabilities, LGBTQIA+ individuals and those from lower socioeconomic backgrounds (Mueller et al, 2019; Waller et al, 2021). Thus, the consequences of violence and sexual violence are far-reaching, they exist on multiple levels and span victims' life course.

Clarity of what violence is and what it is not is central to empirical examination so that effective 'surveillance, identification of causes and consequences, providing appropriate prevention and intervention, and conducting outcome studies' (Hamby, 2017, p 167) can be ensured. Before a definition of violence is presented, it is worth first making the distinction between aggression and violence.

Defining aggression and violence

Social psychologists argue that rather than separate entities, violence and sexual violence are subdomains and extreme manifestations of aggression. Thus, an understanding of aggression is needed before beginning to explore violence (Allen et al, 2018). While all acts of violence can be perceived as aggression, not all acts of aggression are violent or sexually violent. For example, a lawyer cross-examining a witness may use aggressive verbal tactics such as interrupting, shouting or undermining the witness, but this would not be deemed violent. Some social psychologists consider aggression to be a learned behaviour, informed and nurtured by an individual's environment and life experience. Through the observation of reward and punishment, individuals learn to adopt aggressive behaviours when they see others benefit and adopt alternative strategies when they witness others punished for the use of aggression. Others believe there is some innate element of aggression within humans, with striking similarities to the animal kingdom, and this is either heightened or dampened through learning. The position adopted when understanding and explaining aggression is important, because it informs responses to the prevention, treatment and management of those who are aggressive and or violent. If aggression is perceived as innate, mechanisms that control natural urges to act aggressively and even violently are limited, whereas if it is believed that aggression is learned and not inevitable, factors known to influence aggression such as environments, situations and other psychosocial factors can be controlled.

Although not all aggression is perceived to be problematic, it is generally agreed harmful aggression, that is, the intention of at least one person to cause harm to another who is motivated to avoid that harm, is a problem (Felson, 2013). The scale and scope of this type of aggression tends to manifest through violent acts and is diverse in its form. Harmful aggression ranges from state-sponsored acts of war, female genital mutilation, female infanticide and ethnic cleansing to corporate aggression, including illegal dumping of toxic waste, unsafe working conditions and violence to consumers through unsafe pharmaceutical products, to interpersonal aggression and violence such as gang/street, domestic and familial. Aggression can be carried out in private or public spaces and at individual and group level, and victims and perpetrators can be adults, children, people with power or people without and so on. Yet not all aggression, or even all violent behaviour, is criminal. Indeed, some forms of violence are legally recognised as justifiable, for example the use of legitimate force to restrain a person for medical or criminal reasons, violence in self-defence, the infliction of the death penalty and even violence for pleasure in sports such as boxing or hunting.

A definition of violence is more contentious. Violence is often defined as a behaviour that is intended to harm another person or persons through physical, emotional and/or psychological means. However, definitions of violence, abuse and aggression are often conflated and defined through the use of typologies and classifications, rather than through the construction of clear and precise elements. Typologies of violence often take one of two forms (Allen and Anderson, 2017). Firstly, the 'hostile' versus 'instrumental' typology finds that a perpetrator reacts to an (often) external trigger as a personal transgression and, as such, reacts with violence (hostile); or, if violence is instrumental, it is a means to achieve a goal or desire (the goal could be material, or the desire to inflict harm on another person). Either way, the act is organised and planned. There are problems with this classification in that an explanation of violent behaviour is far more complex, as even these two motivations are fluid. It could be the case that an initial reaction to an incident might be reactionary (hostile), but over time, a perpetrator shifts into a more predatory (instrumental) position.

A second typology relates to the proximity of the victim, through acts of direct or indirect violence. Direct violence occurs when the victim and perpetrator are present (for example, a physical assault) whereas indirect violence happens even when the victim is absent (for example, rape threats made over social media). Like the hostile and instrumental typology, these too can co-occur in the commission of violence. For example, in an email dispute, a man might threaten to rape his boss (indirect violence) but later that day follow her home and carry out the threat (direct violence). Are these separate incidences of violence, or are they one act protracted over time?

Hamby (2017) is critical of a lack of clear definition of violence and the overuse of such typologies. While there is strength in classifying acts of violence with shared characteristics, these exemplar approaches fail to define the boundaries for all types of violence. Hamby neatly brings together common approaches from the fields of social psychology, public health and animal studies to define violence precisely. She outlines four essential elements required when making a precise definition of violence. She argues that a behaviour can only be defined as violent when each of these four aspects are present; that is the act is: (a) intentional, (b) unwanted, (c) non-essential, and (d) harmful. An important note that Hamby also makes is what should be excluded from definitions of violence. She details how the use of social norm violations are problematic when defining or providing examples of violence and thus should be excluded. When considering the problems and solutions to violence through a criminal justice lens, this is crucial. Effectively, because legal and CJSs are socially, politically, culturally, geographically and historically constructed, definitions that require legal and criminal frameworks are limited within the social norms in which they exist. Rape and other sexual assaults are defined under Hamby's four criteria as violence, as the act of rape is intentional (motivation might be varied; for example, exploitation, coercion, sexual gratification and so forth), harmful, unwanted and non-essential. While having clear and precise definitions allows for greater accuracy in theory development, definitions alone do not explain why rape occurs or what causes it.

Furthermore, typologies and categorisations of violence fail to centralise a gendered understanding of violence. Although men are much more likely to both perpetrate and be victims of violence, women are overwhelmingly more likely to be victims of domestic and sexual violence. Such violence is commonly referred to as gendered violence. Gendered violence is much more likely to be committed by someone known to the victim, challenging the myths of 'stranger danger' commonly perpetuated in the media. One such example is domestic violence, a pattern of behaviour which is controlling, coercive, violent, threatening and degrading, in the majority of cases perpetrated by a partner or ex-partner, but also by a family member or carer. The gendered nature of such violence is well documented, with Hester (2013) highlighting that men are not only more likely to perpetrate such violence against women, but also that male violence is more severe and more likely to involve fear and control of female victims.

Using a feminist lens to define violence

Feminist perspectives provide a useful lens through which to understand domestic and sexual violence. Such perspectives situate women's experiences within the broader context of patriarchy and gender inequality, as well as considering the ways in which structural constraints such as race, class and disability intersect with gender. A key contributor to the feminist theorising of violence is Liz Kelly. Kelly's (1988) notion of a continuum establishes the common characteristics between different gendered experiences of abuse and assists understanding of the continuous nature of women's experiences in a patriarchal culture. Kelly is not suggesting that women cannot distinguish between an unwanted pat on the backside by a co-worker and being raped, for example. Rather, the continuum allows an understanding of the ways in which individual acts of sexual aggression are embedded within existing relationships and power structures.

McPhail's (2016) framework provides a further useful example of feminist conceptualisations of sexual violence in particular. McPhail knits together five feminist theories to explain the act of rape. The framework is further strengthened through the addition of empirically supported psychological, environmental, developmental, situational and biological factors. The five theories include: (a) radical liberal feminism, under which rape is perceived as a political act in which perpetrators are motivated by power and control and efforts are made to secure male domination and female subordination; (b) radical feminism, which views rape on a continuum of normative heterosexual sex, with rape eroticised; (c) intersectional feminism, which sees race, class and gender at the core of understanding the unique experiences and consequences of women across the intersection; (d) social constructionism, which perceives rape as a mechanism for men to achieve and sustain their masculinity and, as such, views motivations for rape as being multiple; and (e) post-modern feminism, which views rape as a sexually specific act upon both the body and identity, where the specificities of rape are important because the act itself is specific to the body and mind. Similarly to Kelly (1988), these five theories integrate important areas of power, patriarchy, gender dynamics and feminist perspectives. However, McPhail fortifies the model further using empirically evidenced gender violence factors, such as sexual entitlement, hostility towards women, the belief in rape myths and traditional gender roles, the emphasis on heterosexuality and the existence of the patriarchy and gender inequality.

By knitting together feminist perspectives along with single-level theories McPhail generates a superior explanation for rape, assisting researchers, practitioners and policy makers to make sense of a highly complex phenomena. The model provides a clear roadmap of the aetiology of rape in which hypothesis models can be tested to support future prevention, education and treatment interventions. However, the model is not without its limitations. The explanatory power for female and same-sex perpetration is weak and the model fails to explain sexual assault outside male-to-female/child violations. While the model provides explanatory power for the act of rape, the model itself is highly complex and thus articulation of it to a broad range of audiences will be a challenge. But rape is, of course, a complex phenomenon and cannot be fully explained by single factor theories. An integrated and multiple-level model is required.

Conclusions

As this short overview has shown, developing a clear definition of violence is complex, although Hamby's (2017) four key domains provide a useful foundation. Typologies or single-level theories are insufficient in explaining all types of violence, and as such gender-based violence, with Kelly's (1988) continuum and particularly McPhail's (2016) integrated feminist theory approach, provide more nuanced explanations. In summary, violence is perceived as an extraordinary issue when the evidence suggests it is anything but that. It is essential that policy makers develop effective policies and deploy resources to interventions and strategies that target those at risk of perpetrating and/or becoming a victim of violence, work to prevent violence occurring in the first place, advocate on behalf of victims and their families, and provide appropriate treatment and management options for perpetrators of violence. However, to do this effectively, they must draw on more precise definitions and address the ways in which violence is influenced by structural constraints such as gender, race and disability.

References

Allen, J.J. and Anderson, C.A. (2017) 'Aggression and violence: definitions and distinctions', in P. Sturmey (ed) *The Wiley Handbook of Violence and Aggression*, Chichester: Wiley, pp 1–14, DOI: https://doi.org/10.1002/9781119057574.whbva001.

Allen, J.J., Anderson, C.A. and Bushman, B.J. (2018) 'The general aggression model', *Current Opinion in Psychology*, 19: 75–80, DOI: https://doi.org/10.1016/j.copsyc.2017.03.034.

Bindler, A. and Ketel, N. (2021) 'Scaring or scarring? Labour market effects of criminal victimisation', Institute of Labor Economics, [online] Available from: https://docs.iza.org/dp12082.pdf [Accessed 6 June 2022].

Felson, R.B. (2013) 'What are violent offenders thinking', in B. Leclerc and R. Wortley (eds) *Cognition and Crime: Offender Decision Making and Script Analyses*, London: Routledge, pp 12–45.

Hamby, S. (2017) 'On defining violence, and why it matters', *Psychology of Violence*, 7(2): 167–80, DOI: https://doi.org/10.1037/vio0000117.

Hester, M. (2013) 'Who does what to whom? Gender and domestic violence perpetrators in English police records', *European Journal of Criminology*, 10(5): 623–37, DOI: https://doi.org/10.1177/1477370813479078.

Kelly, L. (1988) *Surviving Sexual Violence*, London: Polity Press.

McPhail, B.A. (2016) 'Feminist framework plus: knitting feminist theories of rape etiology into a comprehensive model', *Trauma, Violence, & Abuse*, 17(3): 314–29, DOI: https://doi.org/10.1177/1524838015584367.

Mueller, C.O., Forber-Pratt, A.J. and Sriken, J. (2019) 'Disability: missing from the conversation of violence', *Journal of Social Issues*, 75(3): 707–25, DOI: https://doi.org/10.1111/josi.12339.

ONS (Office for National Statistics) (2021) 'The lasting impact of violence against women and girls', [online] Available from: https://www.ons.gov.uk/peoplepopulationandcommunity/crimeandjustice/articles/thelastingimpactofviolenceagainstwomenandgirls/2021-11-24 [Accessed 6 June 2022].

Rivara, F., Adhia, A., Lyons, V., Massey, A., Mills, B., Morgan, E., Simckes, M. and Rowhani-Rahbar, A. (2019) 'The effects of violence on health', *Health Affairs*, 38(10): 1622–9, DOI: https://doi.org/10.1377/hlthaff.2019.00480.

Soares, R.R. (2015) 'Welfare costs of crime and common violence', *Journal of Economic Studies*, 42(1): 117–37, DOI: https://doi.org/10.1108/JES-05-2012-0062.

UN Women (2022) 'Facts and figures: ending violence against women', [online] Available from: https://www.unwomen.org/en/what-we-do/ending-violence-against-women/facts-and-figures [Accessed 6 June 2022].

Walklate, S. and McCulloch, J. (2020) 'Rendering the ordinary extraordinary in order to facilitate prevention: the case of (sexual) violence against women', in S. Kewley and C. Barlow (eds) *Preventing Sexual Violence: Problems and Possibilities*, Bristol: Bristol University Press, pp 9–24.

Waller, B.Y., Harris, J. and Quinn, C.R. (2021) 'Caught in the crossroad: an intersectional examination of African American women intimate partner violence survivors' help seeking', *Trauma, Violence, & Abuse*, 23(4), DOI: https://doi.org/10.1177/1524838021991303.

25

Criminal justice, risk and vulnerability

Eric Halford

Introduction

Both risk and vulnerability are ever present in society. This is not a contemporary concept but rather one that has been widely accepted for centuries. However, the contemporary landscape within the criminal justice system (CJS) has thrust into the limelight a very modern discussion around the fundamental meaning of risk and vulnerability and, vitally, the role of the CJS to deliver on its fundamental principles of preventing crime and disorder while considering such concepts. When examining these issues, it is important to understand them in the language of the CJS, which is not always straightforward within an environment that is both multidisciplinary and multi-agency. The many chains and cogs that make up the CJS are directly responsible for the apprehension, prosecution, sentencing and punishment of those who are suspected or convicted of criminal offences. The *Oxford Dictionary* definition of risk is that it is 'a situation involving exposure to danger' and vulnerability is defined as 'the quality or state of being exposed to the possibility of being attacked or harmed, either physically or emotionally'. In an ideal world the definitions of risk and vulnerability and the key role of the CJS should not be difficult to comprehend. However, simultaneously preventing, reducing and responding to risk and vulnerability is increasingly complex in an ever more globalised world where the volume and complexity of crime has evolved to such a degree that public sector organisations charged with delivering criminal justice are often doing so by playing catch-up in the face of both significant budgetary and resourcing constraints.

Defining and responding to vulnerability

Ever conscious that the role of the CJS is to 'be answerable to law and democratically responsive to the people they serve' (Loader, 2016, p 435), public sector organisations such as the police and Crown Prosecution Service (CPS) have sought to rise to the challenges of the contemporary criminal landscape by responding in a systematic fashion. To enable more equitable prioritisation of demand the definition of vulnerability has been significantly developed (Walley and Adams, 2019). Evolving from a position where it was generally accepted that everyone can be vulnerable at any point of their life, the definition has been refined to consider physical, social and environmental attributes that contribute towards a person or community's vulnerability (Keay and Kirby, 2018, p 433).

The UK's College of Policing (CoP) has defined a vulnerable person as 'a person who is vulnerable if, as a result of their situation or circumstances, they are unable to take care of or protect themselves or others from harm or exploitation' (CoP, 2021). As a result of reaching a consensus in defining vulnerability the CJS in the UK, and in particular the police, have been able to move forward and build upon this to provide a structured framework for responding to it by advocating a simple four-step response.

Firstly, police officers are encouraged to identify a person's individual vulnerability (CoP, 2021). This is a complex undertaking but is most commonly achieved by taking into consideration factors such as the individual's physical attributes including gender, sexuality, health and psychological well-being. Identifying vulnerability can also include consideration of the individual's social attributes such as their race, class, familial relationships and socioeconomic status. In addition, environmental attributes of vulnerability include neighbourhood characteristics, repeat victimisation, housing, isolation and, significantly, deprivation. In considering the latter, the CJS is reinforcing its commitment to confronting and responding to a significant cause of crime and human rights violations. For example, evidence obtained from developing countries has repeatedly shown that more than any other factor poverty is the greatest predictor of victimisation from violence, especially sexual violence committed towards women and young girls (Iorfa et al, 2022). In countries afflicted by epidemic levels of violence it is the vulnerable poor who most crave protection from a fully functioning effective CJS.

Secondly, once vulnerability is identified, police officers are then encouraged to consider if and how they create a risk of harm for the individual (CoP, 2021). If a risk is identified, it is then important to assess the level of harm that would occur if the risk is not addressed. This assessment in itself creates a further layer of complexity which is not eased by a lack of a formal definition of harm. Consulting the *Oxford Dictionary* again, harm is defined as 'damage or injury that is caused by a person or an event'. In the absence of a commonly accepted definition, those working within the CJS are often relied upon to make their own subjective decision on what constitutes harm, thus creating inconsistency across organisations such as the police and CPS. Based upon this assessment, action should then be taken to eliminate or mitigate the risk, reducing its likelihood of occurrence. The form of action which can be taken by the CJS and its partners to attempt to mitigate harm that may occur as a result of an individual's vulnerability is wide and varied and a detailed description is beyond the scope of this chapter. To summarise, however, at a strategic level it can range from new or amended laws or legal protections for victims. At an operational level members of the CJS can use their capacity and capability to address the underlying causes. At a tactical level the police service can pursue prosecutions, utilise prohibitive orders against offenders to protect vulnerable people or even resort to simply patrolling the immediate vicinity of the home of a person at risk of harm. Regardless of the final action taken, it is a complex and multifaceted response that often carries serious consequences if not considered and responded to effectively.

The national decision model

To reduce the risk of serious failures in responding to the dangers faced by vulnerable people, police services at the front line of this wicked problem have devised decision-making models to guide them. Embedded in police services in the UK by the CoP, the national decision model (NDM) provides decision makers with a structured process to underpin their assessments (CoP, 2013). The NDM contains six key elements. At its core are the police Code of Ethics and principles and standards of professional behaviour (CoP, 2014). While abiding by the Code of Ethics, decision makers then seek to gather information and intelligence regarding the threat or risk. As outlined previously, they then make an assessment and begin to develop a working response to the issue in hand. In doing so, the decision maker must then consider all legal powers and policies, followed by paying due attention to all possible options available to them. Finally, they must take action and, at the earliest convenience, review the response and, if required, adapt it accordingly. Even with the aid of the NDM, navigating a response to the complex problems vulnerability presents is a significant challenge. However, in defining the key elements and providing guidance on how to respond to vulnerability, the UK CJS is transitioning to a position that is more compatible with contemporary expectations.

Risk-based demand management

In an effort to better manage demand, the CJS is also evolving how it prioritises the challenges it faces. No longer can the organisations that make up the system respond to all forms of demand. Excluding crime statistics from 2020 and 2021 due to the anomalous impact of the coronavirus pandemic on the volume of crime and disorder (Halford et al, 2020), recent years have seen a shift from low-harm and complexity crime to high-harm, complex offending. The Crime Survey for England and Wales indicates that although crime counts have remained relatively consistent in recent years, traditional core functions of the CJS, such as responding to acquisitive crime including burglary, theft and vehicle-related crime, have all experienced continuous reductions in volume (ONS, 2019).

In contrast, high-harm and complex crime types such as homicide, robbery, fraud and sexual offences, including sexual exploitation, have all experienced increases (ONS, 2019). As a result, although the CJS has responded to stabilise overall crime levels, the shift in complexity has meant significant rises in the time and cost of responding to crime (Walley and Jennison-Phillips, 2018). To absorb the dramatic shift in crime the CJS has adopted a 'risk-based approach'. In doing so, resources, time and available budgets are increasingly being utilised to respond to and support incidents, investigations, victims and offenders that present the highest risk. As a result, issues such as organised crime, county lines drug trafficking (which is the practice of using vulnerable children to traffic drugs from urban to rural areas), sexual exploitation, domestic violence and counterterrorism, all potential situations involving high levels of exposure to danger, have understandably received the greatest attention, time and resources (Walley and Adams, 2019). As a by-product, crime and disorder that fall below what are often inconsistent, localised and highly subjective thresholds have been managed by contemporary criminal justice solutions such as conditional cautions, restorative justice and early intervention. A positive aspect of this approach is that the multi-agency response of the CJS has grown and now often includes agencies from health, social care and education in delivering prevention approaches such as early intervention, which is the practice of intervening with support measures earlier in an individual's life. This approach focuses on preventing or diverting potential vulnerable victims and offenders from the CJS by using holistic or therapeutic approaches, and is widely supported by the UK government (Boyd and Bermingham, 2019). Such approaches provide intuitive benefits while reduced victimisation and recidivism potentially enables the opportunity for realignment of the resources within the CJS to reacquire equitability against demand.

The impact on the CJS

A potentially negative, unintended consequence as a result of this risk-based approach has seen the past decade experience unprecedented falls in criminal justice outcomes in England and Wales. In the year ending March 2020 police forces finalised 43 per cent of cases without identifying a suspect (Home Office, 2020). Cases closed due to evidential difficulties have also significantly increased, from 17 per cent in 2015 to 35 per cent in 2020, with case complexity being cited as a primary factor (Home Office, 2020). In light of the impact of the shift to risk-based responding it is natural to make an intuitive deduction that a 'squeezed middle' is emerging within the contemporary CJS. With high-harm offending being prioritised in key resource and budgetary decision-making processes and low-harm early intervention being used to address present and potential future repeat victimisation and recidivism, mid-level crime and disorder are, unwittingly, under-resourced. This has potentially contributed to the significant impact on effectiveness the CJS is presently experiencing in cases such as rape.

The long-term ambition of tackling repeat victimisation, recidivism and prevention, enabling the CJS to respond effectively to risk and vulnerability, is an admirable, evidence-based approach. However, this will not be achieved overnight and what cannot be overlooked is the immediate and longer-term impact of reduced effectiveness. Efforts to meet the shift to high-harm crime and increased complexity by prioritising risk and vulnerability has potentially contributed to some of the identifiable, negative but unintended consequences the justice system is experiencing. Most significantly is a worrying trend of reducing confidence and legitimacy (Fleming and Grabosky, 2009; Cook, 2015).

Confidence and legitimacy are cornerstones of the CJS and both are significantly negatively impacted by failures in effectiveness.

If the CJS does not effectively deliver justice it loses its legitimacy. In doing so it also loses the confidence of the public it is in place to protect. This is a principle founded by Sir Robert Peel, who understood that to achieve effectiveness the CJS requires the willing cooperation of the public, in voluntary observance of the law, to be able to secure and maintain the respect of the public. By way of example, the CJS must be considered to be effective. If it is not, the public lose confidence in its ability. As a result, they are less likely to report, cooperate or support the system in pursuit of justice, beginning a cycle that feeds further ineffectiveness (Cook, 2015). Those who would prey on the vulnerable also recognise this and, in its worst-case scenario, no longer consider the CJS as a legitimate deterrent, further contributing to the problem. Indicators of this emerging risk can be seen within England and Wales, where only 1.4 per cent of rape cases reported lead to a charge (Home Office, 2020). As a result, women, young girls and other victims of rape often lack confidence to report sexual violence against them and, as such, the UK now experiences two out of every five rape investigations being closed because the victim is unwilling to support further police action against the suspect.

It can be argued that such a situation is further compounded through certain elements of the delivery of the criminal justice prosecutorial system. This is especially acute where key decisions on cases with people being charged or proceeding to trial are made based upon subjective assessments of credibility, competence and reliability of victim evidence. These judgements are routinely made by law enforcement and prosecutors alike, who often conclude there is 'no realistic prospect of conviction' (Hohl and Stanko, 2015, p 324). It could be argued that this approach is unwittingly 'rigged' against the vulnerable who are the very people that the CJS is trying to protect. For example, factors of vulnerability that have been defined in this chapter, such as poverty and deprivation, are often inherently linked to crime, substance abuse and mental illness. These are key factors that influence decision makers' assessments of credibility, competence and reliability, and in doing so contribute to the reduced likelihood of successful case outcomes for crimes committed against the vulnerable (Hohl and Stanko, 2015).

Conclusion

The paradigm shift in crime towards harm and complexity has driven a rise in demand for the CJS. In response, the multiple agencies within criminal justice have adapted through increased effectiveness in prioritisation. The use of vulnerability and risk-based decision making emerged as key conceptual approaches. This transition was well meaning and had intuitive moral and practical advantages, but also unintended consequences. The most significant of these has been a shift in resourcing and budgets to the highest-risk areas within policing and an investment in partnership working to prevent and intervene earlier, thereby stopping or reducing recidivism and victimisation. In doing so, it has emerged that other areas are now under-resourced and have begun to suffer the impact of these changes. In a system that has arguably not yet evolved enough to support vulnerable victims and witnesses who often have a higher presence of traits deemed to undermine credibility, reliability and, ultimately, likelihood of conviction, cases with evidential difficulty or perceived to have no realistic prospect of conviction have been discontinued in large volumes. As a consequence, successful investigation and prosecution of crimes such as rape and violence against women have suffered significantly; this has potentially had a pronounced impact on public confidence and overall legitimacy may have been greatly affected. This impact risks causing a cyclical effect in declining public trust in the CJS. Solutions to these emerging problems include increased budgets and resourcing within the CJS that are initially focused on areas where confidence and legitimacy is at its lowest, such as rape and sexual violence against women. Such future investment should continue to be underpinned by transforming culture, policy and legal frameworks to enable increased compassion, empathy and a trauma-informed approach within the CJS that recognises and accepts the fallibility of vulnerable victims, witnesses and communities that are a by-product of systemic disadvantages such as poverty and deprivation.

References

Boyd, F. and Bermingham, R. (2019) 'Research briefing on early interventions to reduce violent crime', United Kingdom Parliament, [online] Available from: https://researchbriefings.files.parliament.uk/documents/POST-PN-0599/POSTPN-0599.pdf [Accessed 26 May 2021].

Cook, P.J. (2015) 'Will the current crisis in police legitimacy increase crime? Research offers a way forward', *Psychological Science in the Public Interest*, 16(3): 71–4, DOI: https://doi.org/10.1177/1529100615610575.

CoP (College of Policing) (2013) 'National decision model', [online] Available from: https://www.college.police.uk/app/national-decision-model/national-decision-model [Accessed 25 May 2021].

CoP (College of Policing) (2014) 'Code of Ethics', [online] Available from: https://assets.college.police.uk/s3fs-public/2021-02/code_of_ethics.pdf [Accessed 25 May 2021].

CoP (College of Policing) (2021) 'Introduction to vulnerability-related risk', [online] Available from: https://www.college.police.uk/guidance/vulnerability-related-risks/introduction-vulnerability-related-risk [Accessed 25 May 2021].

Fleming, J. and Grabosky, P. (2009) 'Managing the demand for police services, or how to control an insatiable appetite', *Policing*, 3: 281–91, DOI: https://doi.org/10.1093/police/pap019.

Halford, E., Dixon, A., Farrell, G., Malleson, N. and Tilley, N. (2020) 'Crime and coronavirus: social distancing, lockdown, and the mobility elasticity of crime', *Crime Science*, 9(11): 1–12, DOI: https://doi.org/10.1186/s40163-020-00121-w.

Hohl, K. and Stanko, E.A. (2015). 'Complaints of rape and the criminal justice system: fresh evidence on the attrition problem in England and Wales', *European Journal of Criminology*, 12(3): 324–41.

Home Office (2020) 'Crime outcomes in England and Wales 2019 to 2020', [online] Available from: https://assets.publishing.service.gov.uk/government/uploads/system/uploads/attachment_data/file/901028/crime-outcomes-1920-hosb1720.pdf [Accessed 4 April 2021].

Iorfa, S.K., Onyishi, A.B., Anozie, E.U., Chukwuorji, J.C. and Ifeagwazi, C.M. (2022) 'Sexual violence and child poverty: lived experiences of child sexual violence survivors in Nigeria', *Journal of Social Service Research*, 48(1): 134–44.

Keay, S. and Kirby, S. (2018) 'Defining vulnerability: from the conceptual to the operational', *Policing: A Journal of Policy and Practice*, 12(4): 428–38, DOI: https://doi.org/10.1093/police/pax046.

Loader, I. (2016) 'In search of civic policing: recasting the "Peelian" principles', *Criminal Law and Philosophy*, 10(3): 427–40.

ONS (Office for National Statistics) (2019) 'Crime in England and Wales: year ending March 2019', [online] Available from: https://www.ons.gov.uk/peoplepopulationandcommunity/crimeandjustice/bulletins/crimeinenglandandwales/yearendingmarch2019 [Accessed 4 April 2021].

Walley, P. and Jennison-Phillips, A. (2018) 'A study of non-urgent demand to identify opportunities for demand reduction', *Policing: A Journal of Policy and Practice*, 14(2): 542–54, DOI: https://doi.org/10.1093/police/pay034.

Walley, P. and Adams, M. (2019) *An Evaluation of Demand Management Practices in UK Police Forces*, Centre for Policing Research and Learning: Open University.

26

Criminal justice, risk assessment and dangerousness

Jennifer Murray

Introduction

Risk assessment is a key competency for practitioners within forensic psychology and the criminal justice system (Singh et al, 2014). In a survey of 2,135 risk assessment practitioners across 44 countries, Singh et al (2014) identified that participants carried out an average of 435.5 formal risk assessments across their working lifetime and a reported average of 34.5 completed risk assessments per week. Despite the prominence of risk assessment within criminal justice practitioners' daily practice and the potential impact that the outcomes of these assessments can have on individuals' lives, there remains uncertainty and disagreement over what it is and how it should be carried out in practice (Viljoen et al, 2021).

This chapter provides a broad definition of what risk assessment is within the criminal justice context. It will then discuss risk assessment's relationship to 'dangerousness' and the different approaches to risk assessment available to practitioners. Effective risk assessment practice and the knowledge of different approaches and their application are imperative for improving not only practitioner understandings but also outcomes for the people involved in the assessment (Murray and Enang, 2022).

What is risk?

It is first useful to understand what is meant by 'risk'. While this should be relatively simple – as in everyone knows what risk is – when trying to pin down a clear definition there is some possibly unexpected complexity. For instance, definitions from the majority of criminal justice and forensic-related fields convey risk as a negative thing to be mitigated and avoided (Litwack et al, 2006), while other fields such as health and policing treat risk as something which is expected and accepted as part of the day-to-day working environment (Murray and Enang, 2022). Health and social care professions take this a step further, openly embracing risk and uncertainty through the implementation of positive risk-taking strategies within their practices (Felton and Stacey, 2008). For this chapter, and to embrace the breadth of risk definitions and conceptualisations, risk will be operationally defined in line with the International Organization for Standardization's (ISO,

2018) definition. The ISO is an international organisation which aims to bring together expertise, share knowledge and develop consensus-based and voluntary international standards relevant to real practice. ISO's definition outlines that risk is the effect of uncertainty on objectives (ISO, 2018). This effect can be positive or negative; it is simply the deviation from the norm or from the expected outcome. Positive effects resulting from the risk are seen as opportunities, while negative effects are seen as threats. There is, therefore, a balance between removing or reducing risks (threats) and taking risks (opportunities). Further, risk is both flexible and dynamic.

Risk assessment and related terminology

Risk assessment within the criminal justice context is a process through which a practitioner seeks to assess the extent to which a risk or set of risk factors are present, whether these are relevant to the individual or situation being assessed, and what potential impacts these may have on an outcome (Hogan, 2021). Essentially, risk assessment aims to reduce negative outcomes for the person and for society, while balancing the need for positive risk taking and informing intervention and risk-management planning (Murray and Enang, 2022). More recent risk assessment practices also incorporate consideration of protective factors, for example, factors which may reduce the negative effects of risk (de Vries Robbé et al, 2013).

Historically, the term 'dangerousness' was used rather than risk. In more recent years, this focus on a person being dangerous and assessing dangerousness has been acknowledged as problematic, with Cooke et al (2001) indicating that when discussing an individual's propensity for violence, the term 'violence risk' should be preferred. This reduces the potential negative impact of unconscious biases associated with over-ascribing an internal cause to a person's behaviours and under-ascribing the impact of contextual or external factors. On the one hand, when an internal cause is applied to a person's behaviour they are seen as more in control of and responsible for their actions. When an external cause is applied, on the other hand, the behaviour is seen as situational and something that they are less responsible for (Murray et al, 2011). This process is described within Kelley's (1967) attribution theory: a core theory within social psychology. It can lead to unintended and unconscious biases – errors in judgements – affecting decision making, responses and behaviours towards others (Murray et al, 2011). The over-ascribing of internal causal labelling to a person's behaviours has been found to increase recommended sentence lengths, perceptions of severity of a person's violent behaviour and the level of risk attached to the person (see Murray et al, 2011). This has clear potential consequences for the person's liberty and future decision making around risk management.

Similarly, the labelling of a characteristic (such as being dangerous) as the cause of or outcome of a behaviour (for example, being dangerous) is misleading and inappropriate; the state or behaviour enacted by an individual logically cannot be the cause of the individual's state or behaviour (Kriegman, 2007). Through implying causality via terminology such as this a practitioner may be unconsciously influenced to create causal theories relating to the case at hand and issues may arise when these causal theories are influenced by erroneous or leading information, resulting in bias in the assessment (Kim and Ahn, 2002). It is therefore suggested, in line with Cooke et al's (2001) recommendation, that the term 'dangerousness' is avoided and that 'violence [or other] risk' should instead be the focus of an assessment.

Recent discussions within forensic mental health and law enforcement and public health literatures have discussed the replacement of the term 'risk' in specific forms of assessments, such as safety planning when assessing risk of self-inflicted violence and self-inflicted death (Cole-King and Platt, 2017), or by discussing a person's vulnerability rather than risk (for example, Enang et al, 2022). These are important considerations as the framing removes the negative connotation that is often associated with the term 'risk' and focuses the assessment on the person within their context and on care/risk-management planning. While the current chapter will retain a focus on risk assessment, this is something that readers ought to be mindful of – the use of 'risk' within the current chapter is not inherently negative as per the ISO (2018) definition presented earlier.

Approaches to risk assessment

The remainder of the chapter will outline and discuss the three main approaches to risk assessment used within the criminal justice context: the clinical judgement approach, the actuarial approach and the structured professional judgement (SPJ) approach. Through discussing the core aspects of these approaches, their strengths and their weaknesses, the reader should be able to critically evaluate the usefulness of the approaches for their own practice and needs. This chapter is not exhaustive and a more detailed discussion is available in Murray and Thomson (2010).

Clinical judgement

The clinical judgement approach to risk assessment is the oldest and one of the most commonly used approaches (Cooke et al, 2001). In their survey, Singh et al (2014) found that half of their sample used clinical judgement approaches to assess risk rather than using a tool, and that on average these assessments took participants 2.8 hours to complete. The clinical judgement approach is essentially where the assessment is made using the practitioner's judgement without the use of a formal tool (Murray and Enang, 2022). This approach is also called the unaided clinical judgement approach, the clinical reasoning approach or the practitioner judgement approach.

Despite some authors in the 1980s and 1990s calling for clinical judgement approaches to be completely replaced with more rigid, standardised risk assessment tools (Quinsey et al, 1998), and a commonly cited figure of two out of every three clinical assessments of risk being wrong (Monahan, 1984; see a full discussion on this specific argument within the literature in Murray and Thomson, 2010), this approach clearly remains important in the everyday practice of risk professionals. Practitioners using this approach apply their expertise (developed through education and training), experience and intuition (developed through years of practice) in combination with their knowledge of the person and the person's situation to develop a holistic interpretation of risk, to inform the intervention and risk-management planning (Murray and Enang, 2022).

This is a highly idiographic approach which is difficult to externally assess in terms of objectivity in the decision-making process. Some also argue that, like all human decision making, this approach is prone to unconscious biases within the assessment which may negatively affect the outcome (Viljoen et al, 2021). In response to these concerns around the subjectivity and accuracy of clinical judgements of violence risk, a range of tools were developed which aimed to predict the likelihood of a risk occurring. This predictive approach is known as actuarial risk assessment.

Actuarial assessment

The actuarial approach to risk assessment is designed to reduce the variation between and within clinician judgements of risk, replacing the clinical judgement with an assessment of likelihood based on the completion of a risk assessment tool. Actuarial tools contain risk factors which are drawn from the academic literature and which have been determined through rigorous study to be statistically predictive of the form of risk being assessed (Fazel et al, 2012). These risk factors are weighted within the scoring of the tool and the final scoring provides an indication of the likelihood of the risk occurring within a set timeframe or a scoring for how at risk the individual is.

Most actuarial tools measure only static risk factors (for example, historical risk factors such as pre-offence history). Most also do not consider dynamic risk factors (that is, risk factors that are changeable, such as socioeconomic status). This has led to criticisms of the approach for being too rigid and lacking sensitivity to change, and for being poorly applicable to populations outside the sample on which the tools were based (Scott and Resnick, 2006). An important ruling (*Ewert* v *Canada* 2018) challenged the appropriateness of the use of well-established and widely used actuarial measures for Indigenous people within Canada due to cultural differences and potential for bias. It is of great importance when selecting a risk assessment tool, actuarial or otherwise, to ensure that it is culturally appropriate for the person being assessed to prevent unintended harm.

A great deal of literature seeks to compare the predictive accuracy of clinical assessments to that of actuarial tools (for example, Viljoen et al, 2021). These comparisons, while interesting from an academic perspective, present a false comparison. The purpose of clinical approaches to risk assessment is not, and has never been, to predict likelihoods of risks occurring. Instead, these approaches seek to inform intervention, care and risk-management planning to prevent and reduce risks from occurring. A successful risk-management strategy devised from a risk assessment using a clinical judgement approach should ideally lead to the original assessment being 'incorrect' – the aim is to reduce risk, not keep it constant. This may then be turned around to form a key critique of the actuarial approach. Their focus on predicting risk does not (generally speaking) helpfully inform the risk-management planning stages which practitioners need. In addition, their focus on mainly historical or static risk factors reduces their helpfulness in identifying which of the more changeable, dynamic or situational risk factors may be key in reducing a person's risk.

Structured professional judgement

Taking the two approaches into consideration and trying to balance the strengths of having an evidence-based and standardised objective assessment tool with the need for clinical flexibility, the SPJ approach was developed. It is often posited as representing a step towards more effective decision-making practice, being based upon combining empirically established risk factors with clinical judgement (Douglas et al, 2003).

In this approach, the clinician is supported through the use of a set of risk (and/or protective) factors which have been drawn from the evidence base. Validated SPJ tools are usually accompanied with dedicated training and detailed instruction manuals. This approach is not a 'check-box' approach and does not seek to predict risk. SPJ tools are used as guidelines to support and structure the assessment (Douglas et al, 2003). These take longer to complete than unaided clinical judgement assessments (7.8 hours on average; Singh et al, 2014), reducing their practical utility in busy areas of clinical and frontline practice. However, the process is more involved and leads to an objective and traceable decision-making process which is based on evidence-informed risk and protective factors.

The SPJ approach has several steps, as outlined more fully in Hart et al (2016). The key steps for SPJ are relatively consistent across different tools and across the application of the SPJ approach within risk assessment, and are summarised briefly as follows. Firstly, information gathering, including case reports, related documentation and speaking to the person and others associated with the case. Secondly, using the SPJ tool (or relevant evidence base) to draw out from the case information about which risk factors are present and whether these are relevant for the risk being assessed. These are structured under a series of headings or 'risk factors' for ease of reference. The practitioner then engages with the information and draws together the key information to form a meaningful interpretation of the risks and protective factors, how these interact and under which circumstances, via a process of formulation. In formulation, the practitioner is not simply summarising or listing information, but instead should be seeking to better understand the key information, to identify any causal influences on behaviour and to help inform management and intervention planning (Hart et al, 2016). Following this, a process of scenario planning and risk-management planning is carried out, considering different contextual scenarios and possible outcomes that may occur. The practitioner deliberates on how best to mitigate the potential risks, apply successful interventions and support the most optimal outcome for the person in a realistic manner for each scenario.

This approach is considered advantageous as the practitioner is given some level of flexibility and discretion (Hart, 2000). In addition, working to non-weighted guidelines that are easily adapted to new cases means the factors on which the final judgement is made are explicit, and as with actuarial tools, the level of inter-rater reliability is higher than would be the case with clinical judgement alone.

Conclusions

To summarise, there is no single 'best' approach to risk assessment; each has strengths and weaknesses depending on the purpose of the assessment and the time and resources available. Critically considering the suitability of the assessment approach/tool being applied is imperative in improving risk assessment practice. Risk is complex, as is risk assessment, and adequate risk assessment requires training, time, careful thought and consideration for its most optimal use in practice. Importantly, when considering risk assessment practitioners should consider not only person-focused risk factors but also situational and protective factors to allow a holistic and meaningful assessment and management plan to be developed.

References
Cole-King, A. and Platt, S. (2017) 'Suicide prevention for physicians: identification, intervention and mitigation of risk', *Medicine*, 45(3): 131–4, DOI: https://doi.org/10.1016/j.mpmed.2016.12.012.

Cooke, D.J., Michie, C. and Ryan, J. (2001) 'Evaluating risk for violence: a preliminary study of the HCR-20, PCL-R and VRAG in a Scottish prison sample', Scottish Prison Service Occasional Paper Series 5/2001.

De Vries Robbé, M., de Vogel, V. and Douglas, K.S. (2013). 'Risk factors and protective factors: a two-sided dynamic approach to violence risk assessment', *Journal of Forensic Psychiatry & Psychology*, 24(4): 440–57, DOI: https://doi.org/10.1080/14789949.2013.818162.

Douglas, K.S., Ogloff, J.R.P. and Hart, S.D. (2003) 'Evaluation of a model of violence risk assessment among forensic psychiatric patients', *Psychiatric Services*, 54(10): 1372–9, DOI: https://doi.org/10.1176/appi.ps.54.10.1372.

Enang, I., Murray, J., Dougall, N., Aston, E., Wooff, A., Heyman, I. and Grandison, G. (2022) 'Vulnerability assessment across the frontline of law enforcement and public health: a systematic review', *Policing and Society*, 32(4): 540–59, DOI: https://doi.org/10.1080/10439463.2021.1927025.

Fazel, S., Singh, J.P., Doll, H. and Grann, M. (2012) 'Use of risk assessment instruments to predict violence and antisocial behaviour in 73 samples involving 24 827 people: systematic review and meta-analysis', *British Medical Journal*, 345: e4692, DOI: https://doi.org/10.1136/bmj.e4692.

Felton, A. and Stacey, G. (2008) 'Positive risk taking: a framework for practice', in T. Stickley and T. Basset (eds) *Learning about Mental Health Practice*, Chichester: Wiley, pp 195–212.

Hart, S.D. (2000) 'The promise and peril of sex offender risk assessment', R. Laws (Chair), Structured professional guidelines for assessing risk in sexual offenders. Symposium presented at the Annual Conference of the Association for the Treatment of Sexual Abusers, San Diego, CA.

Hart, S.D., Douglas, K.S. and Guy, L.S. (2016) 'The structured professional judgment approach to violence risk assessment: origins, nature, and advances', in L. Craig and M. Rettenberger (eds) *The Wiley Handbook on the Theories, Assessment, Treatment of Sexual Offending, Vol. 2: Assessment*, Chichester: Wiley, pp 643–66.

Horgan, N.R. (2021) 'Critical considerations in the development and interpretation of common risk language', *Psychiatry, Psychology and Law*, 28(2): 218–34, DOI: https://doi.org/10.1080/13218719.2020.1767719.

ISO (International Organization for Standardization) (2018) 'ISO31000:2018 risk management: guidelines', [online] Available from: https://www.iso.org/standard/65694.html [Accessed 15 April 2021].

Kelley, H.H. (1967) 'Attribution theory in social psychology', in D. Levine (ed) *Nebraska Symposium on Motivation*, Lincoln: University of Nebraska Press, pp 192–38.

Kim, N.S. and Ahn, W. (2002) 'Clinical psychologists' theory-based representations of mental disorders predict their diagnostic reasoning and memory', *Journal of Experimental Psychology: General*, 131(4): 451–76, DOI: https://doi.org/10.1037/0096-3445.131.4.451.

Kriegman, D. (2007) 'Affidavit in support of a Daubert challenge to the admissibility of scientific testimony to support Sexually Dangerous Person commitment under the Adam Walsh Act', Case 1:06-mc-PBS Documents 12–1 to 12–13, filed 16 May.

Litwack, T.R., Zapf, P.A., Groscup, J.L. and Hart, S.D. (2006) 'Violence risk assessments: Research, legal, and clinical considerations', in I.B. Weiner and A.K. Hess (eds) *The Handbook of Forensic Psychology*, Chichester: Wiley & Sons, pp 487–533.

Monahan, J. (1984) 'The prediction of violent behaviour: toward a second generation of theory and policy', *American Journal of Psychiatry*, 141: 458–71, DOI: https://doi.org/10.1176/ajp.141.1.10.

Murray, J. and Thomson, M.E. (2010) 'Clinical judgment in violence risk assessment', *Europe's Journal of Psychology*, 1: 128–49, DOI: https://doi.org/10.5964/ejop.v6i1.175.

Murray, J. and Enang, I. (2022) *Conceptualising Risk Assessment and Management across the Public Sector: From Theory to Practice*, Bingley: Emerald Publishing.

Murray, J., Thomson, M.E., Cooke, D.J. and Charles, K.E. (2011) 'Influencing expert judgment: attributions of crime causality', *Legal and Criminological Psychology*, 16(1): 126–43, DOI: https://doi.org/10.1348/135532510X490183.

Quinsey, V.L., Harris, G.T., Rice, M.E. and Cormier, C.A. (1998) *Violent Offenders: Appraising and Managing Risk* (4th edn), Washington, DC: American Psychological Association.

Scott, C.L. and Resnick, P.J. (2006) 'Violence risk assessment in persons with mental illness', *Aggression and Violent Behaviour*, 11(6): 598–611, DOI: https://doi.org/10.1016/j.avb.2005.12.003.

Singh, J.P., Desmarais, S.L., Hurducas, C., Arbach-Lucioni, K., Condermarin, C., Dean, K., Doyle, M., Folino, J.O., Godoy-Cervera, V., Grann, M., Mei Yee Ho, R., Large, M.M., Hjort Nielsen, L., Pham, T.H., Rebocho, M.F., Reeves, K.A., Rettenberger, M., de Ruiter, C., Seewald, K. and Otto, R.K. (2014) 'International perspectives on the practical application of violence risk assessment: a global survey of 44 countries', *International Journal of Forensic Mental Health*, 13(3): 193–206, DOI: https://doi.org/10.1080/14999013.2014.922141.

Viljoen, J.L., Vargen, L.M., Cochrane, D.M., Jonnson, M.R., Goossens, I. and Monjazeb, S. (2021) 'Do structured risk assessments predict violent, any, and sexual offending better than unstructured judgment? An umbrella review', *Psychology, Public Policy, and Law*, 27(1): 79–97, DOI: https://doi.org/10.1037/law0000299.

27

Criminal injustice

Amy Hughes-Stanley

Introduction

The criminal justice system (CJS) is thought to be rooted within values of fairness, equality and due process. However, there are many facets of criminal justice which can be considered unjust. This chapter provides an overview and exploration of some of the key issues concerning the criminal *injustice* system.

What is a miscarriage of justice?

A miscarriage of justice occurs when the criminal process fails to work in a way which achieves a 'just' outcome. This may be for victims, offenders or the community that is impacted by a crime (Belloni and Hodgson, 2000). Put simply, a miscarriage of justice is a breach of an individual's rights by the state or its agencies (Poyser and Grieve, 2018). Naughton (cited in Case et al, 2017) highlights that much of the focus regarding miscarriages of justice relates to the overturning of wrongful convictions. However, this is just a small area of the broad spectrum of criminal injustices which occur daily. As such, it is important to note that criminal injustice can occur at any stage of the criminal justice process: during the first stage of identifying a potential suspect, the investigation process, pressing charges, and prosecuting and punishing offenders (Poyser and Grieve, 2018).

Police injustices

Within policing practice, injustices can occur when police power is deliberately misused; however, injustices can also occur throughout the performance of seemingly routine activities, such as a stop and search. These forms of injustice are often seen as invisible and can be difficult to challenge (Belloni and Hodgson, 2000). An area of significant injustice is the overpolicing of, and disproportionate use of stop and search against, minority ethnic populations in England and Wales. Black people are stopped and searched at more than eight times the rate of White people, despite the 'find' rate for drugs being lower for Black people than for the White population. This suggests that the disproportionate targeting of those from minority ethnic groups is not the result of a higher crime rate among minority ethnic populations, but rather is a result of ethnic profiling and racial bias among officers (Shiner et al, 2018). Bowling and Phillips (cited in Case et al, 2017) note that while there is overt racial profiling within the police force, there are also ways in which supposedly neutral police practices and policies reinforce systemic racial inequalities. For example, as police decisions to grant bail can be based upon a suspect's housing status, this can work against people from minority ethnic backgrounds who, as a group, are more likely to have no fixed abode due to socioeconomic adversity, which disproportionately affects those from these groups (Case et al, 2017). In this way, racial and class oppression interact to compound ethnic minorities' experiences of criminal injustice, which is described by Roberts (cited in Case et al, 2017) as a form of ethnic penalty. Moreover, this treatment demonstrates what many have termed institutional racism within the police force (Case et al, 2017; Newburn, 2017; Shiner et al, 2018).

Another area of concern in relation to criminal injustice is deaths of people from minority ethnic backgrounds while in police custody. The work of the charity Inquest, which monitors and provides advice and support to those affected by deaths in custody, has been particularly influential in bringing public attention to this issue (Case et al, 2017). Research conducted by the Home Office (Leigh et al, cited in Newburn, 2017, p 859) found that 'over one-third of cases in which a Black detainee died occurred in circumstances in which police actions may have been a factor ... this compared with only 4 per cent of cases where the detainee was White'. In England and Wales numerous cases of deaths of people from minority ethnic groups in police custody have occurred within recent history, most notably those of Stephen McCarthy, who in November 1970 was allegedly assaulted by police officers and later died in hospital in January 1971; Liddle Towers, who, in 1976, according to eyewitness reports, was severely beaten by police officers and died three weeks later; and Christopher Adler, who died in police custody in Hull in 1998 (Newburn, 2017). Official responses to such deaths in custody can be extremely limited. For example, in the case of Sean Rigg, who died in police custody in Brixton, South London, in 2008, his family are still fighting for justice (Case et al, 2017).

Court injustices

Injustices which occur at the level of the police are compounded within the criminal courts in England and Wales. While miscarriages of justice are more commonly associated with high-profile cases tried in the Crown Court, Belloni and Hodgson (2000) note that injustices also occur within magistrates' courts – arguably at a higher rate. As most criminal offences taken to court in England and Wales are summary offences, the magistrates' courts hear over 95 per cent of all criminal cases and rely heavily upon the use of police evidence in order to try cases. McConville et al (cited in Belloni and Hodgson, 2000) argues that magistrates are ill-equipped to challenge the reliability of police evidence and are in fact keenly inclined to believe police accounts without question. This results in what Gifford (cited in Belloni and Hodgson, 2000) describes as the reversal of the burden of proof, in which defendants must prove their innocence against evidence provided by the police, rather than being found guilty beyond reasonable doubt. With this in mind, criminal injustices may be understood as a product of a flawed adversarial system of justice, whereby convincing a jury or magistrate(s) of guilt beyond reasonable doubt is prioritised over truth (Case et al, 2017).

Moreover, the very structure of the magistrates' courts' hearing of criminal cases can create an environment for injustices to flourish. Defendants in summary cases are not given access to the prosecution's case prior to their hearing, there are long delays in bringing complex cases to court (even more so after the onset of the COVID-19 pandemic) and there are no transcripts of trials heard within the court. These conditions create a situation in which injustice is difficult to challenge and in which appealing magistrates' decisions is increasingly difficult (Belloni and Hodgson, 2000). While injustices that occur in magistrates' courts may not be seen as serious miscarriages of justice, or receive much public attention, Poyser and Grieve (2018) insist that the harms generated from these injustices are just as damaging as those which arise within the Crown Court.

As well as administrative problems which amount to injustices within the criminal courts (as discussed), structural issues such as racism, sexism and classism also contribute to a court system which is arguably unjust. In a landmark study which analysed sentencing patterns from five Crown Court centres in the West Midlands, Hood (cited in Newburn, 2017) found that Black defendants were around 5 per cent more likely to be sentenced to prison than their White counterparts. Moreover, Hood (cited in Newburn, 2017, p 857) also discovered that the treatment of Black defendants was poorer than that of White defendants, in relation to which he stated: 'when one contrasts the overall treatment meted out to Black Afro-Caribbean males one is left wondering whether it is not a result of different racial stereotypes operating on the perceptions of some judges'. Almost two decades later, racism in the courts does not appear to have improved. The 2017 Lammy Review (cited in Shiner et al, 2018), which was an independent review into the treatment of, and outcomes for, minority ethnic individuals in the CJS, similarly asserted that even when factors such as previous convictions are taken into account, minority ethnic defendants at the Crown Court are more likely to receive custodial sentences for drug offences than White defendants. Within both magistrates' courts and the Crown Court, there is an ethnic disparity through every form of sentencing outcome, including immediate custody (Shiner et al, 2018).

Gender also plays a role in creating unjust outcomes in the courts. Regarding women, there are competing narratives about their treatment within the CJS; on the one hand, they are seen to be treated more leniently, and on the other, more harshly (Case et al, 2017; Newburn, 2017). There are also competing evidence bases concerning their treatment in court. Hedderman and Hough (cited in Newburn, 2017), for example, argue that there is limited evidence that women are dealt with in a more severe manner in the courts than men; however, research conducted by Steward (cited in Newburn, 2017) regarding remand decision making in magistrates' courts found that women who defied normative gender roles were *more* likely to be remanded to custody. This, according to Heidensohn (cited in Newburn, 2017) is due to the courts operating on a standard whereby women who deviate from typical femininity (such as through lawbreaking, by being single mothers or not conforming to heterosexuality) are treated more punitively.

Prison injustices

While those from minority ethnic groups experience institutional racism and discriminatory treatment from the police and the courts, they are also over-represented within the prison system. Bowling and Phillips (cited in Case et al, 2017) argue that this visible over-representation is the culmination of the direct and indirect discrimination that people from minority ethnic groups face at each step of the CJS. Those from a Black and mixed ethnic background are the most likely to be sentenced to prison (Case et al, 2017), with Black people sentenced to immediate custody for drug offences at 9.1 times the rate of White people but given suspended sentences at only 5.6 times the rate of White people (Shiner et al, 2018). Moreover, the incarceration rate for Black people is four times higher than that of White people, and those from minority ethnic backgrounds have significantly worse experiences of custody (Newburn, 2017). For example, during the 2008 Race Review (cited in Case et al, 2017, p 277), which was concerned with implementing racial equality into the prison system, the National Offender Management Service found that 'Black prisoners were 30 per cent more likely than White prisoners to be on basic regime without privileges, 50 per cent more likely to be held in segregation, and 60 per cent more likely to have force used against them.' This discussion paints a stark picture of the channels of racial injustice experienced by people from minority ethnic groups throughout the so-called justice system.

The provision of prison for women has also been critiqued as unjust. Following the deaths of six women in HMP Styal over a 13-month period, Baroness Corston was commissioned by the Home Office to conduct a review of the CJS for women with particular vulnerabilities. She found that 'women have been marginalized in a system largely designed by men for men', which meant that there was a lack of understanding of women's gendered needs and how these were different from those of the male population (cited in Newburn, 2017, p 882). Baroness Corston made 43 recommendations following her review: that the strip-searching of women on entry to prison should be abolished, that the government should replace women's prisons with small, geographically dispersed, multifunctional custodial centres, and that custody for women should be reserved only for the most violent and dangerous offenders. Unfortunately, only two of the 43 recommendations were implemented and the report made little operational change to prisons for women.

In 2018, the Ministry of Justice (MoJ) launched the Female Offender Strategy. The strategy highlighted the unique position of women in the CJS and noted, like the 2007 Corston Report, that women offenders have higher levels of need than their male counterparts. The Female Offender Strategy (MoJ, 2018) noted that levels of self-harm in women's prisons, at that time, were nearly five times higher than those in the men's prison estate. An aim of the Female Offender Strategy was therefore to drastically reduce incidences of self-harm in custody. Despite such goals, self-harm incidents have in fact increased in the women's prison estate since the publication of the Female Offender Strategy. In December 2021, data from the MoJ revealed that over the previous 12 months the rate of self-harm incidents per 1,000 prisoners had increased by 4 per cent in female establishments, yet had decreased by 1 per cent in male establishments. As such, in comparison to the male estate, which saw 561 incidents of self-harm incidents per 1,000 prisoners, the rate of self-harm was over six times higher in the female estate, with 3,697 self-harm incidents per 1,000 prisoners (MoJ, 2021). Such high rates of self-harm across the women's prison estate, particularly in comparison to the male estate, suggests that the state is failing in its duty of care towards women housed within its prison establishments.

Moreover, the patterns of racial inequality evidenced throughout the CJS are also replicated within the female prison population. As such, 'ethnic minority groups represent around 29 per cent of the female prison population, compared with 22 per cent of the male population' (Newburn, 2017, p 882). Black women (as well as men from Black and minority ethnic groups) were consistently more likely to receive a custodial sentence for drug offences than those of a White background. This suggests that minority ethnic women not only experience gendered injustice within a prison system designed by and for men, but also racial injustice within a prison system in which those from minority ethnic backgrounds experience worse treatment and outcomes (Case et al, 2017).

Conclusion

To conclude, as demonstrated throughout this chapter the CJS in England and Wales cannot be assumed to deliver justice for all. It may be argued that the very structure of adversarial justice lends itself to questions regarding the aim of justice; is it to seek truth or to win over a jury? Perhaps this is best demonstrated by the many attempts to reform criminal justice, despite which inequality and injustice persist. Given that the CJS is merely a microcosm of society, in which classism, sexism, racism and many other forms of oppression are still very much alive, it is no wonder that the justice system is flawed.

References
Belloni, F. and Hodgson, J. (2000) *Criminal Injustice: An Evaluation of the Criminal Justice Process in Britain*, Basingstoke: Macmillan.

Case, S., Johnson, P., Manlow, D., Smith, R. and Williams, K. (2017) *Criminology*, Oxford: Oxford University Press.

MoJ (Ministry of Justice) (2018) 'Female Offender Strategy', [online] Available at: https://assets.publishing.service.gov.uk/government/uploads/system/uploads/attachment_data/file/719819/female-offender-strategy.pdf [Accessed 10 June 2022].

MoJ (Ministry of Justice) (2021) 'Safety in custody statistics, England and Wales: deaths in prison custody to March 2022, assaults and self-harm to December 2021', [online] Available at: https://www.gov.uk/government/statistics/safety-in-custody-quarterly-update-to-december-2021/safety-in-custody-statistics-england-and-wales-deaths-in-prison-custody-to-march-2022-assaults-and-self-harm-to-december-2021#contents [Accessed 10 June 2022].

Newburn, T. (2017) *Criminology* (3rd edn), Abingdon: Routledge.

Poyser, S. and Grieve, J.D. (2018) 'Miscarriages of justice: what can we learn', in A. Griffiths and R. Milne (eds) *The Psychology of Criminal Investigation: From Theory to Practice*, Abingdon: Routledge, pp 24–44.

Shiner, M., Carre, Z., Delsol, R. and Eastwood, N. (2018) *The Colour of Injustice: 'Race', Drugs and Law Enforcement in England and Wales*, London: StopWatch.

28

Criminal justice:
future directions

Noel Cross

Introduction: criminal justice at a crossroads?

Currently, criminal justice in England and Wales feels very much as if it is at a crossroads. The impact of the ongoing COVID pandemic on criminal justice continues to be immense. In January 2021, a joint report by the chief inspectors of police, the Crown Prosecution Service, and HM Prison and Probation Service estimated a backlog of outstanding court cases of close to half a million, with many Crown Court cases already delayed to 2022 and thousands more people stranded in the limbo of remand. Elsewhere, criminal justice's scope for harm and discrimination has been highlighted in a range of different ways. Research by Bebbington et al (2021) re-emphasised the greatly increased prevalence of mental illness among ex-prisoners, adding to the crisis of COVID-19 infection rates among current prisoners. Government crime statistics suggested a drop in property offences during lockdown but a sharp increase in rates of domestic violence. The largest-scale anti-racism demonstrations in recent memory have taken place across the country, as part of the Black Lives Matter movement and as a response to police racial discrimination in the UK and internationally. Further demonstrations took place in March 2021 in response to the unlawful killing of Sarah Everard in London. All these developments pointed not only to the presence of deeply embedded structural discrimination on the grounds of race, gender, class and sexuality in English society, inside and outside the criminal justice system (CJS), but also to the intolerance of that discrimination by at least some sections of society.

Which strategies is the state using to respond to the criminal justice crisis?

The response of the state, however, has been characterised by the criminalisation of social problems and a punitive approach. Using the typologies of Cavadino et al (2020), this approach is Strategy A, involving harsh and exclusionary criminal justice policy. Cavadino et al's (2020) other strategies are Strategy B, characterised by using managerialist and bureaucratic policies designed to make criminal justice as cost-effective as possible; and Strategy C, which prioritises the human rights of perpetrators, victims and potential victims of crime, minimises punishment, and promotes fairness and inclusivity within criminal justice. The police responded aggressively to the protests mentioned earlier, regularly using tactics such as kettling (a method of crowd control in which police officers form a cordon around a group of people so as to prevent those people from leaving a particular area) against unarmed and non-violent protestors. The UK government has introduced new legislation (the Police, Crime, Sentencing and Courts Act 2022) which has greatly expanded police powers to limit and prevent legitimate protest. The government also did very little to reduce the prison population despite the obvious health risks posed by COVID-19, either through early release or by directing courts to use custodial sentencing less. Taking a more long-term view, the prison population in England and Wales remains high, with average prison sentences increasing in length and usage of community sentences decreasing. There are also plans to increase the harshness of sentencing for serious and persistent offenders and to build more prisons – all hallmarks of Cavadino et al's Strategy A.

A utopian blueprint for criminal justice reform

It therefore seems an appropriate time to imagine alternative futures for criminal justice, based on an approach which goes beyond current government strategies of punitivism and repression and which draws on evidence of public resistance to such strategies in recent public protests. The remainder of this chapter offers a utopian and normative blueprint for shaping the future of criminal justice, using principles based on Cavadino et al's (2020) Strategy C. Four of these principles address the external context of crime and criminal justice and three address issues internal to the operation of criminal justice itself.

Principle 1 concerns the reform of criminal law to improve justice and effectiveness. Criminal law must be the starting point for the reform of criminal justice because the enforcement of criminal law to maintain social order is the main function of CJSs. The proposal here is the creation of a Criminal Code covering all criminal offences and defences. Such a move would end the involvement of common law in defining the shape of criminal law and reorganise criminal law on more principled and consistent grounds. These principles should take a holistic view of what causes harm in society. The principles should also recognise the ways in which responsibility for crime is limited by social exclusion and vulnerability. As such, the principles should also use defences to crime to limit liability on the grounds of social exclusion. One example of the outcomes that such an approach might produce is an increase in the minimum age of responsibility for crime, given the scientific evidence on continuing brain and cognitive development throughout the teenage years. Focusing on harm allows the consideration of socially harmful activities which are normally outside criminal law's boundaries, such as corporate crime and state crime. Levels of harm caused by different behaviours could be reviewed regularly by a panel of legal and academic experts, from the point of view of whether the harms should be criminalised and what the appropriate punishment for them should be. Minor offences could become formally dealt with administratively (as in Germany and elsewhere), resulting in fines but avoiding the stigma of criminal justice, as well as the financial costs associated with court hearings.

Principle 2 involves education – education of the public about the true nature and effectiveness of criminal justice policy and practice and about the limits of what criminal justice can do about crime. An expansive human rights approach to crime and criminal justice recognises the social roots of crime in factors such as social and economic inequality, neoliberal and materialistic economic policies, and insufficient support for vulnerable communities who are more at risk of both committing and being victimised by crime (Reiner, 2016). It would give rights to reasonable standards of education and healthcare. Such an approach would take lessons from socioeconomic policies used by countries which have a greater level of social happiness, less socioeconomic inequality and lower reported crime rates – such as Finland for example (Dorling and Koljonen, 2020).

Principle 3 involves greater trust of experts with specialist knowledge of crime and criminal justice from outside the criminal justice sector. This would mean a much stronger role being played in criminal justice policy development by reliable academic research evidence than is currently the case. It would also mean the clear consideration of both quantitative and qualitative academic data in policies on crime and criminal justice, through the direct involvement of academics in policy development as well as through the perspectives of practitioners working in key roles within CJSs. Principle 3 would also promote a 'public health' approach to criminal justice. It would draw on the expertise of practitioners from health and education sectors to provide a holistic response to the harm caused by crime, one which can provide alternatives to a criminal justice response on primary, secondary and tertiary prevention levels. A 'public health' approach could and should target whole populations through education and preventative work, not just particular 'at risk' individuals. Projects such as Violence Reduction Units in Scotland and elsewhere, and the safeguarding-focused domestic violence initiative Operation Provide in Lancashire, show how a multi-agency 'public health' approach can be used as an effective response to crime that goes beyond the punitive use of a CJS which deals with only a small percentage of criminal activity.

Principle 4 advocates a more proactive use of technology to serve the aims of criminal justice. The COVID-19 pandemic has forced courts to rely on remote hearings, but the technology allowing this to happen encountered problems following the first lockdown of spring 2020, causing further delays. Greater investment in reliable technology and online document sharing could save both time and money in the future. COVID-19 crime statistics also highlighted the endemic nature of cybercrime in society in the UK. In line with Principles 2 and 3 (previously discussed) and Principle 5 (to be discussed next), the police could share the response to cybercrime with specialist technology experts for a more effective public education, prevention and prosecution strategy.

Principle 5 involves reform of the police in line with the 'public health' strategy defined under Principle 3. This would involve formal merging of the police with workers from the other emergency services to improve community safety, responding to the harm caused by crime in a public health-focused approach which recognises the rights of both perpetrators and victims. A review of the Police and Criminal Evidence Act 1984, as well as other legislation governing police powers, should take place in line with public health and human rights values. Finally, and in recognition of recent public unrest about police discrimination and lack of accountability, police and crime commissioner roles should be abolished in favour of a greater role for local authorities in relation to how police resources are allocated in each area. Local-level, independent community panels should respond to allegations of police wrongdoing in place of formal police complaints agencies.

Principle 6 involves the reform of court processes around a restorative justice approach, which would provide mandatory diversion from the court process for less serious offences and optional diversion from court for offences of intermediate seriousness. The court process would be activated only where restorative justice was not suitable or supported by the parties involved. Restorative justice does, and should, involve a range of different forms of intervention, but it also promotes the human rights of both perpetrators and victims in line with Cavadino et al's (2020) Strategy C approach, by including them both in the process of responding to crime. For those more serious cases which did necessitate a formal court process, sentencing should prioritise restoration and rehabilitation and should take place in line with a comprehensive set of guidelines developed by the Sentencing Council. These guidelines could use a living standard approach of the type suggested by von Hirsch and Jareborg (1991) to assess harm and establish proportionality between crime and sentence, but would aim to reduce the use of imprisonment as a sentence to the status of last resort and would also remove minimum and mandatory sentences as a means of reducing the prison population and average sentence length. Courts should use the template of the North Liverpool Community Justice Centre – in operation between 2005 and 2013 – in taking a problem-solving approach to criminal justice, engaging with agencies inside and outside criminal justice in making decisions and offering resources to, and engagement with, the local community.

Principle 7 addresses methods of criminal justice punishment, including probation and prison activities. Here, recognising the importance of accountability for the deprivation of liberty which criminal justice has the power to impose, privatisation should be scaled back and eventually abolished. Probation work, based on the academic literature in the field of desistance, should prioritise positive compliance with the conditions of community punishment, as well as reintegration into the wider community after punishment has ended. In line with Principle 6, a much-reduced prison population would allow a focus on therapeutic intervention, of the kind seen in prisons such as HMP Grendon, throughout the prison estate. The kind of public health approach promoted earlier on in the discussion would also allow for greater diversion of those with mental health or substance use issues away from prison and into health treatment and care systems. Prisons should be community based to reflect the community nature of courts under Principle 6, with maximum population numbers, minimum living conditions and a proactive grievance process, all enforced by statute law.

Conclusions: what are the chances of making utopia a criminal justice reality?

It could be argued that the reform programme set out earlier is hopelessly idealistic and utopian, never capable of realisation in the real world. Three points can be made in response to this argument. The first is that there is extensive evidence that the current, punitive approach to criminal justice is expensive, discriminatory and ineffective in terms of reducing the harm caused by crime and criminal justice. This evidence alone justifies alternative ways of thinking about these issues in the future. Secondly, current resistance to government and police policies and practices suggests an appetite for alternative thinking about criminal justice, especially among younger age groups. Thirdly and finally, no matter how fixed particular crime justice attitudes and policies may seem to be, it is always important to remember that, like the definition of crime itself, nothing is really inevitable in criminal justice policy and practice. Eighty years ago, Finland's crime rates and prison population were considerably higher than they are now, and many of the social and economic factors which explain Finland's current crime and prison rates (as well as explaining Finland's current status as the world's happiest country according to the World Happiness Index), such as low socioeconomic inequality and high levels of education and literacy, were not present. There is therefore reason for optimism about the future of criminal justice in England and Wales, however punitive and repressive its current status may be.

References

Bebbington, P.E., McManus, S., Coid, J.W., Garside, R. and Brugha, T. (2021) 'The mental health of ex-prisoners: analysis of the 2014 English National Survey of Psychiatric Morbidity', *Social Psychiatry and Psychiatric Epidemiology*, 56: 2083–93, DOI: https://doi.org/10.1007/s00127-021-02066-0.

Cavadino, M., Dignan, J., Mair, G. and Bennett, J. (2020) *The Penal System: An Introduction* (6th edn), London: SAGE.

Dorling, D. and Koljonen, A. (2020) *Finntopia: What We Can Learn from the World's Happiest Country*, Newcastle: Agenda Publishing.

Reiner, R. (2016) *Crime: The Mystery of the Common-Sense Concept*, Cambridge: Polity Press.

Von Hirsch, A. and Jareborg, N. (1991) 'Gauging criminal harm: a living-standard analysis', *Oxford Journal of Legal Studies*, 11(1): 1–38.

PART III

Police and policing

29

Policing:
past and present

Kate Bates

Policing in the 21st century is more complex and diverse than it has ever been. Yet to understand this, it is important to trace policing's history and evolution. For decades now academics, historians and criminologists alike have charted the creation and development of policing in the UK, but most focus mainly on the birth of the 'new' police in the early 19th century. While obviously a crucial period, 'policing', in one form or another, has existed ever since the emergence of ancient city-states, with the word itself deriving from the Greek *polis* meaning a body of citizens or citizenhood. Thus, the regulation and control of communities of people has always been at the very core of policing. However, as societies have changed and become more complex, so too have the practices and politics of the police.

Early policing: from medieval to metropolitan

In the Middle Ages (600–1350), the community was central to the enforcement of laws based upon customary practices and principles and was crucial in terms of criminal intervention. The people would police themselves in various ways, from retaliation via blood feuds, to methods such as the 'hue and cry', which involved the cooperation of the whole village in chasing and catching miscreants. These responsibilities were taken so seriously that the community would compensate the victim if the criminal managed to escape. These amateur methods adequately dealt with most crimes until the middle of the 14th century when the feudal system of existence began to fail. Local communities became unstable due to famines, plagues and the resultant labour shortage, and there was a need for more official control of crime. This is the period that witnesses the rise of the official, when the obligations for law enforcement transferred from the people to officers of the parish (Rawlings, 2003). The post of constable was created, whereby a local male would be appointed to police his local area and be answerable to a justice of the peace, who mainly came from the landowning gentry. This was the literal start of bringing people to justice. Another development during this period was the expansion of the watch, whereby every local community was required to appoint men to guard parish boundaries and patrol the streets. The watchman's main purpose was to maintain order by challenging those who were unknown to the community, or who appeared suspicious, especially at night.

This system remained the main form of local policing until well into the 18th century, when the expansion of towns and cities began to create challenges beyond the constable's and watchman's crude capabilities. The main problem was that these 'official' roles were mostly unpaid and increasingly unpopular to perform. Usually, ordinary householders would be appointed yearly to serve, and although increasingly given powers to stop, search and arrest, they could be incompetent or caught between their duties and diplomacy, since they were policing a population to which they would return as private citizens once their term of office was over. This could often lead to difficulties, and the constables, especially in more rural areas, would have to rely on their discretion when deciding which criminals to pursue or ignore. Despite this, the parish constables and men of the watch functioned sufficiently and their roles survived until well into the early 19th century. However, detention, not detection, was their main focus, and from the early to mid-1700s they had been joined by other players in policing, such as thief-takers and the Bow Street Runners. Based in London, both applied their skills to mainly private client work and the return of stolen property. For the thief-takers especially this became very lucrative work, as the rewards they received from grateful customers could be high. This tempted many to create their own opportunities, such as the Thief-Taker General Jonathan Wild who was executed in 1725 for receiving stolen goods (Godfrey and Lawrence, 2005). By the late 18th century, the Bow Street Runners, which had been created by the magistrate and novelist Henry Fielding, were joined by new street and horse patrols; this new policing force, funded in part by the government, became the most comprehensive outfit in the capital and by 1829 the number of its constables had reached 400 (Rawlings, 2003).

Thus, by the late 18th and early 19th centuries, policing was a combination of public and private schemes and many were content for it to remain so. Indeed, there had been continual resistance to repeated attempts at reform and a move towards a more centralised and government-controlled body. The landowning elite had long cherished their liberty and personal authority and were apprehensive of any threat to that. Also, they were suspicious that a larger and more organised police force would be too militarised and political in nature. There were also concerns about the cost, with many parishes and counties preferring to continue to fund their own policing arrangements rather than a police force over which they would have no control. However, criticisms about the old style of policing were also beginning to grow during this period, due to apparent rising surges in crime and disorder, and when Sir Robert Peel became Home Secretary in 1822 he was determined to transform policing as part of his plans for a new and improved criminal justice system (Emsley, 2003). Peel was a skilled politician and knew he had obstacles to overcome if he was to achieve this so, when the Metropolitan Police was established in 1829, he ensured several things. Firstly, the new constables would wear a blue uniform, as opposed to the red one worn by the army; secondly, they would be a professional and disciplined force answerable to, and overseen by, two commissioners, Charles Cowan and Richard Mayne;

thirdly, they would be unarmed except for wooden batons to be discreetly hidden under their coats; and lastly, and perhaps most importantly, the 'new' police would be recruited mainly from the working classes. Peel's strategy was to ensure that his police would gain public approval and legitimation by enshrining certain principles of law enforcement. His aim was that the police would serve to prevent crime and disorder by working with and for the public, and that his officers would be seen as impartial and approachable 'citizens in uniform'. It has been well documented, however, that the 'birth of the blues' was not so easily achieved and that there was continued resistance and resentment for several years, but ultimately there was an uneasy acceptance that the Metropolitan Police was here to stay (Bowling et al, 2019).

The decades following 1829 saw the spread of Peel's policing model across the whole country but this too was a fractious and contested process. The old systems and styles of policing were still functioning outside of the metropolis and many local boroughs and counties were reluctant for that to change. They wished to remain in control of their own law enforcement arrangements and were sceptical that the new police would be any improvement on these. However, in 1835, the government passed the Municipal Corporations Act, which required all incorporated boroughs to set up police forces under the control of a watch committee who would be responsible for supervising appropriate policing for their communities. Further legislation soon followed under the 1839 Rural Constabulary Act, which empowered counties to establish police forces if they so desired. It was not until the mid-1850s that further moves were made to establish more centralised control when the County and Borough Police Act of 1856 was enacted and mandated that all provinces had to form a police force. The Act also created an Inspectorate of Constabulary responsible for overseeing efficiency in the provincial police and for making annual reports to government. So, despite apparently acknowledging that local policing should be locally managed on one hand, on the other hand government was slowly creeping towards a system of centralised control without yet actually having the nerve to enforce it (Emsley, 2003).

The challenges and changes of modern policing

By the late 19th century, the new formation of policing was firmly embedded and it would take the two world wars to compel the need for further change. World War I (1914–18) saw the need for women officers and special constables to be introduced in order to replace the men who were fighting on the front. The lack of labour force and resources, as well as other wartime pressures, also led to the abolition and amalgamation of several smaller forces. The pressures placed upon the police during both wars was immense but did much to cement the cherished image of the British 'bobby' (Godfrey and Lawrence, 2005). Indeed, the immediate postwar period would see the peak of police popularity, but it was not to last. Social, economic and political changes, as well as rising crime rates, would lead to increased tensions between the police and public. Furthermore, by the 1960s, the policing institution had become embroiled in several corruption scandals and controversies leading to calls for more accountability and reform. The Police Act 1964 made changes to the way complaints against the police would be recorded and investigated, but further crises were soon to follow. Continued social challenges and changes to the way policing was implemented throughout the 1970s would annihilate the positive public image of the police and transform the 'citizen in uniform' to that of 'a firm within a firm' with criminal tendencies of its own (Bowling et al, 2019). The perceived increasing politicisation of the police would also have far-reaching repercussions, especially with regards to its public order response to the miners' strike and race riots of the early 1980s. A Royal Commission on Criminal Procedure was set up, which would lead to the implementation of the Police and Criminal Evidence Act (PACE) in 1984. PACE aimed to rebalance police powers with stringent safeguards against their abuse. In addition, the Crown Prosecution Service was created in 1985, which removed the responsibility of prosecuting offenders from the police and in so doing added an extra layer of accountability.

Despite these significant changes, the Metropolitan Police especially would continue to be the focus of major failings, culminating in the Macpherson Report in 1999, which found it to be institutionally racist following the murder of Stephen Lawrence. This, coupled with the realisation that crime was still rising despite substantial increases in government funding in the 1980s, meant that there was an obvious need for a fundamental shift in the attitudes and ambitions of the police. The result was the emergence of community safety initiatives and a renewed focus on crime prevention. The Crime and Disorder Act 1998 placed a statutory duty on chief constables, local and police authorities to cooperate in formulating and implementing a plan for the reduction of crime and disorder in their area. The emphasis now was on multi-agency partnerships in the fight against crime and on a determination to present policing as a public service, not a partisan force. In the 21st century there have continued to be considerable changes to policing. Notably, it has become increasingly pluralised and there is now a plethora of public and private organisations and agencies involved in the protection of society. For example, the Police Reform Act 2002 introduced community support officers and other accredited authority figures, such as neighbourhood wardens, to work alongside the police in a formal capacity (Newburn, 2003). Then, the Police Reform and Social Responsibility Act 2010 transformed police governance and re-localised policing further by creating the powerful role of police and crime commissioners, who are publicly elected, to hold chief constables and their local police to account and to ensure that they are answerable to the public they serve.

In charting the creation and development of policing over the centuries it is obvious that there have been major changes in policing's politics, practices and principles. Policing has always had to reflect and respond to the society it serves and throughout its history there have been times of challenge, crisis and controversy. However, in chronicling its past it is also evident that there are constants as well. The 'thin blue line' has always been fragile. There has been constant tension between policing and the government of the day, and the former has had to adapt to combine both public and private elements since its inception. More importantly though, the community has been at policing's very core, and the relationship between the two has been surprisingly cyclical – sometimes cooperating, sometimes controlled, but always crucial. In some ways, policing in the 21st century is more similar to Peel's vision of it being of the people and for the people than ever before.

References

Bowling, B., Reiner, R. and Sheptycki, J.W.E. (2019) *The Politics of the Police* (5th edn), Oxford: Oxford University Press.

Emsley, C. (2003) 'The birth and development of the police', in T. Newburn (ed) *The Handbook of Policing*, Cullompton: Willan, pp 66–83.

Godfrey, B. and Lawrence, P. (2005) *Crime and Justice 1750–1950*, Cullompton: Willan.

Newburn, T. (2003) 'Policing since 1945', in T. Newburn (ed) *The Handbook of Policing*, Cullompton: Willan, pp 84–106.

Rawlings, P. (2003) 'Policing before the police', in T. Newburn, (ed) *The Handbook of Policing*, Cullompton: Willan, pp 41–65.

30

Police and policing models

Adrian James and Vesa Huotari

Introduction

A plethora of structural and institutional factors influence individual and group behaviour, but the primary agents of social control are groups of people, sanctioned by the state according to its laws, to safeguard citizens and to arrest lawbreakers. It is to those bodies that the label 'police' ordinarily attaches. Britain's first public police force, London's Metropolitan Police, was established in 1829.

This chapter explores a pillar of policing in the UK, namely the institution's commitment to the principle of consent and to the traditional, community-centred policing model it inspires. The chapter also explores other policing models that emerged in the modern era and assesses whether they are intellectually coherent and conceptually cogent. Can these models offer alternative practically relevant models for policing?

The chapter will begin with a discussion of the UK policing model. Unlike the militarised, state-controlled model of 'policing by law' that developed in continental Europe, UK policing is founded on the principle of consent, enshrined in the 'Peelian Principles' (named after Home Secretary Sir Robert Peel, 1788–1850, the principal architect of UK's police service; their authorship is usually attributed to the force's first commissioners). Rather than *gens d'armes* (later *gendarmes*), armed representatives of the state who control by force, the UK's police officers are civilians in uniform. They are members of the public, paid to give attention to duties which, in the interests of security, welfare and community cohesion, are the responsibility of every citizen.

The principle underpins policing but its inherent contradictions have never been resolved. These contradictions include the fact that police work often is undertaken during conflict; that police officers alone are entitled to exercise force; and that there is often a lack of consent from those being policed to police action. Such contradictions are by-products of the service's genesis; the executive's promotion of democratic, reflexive policing was intended to overcome massive and widespread hostility to the new institution.

In that sense, this plan was successful. Opposition to the police was overcome slowly but progressively. Public support peaked in the 1950s, which scholars consider to be the 'golden era' of policing (Reiner, 2010). Although support for the institution has never reached that level since then, the UK's police are trusted by the majority of citizens.

Nevertheless, the world is not in stasis. Society is changing rapidly and fundamentally because of, among other factors, social fragmentation, an ageing and more diverse population, artificial intelligence and – as the COVID pandemic has shown – globalisation. Policing has had to change, to meet challenges such as the growth of organised transnational crime, increasing legislative and administrative burdens on the institution and its officers, and the widespread availability of sophisticated information technologies that offer communities new ways to hold the police to account, but also present criminals with many new ways to exploit the vulnerable.

Models of policing

The chapter will now consider different approaches to policing. The police have always recognised that they need communities' help to control crime and to keep them safe. Help will not be forthcoming if the institution's legitimacy is in doubt. In large part, maintaining legitimacy relies on convincing people that their police are effective, efficient, procedurally fair and at their service, regardless of their race, ethnicity, age or social status. Alternative or complementary models that promise greater effectiveness, efficiency, accessibility and fairness have emerged in the modern era.

Since the 1990s, the term intelligence-led policing (ILP) has been applied to 'crime-fighting' processes that rely on the efforts of specialists to collect and analyse data to produce narratives that inform patrol patterns and operational deployments. The term is also applied to the work of teams of specialists who use covert methods to target groups or individuals suspected of involvement in crime, usually serious organised crime. It is in this field that ILP methods are used most extensively.

Policy makers' enthusiasm for ILP was founded on its business-focused principles and on its promise to do more with less by employing a more targeted, coordinated and focused approach to policing problems. Police managers seem to value ILP for its rigour in analysing problems and in documenting solutions, in the form of knowledge products such as strategic and tactical assessments and problem and subject profiles (see James, 2013, 2014).

Evidence-based practice is the dominant policy-making paradigm around much of the world. Evidence-based tactics and methods, backed by rigorous empirical evidence, are increasingly seen as the trademark of true professions. They have a firm foothold in the policing sphere too (see Sherman, 2013; Lumsden and Goode, 2018; Fielding, 2020).

The College of Policing (CoP) is the professional body for policing in the UK (see Crawford, 2020). Evidence of the CoP's commitment to EBP (the acronym in this sense is commonly used for evidence-based policing rather than practice) can be found in its establishment of a 'what works' research centre; in its burgeoning relationship with higher education institutions following the introduction of the Police Education Qualifications Framework

(PEQF), which mandates degree-level qualifications for new joiners, and will eventually deliver programmes of training for all officers; and its embedding of EBP principles in the teaching and learning of new recruits (see Brown et al, 2018.)

Economically, EBP promises sustainability for the police service. Politically, it is central to the governance, accountability and legitimacy of policing. Socially, it stands for true police professionalism and is key to policing's professionalisation, a long-held desire of the institution (Fyfe, 2017). EBP's claim to deliver a transition from tacit, intuitive, personally meaningful and situationally articulated direction to explicit, rational and organisation-anchored control has validity. Certainly, in harnessing itself to the CoP (in terms of the PEQF, which is delivered in partnership with universities, and its commitment to underpin practice with scholarly research, see Holdaway 2020), policing has opened itself up to scrutiny at every level.

Knowledge-based policing (KBP) lacks the distinctiveness of EBP and ILP, which are formulated as models and discussed more widely in the research literature (see Brodeur and Dupont, 2008). Arguably, what appears a conceptual weakness of KBP is its greatest strength. Building on knowledge, policing could develop organically through a process of continuous learning and understanding which is actively promoted and valued. KBP does not rely on customised, ready-made, actionable knowledge products, but on tacit and explicit knowledge. History is important; tacit knowledge, often gained from many years of experience, can provide context for assessing problems and delivering policing services effectively. Explicit knowledge is captured from extant scholarly research.

Advocates of KBP (see, for example, Williamson, 2008; Huotari, 2021) argue that the police operate in a dynamic environment, which changes as a response to police tactics. Thus, as valuable as knowledge may be in the short term, the lessons learned and knowledge acquired may have diminishing validity and value as offenders adapt to police tactics. Therefore, knowledge must be continuously updated and refreshed and that places a huge burden on institutions. This is true particularly when, as in recent years, public finances are squeezed.

There is a case for change. The image of a golden era typified by community focus and founded largely on the delivery of policing services by the 'bobby on the beat' endures. The policing institution retains that focus, operationalised through its neighbourhood policing programmes and a steadfast commitment to responding to calls for help from the public (even if that response sometimes is not as rapid as the public would like, or the police themselves would hope). Recognising that it needs to evolve, policing has experimented with other models that rely on the acquisition of intelligence and knowledge and on evidence of 'what works' as bases for the delivery of policing services.

For a time, ILP was the great hope for policing's modernisation, but leaders now seem to understand that it can succeed only if policing fundamentally changes both its structure and culture to a degree that neither stakeholders nor communities want. Leaders recognise that ILP can send shockwaves through an organisation, challenging hierarchies of experience, status relations and positional bases. Moreover, ILP's reliance on intrusive methods of data collection (in terms of the interception of communications and the tracking of suspect individuals and groups) is unpalatable to some. In many places, an 'ILP lite' version has developed, in which ILP practices have complemented rather than replaced traditional approaches. When ILP has been used successfully, it has addressed either a particular crime type or, over a strictly limited period, crime more broadly. In that way, the dislocation of ordinary policing services is not interrupted, intrusion is minimised and traditional ways of working are not disrupted.

Essentially, KBP is more a philosophy than a policing model, an endless pursuit of better understanding of the social and professional worlds. With hindsight, KBP appears to be an innovation that could have flown, but never had enough momentum and therefore failed to leave the ground. Knowledge is a much more fluid concept than evidence and perhaps that is why EBP, with its commitment to methodological tools supported by rigorous empirical evidence, has largely superseded it in both policing and scholarly discourses (on comparisons between ILP, EBP and KBP, see Huotari 2021).

EBP does not threaten traditional policing arrangements in the same way as ILP. It is a philosophy and a process that complements the consent model and its ways of working. Gathering evidence is nothing new to the police, who know from their experience and training what to look for in investigations in order to build a case for a court or other tribunal. In that context, the clearest evidence often comes from properly isolating the crime scene. Scientific research also comes from conducting experiments in closed conditions where variables can be manipulated as researchers wish. In daily life, evidence tends to be much more ambiguous and findings based upon it much less certain.

That potential for uncertainty is recognised in evidence-based medicine where scientific knowledge is just one of three sources used for the purposes of diagnosis and problem solving. Medical practitioners also draw upon their clinical experience and their knowledge of the patient to make treatment decisions (Greene, 2019). The emphasis is on effective integration of the discrete elements, not on establishing a hegemony for one of them. Fyfe (2017) agrees; he argues that research evidence is only one element in police decision making and that professional judgement and experience must also be considered.

Conclusion

To conclude, arguably one of the few constants in public policing has been change, but the institution's commitment to the principle of consent never has wavered. The police and their stakeholders recognise, and seem always to have recognised, that consent is a fundamental requirement for democratic policing. The continuing relevance of this model in an age of globalisation, social fragmentation and technological change may be questioned, but its values, in the context of the rule of law and of police legitimacy, are eternal. Even if the rhetoric does not always match the reality, it remains a powerful statement about British policing's philosophy and guiding principles.

This is not an argument against change per se. Policing needs to retain its core values but it must evolve to meet its increasingly diverse communities' needs. Policing seems to have set aside ILP and KBP from mainstream policing and settled on EBP as a key means of delivering a professional policing service. All have value. ILP's focus should remain on the investigation of serious organised crime, where intrusions into citizens' privacy, routinely associated with its methods, can more easily be justified. The pursuit of better understanding the central feature of KBP should be the aim of every profession.

Objectively, EBP certainly has merit. Policing could thrive on research-based evidence that helps it build on its alliance with the CoP to develop knowledge of what works – knowledge it can use in the interests of all its communities. However, policing must recognise and accept that evidence is invariably subjective; normatively, it reflects power, politics and status. Learning from 'what works' in medical practice, the institution's commitment to EBP should embrace inside, situational, knowledge so that concerns over policing's impact on individual rights, freedoms and diverse ways of life are better reflected and police actions are adapted appropriately and proportionately. Arguably, that is what the British policing model has delivered successfully for the greater part of two hundred years. To do otherwise risks offending people's senses of morality, reasonableness and fairness. Ultimately, unless communities trust the police, the police will not attract support for their efforts, no matter how much evidence the institution brings forward or how well it feels it can argue its case for change.

References

Brodeur, J. and Dupont, B. (2008) 'Introductory essay: the role of knowledge and networks in policing', in T. Williamson (ed) *The Handbook of Knowledge-Based Policing: Current Trends and Challenges*, Chichester: John Wiley & Sons, pp 9–25.

Brown, J., Belur, J., Tompson, L., McDowall, A., Hunter, G. and May, T. (2018) 'Extending the remit of evidence-based policing', *International Journal of Police Science & Management*, 20(1): 38–51.

Crawford, A. (2020) 'Effecting change in policing through police/academic partnership', in N. Fielding, K. Bullock and S. Holdaway (eds) *Critical Reflections on Evidence-Based Policing*, Milton Park: Routledge, pp 175–97.

Fielding, N. (2020) 'Evidence-based practice in policing: future trends', in N. Fielding, K. Bullock and S. Holdaway (eds) *Critical Reflections on Evidence-Based Policing*, Milton Park: Routledge, pp 201–13.

Fyfe, N. (2017) 'Evidence-based policing', in the Scottish Institute for Policing Research (eds) *Policing 2026 Evidence Review*, [online] pp 9–19, Available from: https://rgu–repository.worktribe.com/preview/1001194/FYFE%202 017%20Policing%202026%20evidence%20review.pdf#page=10 [Accessed 5 May 2021].

Greene, J. (2019) 'Which evidence? What knowledge? Broadening information about the police and their interventions', in D. Weisburd, G. Mason and A.A. Braga (eds) *Police Innovation. Contrasting Perspectives* (2nd edn), Cambridge: Cambridge University Press, pp 457–81.

Holdaway, S. (2020) 'The development of evidence-based policing in the UK', in N. Fielding, K. Bullock and S. Holdaway (eds) *Critical Reflections on Evidence-Based Policing*, Milton Park: Routledge, pp 15–32.

Huotari, V. (2021) 'Innovations of police science: remarks from the point of view of customer protection', in V. Huotari (ed) *Innovations and Innovativeness in the Police and Policing: Essays on History, Theory and Philosophy*, [online] Police University College Research Reports 46, pp 165–94. Available from: https://www.theseus.fi/bitstream/handle/10024/502515/Research46POLAMK_web.pdf?sequence=1&isAllowed=yJames [Accessed 5 May 2022].

James, A. (2013) *Examining Intelligence-Led Policing: Developments in Research, Policy and Practice*, Basingstoke: Springer.

James, A. (2014) 'Forward to the past: reinventing intelligence-led policing in Britain', *Police Practice and Research*, 15(1): 75–88.

Lumsden, K. and Goode, J. (2018) 'Policing research and the rise of the "evidence-base": police officer and staff understandings of research, its implementation and "what works"', *Sociology*, 52(4): 813–29.

Reiner, R. (2010) *The Politics of the Police* (4th edn), Oxford: Oxford University Press.

Sherman, L.W. (2013) The rise of evidence-based policing: targeting, testing, and tracking, University of Chicago, pp 377–451. Available from: https://cebcp.org/wp-content/evidence-based-policing/Sherman-TripleT.pdf [Accessed 10 June 2022].

Williamson, T. (ed) (2008) *The Handbook of Knowledge-Based Policing: Current Conceptions and Future Directions*, Chichester: John Wiley & Sons.

31

Police and crime commissioners

Helen Selby-Fell and Jason Roach

The role of police and crime commissioner (PCC) was created in England and Wales in November 2012 by the Conservative and Liberal Democrat Coalition government. Until 2012, the management and operation of the individual 43 police forces in England and Wales had been overseen by police authorities, which consisted of councillors and independent members. Except for London, where policing became the responsibility of the Mayor's Office, PCCs were elected in the remaining 42 police force areas of England and Wales. PCCs were retained by the Conservative government that took office in 2016, and a second round of PCC elections took place in May 2016. The Police and Crime Act 2017 introduced opportunities for PCCs to take on responsibility for fire and rescue governance. The new arrangements have however, been criticised, both for the election process itself and for some of the ways in which elected PCCs have operated (Mawby and Smith, 2017).

The Police Reform and Social Responsibility Act 2011

The Police Reform and Social Responsibility Act 2011 introduced the most radical transformation in the governance and accountability arrangements for the police service in England and Wales for almost 50 years (Lister and Rowe, 2015). The Act dismantled the 'tripartite' model of police accountability established by the Police Act 1964, which consisted of police forces, police authorities and central government. The Act instead introduced a 'quadripartite' model whereby a more complex framework of institutional arrangements governs the police (Lister and Rowe, 2015). Police authorities were abolished and replaced with entirely new legal entities in the form of PCCs and Police and Crime Panels (PCPs). The creation of PCCs politicised police forces by giving an elected official responsibility for local policing and made it probable that the elected official would be the representative of a political party (Mawby and Smith, 2017).

The Police Reform and Social Responsibility Act 2011 followed a review of policing by Sir Ronnie Flanagan (2008), the then Chief Inspector of HM Inspectorate of Constabulary. The review concluded that police authorities lacked public profile, a democratic component and citizen involvement (Lister and Rowe, 2015). Similarly, other reports had also argued that both local communities and the police service had become disempowered, with the central government influence being too strong (for example, Home Affairs Committee, 2010; Home Office, 2010).

The PCC elections

The inaugural elections of PCCs were controversial even before the elections took place (Lister and Rowe, 2015). The decision in 2012 to postpone the elections from May to November was contentious, due to the likelihood of poorer weather and the lack of other polls on the same day (which is often likely to adversely affect turnout numbers), thereby immediately undermining the mandate of the elected PCCs (Mawby and Smith, 2017). In addition, unlike mayoral elections, the public had not been consulted on whether they wanted the new system (namely PCCs) in the first place. Two months prior to the elections, the Electoral Reform Society called on the then Home Secretary to take steps to raise public awareness in order to try to increase voter turnout. However, the Home Secretary failed to do so.

Commissioned opinion polls had suggested that between 15 per cent and 20 per cent of eligible voters would take part in the elections (Lister and Rowe, 2015), with one poll, in August 2012, conducted by RUSI/You Gov, predicting a low turnout that proved to be accurate (Gilmore, cited in Mawby and Smith, 2017). The proportion of the electorate who voted was only 14.7 per cent, even lower than predicted, and was the lowest on record for any national elections in England and Wales. The turnout varied between the different police force areas; it was low as 11.6 per cent in Staffordshire and 12 per cent in the West Midlands (Mawby and Smith, 2017).

The proportion of the electorate who voted in 2016 was higher than in 2012, with an average of 26 per cent. However, the increase was most marked in Wales, where there were simultaneous elections for the Welsh National Assembly, and those parts of England where local elections were also taking place. Between police forces the proportion voting again showed considerable variation, ranging from 17.4 per cent in Durham to 49.1 per cent in Dyfed-Powys. However, in all 42 police force areas the turnout was higher than in 2012 (Mawby and Smith, 2017). In terms of the comparison to 2012, again there were considerable variations, from a 3 per cent increase in Durham to a 32.7 per cent increase in Dyfed-Powys. The four Welsh police force areas registered the highest turnouts and greatest increase since 2012 (Mawby and Smith, 2017).

Election results

In 2012, Conservative candidates were successful in 16 police force areas, winning 39 per cent of the posts, with Labour winning 13 (31.7 per cent). However, an unexpected outcome was the relative success of independent candidates, who were elected in 12 (29.3 per cent) of areas, and included ex-teachers and ex-police officers (Mawby and Smith, 2017). No other parties were successful. Labour tended to win the larger metropolitan police force areas that had greater police officer strength, whereas the Conservatives and independents were more successful in the smaller forces with smaller populations (Mawby and Smith, 2017).

In 2016, Conservative candidates were successful in 20 police force areas, winning 50 per cent of posts, with Labour winning 15 (37.5 per cent) and Plaid Cymru, the Welsh Nationalist Party, winning two. However, the most notable change was the demise of the independent vote, with only three independent candidates elected. No other parties were successful, although UKIP came second in three areas (Mawby and Smith, 2017).

In 2012, the claim that PCCs could represent their local constituencies gained credence from the relatively large number of independents elected. However, the elected PCCs were generally White males (Lister and Rowe, 2015). Only 17.1 per cent were women and no non-White candidates were elected. Further, 19.5 per cent of successful candidates had previously served as police officers and 26.8 per cent as members of police authorities (Mawby and Smith, 2017). Of the 26 PCCs who stood for re-election in 2016, 20 were successful (76.9 per cent). It has been argued that 'quality control' is lacking in the electoral process, as anyone can stand for election and there is no skills training on offer to those who win (Loveday, 2018).

The role and responsibilities of the PCC

So, what do PCCs do? PCCs have responsibility for governance and executive functions, including holding the police force (for example, chief constables) to account, hiring and firing chief constables, setting out local policing priorities and managing the police budget (Home Office, 2010). One of the primary aims of the PCC role was to fundamentally change the relationship between the chief constable and the civilian authority. The Home Office encouraged the creation of a 'principal–agent' relationship, in which the PCC was principal (Loveday, 2018). Overall, PCCs have an overarching responsibility for securing and maintaining an 'efficient and effective' police force. How they achieve this differs between forces due to the idiosyncrasies of the areas and public they serve; however, many PCCs have instigated regular 'performance meetings' where police force crime data is scrutinised.

The Police Reform and Social Responsibility Act 2011 required PCCs to also work with local Community Safety Partnerships to facilitate joined-up approaches to reducing crime and disorder and promote public safety (Lister and Rowe, 2015). Within this broader remit PCCs have responsibility for commissioning community safety services, as well as services for victims of crime, by awarding grants to local agencies, whether from statutory, private or third sector providers. Central government funding that was previously routed either to local service providers directly or indirectly, for example, via local authorities (under the Community Safety Fund), now falls under the responsibility of PCCs.

Accountability

In terms of accountability of PCCs themselves, in each force area the performance of the PCC should be scrutinised by a PCP, designed to be the formal institutional means by which PCCs can be held to account between elections (Lister and Rowe, 2015). Comprising at least ten (but no more than 18) local councillors nominated from each local authority in the force area, and two co-opted independent members, PCPs are intended to provide an additional layer of local political accountability for the governance framework. However, it remains unclear how robust a mechanism of 'accountability' they actually provide (Lister and Rowe, 2015). The legislation describes the function of PCPs as placing 'checks and balances' on the authority of the PCC. However, conversely the legislation also states that PCPs will be 'supportive' of the work of the PCC. It has been suggested that the creation of PCPs was an 'afterthought' pushed through into the legislation by the Liberal Democrat Coalition members (Loveday, 2018), and that PCPs were actually given very limited powers and few resources.

The fourth constituent of the 'quadripartite' framework is the Home Secretary, who retains authority to intervene in the functioning and operation of any police force seen to be failing. The different roles and responsibilities of each constituent within the new governance model, and the boundaries between their respective areas of authority, are defined in the Policing Protocol, a secondary piece of legislation required by the Act (Lister and Rowe, 2015). In the Policing Protocol, the government stated its intention to protect the operational discretion of chief constables from political interference. However, where police chiefs are accountable to locally elected 'managers' the evidence suggests that potential conflict between the police chief and their elected official may arise, in particular the level of involvement of the elected 'manager' in operational matters (Lister and Rowe, 2015). Conflicts between PCCs and chief constables have been widely reported (Mawby and Smith, 2017). However, some commentators have argued that this is not necessarily a bad thing (Loveday, cited in Lister and Rowe, 2015). The extent to which PCCs have created their own 'fiefdoms' (Mawby and Smith, 2017) or indulged in 'cronyism' to the detriment of their accountability to local constituencies has been debated (Lister and Rowe, 2015).

Public engagement

One of the aims of the PCC role was to deliver wider and deeper forms of engagement with the public; however, how each PCC sets about operationalising the requirement to consult remains largely a discretionary decision. The Act does not specify details of the mechanisms by which PCCs are expected to deliver greater public consultation. Nor does it specify how frequently and by what method PCCs should consult the public, or what the content of engagement should be. As a result, these issues remain unclear (Lister and Rowe, 2015). Although some PCCs pledged to consult widely with specific interest groups (such as hate crime victims and young people) on gaining office, questions exist over how the results of such consultations are interpreted and subsequently transformed into practice. Research has often found that it is those (sub)communities and groups with the 'loudest voices' whose concerns tend to be most reflected in the crime areas prioritised and the inevitable conflicts over how police resources should be used (Jones and Newburn, cited in Lister and Rowe, 2015). Furthermore, the needs of communities for policing are often complex and contradictory and so the allocation and use of resources cannot simply meet 'the community view'. A potential challenge for PCCs is to explain the choices involved when prioritising the use of finite police resources. In addition as Wells (2008) concludes, PCCs need to cautious that they do not create a 'demand' that cannot be satisfied when they engage with the public by asking them what kind of policing they would like to receive.

Conclusion

Although PCCs continue, for the time being, to represent a significant component within the new governance arrangements, they are only one institution within a web of local and national stakeholders (Lister and Rowe, 2015). As presented here, the role of the PCC is inherently limited and there are a number of issues that need to be addressed within the PCC model (Loveday, 2018). However, it can be argued that the democratic value of PCCs should be considered in light of how they fulfil their role in practice, as well as the manner of their initial electoral mandate (Lister and Rowe, 2015). The reintroduction of a local model of policing might be best managed by a continued commitment to openness and transparency within police governance (Loveday, 2018). Future changes in UK government may well see PCCs consigned to history or their powers and remit widened or narrowed but, for now at least, PCCs seem here to stay.

References

Flanagan, R. (2008) 'The review of policing: final report', London: Home Office.

Home Affairs Committee (2010) 'Policing: police and crime commissioners: second report of session 2010–11', [online] Available from: https://publications.parliament.uk/pa/cm201011/cmselect/cmhaff/511/511.pdf [Accessed 30 March 2021].

Home Office (2010) *Policing in the 21st-Century: Reconnecting Police and the People*, London: Home Office.

Lister, S. and Rowe, M. (2015) 'Electing police and crime commissioners in England and Wales: prospecting for the democratisation of policing', *Policing and Society*, 25(4): 358–77.

Loveday, B. (2018) 'Police and crime commissioners: developing and sustaining a new model of police governance in England and Wales', *International Journal of Police Science & Management*, 20(1): 28–37.

Mawby, R.I. and Smith, K. (2017) 'Civilian oversight of the police in England and Wales: the election of police and crime commissioners in 2012 and 2016', *International Journal of Police Science & Management*, 19(1), 23–30.

Wells, H. (2018) 'The angered versus the endangered: PCCs, roads policing and the challenges of assessing and representing "public opinion"', *British Journal of Criminology*, 58: 95–11.

32

Police codes of conduct

Nicoletta Policek

A code of conduct sets out the principles which guide police officers' behaviour. It does not seek to limit officers' discretion; rather, it aims to demarcate the parameters of conduct within which that discretion should be exercised. However, any breach of the principles enshrined in any code of police conduct may result in action being taken by the organisation and, in serious cases, it could involve dismissal. A code of conduct applies to the conduct of police officers of all ranks while on duty, or while off duty if the conduct is serious enough to indicate that that person is not fit to be a police officer. Due regard is paid to the degree of negligence or deliberate fault shown and to the nature and circumstances of an officer's conduct. Where off-duty conduct is in question, this will be assessed against the generally accepted standards of the time.

Police officers are the executive agents of the legal system and are expected to both enforce and uphold the law. Across different national jurisdictions, specific laws have been established to define the limits of police powers. The need for general applicability of UK law means that when applied to highly specific or unique situations, such as the conduct of the police, the results may not reflect the severity of their deviation from the law within the context of their profession. Accordingly, a police code of conduct promulgates core ethical guidelines that can be built into police training and disciplinary processes. These provide clarity to police officers of all ranks about what conduct is appropriate. A police code of conduct, therefore, is more than just ideals. It serves as practical guidelines that comprehensively cover as many areas of ethical concern as possible. By and large, professional codes seek to foster trust through a commitment to excellence. This is particularly important to the police, as the public demands assurances from law enforcement agencies because of the substantial power that has been vested in them.

Managing police integrity

The police code of conduct does not exist in a vacuum and, undeniably, the political and social environment within which the police operate dictates the conditions for police work and police management. The political culture and structures, social and economic conditions and societal norms and values relating to aspects of integrity often limit the possibilities of police management to manage integrity. In fact, often environmental factors contain a major limitation for the improvement of the integrity of the police in many countries. The integrity of the police undoubtedly cannot be much higher than the integrity of the relevant environment. This limitation also applies to the social reality in which the police operate. Non-integrity in the environment of the police hampers efforts to improve police behaviour (Westmarland, 2005). Despite the advantages of adopting a number of measures to prevent breaches of integrity, managing integrity is not only about what measures are adopted. Integrity management tries to improve the way in which police officers are encouraged to realise the legitimate fundamental expectations of stakeholders. A written code of conduct is an appropriate instrument to achieve this.

Policing by consent: the UK Code of Ethics

In the UK in recent decades, a series of high-profile misconduct and corruption cases involving all ranks of the police, together with the need to implement the police professionalisation agenda, have been partly responsible for the College of Policing (CoP) introducing a formal Code of Ethics in 2014. The work was carried out by the CoP's Integrity Programme in association with the national policing leads for Ethics and Professional Standards and a comprehensive selection of key stakeholders, including chief constables, staff associations and trade unions, and police practitioners. The CoP has issued the Code of Ethics as a code of practice under section 39A of the Police Act 1996 (as amended by section 124 of the Anti-Social Behaviour, Crime and Policing Act 2014). As a code of practice, the legal status of the Code of Ethics applies to all police forces in England and Wales. The scope of the Code of Ethics extends beyond its statutory basis as a code of practice. The expectation of the professional body and the public is that every person working in policing will adopt the Code of Ethics. This includes all those engaged on a permanent, temporary, full-time, part-time, casual, consultancy, contracted or voluntary basis. It also includes all forces not funded by the Home Office and any other policing organisations outside the remit of the Code as a code of practice.

Inspired by the principles embedded in the philosophy that Sir Robert Peel and others developed around 1829 to define an ethical police force, the Code of Ethics supports a philosophy which is commonly known as policing by consent in the UK and other countries such as Canada, Australia and New Zealand. The main components of the Code are sets of principles and standards of professional behaviour. The policing principles are accountability, fairness, honesty, integrity, leadership, objectivity, openness, respect and selflessness. The standards of professional behaviour are honesty and integrity; authority, respect and courtesy; equality and diversity; use of force; orders and instructions; duties and responsibilities; confidentiality; fitness for work; and conduct and challenging and reporting improper conduct.

The nine policing principles originate from the Principles of Public Life published by the Committee on Standards in Public Life in 1995, as these continue to reflect public expectations. The Code adds the principles of fairness and respect because of their importance to the public. The ten standards of professional behaviour originate from the Police (Conduct) Regulations 2012 and from the Police Staff Council Joint Circular 54. In the Code the wording of the standards has been adapted so that it applies to everyone. Where something applies exclusively to police officers, this is made clear. The combination of policing principles and standards of professional behaviour encourages stability and accountability between what people aspire to and what they do.

The vast majority of those working in policing are already upholding these principles and working to these standards. The Code simply defines the expectations more clearly and brings policing into line with other professions that have codes of professional conduct, such as the medical and the legal professions (Kleinig, 1996). The Code provides supplementary information on how to use it to guide ethical decision making and how breaches of the Code will be dealt with. Specific guidance is given on the types of possible actions for managing unprofessional behaviour and relevant considerations in determining whether behaviour reflects the principles and standards in the Code.

Breaches of the Code of Ethics do not always involve misconduct or require disciplinary proceedings. Breaches can range from relatively minor shortcomings in conduct, performance or attendance, through to gross misconduct. Different procedures exist according to the type of unprofessional behaviour or misconduct alleged. For example, relatively minor breaches of the Code will normally be dealt by a line manager, whereas any breaches that are deemed to require formal action will be dealt with under the existing disciplinary regimes for police officers and staff.

International codes of ethics

Worldwide, most police forces use a code of ethics to standardise the conduct of the police officers and others involved in law enforcement (Caldero et al, 2018). In the wake of the abuses that occurred during World War II, states have paid far more attention to the creation and implementation of international standards of behaviour. However, while this has made deviant and corrupt activities by individual states harder to conceal, corruption and abuse still exist. Indeed, applying international codes of ethics at both global and local levels offers some difficult challenges to law enforcement agencies and personnel (Westmarland and Conway, 2020). The two key challenges faced by police officers are the universal applicability of the international codes, and their relevance to non-democratic contexts. Both the United Nations (UN) Code of Conduct for Law Enforcement Officials and the International Association of Chiefs of Police (IACP) Law Enforcement Code of Ethics are recognised as the universal international codes which regulate the police code of conduct.

Both of these international codes have been created by stakeholders that can claim differing types of international membership, whether it is the UN, of which almost all of the world's states are members, or the IACP, which claims the membership of police executives from over a hundred countries. The fact that the codes are promoted by a diverse membership supports the claim that they encompass universal policing norms. For example, the IACP code has been adopted as a standard code by many agencies throughout the US and internationally. The language of the codes themselves indicates that they are designed for wide application. Both are officially categorised as police codes of conduct, thus applying not just to police, but also to other security services engaged in law enforcement and in policing. It is worth highlighting here that one major issue concerns the question of whether the codes are universal. They could be interpreted as an attempt at cultural imperialism and are often viewed as 'foreign' value impositions. Differing cultural contexts are not incompatible with the idea of ethical principles, which can still be universally applied if cultural perspectives are acknowledged.

Furthermore, the ethical principles espoused in the UN and IACP codes of police conduct confront another set of problems when applied to a non-democratic context. Both the codes emphasise that the key responsibility of the police is to serve the community, an unquestionably democratic idea that can be very problematic to accomplish in a non-democratic context. Often the police can be turned into a tool of the ruling elite, thus justifying policies of suppressing dissidents, opposition groups and public demonstrations. Often law enforcement oppresses citizens in the supposed interests of the state or of some higher ideal (Neyroud and Beckley, 2001). This places the state at odds with the ethical principles outlined in each of the international codes. Therefore, if policing is a tool of the state and the state ignores the ethical principles espoused in each of the codes, individual police personnel are then placed in a difficult, if not precarious, position. While they may individually seek to form direct links with the community, police officers may ultimately be forced to choose whether to contravene ethical principles or to contravene domestic law. Police officers cannot create democracy by themselves, yet they can forge ahead of repressive government and engage in positive ethical policing conduct. While this represents a risk, through this behaviour police officers may reflect democracy to the general population, thus encouraging citizens to set democratic change in motion. This means that the codes are relevant to non-democratic contexts, because the very reasons that make them hard to implement in such an environment also make them worthwhile. Police codes of conduct need to cover as many ethical concerns as possible if they are to act as practical measures for law enforcement behaviour. If these codes are to be used as yardsticks and remain practically relevant to law enforcement organisations, as well as acting as guides for the construction of domestic codes, they need to address these emerging ethical dilemmas. A failure to address these issues may render the codes irrelevant to the day-to-day operations of police officers and thus make the codes futile as both a training and a disciplinary measure. Therefore, the international codes of police conduct should cover the following ethical issues: difficulties associated with applying the international codes; human rights and the use of force; misconduct and integrity; and enforcement and accountability (Neyroud and Beckley, 2001).

The codes outline appropriate forms of law enforcement behaviour, and if law enforcement organisations within non-democratic states do not follow these norms, it is clear that they are not operating as they should be. The codes, therefore, can be used as a benchmark for measuring not only individual law enforcement official conduct, but also that of entire organisations when compared to their modes of operation.

Use of force

Police officers are expected, on occasion, to restrain suspects physically, and doing so can involve serious injury or even death. The right to use force entails the potential for officers to misuse this authority and engage in unnecessary or excessive force. Consequently, criminal and civil laws normally specify conditions under which police may use force lawfully. Incidents of police use of excessive force have included beating civil rights protestors, deliberately kicking and choking someone while making arrests, and unprovoked use of deadly force when attempting to control riots and disturbances.

Police codes of conduct normally make explicit the requirement that police use the minimal force which would be considered reasonable in the circumstances, in proportion to the threat or seriousness of the offence, and only as a last resort option. The UN Code of Conduct for Law Enforcement Officials emphasises that the principle of minimal force should apply irrespective of the specific law or policies in any jurisdiction. The use of firearms is considered the ultimate measure and every effort should be made to avoid this. In every instance in which a firearm is discharged, a report should be made promptly to the competent authorities (Code of Practice on Armed Policing and Police Use of Less Lethal Weapons; CoP, 2020). Within these legal and ethical frameworks, police officers can be disciplined for unjustifiable force and they can also face criminal charges for assault. There is usually also a capacity for citizens who believe they have been victims of excessive force to make an official complaint or seek a remedy by suing police officers or the police in the civil courts. Despite various internal and external controls, inappropriate and excessive force by police officers has been an ongoing major problem in many countries. A written police code of conduct not only makes police officers more accountable within communities, but also encourages forces to challenge their own police culture, often deemed as the most plausible justification for the conduct of the police (Westmarland and Conway, 2020).

References
Caldero, M.A., Dailey, J.D. and Withrow, B.L. (2018) *Police Ethics: The Corruption of Noble Cause*, Abingdon: Routledge.

CoP (College of Policing) (2020) 'Code of Practice on Armed Policing and Police Use of Less Lethal Weapons', [online] January, Available from: https://assets.publishing.service.gov.uk/government/uploads/system/uploads/attachment_data/file/857699/CCS207_CCS0120853800-001_Code-of-Practice-on-Armed-Policing_web.pdf [Accessed 14 June 2022].

Kleinig, J. (1996) *The Ethics of Policing*, Cambridge: Cambridge University Press.

Neyroud, P. and Beckley, A. (2001) *Policing, Ethics and Human Rights*, London: Routledge.

Westmarland, L. (2005) 'Police ethics and integrity: breaking the blue code of silence', *Policing and Society*, 15(2): 145–65.

Westmarland, L. and Conway, S. (2020) 'Police ethics and integrity: keeping the "blue code" of silence', *International Journal of Police Science & Management*, 22(4): 378–92.

33

Police professionalisation

Tim Kelly

Does the police service in England and Wales need to be professionalised? Film and television programmes like *Dixon of Dock Green* over the years created a mythic archetype of the 'British bobby'; however, this perception has been challenged. The investigations into the deaths of Sarah Everard, Jean Charles de Menezes and Stephen Lawrence; the Hillsborough inquiry; the fallout from Operation Midland; and Black Lives Matter protests in 2020 highlight a need for a fresh look at the education of police officers. One part of the service response, via the College of Policing (CoP) could be a revitalisation of the on–off relationship between police and academia.

Consider this – to qualify as a medic, a doctor has to study for over five years, and in the post-Shipman era must also show continuous professional development. Nurses, probation officers and social workers must complete an undergraduate programme, followed by portfolio building to an occupational standard. Prior to January 2020 all police officers had an Initial Police Learning and Development (education) Programme (IPLDP) to complete (taking around six months), followed by a portfolio build and a two-year probationary period (Peace, 2006, p 336). After that – and some compulsory programmes familiar in the public sector, such as the use of police personal protection equipment and driving assessments – little further core learning was required unless until an officer sought promotion or specialisation. It is arguable that the focus of education for police officers has been squarely on the shoulders of new entrants and senior management (with the staff college at Bramshill, which closed in 2015). The concept of professionalisation though, had become a regular part of the policing conversation, following publication of the Neyroud (2012) report into police leadership and training.

Police education before 2005

Before 1990 the service provided some opportunities for promising officers; those who passed the written sergeants' exam in the highest category could apply for bursaries or secondments to undertake degree programmes at university. Alumni from those programmes became senior officers, others academics, for example, Professor Simon Holdaway (1983) whose experience returning to the police from university was part of his seminal ethnographic research. It may be at that time, the police service was unready to embrace higher education (HE) as the way forward. Accelerated promotion schemes (where officers could progress more quickly) in several forms may also have suffered from indifference across the rank and file. Whether acceptance for the idea of the (qualified) professional police officer has grown over time may not be possible to answer just yet, but research continues.

Prior to 2005, police education (outside of the Metropolitan Police who had their own version at Hendon) delivered a coordinated programme of initial training to new police recruits via a number of District Training Centres (DTCs), administered by National Police Training (later Centrex, then the National Police Improvement Agency, established in 2006 under the Police and Justice Act). In 2005, this process changed with devolved training starting to be delivered by forces (Peace, 2006, p 340). At the launch of the new devolved IPLDP, many forces opted for a familiar competence-based assessment format. A small number opted for an HE collaborative approach, partnered with universities including Kent (Canterbury) and Teesside. This coincided with work to develop Core Investigative Doctrine and the Professionalising Investigation Programme (PIP) in 2005 to 2007. It is true that the subsequent development of the PIP programme improved approaches to investigations, but this pre-dated the formation of the CoP as a professional statutory and regulatory body. It might be argued that the PIP model could have been utilised as a basis for a professionalising programme outside the investigative sphere, geared more towards general policing.

Partnerships with HE

Subsequently, more forces saw merit in, and developed partnerships with, various higher education institutions (HEIs) to deliver foundation degrees in policing. Those foundation programmes were initially able to access funding, and so became popular with forces, possibly because they also answered the growing call from police officers to recognise the skills and knowledge that they acquired during their service. Top-up programmes to full degree level became available to officers, leading to a number of existing police education programmes becoming more widely available, thus beginning to cater for an increased demand across the service for recognition of officers' experience and learning.

Professionalisation by education

The approach of the regulatory body – the CoP – has been to implement a Police Education Qualifications Framework (PEQF) for the service. This project was intended to address the ways officers make decisions, improve their knowledge base and raise standards (Marshall, 2016). The aspiration: to address issues around performance and trust, thereby improving public confidence. PEQF would do this by creating a framework of qualifications across ranks to achieve the stated aims. Rather than a foundation degree, constables would require a bachelor's degree, with senior managers expected to undertake postgraduate qualifications, benchmarking master's level for superintendents. Eventually this focus would place policing on a par with recognised professions such as medicine and the law, developing a more highly skilled, efficient workforce and with less supervision. Debate across the service made it clear that agreement over what might be a suitable qualification for senior managers was less straightforward. Many already hold qualifications from HEIs (several Cambridge programmes for example), others perhaps do not wish to engage. Discussion around level and scope reached an impasse. Following consultation with staff associations and the National Police Chiefs' Council, the CoP decided to focus on the initial entry routes, before agreeing qualification levels for middle and senior managers.

Consequently, since the beginning of 2020, each of the Home Office forces across England and Wales have been able to recruit new starters from any one of three new entry routes. Firstly, a police constable degree apprenticeship that includes a degree in 'professional policing practice' as well as an occupational competence element, which could be categorised as earn while you learn, and utilising the apprenticeship levy. Secondly, a degree-holder entry programme, which incorporates a *graduate*-level diploma in policing, to encourage applicants from academic disciplines, and finally a traditional undergraduate degree completed prior to application to the police. Each applicant would still complete a probationary period of occupational assessment.

Policing and HE

The promotion of partnerships and collaboration with HEIs into police training was seen by the CoP as key to address the requirement to develop critical thinking skills in police officers at all level, and across all areas of work, from intelligence to roads policing. Considering the events of summer 2020 and into early 2021, with criticism of police approaches to managing protest, it is very clear that the police in England and Wales are firmly under the spotlight, and promoting a more professional approach must be key to improvement. If this approach were to prove successful, it would provide a more emotionally intelligent workforce that recognises and develops the leadership and problem-solving skills already present in the service.

However, one might suggest that, given the emerging criticisms of police actions in mainstream and social media, a concerted, dual focus on senior as well as junior staff qualifications (and thereby, in an existential way, professionalisation at both ends of the organisation) would be not only pragmatic but also in line with the desired improvements in public confidence, demonstrating an understanding of the expectations of individuals and communities as well as of government. Certainly, it is a complex issue, but government aspirations are evident. Degree qualifications, to keep up with Scandinavian and other Northern European countries, were part of the '2020 Apprenticeship Vision'.

Furthermore, Neyroud (2012, p 85) also recommended a (consistent) national pre-entry qualification to the police. It would be easy to suggest this was highlighting the obvious, not least because, as noted, by 2012 there was less consistency between the forces in England and Wales in terms of entry routes than had previously been the case. This crystallises an issue – with chief constables all wanting slightly different things from their officers, it could be argued that the dissolution of 'national' police training was particularly counterproductive. Especially *if* the government agenda really was to create a 'professional police force' – simply because what had been a fairly consistent product was devolved out to the 43 separate forces, each with different approaches and local requirements (Holdaway, 2017). This may also be said to be exacerbated by the introduction of police and crime commissioners in 2012, which also localised interest in the recruiting and initial learning of frontline officers.

In the Independent Police Commission Report, 'Policing for a better Britain' (Neyroud et al, 2016, pp 112–13), Peter Neyroud, Ian Loader and Jennifer Brown, all eminent commentators, discuss a range of pertinent issues – leadership, 'diversity', relationships and governance. Chapter 5 in the document is highly relevant, where they consider skills and qualifications in the light of Sir Tom Winsor's 2012 review of police pay and conditions, which notes that graduates were more likely to succeed in the police recruitment process (Winsor, 2012, p 87). Winsor provides no prescription for all recruits to the police to be graduates; however, the report accepts that aspects of modern policing require 'the brightest and best in our society' (Winsor, 2012, p 94). Winsor also promulgated direct entry at both inspector and superintendent levels, an approach to provide new thinking at several levels across the police service. It is clear that the ethos of PEQF, and encouragement from middle and senior managers to access numerous HE courses developed over the last ten years, would support a policy of direct entry. As yet, limited numbers of direct entrants have not changed policing attitudes. New starters may take time to progress; it would seem helpful to unlocking existing potential and recognising public expectations for them to have the chance.

Neyroud et al (2016, p 114) also argue that the lack of universal requirement for specific educational qualifications 'may operate as a deterrent to intellectually able young people'. Pertinently for PEQF, they note that some cultures may frown on their members joining the police as an inferior career path because it lacks 'professional credentials' (Neyroud et al, 2016, p 117).

Policing: profession or craft?

On 15 December 2016, Alex Marshall, in his blog launching the PEQF, talked at length about the strengths of policing, but was also clear that he wanted all current staff to access opportunities of their own and 'to ensure that the complex activities undertaken by people working in policing are properly recognised' (Marshall, 2016). He reiterated the core values of the CoP, but was clear that officers and staff deserved recognition for working 'at a graduate level now' (Marshall, 2016). This chimes well with the observations of Neyroud et al

(2016) and also with the findings in Winsor (2012), but with one fundamental difference, that neither report endorsed the idea of all police recruits needing to be degree holders.

The opposite view is manifest from those who consider policing to be an experience-based function, of quasi-artisans learning a lore passed on from one generation to the next. This can be characterised as the 'craft' (as opposed to profession) argument. Where police staff adhere to this paradigm it can provide a tension between the progressives (and researchers) and practitioners (see Heslop 2011; Lumsden, 2017).

Very clearly there is a drive to promote evidence-based policing, looking to provide a cultural shift to a more scientific, considered approach. The CoP view of professionalisation fits well with this cultural shift for policing; however, the degree to which progressives can convince those who view policing as a 'craft' that HE is imperative for all ranks will be key to success. Therefore, a holistic all-levels programme such as PEQF would seem to make a great deal of sense. At this time (2023), the envisaged middle and senior qualifications are in hiatus, probably for good reason in terms of development and approach, although that may not be the whole story. Whether a top-down approach would improve acceptance is not clear, certainly it would drive change. It remains to be seen whether professionalising initial entry is enough to make the necessary difference.

References

Heslop R. (2011) 'The British Police Service: professionalisation or "McDonaldization"?' *International Journal of Police Science & Management*, 13(4): 312–21, DOI: https://doi.org/10.1350/ijps.2011.13.4.238.

Holdaway, S. (1983) *Inside the British Police: A Force at Work*, Oxford: Basil Blackwell.

Holdaway, S. (2017) 'The re-professionalization of the police in England and Wales', *Criminology & Criminal Justice*, 17(5): 588–604.

Lumsden K. (2017) '"It's a profession, it isn't a job": police officers' views on the professionalisation of policing in England', *Sociological Research Online*, 22(3): 4–20.

Marshall, A. (2016) 'PEQF launch' [Blog], Available from: http://www.coll ege.police.uk/News/Collegenews/Pages/PEQF_media_launch_blog.aspx. [Accessed 18 April 2019].

Neyroud, P. (2012) 'Review of police leadership and training', GOV.UK, [online] Available from: https://www.gov.uk/government/publications/review-of-pol ice-leadership-and-training [Accessed 24 March 2021].

Neyroud, P., Loader, I. and Brown J. (2016) 'Policing for a better Britain: report of the Independent Police Commission', [online] Available from: https:// www.researchgate.net/publication/303873773_Policing_for_a_Better_ BritainReport_of_the_Independent_Police_Commission/citations [Accessed 28 January 2021].

Peace, R.J. (2006) 'Probationer training for neighbourhood policing in England and Wales: fit for purpose?' *Policing: An International Journal of Police Strategies & Management*, 29(2): 335–46.

Winsor, T. (2012) 'Independent review of police officer and staff remuneration and conditions (Winsor Report)', [online] Available from: http://library.coll ege.police.uk/docs/Winsor–Part2–vol1.pdf. [Accessed 2 April 2021].

34

Policing and decision making

Laura Boulton

Psychology has made a range of important contributions to policing, from how police carry out their duties and how the force works as an organisation, to how police work affects individual officers and staff. In particular, decision-making research can help explain how decisions are really made in policing-related circumstances as well as inform the development of decision-making tools and aids. In policing, decisions must be made all the time, often under extremely challenging situations, and the outcomes of police decisions can be life changing both for the officer themselves and the general public. Although there is a big difference between tactical, strategic and investigative policing tasks, the common thread in all types of policing roles is the need for appropriate decision making.

Intuition vs analysis

In his bestselling book *Thinking Fast and Slow*, Daniel Kahneman (2011) talks about how thinking is generally split between two dichotomous modes which he calls System 1 and System 2. They can also be referred to as intuitive and analytical thinking. System 1 is in charge of those decisions that individuals make that they don't even really think about: they are instinctive, fast, led by emotion and reflect experience. This experience allows for pattern recognition within a situation and helps the decision maker draw upon previously learned associations to quickly arrive at a choice, even with limited information and without the cognitive demands of careful and systematic alternative comparison. Once things are learned well through reinforced practice and feedback, responses become automatic. This approach enables flexibility in judgement, an ability which is crucial in fast-moving and dynamic environments. However, because of the automatic nature, it can be hard for decision makers to be aware of the processes underlying System 1 thinking or be able to explain how they came to their decisions. In contrast, System 2 is that analytical thinking that individuals do when things require conscious effort to figure out and may even require some sort of calculation. Analytical decision making is assumed to be a goal-orientated and systematic process which evaluates alternative options in terms of associated strengths, weaknesses, opportunities and risks in order to identify the best alternative.

According to classical decision-making theories such as Bayesian decision theory, which are concerned with identifying the best decision to take, analytical decisions which identify hypotheses, evidence and action outcomes before evaluating the utility of those options via probability estimates are superior to unaided human judgement (Gärdenfors and Sahlin, 1982). However, such analytical processes are time intensive, reliant on complete situational information in order to systematically compare alternatives and do not promote flexibility. As such, analytical decision making may be impractical in real-world contexts which are defined by time restrictions, uncertainty, incomplete information, risk and dynamically changing circumstances (Klein, 2008). The naturalistic decision-making movement sought to explore how people made decisions during these sort of situations.

Real-world decision making

In reality, decision makers are not often faced with situations in which all the information needed is available or they have enough time to evaluate the information and options, so they cannot use laws of logic to make the 'best' choice. In policing, decision makers will often have to make judgements under uncertainty, time pressure and stress. Uncertainty (such as inadequate understanding, incomplete information and/or undifferentiated alternatives) can cause doubt and increase hesitation, especially with regard to decisions that carry a higher risk. Similarly, time pressure can result in a speed–accuracy trade-off. In these situations, decision makers instead rely on quicker strategies such as intuition and heuristics rather than the accuracy of analysis. Heuristics serve as general and automatic cognitive shortcuts for simplifying complex tasks (Schaeffer, 1989). They are strategies which individuals, as humans, use every day to come to an acceptable decision quickly while reducing cognitive load on the decision maker. A wide range of heuristics have been identified, described and researched by researchers like Kahneman and his academic partner, Amos Tversky (Tversky and Kahneman, 1986). Two of the most commonly discussed with relevance to policing are briefly described here. The availability heuristic is the tendency of individuals to base judgements on information that is readily available. The easier something is to recall, the more important it seems, and so the impact of those things are overvalued and overestimated. For example, more people fear flying than fear driving in a car, despite flying being statistically less risky than driving. This is thought to be because the media gives much more attention to air accidents and, as such, these events have a higher availability in people's minds. A concept's availability can also be affected by how recently and how frequently it has been brought to mind. In a policing setting, this heuristic may impact on decision making. For instance, the salience of a particularly emotional or impactful case may influence the reaction to a current one: the investigation of a missing person may be prioritised as high risk immediately after a high-profile case of a missing person was found to be a homicide. The representativeness heuristic uses categories. An individual or a thing has a high representativeness for a category if it is very similar to a prototype of that category, for example when deciding whether or not a person is a criminal. While it is effective for some problems, this heuristic involves attending to the particular characteristics of the individual, ignoring how common those categories are in the population (called the base rates). Thus, people can overestimate the likelihood that something has a very rare property, or underestimate the likelihood of a very common property.

Heuristics are the mental shortcuts that humans use to make decisions quickly and generally efficiently. These work as effective techniques that are successful in a lot of day-to-day circumstances, particularly in time-pressured and uncertain settings where analytical strategies cannot be used. However, sometimes they can lead to inaccurate or biased decision making and judgement errors. The resulting errors are called cognitive biases and many different types have been documented. In day-to-day life these biases and errors don't often have major consequences so individuals go on using them as they are an adaptive and useful shortcut in most cases. However, in policing-related circumstances, the consequences of biased or erroneous decision making can have critical consequences.

Confirmation bias is the tendency to search for and favour information that confirms an individual's beliefs while simultaneously ignoring or devaluing information that contradicts it (for example, tunnel vision; see Klein, 1999). The confirmation bias can operate by means of two mechanisms: (1) selective information search; and (2) biased interpretation of available information. Changing one's mind is harder than it appears – the more a person believes they know something, the more they filter or ignore information to the contrary. In a police investigation setting, this bias can be catastrophic, especially under conditions of uncertainty or time pressure. In a policing setting, uncertainty and framing of information has been found to impact evidence search strategies and interview question style, resulting in search strategies based on initial assessment of guilt or innocence (Rassin et al, 2010). Furthermore, when under time pressure, the confirmation bias has been found to influence investigators to seek evidence to support their immediate hypothesis of who is guilty of a crime and ignore or devalue evidence which contradicts this theory (Ask and Granhag, 2005). This can be detrimental to the efficiency and objectivity of a police investigation, whereby investigators become too focused on finding incriminating (as in, confirming) evidence against a prime suspect, while no efforts are made to find potentially exonerating (that is, disconfirming) information.

Expert decision makers?

It is often assumed, perhaps based on TV depictions, that to be a police officer is to be an expert decision maker, and police officers should behave expertly based on their intuition and hunches. This perception also appears to be evident in academia, where researchers often compare police officers as an expert group to a student control sample on a range of skills (such as an ability to detect deception). However, policing is a profession that involves a wide range of roles and responsibilities which require a combination of skills, including, but not limited to, standard patrol, investigation, community support, covert operations, firearms response, negotiation, counterterrorism and surveillance. Furthermore, in reality police officers are human and are susceptible to the same human cognition limitations, heuristics and biases that have been discussed previously, just as the rest of society are.

Internationally, and particularly in the US, police actions continue to be scrutinised due to high-profile incidents, such as the shooting of unarmed Black men. As a result, there has been much debate about the validity of police officers' intuitions, hunches and gut instincts as a basis for forming high-risk decisions in situations where time is available for more analytical methods such as suspicions about who to stop and search (Suss and Boulton, 2018). Studies which explore racial bias in police decisions to shoot or not to shoot suspects have typically found a reduced racial bias in the decisions of officers compared to civilians. However, these studies also identify important complexities within this finding that are impacted by situational features. Correll et al (2014) found that the police officers were faster, more accurate and less racially biased in terms of errors compared to non-police civilians on a first-person shooting task; however, officers still exhibited a bias towards shooting unarmed African-American males. These findings suggest that expertise has the potential to enable officers to minimise behavioural consequences of stereotypes, via exercise of cognitive control and analytical reasoning. A working definition of expertise in law enforcement is provided by Suss and Boulton (2018, p 768) as being 'characterized by the ability to adaptively apply one's skills, knowledge, and attributes to novel and complex (e.g., uncertain, time-pressured, dangerous) situations and environments'. Therefore, while errors in police decision making are predictable on the basis of decision-making and heuristics research, these errors can be reduced if people are aware of them and strive consciously to avoid them – for example, through the use of aids or decision support tools that recognise the central role of intuitive reasoning, but offer systematic methods for encouraging and facilitating analysis.

Making better decisions

One way to encourage analytical decision making in police setting is to implement the use of a decision aid or model. The national decision model (NDM) is a cyclical model with six elements which the decision maker can use as an area for focus and consideration. These elements can be summarised by the mnemonic CIAPOAR, which is said to act as an aide-memoire for decision making: (1) use a code of ethics (C) (central to the model) which relates to the principles and standards of professional behaviour; (2) gather information and intelligence (I); (3) assess threat and risk and develop a working strategy (A); (4) consider powers and policy (P); (5) identify options and contingencies (O); and finally (6) take action and review what happened (AR). The College of Policing say that the NDM is suitable for all decisions and should be used by everyone in policing spontaneous incidents or planned operations, by an individual or team of people, and in both operational and non-operational situations. Decision makers can use the NDM to structure a rationale of what they did during an incident, while managers and others can use it to review decisions and promote learning. However, there is no academic evidence base for the NDM. There is no empirical support for its use generating better policing decisions, less erroneous or biased decision making, or even for which decisional tasks the NDM works most effectively. Taking the naturalistic decision-making research into consideration, it could be assumed that this sort of analytical tool would be most appropriate for slower policing tasks as opposed to fast-paced operational judgements. However, research is needed to examine this assumption.

Conclusion

Appropriate and effective decision making is a crucial aspect of everyday policing duties. Psychological research has made important contributions to aiding an understanding of the decisions that are made in police settings, as well as how supporting good police judgement can be realised. Through decision-making literature, one can begin to understand the nature of human judgement in naturalistic, real-world situations, like policing, which are characterised by uncertainty, time pressure and high stakes, as well as the limitations of individual cognition in these environments. Understanding how heuristics and cognitive biases can manifest themselves enables an objective evaluation of the decisions that are made. Furthermore, through this understanding, policy makers, practitioners and academics can begin to make evidence-based recommendations to support good decision making in these settings via training and/or decision-making aids and tools.

References

Ask, K. and Granhag, P.A. (2005) 'Motivational sources of confirmation bias in criminal investigations: the need for cognitive closure', *Journal of Investigative Psychology and Offender Profiling*, 2: 43–63.

Correll, J., Hudson, S.M., Guillermo, S. and Ma, D.S. (2014) 'The police officer's dilemma: a decade of research on racial bias in the decision to shoot', *Social and Personality Psychology Compass*, 8: 201–13.

Gärdenfors, P. and Sahlin, N.E. (1982) 'Unreliable probabilities, risk taking, and decision making', *Synthese*, 53(3): 361–86.

Kahneman, D. (2011) *Thinking, Fast and Slow*, London: Penguin.

Klein, G. (1999) 'Applied decision making', in P.A. Hancock (ed) *Human Performance and Ergonomics*, Academic Press, pp 87–107.

Klein, G. (2008) 'Naturalistic decision making: human factors', *Journal of the Human Factors and Ergonomics Society*, 50(3): 456–60.

Rassin, E., Eerland, A. and Kuijpers, I. (2010) 'Let's find the evidence: an analogue study of confirmation bias in criminal investigation', *Journal of Investigative Psychology and Offender Profiling*, 7(3): 231–46.

Schaeffer, M.H. (1989) 'Environmental stress and individual decision-making: implications for the patient', *Patient Education and Counseling*, 13(3): 221– 35.

Suss, J. and Boulton, L. (2018) 'Expertise in law enforcement', in P. Ward, J.M. Schraagen, J. Gore and E. Roth (eds) *The Oxford Handbook of Expertise*, Oxford: Oxford University Press, pp 765–91.

Tversky, A. and Kahneman, D. (1986) 'Rational choice and the framing of decisions', *Journal of Business*, 59(4): 4251–78.

35

Police accountability and legitimacy

Tammy Landau

Introduction

In this discussion of police accountability and legitimacy, specific reference is to the uniformed public police as the body or entity to which these concepts apply. While they are closely related, accountability and legitimacy are quite separate in their definitions and applications. Accountability and legitimacy are normally evoked when discussing the 'routine' activities of the public police and raise specific challenges when applied to the context of forensic policing; that is, accountability and legitimacy as they apply to individuals living with or experiencing mental illness.

Police accountability and legitimacy are critical concepts to democratic policing (Expert Panel of the Future of Canadian Policing Models, 2014). In jurisdictions where the uniformed public police are an arm of democratically elected governments there are crucial expectations, indeed demands, placed on them. As the institution with exceptional powers to arrest and use coercive, even deadly, force, these requirements are particularly critical (Tyler, 2006). To be effective, these mechanisms must be implemented in a clear and enforceable fashion.

Uniformed public police and democratic policing

The institution of the uniformed public police is fairly new. Its roots trace back to the creation of the Metropolitan Police of London in 1829. Often identified as a turning point in the ways in which democratic states police, regulate and protect their citizenry (Zedner, 2006), the uniformed public police were specifically designed to be an integral part of local communities. 'The police are the public and the public are the police' is the central principle on which Sir Robert Peel built this new institution. While policing of the community was presumed to be carried out by consent, a considerable degree of suspicion towards state authorities remained. Thus, along with accountability to the community, independence from operational and political interference became cornerstones of the 'New Police' (Reiner, 2013).

This model of policing is presumed to have spread throughout the western world to most democratic countries. Clearly, there are historical and geopolitical evolutions in the nature of the uniformed public police, but for the most part those early principles are presumed to have prevailed; police operating locally with the consent of the community and democratically accountable either directly to local authorities or through elected representatives (Reiner, 2013).

Accountability and the public police

In its simplest form, '[a]ccountability refers to the ability to demand explanations and justifications from the police for their actions and does not necessarily include a power by those demanding an account to control police behavior' (Expert Panel on the Future of Canadian Policing Models, 2014, p 60). Indeed, accountability is crucial in maintaining trust and legitimacy in the police. While accountability may take different forms (Walsh and Conway, 2011), it must be distinguished from controlling or directing the police, both of which are undesirable and antithetical to policing in a democratic society. Accountability itself takes on multiple forms, and may be achieved through external oversight bodies that govern police organisations, mechanisms to receive and investigate complaints against police officers from members of the public and, indeed, through the courts or judicial inquiries. The main point is that the requirement of accountability is uncontested, if challenging to achieve.

Legitimacy

Equally critical to the existence of the uniformed public police and their ability to function within a democratic framework is the notion of legitimacy. 'Irrespective of whether the focus is on an individual authority or an institution, legitimacy is a property that, when it is possessed, leads people to defer voluntarily to decisions, rules, and social arrangements' (Tyler, 2006, p 376). Rogers and Coliandris (2015, p 99) note that legitimacy is linked to both trust and confidence in policing authorities, in addition to 'whether the police and the public are morally aligned', while limits on the use of those powers remain. These are particularly critical when the police are authorised to use physical or lethal force to carry out their duties; while 'model' policing would only resort to force as a last resort, without legitimacy it would risk becoming a routine or oppressive tool. Homolova (2018, p 103) also points to the importance of 'bounded authority – that the police limit or do not misuse their powers'.

As noted throughout this chapter, accountability and legitimacy are referred to as they apply in particular to the uniformed public police. A number of assumptions challenge and question the very nature of policing for many communities. First and foremost, perhaps, is the notion that 'policing' is carried out by the police. In fact, the public police is only one body that carries out this function; there are more organisations and bodies that 'police' communities, but which are not part of the formal state apparatus (Stenning, 2009; Walsh and Conway, 2011). Indeed, Zedner (2006, p 81) characterises policing as 'an array of activities undertaken by multiple private and public agencies, and individual and communal endeavours'. As non-state agencies, they create challenges for both accountability and legitimacy that have not yet been resolved. To whom are these agencies accountable? What mechanisms would be in place to ensure this? Do they have – indeed, do they need – legitimacy in the specific context in which they are active?

In addition, and perhaps more critical, is the notion that 'the police are the public and the public are the police' and its companion principle of 'policing by consent'. While Peel's ideals have been defined as the foundational model of the police that has been imported to distant lands, many of these communities are not, in fact, policed by consent. Indeed, a different model, one that acknowledges the coercive regimes imposed on colonised peoples, would be more appropriate (Marquis, 1997; Monaghen, 2013). For example, Indigenous peoples across the Americas have never given consent to this policing regime and do not share the values of the colonial forces. Accountability mechanisms do not generally meet the requirement of Indigenous sovereignty and legitimacy is therefore difficult, if not impossible, to achieve with such a model (Canadian Council of Academies, 2014).

Policing mental health and conclusions

Finally, in many jurisdictions there are significant challenges when the uniformed public police are involved in interactions involving someone with mental health issues (Bouveng et al, 2017). While the police have been traditionally viewed as the only 24-hour service providers with both the power and authority to respond to any and all emergencies, their training is limited and does not typically include the skills to deal with psychiatric issues. Indeed, the police's presence (during which they are typically armed) seems to escalate matters, with often tragic, even deadly results (Adhopia, 2020). As just one of many examples, Chantel Moore, a young Indigenous woman experiencing a mental health crisis was shot and killed by police during a 'mental health check'. As a result, many jurisdictions have investigated, or are in the process of investigating, ways to remove police as first responders and replace them with a model that is more professionally suited for this task.

References

Adhopia, V. (2020) 'It's time to rethink police wellness checks, mental health advocates say', *CBA News*, [online] 4 July, Available from: https://www.cbc.ca/news/health/police-wellness-check-alternatives-1.5637169 [Accessed 10 June 2022].

Bouveng, O., Bengtsson, F. and Carlborg, A. (2017) 'First-year follow-up of the Psychiatric Emergency Response Team (PAM) in Stockholm County, Sweden: a descriptive study', *International Journal of Mental Health*, 46(2): 65–73.

Expert Panel on the Future of Canadian Policing Models (2014) *Policing Canada in the 21st-Century: New Policing for New Challenges*, Ottawa: Canadian Council of Academies [online], Available from: https://cca-reports.ca/reports/polic ing-canada- in-the-21st-century-new-policing-for-new-challenges/ [Accessed 10 June 2022].

Homolova, P. (2018) 'Theories of police legitimacy: its sources and effects', *Acta Universitatis Carolinae Philosophica et Historica*, 2: 93–113.

Marquis, G. (1997) 'The "Irish model" and nineteenth-century Canadian policing', *Journal of Imperial and Commonwealth History*, 25(2): 193–218.

Monaghen, J. (2013) 'Mounties in the frontier: circulations, anxieties, and myths of settler colonial policing in Canada', *Journal of Canadian Studies*, 47(1): 122–257.

Reiner, R. (2013) 'Who governs? Democracy, plutocracy, science and prophecy in policing', *Criminology and Criminal Justice*, 13(2): 161–80.

Rogers, C. and Coliandris, G. (2015) 'The expert citizen: the key to future police legitimacy?' *Police Journal: Theory, Practice and Principles*, 88(2): 95–105, DOI: https://doi.org/10.1177/0032258X15585249.

Stenning, P. (2009) 'Governance and accountability in a plural policing environment: the story so far', *Policing*, 3(1): 22–33.

Tyler, T. (2006) 'Psychological perspectives on legitimacy and legitimation', *Annual Review of Psychology*, 57: 375–400.

Walsh, D. and Conway, V. (2011) 'Police governance and accountability: overview of current issues', *Crime, Law and Social Change*, 55: 61–86.

Zedner, L. (2006) 'Policing before and after the police: the historical antecedents of contemporary crime control', *British Journal of Criminology*, 46: 78–96.

36

Police and Criminal Evidence Act 1984

Jo Turner and Karen Corteen

Introduction

The Police and Criminal Evidence Act (PACE) 1984 provides the framework for police powers in relation to individual citizens in England and Wales. Despite the presence of the word 'police' in its title, PACE is used by any organisation in England and Wales that conducts a criminal investigation, such as HM Revenue and Customs and the Ministry of Defence police for example. Different sections of PACE provide directions on stop and search, entry, search and seizure, arrest, detention, questioning and treatment, documentary evidence in criminal proceedings and complaints and discipline, with the final section covering a variety of miscellaneous matters. It came into force during a politically turbulent period in which police accountability and legitimacy was severely lacking, and coincided with the miners' strike, which delayed the implementation of PACE by a year. Brain (2018, p 248) describes PACE as a 'watershed in the history of policing'. For most of its history, the police in England and Wales have been considered citizens in uniform with no extraordinary powers that would differentiate them from the rest of the community. PACE fundamentally changed that history and is generally considered to be the single most important piece of legislation related to policing.

Policing prior to PACE

Since the Metropolitan Police Act 1829, police powers were progressively derived from individual pieces of legislation, resulting from Home Office directives, case law and the 'Judges' Rules'. The Rules had been introduced in 1912 to govern the treatment of those held in police custody so that any evidence collected would be admissible in court. Zander (2017) argues the Rules were often regarded as advisory rather than binding by police officers, due to the arbitrary and isolated way they had been developed and their non-statutory nature. This meant that prior to PACE, police powers were neither consistent across England and Wales nor well defined. Yet this haphazard system of regulating police powers continued until the 1980s when PACE came into force to replace the Judges' Rules.

Factors leading to the introduction of PACE

PACE was a response to public concerns about how the police dealt with suspects and the perception of a deeper institutional malaise, as well as series of scandals around police procedure. The most relevant of those scandals was the wrongful imprisonment of three boys who had falsely confessed to the 1972 murder of Maxwell Confait, a male prostitute. An inquiry conducted by Sir Henry Fisher into the wrongful imprisonment of the three boys made recommendations for policy change regarding the powers and duties of the police in respect of the investigation of criminal offences, the rights of suspects and the responsibility for the prosecution of criminal offences. Fisher had found that the boys had been denied the right to legal advice, were improperly questioned, that there were problems with the charging process and that the officers involved had been unaware of what was required of them by the Judges' Rules (Reiner, 2000). Fisher's conclusions, along with other high-profile cases of police misconduct and the conclusions of the 1981 Scarman Report, which concluded that policing mistakes were a crucial factor igniting the disorder of that year's Brixton riots, led to the establishment of the Royal Commission of Criminal Procedure (1979–81). The Royal Commission, and the general increased attention to police procedure, ultimately culminated in several significant changes to the operation and regulation of criminal justice – with PACE being the first piece of legislation passed, closely followed by the Prosecution of Offences Act in 1985, and the establishment of the Crown Prosecution Service in 1986.

The implementation of PACE

Once in force, Zander (2017) argues that chief constables were quick and successful in implementing the extensive training and procedural programmes suddenly needed to disseminate the significant changes that PACE brought to police practice. Less easy to achieve, though, was the cultural change necessary to adjust attitudes and practices. PACE was largely welcomed by the police as it extended some police powers. However, some, notably rank-and-file police officers, argued that also establishing a statutory framework of rights for those in custody would erode the powers of the police and swing the balance too far in the interests of the suspects. Others opposed any extension to police powers and argued that the procedural safeguards contained in PACE would not be meaningful in practice. Of most concern to this group, were the extensions to police powers in relation to stop and search, taking fingerprints (and other intimate samples) and searching premises. The eight subsequent Codes of Practice, developed since the passing of PACE, deal with these concerns. These Codes provide detailed guidance and clarity on stop and search and detention for example. The Crime and Security Act 2010 has provided further restrictions on the retention of DNA samples where the suspect was not charged. Other PACE powers have been further amended by the Serious Organised Crime and Police Act 2005 and the Protection of Freedoms Act 2012.

The impact of PACE

Described by Reiner (2000, p 176) as 'the most significant landmark in the modern development of police powers', PACE fundamentally and permanently changed how the police interacted with the public in England and Wales. Its impact was dramatic and immediate. For example, section 106 of PACE required police authorities obtain the views of people in their area about policing and aim to secure their cooperation. After the 1981 riots in Brixton, Toxteth, Handsworth, Chapeltown and Moss Side some forces had informally established local liaison committees to help address poor police–community relations, but now everywhere had to have formal committees. However, these committees were to be run by the authorities, not the police.

PACE also meant that now police officers needed a warrant signed by magistrates to enter premises if consent for entry was not voluntarily granted, while magistrates needed to be confident that the search was merited by both the serious arrestable nature of the offence and by the substantial value any evidence expected to be found would add to the investigation. Section 17 of PACE allows police officers to enter premises without consent, and without a warrant, if officers are intending to arrest someone for an offence, to arrest a young person or child in local authority care, to recapture someone unlawfully at large, to 'save a life or limb' or to prevent serious damage to property. Section 32 allows police officers to search the premises at which the suspect is found, or where they were immediately before an arrest. The word 'premises' has been interpreted widely by the courts (Zander, 2017) and has been taken to mean any private property. Section 24 of PACE provides directions on how and when a person can be arrested. It provides three categories of arrestable offences – murder, offences which carry five years or more imprisonment for someone aged 18 years or over with no previous convictions, and a miscellaneous category of other offences that might not carry a five-year sentence. Those suspected of offences which do not fall into any of these categories have to be brought to court with a summons.

Stop and search

In contrast to the arbitrary and unaccountable way the police were able to stop and search people prior to 1984, PACE authorises police officers to stop and search any person or vehicle for stolen or prohibited articles *only* if that officer has reasonable suspicion for suspecting that such articles will be found. PACE defines 'reasonable suspicion' as having 'an objective basis [...] based on facts, information, and/or intelligence'. This definition has undergone several amendments, partly in response to public concerns around the disproportionate use of stop and search powers against minority groups (Bridges, 2015). PACE stipulates that reasonable suspicion be determined by neither personal factors nor assumptions about the differential involvement of certain social groups in criminal activity. Despite this stipulation, stop and search continues to be contentious, largely because 'reasonable suspicion' is a vague term that allows discretion. In response, therefore, section 60 of the Criminal Justice and Public Order Act 1994 further developed those police powers relating to stop and search and also allowed senior officers to authorise their officers to stop and search anyone present in a designated place where serious violence is anticipated, circumventing the original safeguard of PACE that there must be reasonable suspicion of the presence of prohibited articles.

Although ostensibly to be used only in specific circumstances and for a limited time only, concerns have been expressed that these powers have become part of the routine policing of town and city centres and increasing numbers of people are subject to stop and searches where the test of reasonable suspicion has not been met. Stop and search is a highly intrusive power because it effectively detains an individual during a search, depriving them of their liberty. This is particularly controversial with respect to searches under section 60 that do not even require the officer to have reasonable grounds to suspect that the individual is in possession of an illicit item. Use of stop and search continues to be a hotly contested and debated subject. However, by far the most controversial aspects of stop and search are its disproportionate use against people from Black, Asian or minority ethnic backgrounds and the limited evidence for its effectiveness in reducing crime. Despite the College of Policing (CoP, 2017) later finding that the use of stop and search has little bearing on rates of crime, in 1999 William Macpherson claimed that Black people were disproportionately represented in stop and search, the overuse of 'section 60' stop and searches was cited as a causal factor in the 2011 summer disorders, and in 2017 David Lammy found that Black people are over eight times more likely to be stopped and searched than White people, even though drugs are less likely to be found.

Detention

PACE provides the police with the power to detain an arrested individual who is suspected of committing a crime. According to PACE, detaining an individual or individuals in police custody should be a last resort. However, Kemp, in Gibbs and Ratcliffe (2020) argues that PACE is not always adhered to in this respect. The detention of a suspect is a vital aspect of police investigation as it 'allows officers to question them and collect their biometric details', which aids the police in their decision as to whether or not they have grounds to charge a suspect with a crime (Brown, 2021, p 4). In England and Wales, there are approximately two hundred custody suites. Detainees are held in custody suites, which are normally located in large police stations (Brown, 2021). It is the prerogative of individual police forces to decide where to situate custody suites and the number to be in operation. PACE provides the police the power to detain suspects for 24 and 36 hours; in exceptional circumstances a suspect can be detained for 96 hours (Home Office, 2018). An individual can be held without charge for up to

24 hours (section 41) and this can be extended to 36 hours by a senior officer who is a superintendent or above (section 42). If an individual is detained because they are suspected of committing serious indictable offences, a magistrate can increase the period of detention to 96 hours (sections 43–4).

PACE provides guidance on various aspects related to the power to detain. For example, it provides the guidance on the duration of detention, the treatment of individuals held in custody, including the treatment of vulnerable individuals, and the rights of detainees. The custody environment is expected to be clean and safe and detainees should be treated with dignity and respect (Brown, 2021). However, this is not always the case; the police custody environment can be noisy, smelly and lacking in privacy (Dehaghani, 2016). It is a place of deprivation (Wooff and Skinns, 2018), which is closed off from the outside world (Kendall, 2020). While in policy there are protections for the detained, such as the Independent Custody Visiting Scheme and the appropriate adult safeguard, in practice these protections can be highly problematic (Kendall, 2020). The deprivation of an individual's rights can happen on many levels, with the most extreme cases of deprivation resulting in deaths in police custody. It is understandable, therefore, that police custody comprises one of, if not the most, controversial area of criminal justice domestically and internationally.

Conclusion

It has now been over 40 years since the implementation of PACE. There will be few people still working as police officers who worked under the pre-PACE regulations who can compare the two approaches first-hand. There are ongoing problems, debates and controversies associated with stop and search and police custody, among others. Despite this, PACE can be considered as having been valuable for providing comprehensive rules and outlining suspects' rights and entitlements while their case is investigated. It also attempts to ensure protection to police officers with regard to allegations made by suspects of mistreatment while in custody. That said, some amendments to PACE have confused rather than clarified police powers, for example the 2005 reforms which task police officers with undertaking a complex legal assessment prior to arrest. In addition, different governments since the early 1980s have regularly reviewed and amended PACE. Yet, even in the face of these issues, PACE has fundamentally stood the test of time and remains in force.

However, despite the increased accountability these developments suggest, informal practices and cultural norms can result in uneven application of procedures alongside and underneath formal policies and legal procedures. So, while PACE may provide a framework for how police custody, community relations or stop and search for example *ought* to function, the reality can be quite different. It could be argued that much of the real power of the police derives not from the statute books but from the institutional and political framework in which the service operates. In this sense, the 'power' of the police needs to be considered in more complex and nuanced ways. Given the enormous power and authority invested in the police, calls for increased accountability and transparency continue, despite the successes of PACE.

References

Brain, T. (2018) 'Chief constables after PACE 1985–2017: the decline of a professional elite', in K. Stevenson, D.J. Cox and I. Channing (eds) *Leading the Police: A History of Chief Constables 1835–2017*, Abingdon: Routledge, pp 246–63.

Bridges, L. (2015) 'The legal powers and their limits', in R. Delsol and M. Shiner, (eds) *Stop and Search: The Anatomy of a Police Power*, London: Palgrave Macmillan, pp 9–30.

Brown, J. (2021) 'Police powers: detention and custody', [online] August, Available from: https://commonslibrary.parliament.uk/research-briefings/cbp-8757/ [Accessed 17 June 2022].

CoP (College of Policing) (2017) 'Does more stop and search mean less crime?' [online] Available from: https://whatworks.college.police.uk/Research/Documents/SS_and_crime_report.pdf [Accessed 15 February 2021].

Dehaghani, R. (2016) 'The case against custody: exploring the problems with police detention in England and Wales'. Criminal Justice, Borders and Citizenship Research Paper No. 17-5, University of Leicester School of Law, [online] Available from https://ssrn.com/abstract=2858178 [Accessed 10 June 2022].

Gibbs, P. and Ratcliffe F. (2020) '24 hours in police custody: is police detention overused?' Transform Justice, [online] Available from: https://www.transform justice.org.uk/wp-content/uploads/2020/06/TJ_Police_Custody_Report_041.pdf [Accessed 10 June 2022].

Home Office (2018) 'Code C: revised Code of Practice for the detention, treatment and questioning of persons by police officers', TSO, [online] July, Available from: https://assets.publishing.service.gov.uk/government/uploads/system/uploads/attachment_data/file/729842/pace-code-c-2018.pdf [Accessed 10 June 2022].

Kendall, J. (2020) 'Custody visiting: the watchdog that didn't bark', *Criminology & Criminal Justice*, 22(1): 1–17, DOI: https://doi.org/10.1177/174889582 0967989.

Reiner, R. (2000) *The Politics of the Police*, Oxford: Oxford University Press.

Wooff, A. and Skinns, L. (2018) 'The role of emotion, space and place in police custody in England: towards a geography of police custody', *Punishment and Society*, 20(5): 562–79, DOI: https://journals.sagepub.com/doi/pdf/10.1177/1462474517722176.

Zander, M. (2017) *Police and Criminal Evidence Act 1984*, London: Thompson/Sweet and Maxwell.

37

Police and multi-agency safeguarding arrangements

Michelle McManus

Introduction

Safeguarding is seen as the protection of children and adults from abuse, harm or maltreatment, with this being the responsibility of all individuals who work on the front line, particularly with vulnerable groups. Yet, despite the hard work of many professionals within the safeguarding sector in attempting to protect the young and most vulnerable in society, the task can seldom be done by one specific agency or team (Sidebotham et al, 2016; Shorrock et al, 2020).

Multi-agency safeguarding partnerships have been present within England and Wales since the 1980s. The Children Act 1989 established one of the first statutory requirements for inter-agency collaboration and joint working concerning children and young people. Since then, other Acts, policies and guidelines have been introduced to promote a multi-agency approach to safeguarding, including 'Working together to safeguard children' (HM Government, 2018). Despite widespread agreement on the benefits of multi-agency, collaborative approaches in safeguarding, it is widely acknowledged that transferring policies into practice is problematic, with implementation of these models varying greatly across key organisations such as the police and local authorities, but also across areas. Previous reviews have identified overlapping policies, guidance and practice making internal navigation problematic (Ford et al, 2017; McManus and Boulton, 2020). Questions are often raised as to which agencies should be involved and how, with challenges surrounding governance, formalised structures, information sharing, funding and resources (Shorrock et al, 2020). This chapter will discuss safeguarding partnerships, police and multi-agency safeguarding arrangements, Multi-Agency Safeguarding Hubs (MASHs), Multi-Agency Risk Assessment Conferences (MARACs) and multi-agency public protection arrangements (MAPPAs). This will be followed by a summary of the issues.

Safeguarding partnerships

The updated statutory government guidance, 'Working together to safeguard children' (HM Government, 2018), announced changes from existing Local Safeguarding Children Boards to safeguarding partners. Within this guidance, local responsibility for safeguarding now rests with the three safeguarding partners who have a shared and equal duty to make arrangements to work together to safeguard and promote the welfare of all children in a local area. A safeguarding partner in relation to a local authority area in England is defined under the Children Act 2004 (as amended by the Children and Social Work Act, 2017) as either the local authority, a clinical commissioning group for an area, any part of which falls within the local authority area, or the chief officer of police for an area, any part of which falls within the local authority area. This policy change was seen as a positive move in ensuring that key organisations were more joined up at strategic level, with statutory responsibility now shared under the tripartite model mentioned.

Under 'Working together to safeguard children' (HM Government, 2018), these three safeguarding partners should 'co-ordinate their safeguarding services; act as a strategic leadership group in supporting and engaging others; and implement local and national learning including from serious child safeguarding incidents'. The importance of linking in with other strategic partnership work involved in safeguarding children and families locally is also a key function of arrangements and should at minimum link into specific groups within various organisations, such as Adult Safeguarding Boards, Community Safety Partnerships, MAPPAs and Violence Reduction Units (VRUs).

Police and multi-agency safeguarding arrangements

Police hold a legal duty to prevent crime and to protect communities, families and individuals. Within the UK, most police forces manage their responses to safeguarding incidents through their Public Protection Units (PPUs). PPUs work closely with other core agencies, such as child and adult social services, in further safeguarding notifications and information sharing. Ford et al (2020) examined vulnerability-related demand in a Welsh police force. Their study found that from 3,500 safeguarding notifications over a 12-month period, over a half (57.5 per cent) were referred on to a statutory agency (child/adult services). However, only a small proportion of the referrals resulted in any input or action (coded as further screening by a social services team, a case and support plan or social worker input) from these statutory services. Cases involving input or action comprised 4.8 per cent of adult safeguarding notifications and 2.1 per cent of children notifications in Ford et al's (2017) study. They concluded that that over three quarters of police-created safeguarding notifications do not meet the thresholds for intervention from statutory services, resulting in no action for the vulnerable individuals involved. A variety of multi-agency safeguarding arrangements involving policing exist for dealing with vulnerability; these try to ensure the provision of a more joined-up, effective response to safeguarding concerns. Some key arrangements will now be explored in turn.

Multi-agency safeguarding hubs

The introduction of MASHs as more formal arrangements for operational safeguarding, which is accredited to Nigel Boulton, is a recent example of multi-agency practitioners taking shared responsibility to identify and manage vulnerability at the earliest opportunity (Crockett et al, 2013). By co-locating safeguarding agencies, MASHs aim to move towards a more collaborative approach, increasing the likelihood of safeguarding decisions being holistic, effective and proactive. Since 2010, many local authorities in England and Wales have embedded a MASH framework into their safeguarding practices, allowing the gaps within traditional 'silo' approaches to be acknowledged and rectified.

In 2014, a report highlighting the findings of a Home Office project aimed at identifying multi-agency models carried out interviews with 37 local authorities in England. The report noted that 'over two-thirds (26) of the local authorities that were interviewed said that they had multi-agency models in place at the time of interview (between January and April 2013) – around half of these used the term MASH to describe their model' (Home Office, 2014, p 6). Shorrock et al (2020, p 9) have observed that 'unlike previous safeguarding mechanisms, which have typically involved single decision-making processes, Multi-Agency Safeguarding Hubs aim to identify and manage risk at the earliest opportunity by promoting a collaborative approach to safeguarding'.

While a legal definition of MASH does not exist, the Home Office (2014) recognises that most MASH frameworks are based upon three core elements: information sharing, joint decision making and coordinated interventions. It has been acknowledged that without any statutory definition or guidance on implementation and operation within these more formal operating safeguarding arrangements, local authorities and police forces have varied in their approaches, locally and nationally (Shorrock et al, 2020). Transferring the recommendations of statutory Acts of Parliament, policies and guidelines into everyday practice has never been an easy task, since multi-agency partnerships are complex forms of social interaction, crossing professional boundaries. Despite the emphasis that has been placed on the three core elements mentioned, various models and features of multi-agency partnerships have emerged, with academics and agencies unable to agree upon a single framework.

When it comes to safeguarding issues such as child exploitation, particularly child criminal exploitation, there are significant challenges for policing and multi-agency safeguarding, due to the complex processes and diverse risk factors associated with child exploitation of this kind. The recent report by the Child Safeguarding Practice Review Panel (2020) suggested that current guidance is not sufficient in terms of reflecting the increased risks posed to children and young people outside the home, including the risks posed by county lines and serious violence.

Multi-Agency Risk Assessment Conferences

MARACs are voluntary, confidential meetings, which are mainly attended by police, local authority and health services to share information on the highest-risk domestic abuse victims who are seen as being at risk of very serious harm. MARACs focus on how to increase the safety of the victim and provide a coordinated action plan agreed by those agencies attending the MARAC. As stated by SafeLives (2014), the purpose of MARACs is the assumption that 'no single agency or individual can see the complete picture of the life of a victim, but may have insights that are crucial to their safety'. MARACs originated in South Wales in 2003 as a result of concerns about the lack of effective information sharing and risk assessment when dealing with high-risk domestic abuse victims. Due to positive feedback from these early MARACs, further rollout occurred nationally in 2007 through the government's recommended Coordinated Community Response to Domestic Abuse.

In terms of the effectiveness of MARACs, a number of recent reviews of local MARACs have provided insight into their operation. Findings included that MARACs have facilitated more effective information sharing and safety planning, which resulted in reduced re-victimisation in a 12-month follow-up, and have a cost-benefit return, indicating that every £1 invested in MARACs yields a return of £6 (it should be noted that this analysis was conducted in 2010 and that limitations were acknowledged in terms of the many domestic abuse victims who remain hidden from police offence recording). However, reviews such as Adisa (2020) have also commented that MARACs come with a heavy additional workload for practitioners, which is often not considered when implementing action, in addition to the sheer volume of case reviews and monitoring in each meeting. These issues result in high demands on time and resources, with further implications for staff well-being. Finally, as MARACs do not have a statutory footing, attendance and compliance at local level can be problematic, especially when considering the demands imposed by MARACs. Such demands can result in low practitioner and organisation attendance, reducing the effectiveness of MARACs.

In order for MARACs to be effective they are required to engage in enhanced information sharing, have appropriate agency representation and include an independent domestic violence advisor (IDVA) in representing and engaging in the victim in the process. MARAC meetings, using the original guidance from CAADA (Co-ordinated Action Against Domestic Abuse) (now SafeLives) developed a set of ten guidance principles for MARACs (SafeLives, 2017), with additional guidance stating that meetings should last around half a day and discuss approximately 15–20 high-risk cases. However, reviews such as Steel et al (2011) have shown that meeting structure and length vary greatly, with some areas discussing five cases per meeting and others more than 25. Meetings often last for between two and four hours and are sometimes reported to be longer. The meetings occur most commonly on a monthly basis. The police are most frequently reported as chairs of MARACs and are also the most likely organisation to make referrals to a MARAC, followed by IDVAs. Other agencies are seen as less consistent in their attendance and referral to MARACs. Many practitioners who attend MARACs are required to attend more than one MARAC, due to the setup of safeguarding arrangements – for example, due to police and health areas that cover multiple local authority areas.

Given the essential role of police in MARACs, as highlighted, it is evident that although MARACs are seen as a key mechanism in safeguarding high-risk domestic abuse victims, there is more that needs to be done in this context from a multi-agency perspective. With police being the main referrers, the likelihood is that only those recorded domestic abuse (police) incidents are likely to receive this higher-level MARAC review. Recommendations from various reports (Steel et al, 2011; Adisa, 2020; Shorrock et al, 2020) have highlighted consistently that safeguarding is not just a policing responsibility, with a requirement to raise the profile of MARACs with other statutory and non-statutory partners, to ensure that such partners are aware of the existence of MARACs and also aware of local procedures for referring high-risk domestic abuse victims. This is especially the case given that recorded police data often highlights a lack of wider representation of local communities in the reporting of crimes such as domestic abuse within Black, Asian and minority ethnicities and LGBTQ+ communities. In addition, consideration of the statutory footing of MARACs has been a continuous request, in the hope that such a development would help to ensure representation from those key agencies in crucial MARAC meetings that safeguard the most high-risk victims of domestic abuse.

Multi-agency public protection arrangements

MAPPAs were first established in 2001 through the Criminal Justice and Court Services Act 2000. The Criminal Justice Act 2003 (schedule 15) then cemented the creation of MAPPAs for each of the police forces in England and Wales, by providing details on qualifying offences for MAPPA. The purpose of MAPPAs is to protect the public from serious harm caused by sexual and violent offenders. It is an information-sharing system that combines resources to maximise the risk management in place for each offender. The responsible authority is the primary agency for MAPPA. This involves the police, prison and probation services working together to ensure that any risks posed by sexual and violent offenders are managed appropriately. Other agencies, often referred to as 'duty-to-cooperate' agencies, are expected to work with the responsible authority in helping to manage aspects of the offender's life, such as education, employment and housing.

MAPPAs aim to manage the various risks that violent and sexual offenders pose to the public by assessing the level (category) of risk. The primary focus of MAPPAs is the prevention of serious harm through management of, and reductions in, serious offending. Every MAPPA offender is identified in one of the three MAPPA categories, with Category 1 being registered sexual offenders, Category 2 being violent offenders or other sexual offenders and Category 3 including other dangerous offenders. In addition, there are three levels of MAPPA management, which are structured to ensure more intense and joined-up levels of multi-agency are able to manage those judged to pose a higher risk. MAPPA management levels are determined by a robust screening process and are regularly reviewed throughout the MAPPA management period. The three levels of MAPPA management are as follows.

Level 1 is ordinary management, where offenders are subject to management from their lead supervising agency. Most offenders are managed at this level, usually by a single police or probation officer. Level 2 is used where it is deemed that formal multi-agency meetings would add value to the lead agency's management of the risk of serious harm posed and where one, or more, of the following applies: where the offender is assessed as posing a high or very high risk of serious harm; exceptionally, where the risk level is lower but the case requires the active involvement and coordination of interventions from other agencies to manage the presenting risks of serious harm; or where the case has been previously managed at Level 3, but no longer requires Level 3 management. Level 3 cases are those that meet the criteria for Level 2, but where management issues require senior representation from the responsible authority and duty-to-cooperate agencies. Active multi-agency management involves Multi-Agency Protection Panels for offenders who are assessed at the highest risk of causing serious harm. These offenders require the involvement of senior officers to authorise use of special resources, such as police surveillance and specialised accommodation, with ongoing senior management oversight.

Although there is no centrally held database of offenders subject to MAPPA, with information held locally by each police force, each force releases an annual report (released via the government website), with an annual national-level statutory report then released which collates the data from across police forces. Data released from the Ministry of Justice (MoJ, 2020) indicated that in the year ending March 2020 there were 85,709 offenders under MAPPA management in the community in England and Wales. This was a 3 per cent increase from 2019 levels and a 75 per cent increase compared with 2010. The majority were Category 1 offenders (72.8 per cent), followed by Category 2 (26.8 per cent), with the least number of offenders at the highest-risk level of Category 3 (0.4 per cent).

In terms of multi-agency safeguarding, reviews of MAPPA have found that regardless of the guidance requiring that there should be a lead agency for each MAPPA eligible offender, such a lead agency was not always clear or in place. It was found that often, as with other multi-agency arrangements, agencies worked in silos and used the MAPPA meetings to update and exchange information, rather than continuing to work collaboratively outside of formal meetings. Furthermore, a key benefit of multi-agency management meetings is that each agency inputs their expertise and opinion in regard to the risk-management plan. However, a report by the Criminal Justice Joint Inspection (CJJI, 2011) stated that in some cases action plans were not agreed, were too short term, were too vague or were simply not recorded. This report identified that no examples could be found within its review of jointly agreed MAPPA risk-management plans that detailed which agency took responsibility for specific actions and how agencies worked together to manage the individual's risk. Risks tended to be managed through restrictive interventions such as curfews, surveillance and use of approved premises. Recommendations to improve the function of MAPPAs have stated that there needs to be additional work done on the active multi-agency management of offenders, going beyond simple information sharing across agencies. As noted in other multi-agency forums, it is one thing getting the right agencies to attend the meeting, chaired appropriately, with meaningful contributions; however, assigning actions and holding agencies to account outside of the meeting was seen as a weakness within some reviews. However, it is also worth noting that evaluation evidence has shown reductions in reoffending for new MAPPA offenders, suggesting that MAPPAs are making positive contributions to managing these serious offenders and to reducing the risk of serious harm to the public.

Conclusion

In summary, this chapter has highlighted some important forms of multi-agency safeguarding arrangements that exist with the police as the key partner. Safeguarding matters often cross disciplines, organisation accountabilities and thresholds. Furthermore, increased risks from threats and harms outside the family home has moved traditional safeguarding perspectives to consider more contextual safeguarding issues (Firmin and Lloyd, 2020). This does not neatly align to safeguarding policies, processes and procedures, particularly within the child protection system, which is arguably structured to respond to intra-familial harm. This presents challenges around safeguarding ownership, organisational remit and responsibilities.

Reviews, inspections and evaluation reports have consistently come to similar conclusions, regardless of the thematic focus of the multi-agency forum (for example, domestic abuse, violent high-risk offenders, children at risk of exploitation), the demographic details of the cohort, the agencies held 'responsible', other agencies' contribution, and the frequency, volume and aim of the meeting. It is important to ensure that multi-agency meetings have representation from appropriate agencies, but also that the professionals engage in meaningful contributions (added value). This requires the competence and confidence of the professional to appropriately challenge decision making when required. Such challenges have been reported to be more forthcoming when leadership and chairing of multi-agency meetings have encouraged an inclusive culture in providing a safe environment for all voices to be heard. Recommendations are also consistent in the need for clear, recorded, multi-agency agreed action plans that make professionals accountable and able to implement decisions and actions, as well as being able to continually review and liaise with other partners.

Regardless of these continued areas of improvements, there is a growing evidence base within safeguarding partnerships and through the UK VRUs of how multi-agency safeguarding can work effectively. However, it is also clear from research (which runs contrary to the recently announced Beating Crime Plan, 2021) that although the police are often the first responder and the agency on call 24 hours a day, they only provide one piece of the puzzle when responding to safeguarding issues. Consequently, there is a need to ensure that we continue the momentum of effective joint working, especially during the period of recovery from COVID-19 when all key statutory services are suffering from exhaustion, depleted resources and surges in safeguarding and exploitation risk. During the COVID-19 pandemic, much multi-agency working has reportedly been strengthened through the increased use of technology-facilitated multi-agency meetings. This has enabled greater attendance, more contributions and therefore better decision making and actions for safeguarding cases. No single agency can respond to safeguarding alone and, as such, effective safeguarding requires skilled, trusted collaboration between statutory and non-statutory services.

References

Adisa, O. (2020) Professionals' perceptions of MARACs and barriers to attendance: headline findings from the "Are MARACs still fit for purpose?" survey', [online] Available from: https://www.uos.ac.uk/sites/www.uos.ac.uk/files/Are%20maracs%20still%20fit%20for%20purpose_briefing%20paper%202020%20FINAL.pdf [Accessed 25 November 2021].

Child Practice Safeguarding Review Panel (2020) ' "It was hard to escape": safeguarding children at risk from criminal exploitation', [online] Available from: https://tce.researchinpractice.org.uk/wp-content/uploads/2021/03/Safeguarding_children_at_risk_from_criminal_exploitation_review.pdf [Accessed 25 November 2021].

CJJI (Criminal Justice Joint Inspection) (2011) 'Thematic inspection report: putting the pieces together. An inspection of multi-agency public protection arrangements', [online] Available from: https://www.justiceinspectorates.gov.uk/hmicfrs/media/Multi-agency-public-protection-arrangements.pdf [Accessed 25 November 2021].

Crockett, A., Gilchrist, G., Davies, J., Henshall, A., Higgart, L., Chandler, V., Sims, D. and Webb, J. (2013) Assessing the early impact of Multi-Agency Safeguarding (MASH) in London, [online] Available from: https://www.londonscb.gov.uk/wp-content/uploads/2016/04/mash_report_final.pdf [Accessed 11 June 2022].

Firmin, C. and Lloyd, J. (2020) 'Contextual safeguarding: a 2020 update on the operational, strategic and conceptual framework', [online] Available from: https://contextualsafeguarding.org.uk/wp-content/uploads/2020/05/CS-Briefing-2020-FINAL.pdf [Accessed 19 November 2021].

Ford, K., Kelly, S., Newbury, A., Meredith, Z., Evans, J. and Roderick, J. (2017) 'Adverse childhood experiences: breaking the generational cycle of crime', Turning Understanding into Action: Summary Report, Public Health Wales, [online] Available from: https://www.rsph.org.uk/static/uploaded/4cfb1e8b-e427-47fd-a1ec7f29f2b5978f.pdf [Accessed 11 June 2022].

Ford, K., Newbury, A., Meredith, Z., Evans, J., Roderick, J., Davies, A.R., and Bellis, M. (2020) 'The outcome of police safeguarding notifications to social services in South Wales', *The Police Journal*, 93(2): 87–108.

HM Government (2018) 'Working together to safeguard children', [online] Available from: https://assets.publishing.service.gov.uk/government/uploads/system/uploads/attachment_data/file/942454/Working_together_to_safeguard_children_inter_agency_guidance.pdf [Accessed 19 November 2021].

Home Office (2014) 'Multi-agency working and information sharing project: final report', [online] Available from: https://assets.publishing.service.gov.uk/government/uploads/system/uploads/attachment_data/file/338875/MASH.pdf [Accessed 19 November 2021].

McManus, M.A. and Boulton, L. (2020) 'Evaluation of multi-agency operational safeguarding arrangements in Wales (MAOSA)', National Independent Safeguarding Board Wales, [online] Available from: http://safeguardingboard.wales/2021/01/06/national-evaluation-of-multi-agency-operational-safeguarding-arrangements-in-wales-phase-1/ [Accessed 19 November 2021].

MoJ (Ministry of Justice) (2020) 'Multi-agency public protection arrangements: annual report 2019/20', [online] Available from: https://assets.publishing.service.gov.uk/government/uploads/system/uploads/attachment_data/file/930302/MAPPA_Annual_Report_2019-20.pdf [Accessed 21 November 2021].

SafeLives (2014) 'Multi-Agency Risk Assessment Conferences (MARAC)', [online] Available from: https://safelives.org.uk/sites/default/files/resources/MARAC%20FAQs%20General%20FINAL.pdf [Accessed 19 November 2021].

SafeLives (2017) '10 principles of an effective MARAC', [online] Available from: https://safelives.org.uk/sites/default/files/resources/The%20principles%20of%20an%20effective%20MARAC%20FINAL.pdf [Accessed 19 November 2021].

Shorrock, S., McManus, M.M. and Kirby, S. (2020) 'Practitioner perspectives of multi- agency safeguarding hubs (MASH)', *Journal of Adult Protection*, 22(1): 9–20, DOI: https://doi.org/10.1108/JAP-06-2019-0021.

Sidebotham, P., Brandon, M., Bailey, S., Belderson, P., Dodsworth, J., Garstang, J., Harrison, E., Retzer, A. and Sorensen, P. (2016) 'Pathways to harm, pathways to protection: a triennial analysis of serious case reviews 2011 to 2014: final report', Department for Education, [online] Available from: https://assets. publishing.service.gov.uk/government/uploads/system/uploads/attachment_ data/file/533826/Triennial_Analysis_of_SCRs_2011-2014_-__Pathways_to_ harm_and_protection.pdf [Accessed 19 June 2022].

Steel, N., Blakeborough, L. and Nicholas, S. (2011) 'Supporting high risk victims of domestic violence: a review of Multi-Agency Risk Assessment Conferences (MARACs)', Research Report 55, [online] Available from: https://assets.pub lishing.service.gov.uk/government/uploads/system/uploads/attachment_data/ file/116537/horr55-report.pdf [Accessed 21 November 2021].

38

Police and victims of crime

Kate Bates

The concept of what it means to be a victim began in ancient times. The Latin word *victima* referred to living creatures, animal or human, who were offered as sacrifices to a god or other supernatural entity. As such, the term was not associated with crime but religious rituals. However, over the centuries it has come to have a more general meaning and now it commonly refers to individuals who suffer injuries, losses or hardships for any reason. A crime victim is harmed specifically by illegal acts (Karmen, 2016). The role that victims, and the changing conception of victimhood, have played in the prosecution of crime is a complex one and has, in modern times, been inextricably linked with the police. For victims of crime, the police are the most important of all criminal justice agencies and, as the gatekeepers to the system, the police can help or hinder from the very outset of a victim's journey towards justice.

For many victims, the experience of dealing with the criminal justice system (CJS) can be as traumatic as the initial crime itself. Traditionally, as far as agencies of law enforcement are concerned, the victim's only role is to report the crime and aid in the investigation and prosecution by providing evidence. The way they are dealt with throughout this process can have a significant impact upon the emotional and psychological well-being of a victim, which can lead to a form of secondary victimisation, whereby their suffering and trauma can be substantially increased. The main reason for this is that victims have very little control or even participation in their own cases beyond their initial contacts with the police. This is because, for the purpose of modern criminal justice, crimes are considered to be against the state and prosecutions are pursued on its behalf and not for the sake of any one individual victim. This can lead victims to feel abandoned, ignored and powerless in the face of a system that appears to have only its own agenda in mind. Added to this, many victims can fall prey to the often unsympathetic or insensitive behaviour of criminal justice officials and, due to the very nature of their contact, the police are often the focus of victim dissatisfaction. This means, therefore, that issues of respect, trust and participation have been identified as major areas of concern for victims of crime in their interactions with the CJS and especially the police (Hoyle and Young, 2003; Elliott et al, 2012).

The changing role of victims in criminal justice

The roles of victims of crime have not always been so passive and marginal however, and their disappearance from the pursuit of justice is a relatively modern phenomenon. It was only in the late 19th century that the state and other criminal justice agencies took over control of the prosecution of offences. Prior to that, for centuries victims had been the major players in the detection and prosecution of crime. Before the creation of the 'new' police and the centralising of a state-controlled CJS, victims of crime had the responsibility of finding their own redress or retribution for their harm or losses. This meant that the majority of crimes were dealt with by extra-judicial means and it was private action by individuals or communities that initiated and directed any legal proceedings. Indeed, due to the cost of bringing private prosecutions to court, for much of the 18th and 19th centuries the majority of crimes would be settled outside of any official influence. If victims did make use of the formal mechanisms of justice, they would often be responsible for not only the apprehension and detention of the suspect, but also for the providing of evidence and witnesses at trial. The pursuit of justice, therefore, was personal not professional, but this would change during the mid-1900s when major amendments to the CJS would slowly take over the victim's pivotal role. The most impactful change for victims of crime was the fact that increasingly the now established public police forces were beginning to replace them in the judicial process. Indeed, by the start of World War I in 1914, the police conducted 90 per cent of all prosecutions and so private action by victims, and their full participation in the criminal justice process, was now becoming increasingly rare (Godfrey, 2017).

It was not until the second half of the 20th century that things began to change for victims. The impact of World War II led to the rise of a welfarist social and political agenda focused on protecting the most vulnerable in society, including victims of crime; for example, the Criminal Injuries Compensation Board was established in 1964. However, it was the 1980s that would see a real shift in focus, when academics and politicians alike became embroiled in major debates about law and order. The increasing recognition that the public's fear of crime and victimisation was rife led to the implementation of crime surveys. These surveys were designed to explore the 'dark figure' of crime, as well as the extent of unreported victimisation, and were viewed as an important alternative to police statistics. However, they were also soon to expose some shocking revelations with regards to victims' experiences of crime, including the extent of loss and injury suffered by them. Due to this, the second British Crime Survey, which ran in 1984, included questions to help assess the level of emotional impact on victims and was to lead to a renewed focus on their needs and rights (Maguire and Pointing, 1988).

The rise and impact of the victims' agenda

This increased understanding of the plight of crime victims led to a more concentrated resolve from government and criminal justice agencies to ensure that victims' primary harms were addressed and that any secondary victimisation by the system was minimised. The police were central to this process and became increasingly engaged with victims through community-focused initiatives such as restorative justice, which aims to repair the harm suffered by victims of crime through offender–victim interaction. Restorative justice cautioning and conferences gave victims more opportunities to participate in the CJS and have the potential to alleviate the emotional and psychological impact of crime. They can also greatly improve relations between the police and public and bring more satisfaction to victims in the process (Hoyle and Young, 2003). The police also became increasingly involved with the charity Victim Support, which was first established in Bristol in 1974 but by 1986 had a scheme in every county in England and Wales; they routinely work in partnership, with the police referring victims to the service for counselling and assistance. Importantly, this increased willingness on the behalf of the police to engage with other agencies cemented the desire in this period to be seen as a public service which was responsive to the requirements of victims as well as the public at large.

Another major step forward in the victims' movement was the introduction by the government of a Home Office Victims' Charter in 1990. This heralded the UK government's first attempt to cater for the needs of victims within the CJS and to coordinate policy on their behalf. Although the charter was not legally enforceable it contained guiding principles which provided victims with the expectation that they would receive certain services from the relevant criminal justice agencies involved in their case, for example, to be given information from the police about the progress of their investigations and to be treated with respect and sensitivity. In 1996, a second victims' charter introduced both the One Stop Shop and victim statement scheme. The principle of the One Stop Shop was that the police would act as a single point of contact for victims with regard to information about their case throughout the whole justice process and the victim statement scheme was to allow victims to describe the impact of the crime on them, whether emotional, psychological, physical or financial (Hoyle and Young, 2003). Although the One Stop Shop in practice was not much of a success, the victim impact or personal statement has now become a major aspect in the rebalancing of the CJS in favour of victims and the police play an important role in that process. Victims now have the opportunity to make two statements, the first is taken by the police at the same time as the victim's initial witness statement and the second may be made at a later stage in the justice process once any long-term effects have become apparent. These statements become part of the police case papers and are relayed to the Crown Prosecution Service so that they can be taken into account in any prosecution and sentencing decisions. For many victims these statements are their only means of actively participating in the criminal justice process and having their voices heard; the statements have been shown to provide closure and emotional catharsis, as well as increased satisfaction with the system (Turanovic and Pratt, 2019).

In the 21st century the victims' agenda has gathered apace. This has been mainly due to the European Union championing the cause. In 2001 the Council of Europe formulated the 'Framework Decision on the Standing of Victims in

Criminal Proceedings', which took into consideration the rights of victims to receive information, support and assistance, as well as their rights to participate and receive protection throughout the criminal justice process. A further council committee in 2006 on 'Assistance to Crime Victims and Prevention of Victimisation' also recommended European member states ensure that victims' rights are recognised and respected with reference to human rights, and that measures be put in place to provide victims with medical, psychological and social assistance and to assure that vulnerable victims especially have access to special measures to assist them throughout the judicial process. These provisions represented the beginnings of a European appreciation of the importance of addressing victims' needs and including their perspectives in the workings of the CJS. Member states are now bound by duty to ensure that victims are treated with respect and that their rights are recognised, as well as crucially to take steps to prevent secondary victimisation, especially in courts and police stations.

In order to discharge these duties, the UK government introduced the first of now several Victims' Codes in 2006 as part of a wider strategy to transform the CJS by making it more responsive and easier to navigate. This code imposes obligations on various criminal justice agencies but the police feature heavily. At the very first point of contact the police are now required to be the main information provider with regards to victim support and advice, including measures available for their protection and access to specialist provision such as financial, medical or counselling services. More specifically, the police must conduct a needs assessment in order to evaluate whether a victim requires any special rights or if they are to be considered as an especially vulnerable or intimidated witness. This then would lead to enhanced entitlements being put in place throughout the investigation and prosecution of the crime, such as witness anonymity or pre-recorded testimony in court. The police must also provide information regarding every stage of their investigation of the case, as well as explanations for any decisions made regarding arrest, release or bail conditions. The latest Victims' Code came into force in April 2021 and, although core police responsibilities and accountabilities remain largely unchanged from previous versions, this code further enshrines 12 overarching rights which clearly set out how to treat victims with compassion and courtesy, in order to help them engage with the criminal justice process and have those services offered in a professional manner, without discrimination of any kind.

Conclusion

It has taken over a century for victims to be situated back at the core of criminal justice policy and practice, and governments across the world have enacted reforms to provide them with services, rights and compensations. However, for many victim advocates there are still improvements to be made if victims are to genuinely receive redress and reparation. For example, although their rights may be recognised and recommended, these rights are, on the whole, not legally enforceable and only really offer victims an opportunity to complain to the relevant criminal justice agency if the rights are not upheld to their satisfaction. This still leaves victims of crime in a weak position in the face of an often confusing, stressful and traumatising system. It is still possible for the police or prosecution to sidestep their obligations as they are only expected to fulfil victims' needs where applicable or if resources allow. Also, cynics may suggest that any reforms to victims' rights benefit the system more than the victims themselves, by enabling victims to cooperate more effectively in the pursuit of retributive justice. However, it is still undeniable that victims are now more than ever protected by criminal justice practitioners, especially the police, who are committed to ensuring their dignity and trust.

References

Elliott, I., Thomas, S. and Ogloff, J. (2012) 'Procedural justice in contacts with the police: the perspective of victims of crime', *Police Practice and Research*, 13(5): 437–49.

Godfrey, B. (2017) 'Historical perspectives in victimology', in P. Davies, P. Francis and C. Greer (eds) *Victims, Crime and Society* (2nd edn), London: SAGE, pp 66–81.

Hoyle, C. and Young, R. (2003) 'Restorative justice, victims and the police', in T. Newburn (ed) *Handbook of Policing*, Cullompton: Willan, pp 680–706.

Karmen, A. (2016) *Crime Victims: An Introduction to Victimology* (10th edn), Andover: Cengage.

Maguire, M. and Pointing, J. (1988) *Victims of Crime: A New Deal?* Milton Keynes: Open University Press.

Turanovic, J.J. and Pratt, T.C. (2019) *Thinking about Victimisation: Context and Consequences*, Abingdon: Routledge.

39

Police custody

Karen Corteen and Jo Turner

Introduction

> Subjecting an individual to detention is to deprive an individual of their liberty; the process is intrusive, risk laden and for many it is a period of great anxiety and stress. (NPCC, nd, p 3)

Police custody is a fundamental component of the criminal justice process at home and abroad. Every year around the world hundreds and thousands of individuals are processed in police custody blocks. Given contemporary calls for the defunding of the police in the UK and in the US due to the police killing of George Floyd on 25 May 2020, it is fitting to discuss police custody. Also, within academia there has been a renewed interest in police custody (Dehaghani, 2016). Police custody is perhaps one of the most controversial and key aspects of policing in England and Wales and globally. In part, this is because in England and Wales the 'primary purpose of taking and individual into police custody is to make them amenable to the investigation of a criminal offence of which they are suspected' (NPCC, nd, p 3). Furthermore, detainees 'are more likely to confess while in detention in a custody suite' (Kendall, 2021). This chapter will discuss the Police and Criminal Evidence Act (PACE) 1984, police custody, and the two safeguards regarding police custody in England and Wales, namely the appropriate adult (AA) safeguard and the Independent Custody Visiting Scheme (ICVS).

Police custody and PACE

In England and Wales, under the provisions of PACE, the police may detain suspects in police custody for up to 24, 36 or 96 hours in exceptional circumstances (Home Office, 2018). An individual suspected of a summary offence can be held in police custody without charge for up to 24 hours (PACE, section 41) and a senior officer who is a superintendent or above can extend this to 36 hours (PACE, section 42). A magistrate can extend the detention of individuals detained as suspects of serious indictable offences to 96 hours (PACE sections 43–4). Holding people in police custody involves the detention of vulnerable people, this includes children, individuals experiencing substance use and misuse issues, individuals without a home and individuals with mental health or mentally disordered issues. Kendall (2021) contends that being in police custody 'isolates the individual, and it can be a frightening and dangerous experience for detainees'. In addition, holding areas are noisy, smelly and 'place[s] of sanctioned isolation, where detainees are purposefully and legally held in separation from the public and from each other' (Wooff and Skinns, 2018, p 565).

A contemporary understanding of police custody is embedded in PACE, which has undergone numerous revisions. PACE sought to increase the due process rights of suspects. However, it also extended existing police powers and introduced new powers; it introduced the role of custody officer and it regulates the power to detain (Home Office, 2018). Yet, as Dehaghani (2016) states, since its introduction, it has been well documented that greater fairness for arrestees, suspects and detainees has not necessarily been achieved. Provisions in PACE codes of practice include the duration that someone can be detained in custody without being charged, the frequency of checks on those that are held in custody, mealtimes and exercise periods (Wooff and Skinns, 2018).

Police custody: policy and practice

In England, Wales and Northern Ireland, police custody is under the direction and control of individual chief constables within each force area. Custody resources that must be available when required include custody officers and detention staff, who may be police officers, police staff or privately contracted detention staff. There are 45 police forces in the UK and this includes 43 in England and Wales. As a result of Code C in PACE 1984, in England and Wales at least there should be consistency in the manner in which custody is administered (Home Office, 2018). However, the reality is that each station manages custody in its own way. Perhaps in part this is due to unclear guidance regarding Code C provisions and several periodic revisions since its introduction over forty years ago. This is further complicated by the changing landscape of police detention: for example, the introduction of non-designated custody suites, public–private partnerships and private financial initiatives.

If PACE is followed, being detained in a police station should be a last resort, but this is not always the case (Kemp, cited in Gibbs and Ratcliffe, 2020). Police custody policy and practice in England and Wales has been problematic for at least ten years. In 2010 detainees were being held on average for just over nine hours, but in 2020 the average length of custody was 13 hours, an increase of four hours (Kemp, cited in Gibbs and Ratcliffe, 2020). On a more positive note, changes in policing priorities have resulted in a decline in the number of people arrested and detained since 2008. However, the former Home Secretary Priti Patel introduced league tables to assess police forces according to their success in cutting serious crime (Darling, 2021). Chief constables and government sources have denied the new system of 'national and policing measures' is a return to targets. However, the Police Federation of England and Wales and serving officers are sceptical of this measure and have compared it to target setting for police forces in the past (Darling, 2021). If the introduction of this new scheme signals the return of national targets, this may result in full custody suites again. One serving officer who was dismayed with the new measures posted the following on social media: '[t]argets are back. I'll have a lot more to say about this, but once we start nicking people because we have a "league table" and not because they need nicking, it's a dark road' (cited in Darling, 2021).

Despite the significance of and the controversial nature of police custody, this important aspect of policing and criminal justice has previously received little attention inside and outside academia. As Wooff and Skinns (2018, p 576) note, 'literature on police custody is often uncritically linked to the prisons literature'. This is surprising given that in the police operation of custody, the police in England and Wales are subject to very little regulation. Indeed, as Kendall (2021) highlights, regulation takes the form of self-regulation and a full inspection of every custody suite takes place only once every six years.

Police custody is a 'complex environment, where police officers, detainees and other staff interact in a number of different emotional, spatial and transformative ways' (Wooff and Skinns, 2018, p 565). Police custody takes place in a built environment that is infused with emotionality and emotional management. It has been argued that newly built large police custody suites are the equivalent of miniature prisons (Wooff and Skinns, 2018). Police custody suites are at one and the same time in plain sight and yet secretive worlds. They have an external physical built presence in the community and they have an internal covert life. Kendall (2020, p 117) encapsulates the latter point well when he states, '[c]ustody blocks constitute some of the state's secret places and are very much the police's territory'. Custody blocks are closed institutions and they are 'a very locked-down environment, the police's world, which nobody else except custody visitors really get a view into' (Skinns, cited in Kendall, 2020, p 126).

Importantly, police custody is also a distressing experience and even at its best it is an unpleasant one. This can be seen from Dehaghani's (2016, p 8) description of police custody cells:

> [T]he cell conditions are far from pleasant – not only are they dimly-lit, clinical and cold … they have an unusually hostile smell that combines in various quantities, urine, vomit, faeces, stale blood, (stale) alcohol, and body odour. Privacy is not a luxury afforded to those in police custody – detainees who are placed in a CCTV-cell must use the toilet with the knowledge that someone is watching them.

Individuals who are detained in police custody are particularly vulnerable due to the imbalance of power between the police and detained. Despite the intended protections of PACE, which are discussed later, the imbalance of power can and has resulted in the abuse of detainees and deaths in police custody. There were 20 or more deaths in custody in England and Wales per year from 2014 to 2018 and in the 12 months to 31 March 2019 there were 63 apparent suicides (Kendall, 2020, p 117). The pains of police custody can be exacerbated by the immediate deprivation of social media, messaging contact and a clock or watch (Wooff and Skinns, 2018). Within police custody there is nothing to do, nothing to read and nothing to watch and the situation renders detainees vulnerable as it is so bewildering and disconcerting.

With regard to an understanding and analysis of police custody in England and Wales, determining contexts or social variables, such as class, ethnicity, gender and age of detainees, is very difficult due to a lack of data. However, Dehaghani (2016, p 12) comments that while custody 'is or can be, detrimental to all detainees … it is perhaps more problematic for black or minority ethnic (BAME) individuals'. For example, race and ethnicity can impact the increased probability of being strip searched and dying in police custody (Dehaghani, 2016).

Police custody and the AA safeguard

The AA safeguard is in place to provide an important safeguard to young detainees (or juveniles) and vulnerable adults. The safeguard gives vulnerable individuals a right to the provision of an AA who is independent of the police. The AA advises and assists the detainee, observes whether the police are conducting themselves fairly and respectfully with regard to the detainees' rights, and informs an officer of the rank of inspector and above if they believe that this is not the case. The role also includes helping the detainee to understand their rights and assisting them with communicating with the police (Home Office, 2018). Various individuals can act as an AA, namely a friend, relative, guardian or carer, a volunteer, a professional AA or a social worker. Those considered vulnerable include anyone who is or appears (to the custody officer) to be aged under 17, have mental health difficulties or have a learning disability, or have difficulty communicating and understanding things. The policy is laudable, but in practice it is not free from error. For example, police officers may fail to identify vulnerability and this can exacerbate the negative and distressing experience of police custody.

Policy custody and the Independent Custody Visiting Scheme

The ICVS is also supposed to safeguard detainees, vulnerable and otherwise, and 'deter police from misconduct which might lead to deaths in custody' (Kendall, 2020, p 115). The ICVS was introduced in 2002 in response to concerns about deaths in custody. It operates in all parts of England and Wales; Scotland and Northern Ireland have similar schemes. Police and crime commissioners (PCCs) run each local scheme and the Independent Custody Visiting Association (ICVA) provides guidance. All of the members of the ICVA are PCCs who liaise with the Home Office. Thus, there is no national organisation that gives a voice to visitors (Kendall, 2020, 2021). Although officially the scheme is not identified as a regulator, Kendall (2020, p 116) contends 'it is clearly a regulator inasmuch as it forms part of governance aimed at ensuring that the police adhere to standards set for the safeguarding of detainees'. Very little is known about ICVS as, similarly to police custody, this is an under-researched area. The exception to this is the in-depth qualitative doctoral research undertaken by Kendall (2020, 2021), which entailed 76 interviews and 123 hours of observations and found that visitors had no impact on police behaviour and that the ICVS was ineffective. Kendall (2021) also found that '[o]n average, a visit was made to each custody suite once a week. The visits were found to take place at predictable times, and never during the night.' He concluded that 'this watchdog has been debarked as a result of the power of the police' (Kendall, 2020, p 115). In other words, this system of police regulation has no bite and, as such, it is ineffective. The ICVS provides an illusion that there are safeguards for those detained in custody, but this is not the case, and extensive and radical reforms are long overdue.

Conclusions

Due to the competing demands made of the police – for example, ensuring public safety, preventing and detecting crime and investigating offences – the rights of detainees are not a priority. While greater police visibility has been enabled by developments in new citizen-controlled media technologies (mobile phones for example), this has not been true with regard to police custody (and the changing landscape of police custody suites). Although PACE 1984 was intended to tighten up the regulation of police detention, police discretion and the permissiveness of the law means the reality in practice is that this has not happened. PACE provides a veil of legitimacy for the police and it obscures the lack of sufficient and efficient regulation around police custody, including the subordination of detainees' rights to police operations. For Kendall (2020, p 117), 'significant evasions and breaches of detainee safeguards' 'show that all is not well in custody'. The AA and the ICVS should also contribute significantly to police regulation and safeguard the welfare of detainees in police custody yet, sadly, to date this is not the case. In respect of police custody and what is in effect self-regulation, extensive and radical changes are called for. This may entail greater clarity and enforcement of PACE 1984, changes to or the replacement of the AA and ICVS, police reductionism or even police abolitionism.

Finally, COVID-19 has led to a new national protocol which requires the police to restrict the use of holding people in police custody due to the dangers of spreading the pandemic as a result of police interviews in small rooms. Early findings concerned with the impact of COVID-19 on those in police custody are that when the pandemic began, custody work carried on as usual and that between April and August 2020 the total number of detainees decreased slightly; however, after the first lockdown in the five forces that were investigated the numbers returned to the previous levels (HMICFRS, 2021). That aside, a renewed focus on police custody and relevant police powers may offer some hope of an improvement of police custody conditions during and post-COVID-19. This could include less time in police custody and fewer people held in custody.

References

Darling, Z. (2021) '"Targets are back": police officers sceptical about Priti Patel's "league table"', *The Justice Gap*, [online] 23 April, Available from: https://www.thejusticegap.com/targets-are-back-police-officers-sceptical-about-priti-patels-league-table/ [Accessed 20 June 2022].

Dehaghani, R. (2016) 'The case against custody: exploring the problems with police detention in England and Wales'. Criminal Justice, Borders and Citizenship Research Paper No. 17-5, University of Leicester School of Law, [online] Available from https://ssrn.com/abstract=2858178 [Accessed 26 March 2021].

Gibbs, P. and Ratcliffe F. (2020) '24 hours in police custody: is police detention overused?' Transform Justice, [online] Available from: https://www.transformjustice.org.uk/wp-content/uploads/2020/06/TJ_Police_Custody_Report_041.pdf [Accessed 26 March 2021].

HMICFRS (HM Inspectorate of Constabulary (and) Fire and Rescue Services) (2021) 'Custody services in a COVID-19 environment', [online] April, Available from: https://www.justiceinspectorates.gov.uk/hmicfrs/publication-html/custody-services-covid-19-environment/ [Accessed 10 June 2022].

Home Office (2018) 'Code C: revised Code of Practice for the detention, treatment and questioning of persons by police officers', TSO, [online] July, Available from: https://assets.publishing.service.gov.uk/government/uploads/system/uploads/attachment_data/file/729842/pace-code-c-2018.pdf [Accessed 26 March 2021].

Kendall, J. (2020) 'Custody visiting: the watchdog that didn't bark', *Criminology & Criminal Justice*, 22(1): 115–31, DOI: https://doi.org/10.1177/1748895820967989.

Kendall, J. (2021) 'What's going on in police custody?' University of Birmingham [online], December, Available from: https://www.birmingham.ac.uk/news/2021/whats-going-on-in-police-custody [Accessed 17 June 2022].

NPCC (National Police Chiefs' Council) (nd) 'National strategy for police custody', [online] Available from: https://www.npcc.police.uk/documents/NPCC%20Custody%20Strategy.pdf [Accessed 17 June 2022].

Wooff, A. and Skinns, L. (2018) 'The role of emotion, space and place in police custody in England: towards a geography of police custody', *Punishment and Society*, 20(5): 562–79, DOI: https://journals.sagepub.com/doi/pdf/10.1177/1462474517722176.

40

Policing serious, violent and sexual offending

Michelle McManus and Eric Halford

Introduction

This chapter seeks to outline how law enforcement agencies and the criminal justice system (CJS) collectively conduct the management of sexual or violent offenders (MOSOVO). In addition, this chapter will outline the present state of sexual and violent offending in the UK and describe some of the most pressing challenges within MOSOVO. It is first important to define what constitutes serious sexual or violent offending. In theory, this category is extremely broad and could include almost all offences committed against a person. In reality, the scope constitutes high-harm, high-risk offences that are committed by some of society's most dangerous offenders, including rape, sexual exploitation, life-threatening assaults and homicide. Often, the offending is committed by serial and repeat offenders who predominately, though not exclusively, target women and young girls, and it occurs through domestic or intimate partner relations or exploitative grooming, or is committed against strangers.

Sexual assault and rape

Unfortunately, the scale of such offending is high. An examination of serious sexual offending through the Crime Survey for England and Wales (CSEW) in 2020 showed that 1.6 million adults aged between 16 and 74 years have experienced sexual assault by rape or penetration since the age of 16 years, with 49 per cent stating they had been a victim more than once. The volume of recorded sexual offences has tripled in recent years, the figures for the year ending March 2020 were 162,936 reported sexual offences and 58,856 reported rapes (ONS, 2021). Despite such high levels of offending the prosecution of offenders has declined for a myriad of reasons. According to the Crown Prosecution Service's (CPS's) Violence Against Women and Girls Report, rape figures from 2017 to 2019 showed that the number of suspects referred for a charge of rape by the police has fallen by 22.8 per cent. Charges for rape have fallen by 38 per cent, prosecutions have fallen by 32.8 per cent and the number of convictions has fallen by 26.9 per cent. These statistics are extremely worrying, as they only represent those victims who actually come forward and report to the police: approximately one in five female victims and one in six male victims report rape to the police (ONS, 2021).

Domestic abuse and intimate partner violence

In respect of serious sexual or violent offending committed in domestic circumstances or intimate partner relationships, data from the CSEW in year ending March 2020 from the Office for National Statistics (ONS) reported that around 2.3 million adults aged 16 to 74 years had experienced domestic abuse in that year. This was broken down as 1.6 million women and 757,000 men. Domestic abuse crimes were recorded at 758,941 (excluding one major police force). Both statistics showed increases on previous years. However, as with sexual offending, even though rates of self-reporting through the crime survey and official reports to police had increased, charging decisions for domestic abuse had also fallen (by 19 per cent from the previous year). Additional data from March 2020 to June 2020, when COVID-19 hit the world, indicates a 7 per cent increase in police-recorded offences across a range of crime types (Halford et al, 2020), with this increase in demand more pronounced for domestic abuse victim support services. For example, the National Domestic Abuse Helpline, between April and June 2020, reported a 65 per cent increase in calls compared to previous three months prior to the pandemic.

Homicide

Homicide is also increasing. Releases from ONS have shown there were 695 victims in the year ending March 2020, 47 more (7 per cent) than the previous year (this figure includes the Grays lorry incident with 39 homicide victims – if this incident is excluded, homicide showed a 1 per cent increase overall). Fortunately, homicides are rare, with the rate recorded as 11.7 per million population, with the rate higher for males (17 per million population) than for females (6 per million population). Disparities also exist in ethnic groups, for example, over the three-year period to the year ending March 2020 the homicide rate for Black victims was 49.5 per million of the population, approximately five times higher than for the White ethnic group (9.4 per million population). The number of Black victims in 2022, at 105, was the highest seen since the year ending March 2002 (107 victims). Additionally, there has been increases in homicide victims aged 16 to 24 (n = 142). Sadly, a continuous trend in homicides that has been identified has children under the age of 1 as the victims; this was recorded as the highest rate of homicide (28 per million population), followed by those victims aged 16 to 24 years (23 per million population) and 35 to 44 years (18 per million population). Concerns have been raised over the increase in proportion of homicide victims aged 16–24 years of 29 per cent.

The impact of COVID-19 on serious violence and sexual offending

As can be seen, the rate of serious sexual or violent offending is increasing across the board and the impact of the global coronavirus pandemic, COVID-19, has not eased the problem. Despite clear positive declines in lower-harm forms of offending such as acquisitive crimes including theft and burglary, serious sexual and violent offending has been negatively impacted by the pandemic. Much attention has been given to domestic abuse during the pandemic, with concerns about victims being locked in with their perpetrators and the wider, long-term implications of intergenerational victimisation of many children also being home schooled. For example, at the start of the COVID-19 lockdowns in the UK, an increase in women killed by men was recorded. Between 23 March and 12 April 2020, 14 women and two girls were recorded to have been killed by men, representing the highest number since Karen Ingala Smith started 'Counting Dead Women'. While we raise the caveat that this data should be read with caution, as such tragic events very rarely occur in a uniform pattern, Dame Vera Baird, while providing evidence to the Home Affairs Committee, emphasised this data as reflecting the size of the current crisis in terms of the safety and risk associated with domestic abuse during lockdown. In acknowledgement of the concerns around domestic abuse during the lockdown period, the UK government commenced a communications campaign using the hashtag #YouAreNotAlone to encourage victims to seek support, alongside £2 million of funding for online and helpline support services to compliment frontline funding for domestic abuse charities. This was alongside a package of £750 million for frontline charities across the UK, but only time will tell if such efforts were able to curb the increases in serious sexual or violent offending during the pandemic.

Responding to serious violence and sexual offending

Having defined the form and scope of serious sexual or violent offending, how the police and CJS manage and respond to the problem can be outlined. In respect of the academic literature on this there are generally a handful of accepted approaches. These include responses that are focused upon prevention and rehabilitation, often through knowledge-based awareness campaigns (Hamby, 2006), perpetrator-based programmes, early risk identification and victim-focused initiatives (Antle et al, 2011). Although involved in a multi-agency approach in the aforementioned solutions, as can be expected the police and CJS primarily utilise coercive interventions such as investigation and prosecution. Although it should be acknowledged that responding to serious sexual or violent offending is everyone's responsibility within the police and CJS, this chapter will focus on specialist methods delivered through a variety of governance and organisational structural responses (see CoP, 2020). At a localised level the police predominately respond to the management of sexual or violent offenders through dedicated MOSOVO units. These are often multi-agency in nature and the police liaise and engage with a range of public and third sector agencies involved with both victims and perpetrators, such as social services, health, probation, prisons, and housing. Together, this multi-agency approach delivers statutory obligations in respect of managing sexual or violent offenders through formalised procedures, policies and practice around high-risk offenders, such as multi-agency public protection arrangements (HMPPS, 2021), alongside enhanced information sharing and maintenance of national databases such as the Violent and Sex Offender Register. The latter ensures violent and sexual offenders cannot evade supervision by moving across borders.

The role of specialists

In respect of serious sexual and violent offences committed within domestic settings or against intimate partners many forces utilise specialist Public Protection Units. Such units contain domestic and child abuse specialists and often contain 'dedicated domestic abuse or child protection teams'. While not consistent across all forces, there is a minimum requirement that each force has a 'body of specialist officers' who are authorised to practise the investigation of child abuse and have completed the Specialist Child Abuse Investigators Development Programme, who can aid the initial responding officer, supported by specialist supervisors qualified in the investigation and management of serious crime who have an overview of serious sexual or violence-related domestic and child abuse cases (CoP, 2022). For homicide, many police services also deploy a specialist capabilities approach and often use Major Crime Investigative Support (MCIS) units, or the alternatively named Force Major Investigation Teams (FMIT), in their investigative response to major crimes such as murder, manslaughter, kidnap, extortion and stranger rape. Developed in response to the Byford Report into the Yorkshire Ripper investigation (Byford, 1981), local MCIS and FMITs are usually led by a detective superintendent, as known as the senior investigating officer (SIO). The dedicated, experienced team of police officers and staff within these units possess specialised qualifications and are often detectives or assistant investigators qualified under the College of Policing's Professionalising Investigation Programme and experienced in the use of the Home Office Large and Major Enquiry System, which was introduced as a result of failings in the Yorkshire Ripper case. These highly specialised teams operate using the Major Incident Room Standard Administrative Procedures (CoP, 2021), which provide a uniformed national framework for investigating serious sexual and violent offending.

The regional and national response

At a regional and national level, the National Crime Agency (NCA) provides specialist services for police forces across the UK. They do this by working alongside local police services and providing additional support such as specialist research teams, witness intermediary teams, and advice and support from the National Injuries Database team which can assist with identification of unknown injuries, provide case examples of injuries and weapons for case comparisons, and source independent expert forensic and medical opinions. Additional support can also be provided to local police forces through the Expert Advisers Database, which links local investigators with thematic experts in accountancy, toxicology, firearms and psychology (NCA, 2022a). The NCA also provides national SIO advisers, behavioural investigative advisers and geographic profilers. In addition, there are national groups that exist across policing in the UK, such as the National Police Chiefs' Council, National Homicide Working Group and Child Death Subgroup. These working groups bring regional representatives together from across UK policing and other relevant agencies to discuss key trends in homicide and child deaths, ensuring a joined-up approach in prevention and investigation, as well as identification of the training and skills development required, alongside dissemination of key information through newsletters and annual conferences.

From an analytical perspective, the UK Serious Crime Analysis Section (SCAS) identifies serial rapists and murderers at the earliest stages of their offending (NCA, 2022b). All police forces in England and Wales are mandated to submit data to SCAS for cases, including stranger rape, serious sexual assaults, and motiveless or sexually motivated murder cases. The SCAS team holds national responsibility to identify potential serious sexual offenders across the UK and provides support to serious stranger sexual offence and murder investigations by providing specialist behavioural analysis. In regard to recording and coding data, the SCAS team manage the Violent Crime Linkage Analysis System (ViCLAS). Here, behaviours within an offence are indexed in a standardised manner onto ViCLAS, with stringent quality assurance processes in place. There are 500+ options relating to searchable fields concerning offender behaviour, verbal communication, offence locations, victimology and offender details (if known). This data is invaluable to investigations of serious crimes, allowing the narrowing of suspect parameters using previous conviction histories, crime scene behaviours and other offence behaviours to help solve complex, serious cases (Almond et al, 2018).

Challenges in responding to serious violence and sexual offending

Despite the comprehensive framework and highly capable staff and officers from a multitude of agencies, the MOSOVO field is suffering somewhat of a crisis. In order to understand the context of the challenges for the police and wider CJS to protect and prevent serious crimes such as sexual assaults and rapes, it is important to understand the changing landscape of sexual offending perpetration alongside the identification of trends to target prevention strategies and education campaigns. Over the past several decades, research has shown an increase in internet-facilitated rapes, sexual assaults, exploitation and, in the worst-case scenario, murder, such as that seen in the tragic Grace Millane case. Such offending occurs after victims are contacted via social media or dating apps, followed by brief interactions with the perpetrator before a meeting in person. Research from McManus and Almond (2019) has highlighted that these meetings with 'strangers' are happening in isolated locations, such as the victim's or perpetrator's home. Similarly, increased numbers of children are being targeted, groomed through an ever-changing portfolio of social media applications and computer games, often leading to subsequent sexual exploitation and abuse. These changes in interactions between victim and perpetrators indicate emboldened and more overt sexual predatory behaviour, with offenders no doubt taking advantage of victims' subsequent reluctance to report their assault due to concerns about how it might be viewed.

The change in the context of serious offending, particularly sexual offences, has presented the police and CJS with a number of key hurdles to climb. Firstly, the changes in the modus operandi (MO) from 'offline' to 'online' targeting by sexual offenders has resulted in huge increases in digital devices requiring processing. The examination of digital devices such as smartphones is not as simple as 'turning them on and having a look'. To maintain their evidential integrity, police must follow a strict digital forensic imaging and examination process by highly skilled digital technicians. Due to the rapid rise of the digitisation of the MO the police have been unable to keep pace, leading to gross under-resourcing of digital forensics staff and the adoption of novel approaches to address long delays in processing digital evidence (Wilson-Kovacs, 2020) in order to reduce delays in charging decisions, which are frequently in excess of 9–12 months. Secondly, the police and CJS have also struggled to adapt culturally to societal changes in attitudes and language; this has often unwittingly led to a culture of 'victim blaming', leading to survivors of serious sexual violence often feeling humiliation, shame and heightened public scrutiny. In the UK, the 2021 joint thematic inspection of the police and CPS's response to rape by HM Inspectorate of Constabularies and Fire and Rescue Services (HMICFRS) identified 'underlying problems … exist in the mind-set of some police investigators and prosecutors towards rape cases'.

Furthermore, some high-profile cases, such as the murder of Grace Millane, which, although it took place in New Zealand, highlighted the treatment of rape and homicide victims within the CJS, which often starts with a 'digital strip search' of victims, often of information images, text and information completely unrelated to the case. It could be argued that this occurs largely because victims routinely have their medical histories examined for evidence of mental illness or other 'undermining' information that may affect their credibility, leading to what, in essence, often becomes a character assessment of those who are often very vulnerable, with offenders rarely being subjected to the same level of scrutiny. The evidence extracted from the collection and examination of the digital devices, health information and, in some cases, even school records, is shared with the CPS during the 'decision to charge' phase. It can be argued that increasingly officers and prosecutors have interpreted what is societally becoming routine relationship norms, such as proactive contact via dating apps for example, as being 'undermining' behaviour that discredits victim accounts and provides a negative narrative, making the realistic prospect of conviction unlikely. This occurs even before the evidence can be interpreted by a jury, with the CPS often becoming the primary decision maker in whether these serious crimes, with often no witnesses, are even taken forward into a court of law.

The disproportionate focus on the investigation and interpretation of victim credibility has unfortunately led to the third major hurdle facing the police and CJS. This relates to the high level of victim disengagement and a lack of confidence in the CJS to deliver justice while protecting the victim's privacy. Research into this area suggests that victims of serious violence and sexual abuse disengage with the CJS for a variety of reasons; however, a lack of victim support is key in large numbers retracting their original evidence and withdrawing their overall cooperation (Birdsall et al, 2016). The intense scrutiny on the victims' perceived credibility is a major factor in victims not feeling believed and feeling unsupported, which drives their perception that the police do not have their interests at heart. As a result, the CJS again finds itself battling a confidence cycle whereby high levels of disengagement lead to lower conviction rates, which in turn leads to reduced confidence and impacts future reporting and continued engagement. There remains, however, cause for optimism, as recent studies (Halford and Smith, 2022) have shown that police services are working in partnership to provide intense advocacy support for victims, showing a renewed emphasis on supporting victims of serious violence and sexual abuse.

Conclusion

In conclusion, MOSOVO is an integral part of policing and the criminal justice response. MOSOVO can encompass a wide array of offences including rape, other serious sexual offences, exploitation, domestic abuse and homicide. Recent data suggests that the volume of sexual or violent offences is increasing. Pressing issues facing the police and CJS include the rapid and continuing rises in demand for digital forensics examinations. In addition, the culture and attitude within the police and CPS, of practitioners and prosecutors alike, often leave a lot to be desired. These issues have negatively impacted victim engagement and cooperation, significantly underpinning falls in prosecution levels in recent years.

To manage the problem, the police have a specialist capabilities framework in place that functions in a multi-agency environment which consists of dedicated and skilled officers and staff; thus, despite significant challenges in the response to serious sexual and violent offending there is room to be optimistic. The 2021 joint thematic inspection of the police and CPS's response to rape by HMICFRS highlights examples of effective individuals and teams in every force and CPS area (HMICFRS, 2021). Although a relatively damning report, identifying and acknowledging the need for improvement is the first clear step and the report places great emphasis on victim engagement and management from the outset in cases of serious sexual violence. Along with domestic abuse, this is an area where it is known the importance of the initial response and subsequent compassion and empathy shown have the capacity to be transformative and represent a key aspect of effective intervention. Poor responses and victim management result in the withdrawal of engagement and the potential for victimisation and offending to continue, alongside a reduction in the potential of prosecution.

Recent studies conducted on interventions used during the COVID-19 pandemic on specialist domestic abuse responses have shown that broader multi-agency working can be a key facet of effective intervention in responding to, assessing and managing victims of domestic abuse to improve confidence and engagement. Specialist training for officers within the police, the development of specialist Domestic Abuse Units or Public Protection Units that work alongside independent domestic violence advisors, and improved efficiency in engagement at Multi-Agency Risk Assessment Conferences have all been acknowledged as key developments in improving responses to domestic abuse, and it is likely similar improvements could be achieved in cases of serious sexual violence such as rape.

Furthermore, the new Domestic Abuse Act 2021 came into force during 2021 and 2022 and with it came a suite of changes to help improve the response to domestic abuse victims. Some of these changes in the Act include creating a statutory definition of domestic abuse, with emphasis on emotional, controlling/coercive and economic abuse alongside physical abuse; establishing in law the office of domestic abuse commissioner, with enhanced functions and powers; and providing new domestic abuse protection notices and domestic abuse protection orders. Other changes include the prohibition of cross-examination by perpetrators and use of special measures in all civil and family courts. Combined, the recognition of the hurdles faced, along with innovative evidence-based approaches, changes to legislation and the inevitable focus and progress that a report such as the 2021 joint thematic inspection of the police and CPS's response to rape by HMICFRS is likely to instigate, enables a more positive outlook to be tentatively adopted, provided words transition into action and behaviour change within the whole CJS.

References

Almond, L., McManus, M., Bal, A., O'Brien, F., Rainbow, L. and Webb, M. (2018) 'Assisting the investigation of stranger rapes: predicting the criminal record of UK stranger rapists from their crime scene behaviors', *Journal of Interpersonal Violence*, 36(3–4): 1–24, DOI: 10.1177/0886260518756118.

Antle, B.F., Sullivan, D.J., Dryden, A., Karam, E.A. and Barbee, A.P. (2011) 'Healthy relationship education for dating violence prevention among high-risk youth', *Children and Youth Services Review*, 33(1): 173–9, DOI: https://doi.org/10.1016/j.childyouth.2010.08.031.

Birdsall, N., Kirby, S. and McManus, M. (2016) 'Police–victim engagement in building a victim empowerment approach to intimate partner violence cases', *Police Practice and Research*, 18(1): 75–86, DOI: https://doi.org/10.1080/15614263.2016.1230061.

Byford, L. (1981) 'The Yorkshire Ripper case: review of the police investigation of the case', Home Office, [online] Available from: https://assets.publishing.service.gov.uk/government/uploads/system/uploads/attachment_data/file/100353/1941-Byford_part_1_.pdf [Accessed 10 June 2022].

CoP (College of Policing) (2020) 'Major investigation and public protection introduction to managing sexual offenders and violent offenders', [online] Available from: https://www.app.college.police.uk/app-content/major-investigation-and-public-protection/managing-sexual-offenders-and-violent-offenders/ [Accessed 26 July 2021].

CoP (College of Policing) (2021) 'Major incident room standardised administrative procedures: authorised professional practice', [online] Available from: https://www.college.police.uk/app/major-investigation-and-public-protection/major-incident-room-standardised-administrative-procedures-mirsap [Accessed 10 June 2022].

CoP (College of Policing) (2022) 'Investigating child abuse and safeguarding children: authorised professional practice', [online] Available from: https://www.college.police.uk/app/major-investigation-and-public-protection/investigating-child-abuse-and-safeguarding-children [Accessed 10 June 2022].

Halford, E. and Smith, J. (2022) 'Operation provide: a multi-agency response to increasing police engagement in cases of intimate partner violence during the COVID-19 pandemic', *Police Practice and Research*, 23(5): 600–13, DOI: https://doi.org/10.1080/15614263.2022.2033621.

Halford, E., Dixon, A., Farrell, G., Malleson, N. and Tilley, N. (2020) 'Crime and coronavirus: social distancing, lockdown, and the mobility elasticity of crime', *Crime Science*, 9(1): 11.

Hamby, S.L. (2006) 'The who, what, when and where, and how of partner violence prevention research', *Journal of Aggression, Maltreatment & Trauma*, 13(3–4): 179–201. DOI: https://doi.org/10.1300/j146v13n03_07.

HMICFRS (HM Inspectorate of Constabularies and Fire and Rescue Services) (2021) 'A joint thematic inspection of the police and Crown Prosecution Service's response to rape phase one: from report to police or CPS decision to take no further action', [online] Available from: https://www.justiceinspectorates.gov.uk/hmicfrs/wp-content/uploads/joint-thematic-inspection-of-police-and-cps-response-to-rape-phase-one.pdf [Accessed 31 July 2021].

HMPPS (HM Prison and Probation Service) (2021) 'Multi-agency public protection arrangements: updated guidance', [online] Available from: https://www.gov.uk/government/publications/multi-agency-public-protection-arrangements-mappa-guidance [Accessed 10 June 2022].

McManus, M.A. and Almond, L. (2019) 'Rising rape cases, a broken criminal justice system and the "digital strip search"', *The Conversation*, [online] 17 December, Available from: https://theconversation.com/rising-rape-cases-a-broken-criminal-justice-system-and-the-digital-strip-search-127852 [Accessed 28 June 2021].

NCA (National Crime Agency) (2022a) 'Major Crime Investigative Support', [online] Available from: https://www.nationalcrimeagency.gov.uk/what-we-do/how-we-work/providing-specialist-capabilities-for-law-enforcement/major-crime-investigative-support [Accessed 10 June 2022].

NCA (National Crime Agency) (2022b) 'Serious Crime Analysis Section', [online] Available from: https://www.nationalcrimeagency.gov.uk/what-we-do/how-we-work/providing-specialist-capabilities-for-law-enforcement/serious-crime-analysis [Accessed 10 June 2022].

ONS (Office for National Statistics) (2021) 'Nature of sexual assault by rape or penetration, England and Wales: year ending March 2020', [online] Available from: https://www.ons.gov.uk/peoplepopulationandcommunity/crimeandjustice/articles/natureofsexualassaultbyrapeorpenetrationenglandandwales/yearendingmarch2020 [Accessed 31 July 2021].

Wilson-Kovacs, D. (2020) 'Effective resource management in digital forensics: an exploratory analysis of triage practices in four English constabularies', *Policing: An International Journal*, 43(1): 77–90, DOI: https://doi.org/10.1108/PIJPSM-07-2019-0126.

41

Policing and mental health

Tim Kelly

Introduction

A person in crisis. Life and work may be getting on top of them. Feeling that there is nowhere to turn, no one listens to what they say. Got an appointment with the GP, but offered anti-depressants, which may not help. Things go from bad to worse, and then one day a small disagreement with a fellow motorist on the way home from work results in a major meltdown. The person is in a mental health crisis – so who should be coming to help – the police?

It is abundantly clear that arrangements around the management of mental health crisis in public are not seen in a positive light by those who have to use those services, or indeed by their families. The main route into crisis care should be via one's GP, but often this is problematic for those who are actually in the midst of a problem that, characteristically, is not bound by office hours or cannot wait for the setting of a future appointment. Currently, it is more likely that the first call from the individual, friends/family (or potentially a concerned stranger) is via the emergency '999' system. Dependent on how the call is then routed, and the perceived context, it will result in attendance by paramedics, the police and likely both. The question of whether mental health crisis should be a police matter, and whether multi agency approaches to the problem improve the situation for those in crisis, will be discussed.

Currently, the College of Policing (CoP, 2015 pp 9–10) suggests that:

- 17 per cent of police demand is crime-related.
- 15–20 per cent of police demand is mental health-related.
- 83 per cent of all police demand is non-crime-related.

The changing role of the police in responding to mental health needs

It is clear that the police have historically had a role in managing people in mental health crises, ostensibly because of their 24/7 role. However, the health service is arguably more appropriate to deal with those in crisis and is also a 24/7 service. The actions of those in crisis – from the tragic death of Jonathan Zito to the more recent murder of Donald Lock – have caused moral panics ever since the establishment of the Mental Health Act (MHA) 1983 and the move away from institutional care. Headlines in sections of the media have criticised failures of state services in managing crises. Each incident is picked over in detail, with the factors that led to it, and in particular whether they might have been avoided, discussed at length in media and by academics. Then there are other incidents, for example, the death of Thomas Orchard while in police custody, that remind society that the police service has work to do when it comes to actually managing mental health sufferers in crisis. Schug and Fradella (2015, p 16), for example, highlight that the majority of people with a serious mental illness (SMI) who are in crisis are not violent; indeed, research suggests that there is not a great deal of difference between the numbers of SMI and non-SMI sufferers who are violent, and thus the idea of a violent SMI sufferer may be, in part, a construct driven by media and the film industry (Schug and Fradella, 2015, p 3).

This is an issue, then, that can be traced back to representations in drama and the horror genre of TV and film, and possibly to 'shock films' like *Psycho*, with publicity material often predicated around the dangerous SMI sufferer (Schug and Fradella, 2015, p 3). Many researchers make the point that most people who are mentally ill at any given time are not violent and it is often suggested that substance abuse is a much greater factor in the increase of risk of violence. Nonetheless, the perception of the violent SMI sufferer is not entirely without foundation, as discussed in 'Policing and mental health: picking up the pieces' (HMICFRS, 2018). The case study on page 5 of this inspectorate report presents a situation where a person in crisis was unable to access services and saw the possibility of harming another person as the only way to get treatment. It is open to question, then, whether – when people are obviously in a mental health crisis – the misperception of increased violence may be the driver for such situations coming under the bailiwick of the police rather than any other agency. Therefore, any perceptions around the danger of violent behaviour must also be weighed against the frustration expressed by service users and families at not being able to access services when they feel they need them (HMICFRS, 2018, p 5).

The various reviews of procedure and process have shown that the police can do better; indeed, Lord Victor Adebowale's Independent Commission on Mental Health and Policing (ICMHP), in 2013, made the point that managing mental health was always 'core police business' (ICMHP, 2013, p 1). It is a view that has not always been shared by those leading policing. Indeed, in the foreword to his report, Lord Adebowale shared concerns over police involvement in managing mental health crisis (ICMHP, 2013). There is clear tension here; in 2010 for example, the then Home Secretary, Theresa May, famously told the Police Federation that their role was confined to cutting crime. Other commentators, such as former Commissioner of the Metropolitan Police Sir Ian Blair in 2016, were concerned that police focus on mental health was potentially affecting other police business. Another study showed that 15 per cent of police work was related to mental health issues (Cummins and Edmondson, 2016, p 42). Elsewhere, there is a view that, in part, the police role has long overlapped with social work (see Wolff, 2005). All of which begs the question, do the police have the tools available to manage those in mental health crisis?

The police and the Mental Health Act 1983

The MHA 1983 provides the police with an express power to detain anyone acting in a way that gives concern for their own health and safety or that of others, in a public place, under section 136 (1). This means that without all of the other safeguards applied under the Police and Criminal Evidence Act of 1984, those in crisis can be detained (for the purpose of assessment, importantly) for up to 24 hours (as revised). Problems arose with the loose definition of 'public place'. Several of the reports and reviews that have been conducted since 1983 have been scathing about the abuse or potential abuse of the extant definition. The review conducted by the Centre for Mental Health (Durcan, 2014, p 11) reported that service users' experiences supported the notion that police officers misused power under section 136, whether this was to avoid using other powers or for expediency was never clear. What is clear is that guidance was required, but not until 2016, with the revision of the Act, was it forthcoming.

Recent developments in police responses to mental health issues

Driven by increased demand, demonstrated in statistics, including in the aforementioned Adebowale Report (ICMHP, 2013, p 11) and others, and following examples from Australia and New Zealand in particular, forces (Leicestershire and Cleveland) and health trusts began to experiment with types of 'triage' systems (Reveruzzi and Pilling, 2016, p 12). In this approach, the police, psychiatric services, social workers and sometimes paramedics work together to support those in crisis, relieve the pressure on police and ambulance service and create better ways of working. Nine pilots were funded by the Department of Health to evaluate alternative methods (Horspool et al, 2016). Different approaches have subsequently been employed in the wider rollout of these schemes, due to circumstances or limitations of resources. Broadly, the types of triage fall into two categories: 'telephone' (usually in a police/combined control room) or 'street' triage, where a vehicle is employed to take staff to a crisis incident. The general aims of 'triage' in the mental health sense were increasing the percentage of people detained under section 136 who are then referred on for mental health treatment and reducing the amount of time that frontline officers spend dealing with mental health policing incidents (Reveruzzi and Pilling, 2016, p 14). Most importantly, the schemes were charged with improving the quality of at-the-scene interventions. It was also intended that, along with other changes in process, footfall to Accident and Emergency Departments would be reduced.

   Telephone triage can be exceptionally useful when an accredited mental health professional is sited within a police/ambulance control room, largely because of the increased availability of advice for the crises that may occur during any given day. Where it can be properly resourced, a street team consisting of approved mental health professional(s), police officers and other specialists provides an instant resource that can provide much more than police alone. Access to health records in itself can assuage a problematic incident and ideally ensure that unnecessary MHA detentions do not occur. It is, of course, arguable that availability of sufficient resources across services would provide a similar level of assurance, but given the paucity of resources even pre-COVID-19, the triage system does at least offer a level of service to mitigate the number of crises otherwise dealt with by police only. The main thrust of triage was to reduce the overall numbers of people detained under section 136 (Reveruzzi and Pilling, 2016, p 14).

The Policing and Crime Act (PACA) 2017 amendments to the MHA 1983 were important, and fell mostly out of the Review of S136 carried out by the Centre for Mental Health (Durcan, 2014, p 4). Service users had outlined the issues raised earlier, with abuses around the notion of public place in particular. The PACA addresses this (including the addition of a requirement to seek advice before exercising the detention power) and also the difficult issue around the use of police custody premises, by expressly forbidding the use for under-18s and further discouraging the use for adults. It must be understood that there needs to be a focus here on those who are solely detained under section 136 of the Act, rather than for an overt criminal act, for which custody may still be required. The improvements afforded, for example by joint criminal justice liaison and diversion projects across England and Wales, have had a separate effect on custody processes and should be considered independently from the issue of police involvement in mental health crises alone.

In 'Policing and mental health: picking up the pieces' (HMICFRS, 2018), two clear concerns are that the police are more involved than they should be in the area of mental health crisis and that police officers (and presumably, the ambulance service providers) are the only available resources out of 'normal' hours. Most police organisations across the UK now have some form of triage system, which may have improved their performance in dealing with mental health crises. However, the nature of the triage team – that is, the buy-in from partners and resources made available – can have a profound effect on its efficacy in any given policing area (HMICFRS, 2018, p 14).

Revisions to section 136 of the MHA in 2017 made a difference to police forces by explicitly stating it was not appropriate to use section 136 to take people into custody, particularly in circumstances where there were no overtly crime-related issues (and that mental health professionals should be consulted before invoking section 136). This meant that those in crisis were no longer routinely taken to a place they might associate with wrongdoing *on their part*. Taken together with the advent of mental health triage teams, this either encouraged or forced, depending on point of view, health trusts to work together with police and local authorities to find more collaborative ways to deal with those in crisis.

The ICMHP (2013, p 19) and others across the safeguarding/vulnerability arena (see Wood, 2016, p 63) have recommended joint training for police, social work teams and mental health staff, to create a common understanding of each other's role. This was initially embraced by various trusts and local authorities, with connections made and bridges built. Unfortunately, the arrival of a period of austerity put paid to a number of significant programmes and, as a consequence, the joint training petered out. It is to be hoped that changes to police education and in particular the professionalisation programme are able to revive collaborations, or at least improve the training of police officers, as for now at least the first responders to a crisis may well be from that agency.

Conclusions

To summarise, it is not possible to gauge whether process or practice has been the more problematic over time in managing mental health crises. It does seem fairly clear that a joined-up and communicative approach between agencies can create a platform where those in crisis can be better supported and receive better service. This does not mean that every health trust or police service can and will work together in a seamless and productive way, but by trying to adopt a more multi-agency approach the welfare of those in crisis is now at the forefront of the different approaches that are employed, mostly under the guise of triage. Most police work in the 21st century is not expressly crime related, but rather focuses on the other issues that have fallen into their arena and could loosely be defined more as pro-social. In the absence of a new 24/7 service, the improvements to process and the guidelines provided in the reforms to the MHA by the Police and Crime Act 2017 do seem to promote more coherent and safer practice. The immediate management of mental health crisis and its effects remain core policing business.

References

CoP (College of Policing) (2015) 'Estimating demand on the police service', [online] Available from: https://paas-s3-broker-prod-lon-6453d964-1d1a-432a-9260-5e0ba7d2fc51.s3.eu-west-2.amazonaws.com/s3fs-public/2021-03/demand-on-policing-report.pdf [Accessed 7 June 2021].

Cummins, I, and Edmondson, D. (2016) 'Policing and street triage', *Journal of Adult Protection*, 18(1): 40–52, [online] Available from: https://www.emerald.com/insight/content/doi/10.1108/JAP-03-2015-0009/full/pdf [Accessed 9 June 2021].

Durcan, G. (2014) 'Review of sections 135 and 136 of the Mental Health Act', Centre for Mental Health, [online] 18 December, Available from: https://www.centreformentalhealth.org.uk/publications/review-sections-135-136-mental-health-act [Accessed 10 May 2021].

HMICFRS (HM Inspectorate of Constabulary (and) Fire and Rescue Services) (2018) 'Policing and mental health: picking up the pieces', [online] 27 November, Available from: https://www.justiceinspectorates.gov.uk/hmicfrs/publications/policing-and-mental-health-picking-up-the-pieces/ [Accessed 25 May 2021].

Horspool, K., Drabble, S.J. and O'Cathain, A. (2016) 'Implementing street triage: a qualitative study of collaboration between police and mental health services', *BMC Psychiatry*, 16(3), DOI: https://doi.org/10.1186/s12888-016-1026-z.

ICMHP (Independent Commission on Mental Health and Policing) (2013) 'Independent Commission on Mental Health and Policing Report', [online] Available from: https://amhp.org.uk/app/uploads/2017/08/independent_commission_on_mental_health_and_policing_main_report.pdf [Accessed 28 May 2021].

Reveruzzi, B. and Pilling, S. (2016) 'Street triage report on the evaluation of nine pilot schemes in England', [online] Available from: https://www.crisisca reconcordat.org.uk/inspiration/ucl-street-triage-final-report-march-2016/ [Accessed 30 May 2021].

Schug, R.A. and Fradella, H.F. (2015) *Mental Illness and Crime*, London: SAGE.

Wolff, N. (2005) 'Community reintegration of prisoners with mental illness: a social investment perspective', *International Journal of Law and Psychiatry*, 28(1): 43–58.

Wood, A. (2016) 'Wood Report: review of the role and functions of Local Safeguarding Children Boards', [online] March, Available from: https://assets. publishing.service.gov.uk/government/uploads/system/uploads/attachment_d ata/file/526329/Alan_Wood_review.pdf [Accessed 9 June 2021].

42

Policing and non-verbal communication

Elizabeth Peatfield

Humans by design are social animals who spend most of their days, in some way or another, in contact with other human beings (apart from during pandemics). Since prehistoric peoples congregated together for warmth and safety, humans have had a need to communicate before the development of language, to share ideas and concepts such as 'let's take this big rock and go hit something together'. One might suggest that good communication and the ability to work together are the keys to a successful life or tribal survival at the very least. But not all communication is verbal, 'unspoken dialogue' and non-verbal aspects of communication play a large role in communication life. Individuals can often tell what their friends and family mean by a look in their eyes or a facial expression. When someone has that 'not today look' in their eyes, people may tread a bit more carefully round them. All individuals naturally pick up on some level of non-verbal communication (NVC) from others.

When considering policing and criminal justice however, understanding the limitations of NVC are of paramount importance. When evaluating the effectiveness of reading NVC there are a number of variables that make it unreliable such as gender differences, with women able to identify higher levels of both expression accuracy and non-verbal judgement accuracy. Race, culture and age have also been found to show some correlation to non-verbal behaviour and the ability to correctly interpret non-verbal cues. So, the belief that there could ever be a standard guide to NVC is impossible; there is never a one-size-fits-all version when trying to decode the meaning of NVC.

The basics of NVC

To understand the power of NVC a consideration of the basics is required. NVC is constructed from a number of cues, including kinetics, haptics, proxemics and paralanguage. Kinetics is the study of chemical reaction rates. This relates to NVC as it focuses on human action and reaction to stimulus, such as an increased heart rate or flush to the face when someone is aroused, either positively or negatively. Haptics is the subsystem of NVC which conveys meaning through physical contact, such as placing a hand on someone's shoulder to comfort them. Proxemics is concerned with understanding distance or space, such as the amount of distance/space that people feel comfortable setting between themselves and others (intimate, personal, public space for example).

Paralanguage is the non-lexical component of speech communication, such as tone, pitch, speed, gestures and facial expressions. Raising your voice if you are upset or angry for example.

However, to consider NVC as simply a non-speech form of communication would be inaccurate. The complicated nature of NVC was researched by Goldin-Meadow and Alibali (2013), who suggested that non-verbal and verbal communication have to be considered together as there is a complex relationship between the sender of cues and the receiver or the decoder. Non-verbal and verbal have to be considered in conjunction with each other in order to process the meaning correctly. Although every human uses NVC there is no dictionary from which to work as all NVC has to be placed in context. The contextual factors involved in encoding non-verbal cues, the encoder's intentions, behaviour, settings and the relationship with the receiver, all play some part in managing the perception and ultimately the understanding of meaning. Nonetheless, Hall et al (2019, p 272) suggest, when talking about culturally shared meaning, that 'Some discrete gestures (often called emblems) do have meanings that are consensually understood within a given cultural group; examples in North American culture include crossing the fingers for good luck or extending the middle finger toward someone as an insult.'

NVC and criminal justice

Although there is no unified theoretical framework for NVC it can be considered through a dyadic, evolutionary, biological, social or communicative framework among many others (Vrij et al, 2019). Just as the range of NVC is extensive so are the frameworks that seek to explain them. NVC consists of wide-reaching processes that function to express emotion (sadness, anger or happiness), attitudes (positivity or negativity), managing impressions (dignity, decorum or courage) or exerting interpersonal control (dominance, status or authority). NVC can also be used to aid in deception, so, when considering it in the context of crime and crime control, it is important to understand that there is no universal meaning. Like the literature on NVC, the research about deception is also wide ranging, but the need for accuracy in detecting deception cues is high when considering policing and the consequences of misreading a cue (Vrij and Winkel 1992; Otu, 2015). If the ramifications within policing are considered, perceived honesty can be the difference between deciding to investigate an individual or not. An innocent or guilty verdict in court may be based on the jurors' perception of the truth and the appearance of credibility. This has been made even more problematic due to the global pandemic, as the use of digital equipment such as Skype or Zoom dehumanise defendants. Denault and Patterson (2021, p 1) suggest 'the use of such applications also raises a number of commonly ignored issues related to the role of nonverbal communication during in-person exchanges. Because legal scholars and practitioners are rarely trained in research-based principle.'

The misguided belief that deception can often be detected and that somehow the liar will give themselves away by their NVC is simply incorrect. Yet a folk law has developed around deception detection and NVC has leaked into some police interrogation models and been engrained into the justice system. In criminal cases barristers will often ask the jurors to look at the behaviour of a witness or defendant when they are giving their evidence as if daring the juror to spot a lie. Of course, in terms of the media and public interest in NVC, this may be a dangerous game to play.

NVC theories

As with all aspects of NVC there are many theories why truth recallers and deceivers behave differently; one of the most influential was developed by Ekman and Friesen (1969) with their leakage hypothesis. This hypothesis is arguably the basis for many of the theories surrounding NVC and draws on psychodynamic theories of the unconscious, embedded with Darwinian theories of emotion. The theory suggests that deception leakage could be observed by the trained observer as a deceiver would not be able to fully suppress emotions associated with deception, such as heightened anxiety, stress or even exhilaration. The leakage could then be observed as non-verbal cues such as body movements, for example fidgeting and eye movement, alongside tone of voice or pace – all considered cues which could be identified by the observer. But this theory relies on the basis that liars have a specific set of emotions connected to deception and that their cognitive process would be observably different processing deceit to recalling truth.

Cognitive theories contend that the process for lying versus truth telling would also be a similar process; here it is suggested the cognitive process for a deceiver would be more challenging than a truth. The extra cognitive load would in itself betray the deceiver. Theories suggest that formulating a lie is more difficult than drawing from a truthful account. Liars may lack imagination and so to create an account that has the same details of a self-experienced event, alongside plausibility, places more cognitive load on the deceiver. Also, truth is a simple recall process, whereas lying requires a creation process that utilises much more mental effort than truth recall. Again, this theory is dependent on the assumption of difference, as well as on the individual liar, the setting and, of course, the interview protocol being used.

Self-presentational theories argue deception places a higher demand for strategic decision making. With a series of choices to make, the liar has to make choices about what truths to tell and what information to create, skew or omit. A key element of this approach is that the psychology of a liar is driven by planning, strategising and a calculation of risk. It claims that by using a range of investigation techniques that exploit these strategies, such as the Verifiability Approach or the Strategic Use of Evidence an interviewer can identify deception cues and decode that deception (Vrij et al, 2019).

However, self-presentation theory also contends that lying is not an extraordinary form of social behaviour but, rather, that editing occurs as a natural process. Most people edit, both verbally and non-verbally; they tailor their social behaviour to pursue a variety of goals, adjusting as they go. It suggests that humans adapt their own personal narrative to suit a situation, they change and evolve daily to aid their progression and survival in society. In a way, individuals wear a different hat for their different roles in society – child, parent, colleague and employee for example. Each role and presentation may be altered a little to aid success and, with this, micro deceptions take place naturally. In the self-presentational theory, both a liar and a truth teller need to be considered truthful; to achieve this they must present themselves as such, thus engaging in automatic and deliberate self-presentational effort to create a credible impression. This normalisation of the micro deceptions means that not every deception leads to a higher cognitive load.

NVC and deception

So, what is actually known about NVC and deception? It is known that attempting to determine if someone is trying to be deceitful, contrary to what many TV shows say, is not easy. When researchers looked at one of the largest meta-analysis studies in NVC they found that using NVC in order to identify deception was unreliable at best. Verbal cues were far more effective, even if the verbal cues were limited. Yet, no matter what the scientific evidence suggests, interest in NVC is still popular among practitioners such as the police and, of course, the media. The popular nature of the pseudoscientific myth of NVC and the ability to detect deceit is still as popular as ever, as demonstrated by multiple TV shows.

The basic parameter for this mistruth is that the deceiver will be under a higher cognitive load when lying and therefore will have some sort of 'tell' that will alert the decoder to the truth. There are countless books as well as TV shows that claim NVC's ability to decode the truth but, when comparing it to the academic evidence, one should understand its limitations and some of the lies about lying (Vrij et al, 2019).

Therefore, what are some of the most common misconceptions? One theory focuses on micro expressions (ME), suggesting information is leaked to the decoder through fleeting facial movements that indicate emotional concealment by the deceiver. This theory has been used in TV shows suggesting that one can spot a deceiver through training: programme makers tell the tales of experts who can study facial expressions and involuntary body language to expose the truth and allow them solve crimes and other mysteries. Although training does help experts recognise NVC and, along with verbal communication, they are able to decipher if a subject is stressed or evasive, NVC alone (considering the many cultural variations) cannot do this – to claim this is simply incorrect.

Popular not only in the media but also the academic community, ME and NVC interest has grown, but the academic research about ME is limited, finding little evidence in the veracity and reliability of claims that ME can be used to decode deception (Porter and Ten Brinke, 2008). Techniques based on ME have been developed, such as the behavioural analysis interview (BAI). However, this has been criticised not only because of its links to miscarriages of justice, but because the researcher also had concerns over the validity of the findings of the study used to support the technique as they did not know which of the 60 suspects used were actually lying and which were telling the truth (Vrij et al, 2019).

Neurolinguistic programming (NLP) is another technique that has developed with little scientific evidence. Like the BAI, it assumes that a deceiver will behave differently from the truth teller and will give non-verbal cues to allow the decoder to spot the deception. NLP has been developed to help practitioners improve their communication by teaching them how to control their own NVC and to spot those cues in others, such as eye and body movements. However, claims by some in this field have been challenged because they cite studies with no evidence and have been used beyond the scope of the original NVC theories (Vrij et al, 2019).

So why can NVC and the associated techniques developed solely to detect deceit not be relied on? What is the truth about lying? The problem with determining if someone is lying is that there is an assumption that the experience of lying is different to truth recall. It assumes that somehow lying is harder or less natural than telling the truth and that this will have the consequence of betraying the deceivers through their body language. Firstly, there is a need to consider if lying is different? Is there a need to think about lying or is it a natural part of daily life and social interaction with others? Secondly, could high stress situations such as being accused of a crime for example, elicit tension movements, not because of a need to lie, but simply because of a heightened emotional state? The third aspect to consider is if the decoders who are trained to spot these 'tell-tale movements' can pick up on every cue and analyse that cue in a split second to decipher if it is a lie or if it indicates nervousness, fear or any number of other emotions. Not even a so-called base line reading would aid the decoder if the actual act of lying itself is no different from truth recall.

Although there is some evidence to support the ability of some NVC theories to help decode deceit, that evidence is tenuous at best. There is no robust academic evidence base to demonstrate that anyone, trained or otherwise, has the ability to reliably decode deception based solely on NVC cues. To assume that a person can is simply incorrect.

References

Denault, V. and Patterson, M.L. (2021) 'Justice and nonverbal communication in a post-pandemic world: an evidence-based commentary and cautionary statement for lawyers and judges', *Journal of Nonverbal Behavior*, 45(1): 1–10.

Ekman, P. and Friesen, W.V. (1969) 'Nonverbal leakage and clues to deception', *Psychiatry*, 32(8): 8–106.

Goldin-Meadow, S. and Alibali, M.W. (2013) 'Gesture's role in speaking, learning, and creating language', *Annual Review of Psychology*, 64: 257–83.

Hall, J.A., Horgan, T.G. and Murphy, N.A. (2019) 'Nonverbal communication', *Annual Review of Psychology*, 70: 271–94.

Otu, N. (2015) 'Decoding nonverbal communication in law enforcement', *Salus Journal*, 3(2): 1–16.

Porter, S. and Ten Brinke, L. (2008) 'Reading between the lies: identifying concealed and falsified emotions in universal facial expressions', *Psychological Science*, 19(5): 508–14.

Vrij, A. and Winkel, F.W. (1992) 'Crosscultural police–citizen interactions: the influence of race, beliefs, and nonverbal communication on impression formation', *Journal of Applied Social Psychology*, 22(19): 1546–59.

Vrij, A., Hartwig, M. and Granhag, P.A. (2019) 'Reading lies: nonverbal communication and deception', *Annual Review of Psychology*, 70: 295–317.

43

Policing controversies: undercover policing

Margaret S. Malloch

Introduction

Like many aspects of crime and its control, the role of the police in modern society has been a contested and scrutinised issue. Undercover policing involves the covert surveillance of certain groups to obtain intelligence on their activities and generally involves the use of assumed identities, plain-clothes informers and the surveillance of civilians. It was set up to infiltrate groups that the state regarded as being involved in 'serious crime', but the definition of serious crime soon expanded to include any kind of threat to the state, including political dissent, and undercover police have been deployed widely in relation to public order, crime and industrial disputes.

Before the emergence of the modern police force in the early 19th century, military and local regiments had the role of maintaining public order. Government spies and agents were often used where there was perceived to be a threat to the state, to infiltrate political reform organisations. They were used widely in attempts to quell the activities of political reformers and it is claimed that in Glasgow in the years leading to the Radical War of 1820, paid informers, police spies, government spies and 'Secret Men' formed part of a network that was so effective that it infiltrated the very heart of the radical reform movement (Berresford-Ellis and Mac A'Gobhainn, 2016).

Background to contemporary undercover policing

Policing, as it is understood today, originated formally with the Metropolitan Police Act in 1829 and then Home Secretary Robert Peel, although a full-time police force already existed at this time in London to maintain control of the port and the city. Outside London, parish constables policed communities. The introduction of a more centralised and organised police force was consolidated in 1856 when the County and Borough Police Act enforced full-time police forces in all areas. Police identification with the interests of employers, capital and government has been evident in both operational policies and practice as they developed, although opposition to the powers of localised police forces came from workers and local communities and was expressed in Parliament.

The formalisation of undercover policing units developed from the Irish Special Branch, set up in 1883 within the Metropolitan Police, in response to Fenian bombings in London. This unit continued as the Special Branch, tasked with the close surveillance of all potential threats to public order, initially in London, but with the introduction of Special Branches in other police forces in response to political protests of 1967 and 1968. Special Branch's primary roles concern national security (notably terrorism and 'subversion') and the maintenance of public order. It works closely with the security services, especially MI5.

The professionalisation of the police in the mid-20th century, particularly in the UK and the US, resulted in the standardisation of covert methods that have been exported through training and shared knowledge of effective policing practices to many countries. Such practices were augmented by the emergence of technologies that enabled unobtrusive surveillance to extend the infiltration of groups considered threats to public order and have become an institutionalised area of police operations. Surveillance has also been used extensively by corporate business interests. The infiltration of groups and use of informers has raised questions about police accountability, as has the discretionary powers of the police in their negotiation and enforcement of the law (Vitale, 2018).

Areas of controversy

While the modern police force has developed over time (Bowling et al, 2019), the role of the police has continued to be controversial, although the liberal depiction of the localised police officer has remained, in theory, strongly associated with the prevention of and response to 'crime'. However, the public order role of the police has remained a notable priority. The Special Demonstration Squad (SDS) was established in 1968 in the aftermath of violence at anti-Vietnam War demonstrations in London. Set up by the Metropolitan Police, its role became one of infiltrating and monitoring environmental and political groups across the UK. The Home Office was instrumental in the establishment of the SDS and initially provided direct funding. In 1970, the Special Branch Industrial Unit was set up to gather information on trade unions, their activists and their activities. 'Blacklists' were collated that were passed onto a range of industrial sectors, highlighting the collusion between state and private capital (Smith and Chamberlain, 2015).

In 1999 the National Public Order Intelligence Unit (NPOIU) was established by the Association of Chief Police Officers. The NPOIU was funded by the Home Office to gather and coordinate intelligence. Its remit was to reduce criminality and disorder from domestic extremism and to provide support for police forces across England and Wales managing strategic public order issues. The NPOIU is now part of the National Domestic Extremism and Disorder Intelligence Unit with SO15, Counter Terrorism Command. The issue of (upholding) human rights is a continuing tension in relation to undercover policing.

Formation and manipulation of relationships

From the perspective of government and state, undercover policing is intended to identify and thwart attempts to disrupt public order and criminality. It is presented as a mechanism to preventively infiltrate criminal organisations and disrupt their activities. From an operational and psychological perspective, the ability of undercover officers to be skilled at the manipulation of human relationships is crucial in all areas of undercover work. The importance of teamwork, selection and training of officers, ongoing support in preparing for undercover work, contact while undercover, skills in terminating undercover contacts and reintegration into 'real life' are key areas requiring intervention skills and organisational support and accountability.

The basis of undercover work involves the purposeful development of relationships that will ultimately be betrayed and terminated, requiring undercover officers to infiltrate a group by befriending its members with the intention of covertly collecting information. Covert policing operations can include short-term interventions and long-term infiltration. This can be a challenging process requiring the instigation and maintenance of duplicity, potentially adding additional stress to a complex situation. The importance of good interpersonal skills would seem important, backed up by judgement and self-discipline and the ability to stay calm under pressure. No doubt the longer the operation lasts, the greater the ongoing strain involved for the undercover officer. It would seem important to require psychological management to monitor welfare and prevent problems from developing in terms of relationships with those under surveillance as well as the maintenance of personal and family relationships. The longer-term impact on individuals and groups placed under surveillance is often extensive.

Contested infiltration

The exposure of undercover policing practices has evidenced the long-term infiltration of legitimate organisations, notably left-wing groups including trade union branches and political activists with an environmental and/or anti-racist focus. Several reviews have been undertaken to examine concerns about policing practices and, specifically, the role and activities of undercover officers. In October 2011, Operation Herne was set up to investigate allegations of misconduct by undercover officers in the SDS (between 1968 and 2008). This included the practice of using the identities of dead children by some undercover officers. In 2012 Mark Ellison QC was tasked by Theresa May to review the investigation of Stephen Lawrence and to conduct an inquiry into evidence of police corruption and undercover police activity. The initial remit of the review was extended following allegations by Peter Francis, a former SDS officer. Evidence that undercover police monitored the campaign for justice that followed the brutal murder of Stephen Lawrence, while his killers remained at large, resulted in the ordering of a public inquiry by Theresa May.

The Undercover Policing Inquiry (UCPI) was set up in 2015 to investigate the use of undercover police across England and Wales and provide recommendations for the future. The inquiry is expected to run for several years and will consider the deployment of police officers as 'covert human intelligence sources' by the SDS, the NPOIU and by other police forces in England and Wales. It will also review undercover policing practices, identify lessons learned and make recommendations about the way undercover policing is conducted. Requests by the Scottish government to include undercover activities in Scotland in the UCPI was refused by the UK government.

The UCPI aims to draw on extensive evidence of police surveillance and infiltration of political groups. Over a thousand groups are believed to have been infiltrated by undercover police and they include small and large campaign groups with no connections to any form of criminality. The Irish Independence movement, women's rights campaigns, anti-racist struggles, campaigns against nuclear war, animal rights movements and trade union activities have all been subject to infiltration, monitoring and counter-activities (Woodman, 2018). The political nature of this form of policing, and the activities of the SDS and NPOIU, highlight troubling relationships between the police and the state. The role of undercover police officers as agent provocateurs has also been identified as a concern (Evans and Lewis, 2013). SDS operated under the auspices of Special Branch and there has been recent evidence to show that information on trade union activity was passed to various Home Secretaries, a form of industrial espionage, as well as to thwart legitimate legal processes, such as the Stephen Lawrence inquiry. There is evidence of regular liaison between SDS and MI5 from 1974 onwards.

Human rights implications and concerns

Serious concerns around the violation of human rights have emerged with the exposure of undercover police officers who had relationships with women involved in the groups they infiltrated. These personal encounters and, in some cases, long-lasting personal relationships, provided a means of extending undercover operations and increasing efficacy in gathering intelligence on some of the more intimate aspects of people's lives. At least three undercover officers are known to have had children with the activists they were spying on; women who were unaware that the men with whom they were in long-term relationships were serving police officers involved in undercover surveillance. In 2011, several women took civil cases against the Metropolitan Police claiming sexual and psychological abuse as well as the violation of their human rights. In 2015, Metropolitan Police Assistant Commissioner Sir Martin Hewitt apologised to seven women, acknowledging that these relationships were a violation of the women's human rights, an abuse of police power and cause of significant trauma.

Evidence has also emerged of collusion between police spies and big business which were doing their own spying on, for example, environmental activists (Schlembach, 2018). Many issues continue to emerge and will likely do so as the UCPI moves forward, although much of the available material has been, and continues to be, suppressed because of police and governmental secrecy. The evidence that has emerged to date regarding undercover policing shows that the police, as an institution, function as an impediment to democratic change, a limit to political freedom and a barrier to political inclusion. Undercover policing, and the problems that arise from its clandestine and unaccountable activities, serves a highly political function. Much of the controversy surrounds the acknowledgement that there was systematic and strategic use of the police to infiltrate groups and movements.

Future considerations

The planned implementation of the Police, Crime, Sentencing and Courts Act 2022 could see current problems of accountability extended to previously unprecedented levels. To date, the introduction of this Act has resulted in ongoing protests across England. Despite its controversial content, it passed through the House of Commons with virtually no opposition and was enacted on 28 April 2022. Public protest has been widespread against the powers the legislation would give to the police to restrict peaceful protests, including the powers to set conditions on the duration of protests, set maximum noise levels and put restrictions on where protests can take place. Meanwhile, the Covert Human Intelligence Sources (Criminal Conduct) Act 2021 makes provision for the authorisation of criminal conduct in the course of, or otherwise in connection with, the conduct of 'covert human intelligence sources'.

The controversy around undercover policing continues, with delays and limitations characterising the UCPI to date. Meanwhile, related issues emerge and are likely to continue to do so with the ongoing move towards intelligence-led policing (ILP). The shift to ILP is presented as the disruption and prevention of criminal acts and management of the risk of crime (Fyfe et al, 2018; Hestehave, 2018), heralding a shift in 'crime prevention' to the concept of 'pre-crime' and widening scope for police discretion. Partnerships and information sharing are crucial elements here as well as international cooperation between police forces, with no regulatory intergovernmental body to ensure accountability in the international context.

These recent events highlight the controversial nature of policing as an institution and have a long-standing historical (and international) context (Maher, 2021). Claims that people are subject to the principles of universally applied justice and equality before the law have been seriously undermined through evidence of selection bias and specific targeting of certain crimes and groups using 'precautionary logic' and the widening scope for police discretion. The covert nature of undercover policing and the significant ethical dilemmas this continues to raise may prove difficult if not impossible to resolve.

References

Berresford-Ellis, P. and Mac A'Gobhainn, S. (2016) *The Radical Rising*, Edinburgh: Birlinn.

Bowling, B., Reiner, R. and Sheptycki, J. (2019) *The Politics of the Police* (5th edn), Oxford: Oxford University Press.

Evans, R. and Lewis, P. (2013) *Undercover: The True Story of Britain's Secret Police*, London: Guardian Books and Faber & Faber.

Fyfe, N., Gundhus, H. and Vrist Rønn, K. (2018) 'Introduction', in N. Fyfe, H. Gundhus and K. Vrist Rønn (eds) *Moral Issues in Intelligence-Led Policing*, London: Routledge, pp 1–22.

Hestehave, N. (2018) 'Predicting crime? On challenges to the police in becoming knowledgeable organizations', in N. Fyfe, H. Gundhus and K. Vrist Rønn (eds) *Moral Issues in Intelligence-Led Policing*, London: Routledge, pp 62–80.

Maher, G. (2021) *A World without Police*, London: Verso.

Schlembach, R. (2018) 'Undercover policing and the spectre of "domestic extremism": the covert surveillance of environmental activism in Britain', *Social Movement Studies*, 17(5): 491–506.

Smith, D. and Chamberlain, P. (2015) *Blacklisted: The Secret War between Big Business and Union Activists*, London: New Internationalist.

Vitale, A. (2018) *The End of Policing*, London: Verso.

Woodman, C. (2018) *Spycops in Context: Counter-Subversion, Deep Dissent and the Logic of Political Policing*, London: Centre for Crime and Justice Studies.

44

Police abolitionism

Karen Corteen

Introduction

> We live in a world of police, a society built around policing and that presumes their necessity. The world of police is one where those in power see the police as a one-size-fits-all solution for every social problem: poverty, mental health, a lack of opportunity, or inadequate after school or sports programs – just send in the police, and if that doesn't work, send in some more. (Maher, 2021, p 10)

Police reform is a 'mirage' (Maher, 2021, p 74). Historically and contemporarily, efforts to reform the police and prevent police violence have failed and they will continue to fail as 'more than a century of experience proves this beyond reasonable doubt' (Maher, 2021, p 96). The lack of police reform together with the extent of police powers and police violence has impacted on growing calls inside and outside of academia for police abolitionism. This encompasses a campaign to disband, disempower and disarm the police (McDowell and Fernandez, 2018). The police abolition movement is a political movement that is mainly located in the US. However, due to police abuse of power in the UK, together with the high-profile police killing of George Floyd in the US, there have been recent calls in the UK and the US to defund the police – this entails removing any funding for the police. There have also been calls for police abolitionism (Hope, 2014; Vitale, 2017; Maher, 2021). The police killing of George Floyd in 2020 also prompted a discussion about the extent of police brutality in both countries, which joined an existing discussion of the overpolicing of Black communities in the US and in the UK. In the US, Floyd's killing ignited the Black Lives Matters movement. Since then, an international movement For a World Without Police has also been formed (For a World Without Police, 2022). Therefore, now is a good time to revisit the concept of police abolitionism in terms of what this entails in policy and practice. This chapter will begin with a discussion of abolitionism generally, and police abolitionism specifically, and then it will provide an overview of police violence in the US and in England and Wales, arguing that such violence is a powerful reason for police abolitionism. The chapter will also highlight further powerful reasons and arguments for the abolition of the police, concluding with suggestions of what may replace them.

Abolition

The history of abolition is 'long, complicated, and inspiring' and it 'crosses multiple historical periods, social movements, and academic disciplines' (McDowell and Fernandez, 2018, p 375). Abolition is difficult to define as it means different things in different contexts and to different people. For criminologists, abolitionism seeks to 'eliminate punitive responses to "crime"' and they 'criticize the reliance of punitive measures of social control administered through state mechanisms aimed at marginalised populations' (McDowell and Fernandez, 2018, p 378). As Maher (2021, p 11, original emphasis) notes, abolition 'is not simply an *against*, however: it is also a *for*'. Therefore, the shared goal of abolitionism is not simply tearing down or deconstructing institutions, it is about reimagining them, reconstructing them, radically transforming them and proposing long-term, long-lasting effective solutions. It is about the realisation of emancipatory possibilities. It is also about finding new and better ways to respond to harm, crime and public safety and security and it is about securing real justice for all races and for the poor, vulnerable and marginalised.

Police abolition

There has been a previous push for police abolition on the part of activists, movement organisers and academics such as Hope (2014), Vitale (2017), McDowell and Fernandez (2018) and Maher (2021). However, due to recent high-profile racialised police violence there is a greater willingness on the part of the public to imagine such a radical transformation. Hope (2014) states that he 'would give up the police service, particularly the uniformed branch, and its officers'. The reasons he provides for police abolitionism are: the police are ineffective 'in the tasks and functions they set themselves to perform in society', their 'leadership is self-serving and obsessed with the exercise of power and the garnering of status' and throughout the police there is a 'culture of prejudice and blind morality' which results in an attitude of 'us' (the police) and 'them' (the general public) (Hope, 2014). He continues to state that the police resist democratic accountability to the communities they claim to serve, 'while fiddling the figures' and stopping and searching 'populations whom they believe they have an authority to consider suspicious'. Finally, Hope (2014) maintains that the police 'fail to support and protect the vulnerable against the harms they experience to the extent that they are ineffectual against those who cause them harm'. Vitale (2017, p 31) echoes many of these sentiments, he states that crime control is and always has been a small part of policing and that '[m]ost crimes that are investigated are not solved'. These sentiments chime with Maher (2021, p 230) when he states, 'the police simply don't do what they claim to do, nor what many people believe they do'. He maintains that the police do not serve the community and do not protect it, indeed for Maher (2021, p 230) the police 'dehumanize and brutalize entire communities'. He also contends that a world without police exists and this can be built upon and expanded. He concludes that 'in the United States and across the globe, people are sick of cops, and abolition is on the table before us like never before' (Maher, 2021, p 231).

So what is police abolitionism? Police abolitionism is about imagining, visualising and practically planning for a world that does not need police. It is about realising and embracing what seems impossible and unachievable as possible and achievable. It entails finding ways 'to achieve a police-free world' (For a World Without Police, 2022). The contemporary populisation of the call for police abolitionism originated in the US with the slogan 'disband, disempower, and disarm the police' (McDowell and Fernandez, 2018, p 379). This is not just a slogan; it is a strategy and it has policy and practical implications. Disarmament and disempowerment play a role in disbanding the police and in the eventual abolition of this state institution. Police abolitionism would entail taking power and resources from the police and placing them somewhere else. For example, investing them within other civil institutions, within programmes that prevent crime, putting them into alternative methods of dealing with crime and public safety and/or investing in an alternative service – one that could be based on inclusive social policy solutions as opposed to exclusionary criminal justice solutions such as policing. McDowell and Fernandez (2018, p 373) maintain that 'attacking the police as an institution [and] challenging its very right to exist' could have 'the potential to radically transform society'. This is due to the origins and functions of the police being predicated on class and racialised lines. This has resulted in police violence which impacts on particular individuals and identifiable groups.

Police violence in the US

Globally and nationally it is difficult to know the real extent of police violence. However, Mapping Police Violence (MPV, 2020), a research collaborative in the US, is attempting to collect comprehensive data on police killings across the US in order to quantify the impact of police violence on communities. They define police killings as '[a] case where a person dies as a result of being shot, beaten, restrained, intentionally hit by a police vehicle, pepper sprayed, tasered or otherwise harmed by police officers, whether on or off duty' (MPV, 2020). They have found that every day in the US at least three people are killed by the police. Also since 2013 there have been over eight thousand police killings and 97 per cent of the killings happened while a police officer was acting in a law enforcement capacity. In 2020 alone there were over 1,100 police killings and the majority of these could have been prevented. Ninety-six per cent of the deaths were a result of police shooting; the remaining deaths were the result of Tasers, physical force and police vehicles (MPV, 2020).

Officers were charged in 16 of the cases, constituting 1 per cent of the police killings (MPV, 2020). In eight of these cases there was video evidence, five acquired by police body and dash cameras while three were captured by surveillance or bystander video. Most cases involved suspected non-violent offences or instances where no crime was reported. For example, 121 people were killed after police stopped them for a traffic violation. They also found that 'Black people were *more likely to be killed* by the police, more likely to be *unarmed* and *less likely to be threatening someone* when killed' (MPV, 2020, original emphasis). Ninety-seven police killings occurred in response to mental health crises.

Police violence in the UK

Police violence can also be evidenced in the UK as can be seen by the @EndTaserTorture Campaign and the United Family and Friends Campaign. Marc Cole aged 30 and Adrian McDonald aged 34 both tragically died after being tasered by the police while experiencing a mental health crisis (Change. org, 2022). Adrian McDonald was not only tasered, he was also bitten by a police dog. An inquest into his death concluded that 'Adrian McDonald died of stress of incident following police dog bites and Taser use as well as effects of cocaine' (INQUEST, 2018). The Taser is a lethal weapon and it has also been implicated in other deaths (Change.org, 2022). Despite this, in June 2021, the then Home Secretary Priti Patel vowed 'to equip every single officer with a Taser, should they wish to do so' (Dearden, 2021). Also, when addressing the Police Federation at their annual conference she stated that the challenge for the police is to cut crime by 'going out there and actually zapping the really bad people out there, the criminals that perpetrate high harms' (Dearden, 2021). She also stated that she would be 'backing police' with new powers and with funding including for more Tasers. In May 2022, Priti Patel announced that volunteer police officers in England and Wales would be authorised to use Tasers, a move Amnesty International have called a 'dangerous expansion' in their use. This is a worrying development as the use of Tasers increased in 2020/21 from 2019/20 (BBC News, 2022).

Also worryingly, a recent Independent Office for Police Conduct (IOPC, 2021) report found that there was a pattern of more excessive tasering of people in distress, a 'disproportionate use of Tasers against Black people' and that Black people were more likely to be tased for longer periods than White people. The disproportionate levels of police-related deaths of individuals from ethnic minority backgrounds evidenced in the US is mirrored in the UK. In the UK there is a long and violent history of Black people dying as a result of police violence. This can be evidenced in the cases of Christopher Alder, Mark Duggan, Sean Rigg, Sheku Bayoh, Simeon Francis and Dalian Atkinson. In England and Wales, INQUEST is a charity that provides information on state-related deaths, including deaths at the hands of the police. Drawing on the IOPC annual statistics 'on deaths during or following police conduct', INQUEST states, '[i]n the financial year 2019/20, there were 18 deaths in or following police custody, three police shootings, 24 deaths related to road traffic incidents, and 54 apparent suicides following custody' (INQUEST, 2020). There were also 107 'other' deaths 'following contact with the police in a wide range of circumstances' (INQUEST, 2020). The Director of INQUEST, Deborah Coles, commented:

> At a time of real concern about disproportionate and excessive policing, particularly of racialized communities, we still see a disturbing number of restraint related deaths. Mental health and intoxication also continue to feature too heavily. Our casework on police related deaths reveals the systemic failures to safeguard vulnerable people, the excessive use of force and neglect. (INQUEST, 2020)

Alternative solutions

For police abolitionists there are safer ways and systems for dealing with public safety. An example of this can be seen in Coles' response to police-related deaths in England and Wales. Coles comments, '[i]t is clear that not enough is being done. We repeat our point that ultimately to prevent further deaths and harm, we must look beyond policing and redirect resources into community, health, welfare and specialist services'. This is echoed in the 'defund the police' movement in the UK and the US.

According to Hope (2014), the control and prevention of crime can only be accomplished through the institutions of civil society and uniformed police cannot be a civil society institution. Hope (2014) suggests that in order to serve the public good the uniformed police service should be amalgamated 'with the community health, ambulance and fire services to become a harm-response service' with a remit of protecting and supporting victims of crime. In addition, this civil harm-response service should be responsible for the maintenance of public order and safety. This would require training in order to enable those working within a civil harm-response service to work with other public servants such as social workers, teachers and nurses. State functions such as investigation, regulation and law enforcement should be conducted by the formation of appropriate agencies, which should have 'as much, or as little powers of investigation and arrest as their statutory foundations allow them'.

Vitale (2017, p 4), when discussing policing in the US, contends that an attempt to make policing more just, means addressing the problems of 'excessive force, overpolicing, and disrespect for the public'. He explains that in response to these problems much of the public debate has focused on reforms. For example, new and better police training, increasing diversity within the police, implementing community policing strategies and greater means of accountability (Vitale, 2017). However, Vitale (2017) and Maher (2021) strongly believe and argue that reforms will not work as the problem is the police themselves and therefore the solution is to end policing. For Vitale (2017, p 15, original emphasis), the overpolicing of communities of colour is not the result of police bias or misunderstanding but it is actually '*how the system is designed to operate*'. Because the origins and functions of the police in both the US and the UK are underpinned by the management of inequalities, especially those of class and race, Vitale (2017) argues that rather than looking to procedural reforms there is a need to rethink the role of the police, while for Maher (2021) the solution is to make the police obsolete. In so doing, political parties who advocate neoconservative politics and who deem all social problems (for example, mental illness, homelessness, drugs, sex work, immigration) as police problems have to be challenged and changed.

For Vitale (2017, p 28), there is a myth that the police are 'bringers of justice', rather they are 'a tool for managing deeply entrenched inequalities in a way that systematically produces injustices for the poor, socially marginal, and nonwhite'. The modern police force is therefore 'a war on the poor that does little to make people feel safer or communities feel stronger' (Vitale, 2017, pp 53–4). He goes on to say that when the police do actually achieve this it is through 'the most coercive forms of state power that destroys the lives of millions' (Vitale, 2017, p 54). Vitale (2017) describes real justice as restoring people and communities, rebuilding trust and social cohesion and providing people with a way forward. It would also entail reducing 'the social forces that drive crime' and both perpetrators and victims would be treated as 'full human beings' (Vitale, 2017, p 28). Basically, Vitale (2017) and Maher (2021) are saying that society should not look to the police to solve their problems, nor should the emphasis be on the pursuit of wealth; instead, communities should organise in order to secure real justice and in order to produce a society that is designed to meet human need.

Maher (2021 p 140) inspirationally highlights how alternatives to the police 'have been flourishing in recent years'. He advocates that 'the first task is to learn from what people are already doing, to connect these disparate experiences, and to weave from them an ever-expanding community' (Maher, 2021 p 156). For Maher (2021), communities need to be helped to see how much power they actually have and he outlines the institutions that can be relied on to deliver security without resorting to the police. He also proposes a more holistic response to society's problems such as neighbourhood response networks, well-resourced social services, democratically organised self-defence projects and community-based restorative and transformative justice, and he provides example of where such measures have been successful. In sum, communities should be protected from crime and disorder but this should not be sought via 'coercion, violence, and humiliation' and society should be safe and secure, 'but not at the hands of the police. In the end they rarely provide either' (Vitale, 2017, p 228).

Conclusions

> Deep down, we all know what a world without police would look like. We have all seen it. We have all needed help and asked, or called on friends or family in an emergency. We have all experienced moments when we worked together to resolve conflicts with calling in professional violence workers. We have experienced, however

fleeting, the warm embrace of community. We have all trusted the support and generosity of others, and without thinking twice we have been generous in turn. (Maher, 2021, p 127)

At the heart of the problem of the police are their origins and functions, their politicisation, their expansion and intensification, their militarisation and what they are being expected to manage, namely social problems and inequalities. Reform is not enough (Hope, 2014; Vitale, 2017; McDowell and Fernandez, 2018; Maher, 2021). In order to ensure public safety there are alternatives to aggressive, invasive and largely ineffective policing. The police can be defunded and such funds could be used to invest in civil institutions such as education, health and social services (Vitale, 2017). More radically, the police can be abolished and made obsolete (Maher, 2021). The police can be replaced with a more welfarist and non-coercive response, for example a civil harm-response service (Hope 2014). Also, individuals and communities can be supported and empowered to find non-punitive and inclusive solutions (Vitale, 2017; Maher, 2021). Strong communities can be supported and expanded to the extent that they can resolve their own social issues without having to resort to the state. Finally, in the long term, envisioning and transforming the way that society is economically, socially and politically organised and managed is necessary in order to reduce inequalities and human misery which are currently exacerbated by punitive and exclusionary criminal justice systems, including modern policing and police violence. In a nutshell, 'the idealized image of the police is splintering' and 'the tiniest fractures offer glimpses of a new world' (Maher, 2021, p 69) and at present the 'struggle for police abolition is full of potential' (McDowell and Fernandez, 2018, p 388).

References

BBC News (2022) 'Volunteer police officers to be armed with Taser stun guns', [online] 17 May, Available from: https://www.bbc.co.uk/news/uk-61473781 [Accessed 17 June 2022].

Change.org (2022) 'Ban police use of repeated and prolonged tasering of vulnerable people', [online] Available from: https://www.change.org/p/help-us-to-ban-the-deadly-use-of-lethal-police-taser-weapons-against-vulnerable-peo ple-in-mental-health-crisis [Accessed 16 June 2022].

Dearden, L. (2021) 'Priti Patel tells police to start "zapping" criminals as lockdown laws ease', *Independent*, [online] 9 June, Available from: https://www.independ ent.co.uk/news/uk/home-news/police-priti-patel-criminal-taser-b1862623. html [Accessed 16 June 2022].

For a World Without Police (2022) 'Imagine a world without police', [online] Available from: http://aworldwithoutpolice.org [Accessed 16 June 2022].

Hope, T. (2014) 'I would give up … the police service', Centre for Crime and Justice Studies, [online] Available from: https://www.crimeandjustice.org.uk/ resources/i-would-give-police-service [Accessed 28 April 2021].

INQUEST (2018) 'Inquest concludes Adrian McDonald died of stress of incident following police dog bites and Taser use as well as effects of cocaine', [online] Available from: https://www.inquest.org.uk/adrian-mcdonald-conclusion [Accessed 17 June 2022].

INQUEST (2020) 'INQUEST response to latest deaths in police custody statistics', [online] Available from: https://www.inquest.org.uk/iopc-stats-2020 [Accessed 28 April 2021].

IOPC (Independent Office for Police Conduct) (2021) 'IOPC report flags concerns about police use of Taser', [online] Available from https://www.policeconduct.gov.uk/news/iopc-report-flags-concerns-about-police-use-taser [Accessed 17 June 2022].

Maher, G. (2021) *A World without Police: How Strong Communities Make Cops Obsolete*, London: Verso.

McDowell, M.G. and Fernandez, L.A. (2018) '"Disband, disempower, and disarm": amplifying the theory and practice of police abolition', *Critical Criminology*, 26: 373–91.

MPV (Mapping Police Violence) (2020) '2020 police violence report', [online] Available from: https://policeviolencereport.org [Accessed 28 April 2021].

Vitale, A.S. (2017) *The End of Policing*, London: Verso.

45

Policing and occupational cultures

Sean Bell and Nick Kealey

Most discussions about police personality and culture centre on interactions between the police and members of the public as victims, witnesses or suspects. Less has been written about the impact of personality and culture on the internal machinations and interactions between colleagues, managers and subordinates. When this occurs, it is generally based on race, gender and sexuality, and seldom on how those with mental ill health are treated within policing.

Externally, the deaths of George Floyd in May 2020 and Sarah Everard in March 2021 by then-serving police officers Derek Chauvin and Wayne Couzens rightly led for calls to change; however, concern exists that any window of opportunity to reform and strengthen accountability may still need to be prised opened further (Boundreau et al, 2022). The dismissal of police constable Michael Harrison in February 2022 from West Mercia Police for gross misconduct, having abused his position for sexual purposes between 2018 and 2019 (IOPC, 2022b), further amplifies the lack of trust and confidence in policing. In addition, the 15 separate recommendations to change practice following Operation Hotton are still being digested (IOPC, 2022a, p 2), as 'evidence of discrimination, misogyny, harassment and bullying involving officers permanently based at Charing Cross Police Station' was found, thus heightening concerns around the darker aspects of police culture.

Police culture

To those who live away from the policing bubble, the words 'canteen' and 'culture' rarely appear in the same sentence. Culture may relate to ideas, customs or behaviour, but the word canteen is generally accepted to be somewhere provided by an employer, university or factory to eat a hearty breakfast, cellophane-wrapped lunch or overpriced lukewarm meal late in the day. While many look forward to an extra sausage in the morning (vegetarian, halal, gluten and gluten-free options are available), linking the two words to form the phrase 'canteen culture' seems to put some researchers into an apoplectic spin.

Away from policing, Schein (1992, p 3) defines culture as:

> A pattern of shared basic assumptions, invented, discovered, or developed by a given group, as it learns to cope with its problems of external adaptation and internal integration, that has worked well enough to be considered valid, and, therefore, is to be taught to new

members of the group as the correct way to perceive, think, and feel in relation to those problems.

Policing, like other professions, has its own unique culture. Waddington (1999, p 288) referred to this as 'canteen culture' and this is now inextricably linked to policing and how outsiders view policing. A narrative around prejudice and bias may lead some to suggest that policing is dominated by chauvinist males with a self-fulfilling prophecy of self-importance and some form of exaggerated role within society. Chan (Australia) and Loftus (England) do not see it so simplistically. They argue that there is not one but several police cultures and suggest that differing ranks, roles, departments and locations have varied police cultures, implying that police cultures are more diverse than usually considered (Chan, 1997; Loftus, 2009).

Recruitment and police culture

With the drive in England and Wales to recruit 20,000 new officers as part of the wider recruitment and professionalism agenda in 2021, there is the very real possibility that any perceived culture can and must change. It is anticipated that the introduction of younger officers from a more diverse background who understand the importance of diversity, teamwork, professionalism, transparency, integrity and impartiality will change elements of police culture. They may have more modern views about acceptable behaviours, and value community engagement, problem solving and effective communication, rather than the traditionally accepted police culture of physical toughness and crime fighting. It takes courage to speak out against bullying and harassment, and the 'weary woman' (IOPC, 2022a, p 6) must be congratulated for finding the inner strength to stand up to those who do not share the values of policing.

Changes in recruitment may also have an impact on the prevalent culture. Attempts have been made to broaden recruitment demographics from a predominantly White, heterosexual male base towards a more representative composition from English and Welsh diverse communities; however, part of this drive relies on attracting students into university to complete a College of Policing (CoP)-approved professional policing degree. Given universities have their own problems regarding attracting candidates from more diverse backgrounds, it is questionable whether this is a step in the right direction. If policing wants to be more inclusive, police decision makers need to think about how to encourage applications from a wider base and identify those who could make a difference but may not have the means to make the leap from their current role, whether this be due to family, financial, educational or cultural issues. Despite women making up 28 per cent of warranted officers and 60 per cent of police staff, the macho image associated with policing still pervades and policing has plenty of work to do. While policing continues to idealise manliness, cultural change will be difficult.

Positive dynamics of police culture

Despite what many commentators have said, not all aspects of police culture are negative and plenty of observers have argued that canteen culture can have a positive impact on police officers and policing (Waddington, 1999). There is very broad agreement that solidarity and camaraderie are essential policing traits and could be seen as defining elements of police culture where officers are expected to demonstrate loyalty to colleagues above all else. Team spirit and comradeship are essential when striding towards danger, as others run away.

What is the positive impact that Waddington (1999) refers to? It could be argued that positive aspects of police culture, such as a selfless commitment to protecting the public and colleagues from harm, might provide a context for greater tolerance towards mental health issues. For example, policing, with its core networks and close team membership, seems an ideal base to share positive and negative experiences and offer the first opportunity to discuss mental ill health. Where better could this display of camaraderie take place than over breakfast in the canteen.

Storytelling is commonly used as a pedagogical tool in higher education, healthcare, reflection and adult learning and the workplace canteen seems an ideal opportunity to tell stories, recall experiences and share advice. If stories are regularly exchanged and used to initiate recruits, one may believe that policing is a never-ending drama fit for TV, while simultaneously reminding officers of the ever-present possibility that bad things can and do happen and the continuous need for caution. These stories may preserve the established policing culture, and herein lies the problem or one of many problems. The removal of the canteen provides fewer opportunities for officers to learn from each other's experiences, keep up to date on the latest gossip and, most importantly, build trust and offer advice about health through the vehicle of shared humour.

Police culture and mental health

Sadly, officers and staff are still reluctant to disclose mental ill health. Forces may well be supportive of those with mental ill health, but due to cultural pressures the reality is different. Officers reporting stress or depression are seen by peers and supervisors to be malingering or 'swinging the lead', implying mental health-related absences are not genuine (Bell and Palmer-Conn, 2018). Sadly, Bell and Palmer-Conn's national UK study found only 34 per cent of police officers and 44 per cent of police staff would inform their manager if they had a mental illness. Similar findings by the Police Federation of England and Wales in 2021 suggests that there is substantial underreporting of mental ill health and post-traumatic demoralisation syndrome in police officers.

Policing is often described by police officers as a vocation. With greater civilianisation and increasing crossover between warranted and non-warranted roles, this concept of the job extends to police staff. Having joined the force, the majority spend the remainder of their working years committed to policing, so they too become immersed in policing culture. If one lives it, one becomes it or, at least, becomes part of it. This shapes self-identity, which is closely connected to the job and the status of working in the emergency services. Unfortunately for police officers and operational staff, this means a career dealing with vulnerability, tragedy, life, death and everything in between, in a society that appears to regularly challenge their role, perhaps leading to the defensive perceptions of cynicism often associated with those who work in this field.

There are a number of complex factors that contribute to mental ill health. A recent study by Wheeler et al (2021) found that conflicts with the community, a reduction in staff numbers, public disconnection, public pressure and policy demands contributed to loneliness or poor mental health. These are all key phrases linked to policing; however, the study actually set out to address concerns within farming communities. It is not just policing communities that share these fears.

Arguably, the perceived threat of constant danger and having the ability to respond to it promotes a macho culture where physical and mental strength are seen as essential traits. Police officers need to be organised, professional and emotionally aware when dealing with the vulnerable, but they seem unable or unwilling to seek advice about their own fragility. This is worthy of further discussion, as arguably it is the pervading police culture which prevents or suppresses dialogue about officer and staff mental ill health.

When considering the challenges raised by an effective recruitment strategy, it is perhaps important to identify if the common traits associated with policing are acquired on joining the police (sociological paradigm) or are common to police officers (psychological paradigm). Does the recruitment process weed out the non-police personality candidates or are applicants, by their very nature, self-selecting, more ambitious and better organised than the general population?

It is questionable whether police officers' experience and interactions with members of the public with mental health problems in the criminal justice system or pervasive police culture are the major influences on their perception and understanding of mental health. Police officers mirror wider society and hold a number of stereotypical views about mental health (Bell and Palmer-Conn, 2018). If police officers tend to perceive those with a mental illness as dangerous and doubt the integrity or reliability of people with mental ill health, then this stigma remains one of the biggest barriers to the successful community integration of those with mental illnesses and those who seek help. In its own way it becomes a self-fulfilling prophecy. How do you trust a system you don't trust, and one which is regularly highlighted by the media as flawed?

Given police officers are recruited from society, it is likely that they, like the general population, experience the same social-cognitive effects of stigma, which in policing are compounded by their perceived interactions with colleagues. Officers who cannot control their emotions may be viewed as unreliable when responding to critical incidents. With this in mind, a perceived failure to meet the accepted norms or standards can be detrimental to an officer's position, weakening the wider team.

Police officers are reluctant to seek help for mental ill health, and a fear about fitness to practise can result in officers/staff avoiding seeking support, potentially prolonging or intensifying the condition. Despite this reluctance, it could be argued that in large parts of North America, the UK and Australasia much has been done to tackle mental health-related stigma and ensure officers and staff are supported in the workplace. Well-being initiatives in the UK such as MIND Blue Light Campaign, Police Federation Hear 'Man Up' – Think 'Man Down' and, more recently, the CoP Wellbeing Programme have increased the conversation about mental ill health and reduced the stigma associated with it. UK forces have also introduced in-house well-being initiatives and employee assistance programmes, and have employed mental health counsellors to support existing occupational health provision.

More is required, however, as Bell and Palmer-Con (2018) reported that the disclosure of a mental illness to a supervisor or colleague was seen as career threatening, likely to lead to discrimination in the workplace, and seeking help for treatment is seen as a personal failure. This can explain why police officers with mental health problems consider themselves a marginalised community within policing and may have contributed to the very sad news that in the UK more than 20 police officers took their own life each year between 2015 and 2017, a trend which has continued.

It could be argued that the demise of police canteens and related social face-to-face interaction reduce the opportunity to provide support and advice to other members of the team or seek your own, given similar findings around lone-working, long working hours and a reluctance to talk have also been found in the farming community (Wheeler et al, 2021). Challenges with resource management and policing have been exacerbated by an extensive use of single crewing of vehicles, staggered shift and refreshment times and increased use of mobile data further reducing the time officers spend together. It is questionable what these initiatives will have on police culture, but what they do is reduce the informal opportunity to confide in others or seek advice.

If the chances for such opportunities to interact with their colleagues are diminished, what will be the impact on police culture? Will police values and beliefs be reshaped over time? Will the new breed of officers be allowed to flourish within a less masculinised culture where cultural diversity in all its forms are valued and the stigmatisation of mental ill health be removed? And what happens to the colleague who is managing ill health in silence, reluctant to seek more formal advice from a line manager due to believing they will be labelled as weak or a malingerer? Too many questions and not enough answers or, at least, an opportunity for further research.

Summary

So next time the words 'canteen' and 'culture' appear side by side in a policing publication, don't automatically think of the negative aspects often promoted in the media. There are real benefits to sharing a meal and chatting to a colleague. The consumption of calories, protein and carbohydrates should sustain an officer through a shift, but kind words and a simple enquiry such as 'how are you?' may well allow a stranger, friend, colleague, peer or manager the opportunity to share how they really feel and start that long-journey to address the stigma associated with mental ill health.

And don't forget the sausages.

References

Bell, S. and Palmer-Conn, S. (2018) 'Suspicious minds: police attitudes to mental ill health', *International Journal of Law and Public Administration*, 1(2): 25–40.

Boudreau, C., MacKenzie, S.A. and Simmons, D.J. (2022) 'Police violence and public opinion after George Floyd: how the Black Lives Matter movement and endorsements affect support for reforms', *Political Research Quarterly*, 75(2), DOI: https://doi.org/10.1177/10659129221081007.

Chan, J.B. (1997) *Changing Police Culture: Policing in a Multicultural Society*, Cambridge: Cambridge University Press.

IOPC (Independent Office for Police Conduct) (2022a) 'Operation Hotton: learning report' [online] Available from: https://www.policeconduct.gov.uk/sites/default/files/Operation%20Hotton%20Learning%20report%20-%20January%202022.pdf [Accessed 25 May 2022].

IOPC (Independent Office for Police Conduct) (2022b) 'West Mercia police officer dismissed for gross misconduct' [online] Available from: https://policeconduct.gov.uk/news/west-mercia-police-officer-dismissed-gross-misconduct [Accessed 25 May 2022].

Loftus, B. (2009) *Police Culture in a Changing World*, Oxford: Oxford University Press.

Schein, E. (1992) *Organizational Culture and Leadership*, San Francisco, CA: Jossey-Bassey.

Waddington, P. (1999) 'Police (canteen) subculture', *British Journal of Criminology*, 39: 287–309.

Wheeler, R., Lobley, M., McCann, J. and Phillmore, A. (2021) 'Loneliness and social isolation in farming communities: summary of research findings', [online] Available from: https://fcn.org.uk/wp-content/uploads/2021/11/Loneliness-social-isolation-in-farming_FINAL-01.11.21.pdf [Accessed 25 May 2022].

46

Policing: future directions

Andy Rhodes and Michelle McManus

Introduction

The COVID-19 pandemic thrust public services such as policing into the centre of an unprecedented crisis. One for which no government across the world was truly prepared. Policing is often defined by its crisis response, whether that be 999 calls to a myriad of crises 365 days a year, or higher-profile 'big events' such as counterterrorism attacks, firearms incidents and murder investigations. However, despite the police's experience of dealing with crisis, they too were unprepared for a public health challenge that extended volatility, uncertainty, complexity and ambiguity far beyond anything seen in UK society outside of a world war.

So, for researchers and practitioners who, in peacetime, espouse the benefits of police and public health collaboration (and integration), what has been learnt under pressure? There are well-established principles proven to work well for these two systems despite their seemingly unfathomable cultures, quirks and idiosyncrasies, but is the argument that such principles only apply in times of social stability? Or has the pandemic been the coming of age for policing and public health, proving the case for whole system change? The last few years of policing have seen an abundance of changes that have fundamentally altered the role and expectations of police officers themselves, alongside the ever-changing legislative and governance requirements about who and how communities are policed. The stripping away of resources and funding, coupled with a steadily increasing workload involving dealing with vulnerability at all levels, have left many policing professionals exhausted and demoralised in their fight against government decision making. As UK society slowly starts to emerge from lockdown, the police service is reflecting on its experiences and critical roles within that society, with innovative and successful initiatives showing the benefits of a new style of policing. This new policing approach embraces evidence-based approaches focused on the professionalisation of policing at the earliest opportunities and is working alongside other sectors, such as public health, in tackling critical issues, such as responding to the COVID-19 pandemic.

Partnership responses to COVID-19: health and policing

The 2018 Serious Violence Strategy highlighted the importance of partnership working across critical universal sectors. With significant funding from government via the Serious Violence Fund, 18 Violence Reduction Units

(VRUs) were established across England and Wales. These VRUs all have a 'public health approach' as part of their funding requirement, in terms of tackling violence prevention and working closely with vulnerable communities within their local area.

Command and control leadership (CoP, 2018) is often cited as the police's greatest strength as well as their greatest weakness (Martin et al, 2017). In a crisis, the 'can-do' hierarchical structures enable a fast, direct and clear response but hinder effective collaboration in more complex systems, where a reliance on evidence, reflective practice and long-term relationship building is required (Laufs and Waseem, 2020). Policing in the 43 forces of England and Wales is deliberately kept separate from central government, and chief constables are operationally independent, as set out in the secondary legislation of the police protocol under the Policing Protocol Order (2011). It would be naive to suggest that there is no political influence on the way policing is delivered. In fact, the introduction of locally elected police and crime commissioners heralded a shift towards this position. Ultimately, however, the police hold a very privileged position in this regard, namely to maintain legitimacy in the eyes of the public. Health partners are structured in a very different way, with public health devolved to local authorities (top tiers) and National Health Service (NHS) provision centrally funded under the terms of the Health and Social Care Act 2012.

As the COVID-19 crisis started to break, multi-agency Local Resilience Forums (LRFs), who were more accustomed to dealing with local events, were required to behave in a decisive, autocratic way. It soon became apparent that the police were ideally suited to lead the initial response phase. In central government arrangements, the lack of an operational police presence inside the major Gold groups seemed to be at odds with the local direction of travel. Certainly it was the case that in the initial stages of the local COVID response that the police led the multi-agency co-ordination. There are well established arrangements and relationships of trust within these emergency planning groups who exercise regularly and of course respond to crisis events large and small throughout the year, of which health partners often play a key role. In central Government the police are less well represented in relation to civil contingencies around population health matters and are more used to multi-agency working in areas such as Counter Terrorism and protest. As a result there was a need to rapidly stand up national Gold groups without the benefit of an existing infrastructure and more importantly relationships of trust within health. Consequently, the demand on public health resources became intense. Local directors of public health (DPHs) were thrust into the centre of high-pressure decision making, brokering sensitive agreements between local authorities of differing political persuasion (see Local Government Association, 2021). Meanwhile, central government decision making sought to establish consistency and a degree of compliance in response to rapidly changing events (Thorstensen-Woll and Fenney, 2021).

Overall, the LRFs coped admirably, and DPHs stepped up to the challenge with impressive adaptability. Centralisation of decision making in times of crisis is essential, while flexibility and autonomy work equally well at whatever distance from the centre decision making takes place. Clarity of the mission, with clear parameters and boundaries, is proven to work well when systems operate under pressure, while overprescriptive top–down controls can create delays, confusion and unhelpful tension. As a result of this process, the following principles of police and public health emerged in relation to leadership, data and workforce resilience. Each of these principles will now be discussed in turn.

Importance of leadership in partnership working

In terms of leadership, adaptability of leadership styles was a key factor in the successful arrangements at the local and national level. DPHs and other public health leaders coped admirably, and so too did local authority chief executives. Political astuteness in these leadership groups, by necessity, tends to be a stronger feature than in their police counterparts. Yet from time to time the police's bipartisan position was useful in reducing tension during the decision-making process. As a national lead for testing, personal protective equipment, and human resources policy engagement with public health leaders happened almost daily, and on a range of issues. The daily engagement at a national level was required to do three things. Firstly to clarify the scientific advice which was informing Government policy in areas such as new legislation, PPE regimes and public health policy. Secondly to establish supply chains for policing to meet the needs of forces given the huge pressure on the system in the initial stages of the pandemic. And finally to ensure impromptu decisions at a national level were assessed in terms of legislation so they could be quickly translated into understandable operational guidance for the frontline. This highlighted the participants' ability to hold opposing arguments and opinions calmly and with real objectivity, borne out of their confidence in the facts as presented in data or emerging research. It is therefore evident how the pace of a pandemic crisis ebbs and flows, requiring different leadership and management styles to be deployed. Perhaps it is too much to expect all leaders to be able to adapt, and the close working relationships of police and public health leaders has allowed each to play to their strengths.

Information and data sharing

In terms of data, it soon became apparent that a new type of data would form the basis of critical decision making, one that for the police and many other agencies had hitherto been unknown territory. The list of new terminology and accompanying datasets is extensive, and includes such variables as infection rates, the R number, polymerase chain reaction (PCR) and lateral flow tests, symptomatic and asymptomatic cases, and information on IIR and FP3 mask usage and effectiveness. For public health teams this is common ground, and for the police such data became the evidence upon which new legislation and guidance was based. When public health guidance is legislated, often at the last minute, it is important for the police to understand the purpose behind it so that they in turn can explain this to the public when they interact with them. As COVID-19 testing increased the quality of the data and started to drive local decision making, the tensions between the local and national authorities were amplified. As soon as the granularity of data improved, the effectiveness of DPHs and LRFs also improved, providing the sort of agility necessary to tackle outbreaks fast. This should not be seen as an opportunity missed because 'things got done', but results could perhaps have been achieved with far less discord.

Varying public responses to emergency services

In terms of workforce resilience, the frontline NHS workers who were closest to the COVID crisis were already experiencing high level of fatigue and trauma (Whelehan et al, 2021), and the same can be said for many police officers and staff (Hesketh and Tehrani, 2018; Lockey et al, 2021). A national movement to support the NHS emerged early on, with its most visible symbol of mass participation becoming the Thursday night 'clap for carers' (Addley, 2020). Those who work in public service-oriented professions understand the importance of feeling valued by the public, and so this incredible support was perhaps long overdue in the eyes of health professionals. By comparison, the pandemic has placed police officers in new territory, interacting with members of the public with whom they rarely have cause to engage. Many of these new interactions were with those members of the public who are law abiding and were simply confused about what they could and could not do under rapidly changing COVID-19 legislation and policy. Early application of the 'Four Es' (Engage, Explain, Encourage, Enforce) set up a balanced policing style, and most forces set up dedicated teams solely responsible for COVID-related deployments, all of which helped to mitigate the risks of mistakes by the police (HMICFRS, 2021). For the most part this worked well, with around 10 per cent of all COVID deployments attracting a penalty notice.

What cannot be ignored, though, are the numerous points of tension between the police and communities, when anti-vaccination protests and Black Lives Matter protests were added to the ongoing health crisis. The National Police Wellbeing Survey, which covers 23,000 staff, reported a decline in police feeling valued by the public through COVID, but encouragingly also reported an improvement in officers feeling valued by colleagues, supervisors and their organisation (Police Research Unit, 2021). When there is limited control of external factors affecting well-being, the effort to control the controllable internally becomes even more important, and it is contended that such a situation strengthens the argument for a strategic approach to workforce resilience and welfare.

Conclusion

In conclusion, some 18 months on from the crisis, there have been some notable changes which can be attributed to the learning gained from reviews conducted by the NPCC. The establishment of a Chief Medical Officer CMO for policing has been in place since March 2022 and this role is developing relationships within the health ecosystem across a range of issues including crisis management and policy making. The NPCC now have a Chief Scientific Officer who likewise allows for a more effective interface within Government and both are able to provide specialist advice to the NPCC, forces and the College of Policing. Public Health England has been renamed as National Institute for Health Protection and police demand is beginning to return to pre-COVID levels, yet the pressures of today should not lead to a golden opportunity for learning being overlooked. Police and health joint working has been pressure-tested, and there is an urgent need to develop a greater degree of integration at the national level, so that the connectivity to local arrangements (where police have a far more visible and influential presence) is strengthened. Ultimately, the true test of a policy decision is the impact that it has on its intended recipients. Does the policy have the desired effect, or the opposite? How does the policy leave people feeling? Surely the pandemic has reinforced this important issue and presents further evidence for early engagement with frontline workers who interact with the public as part of the policy-making process. Policy, guidance and indeed legislation are all more effective when the person implementing them feels involved in their creation and therefore can see the meaning and purpose behind the change.

References

Addley, E. (2020). 'Clap for our carers: the very unBritish ritual that united a nation', *The Guardian*, [online] 28 May, Available from: https://www.theguard ian.com/society/2020/may/28/clap-for-our-carers-the-very-unbritish-ritual-that-united-the-nation [Accessed 19 July 2021].

CoP (College of Policing) (2018) 'Operations: command and control', Available from: https://www.app.college.police.uk/app-content/operations/command-and-control/ [Accessed 19 July 2021].

Hesketh, I. and Tehrani, N. (2018) 'Psychological trauma risk management in the UK police service', *Policing: A Journal of Policy and Practice*, 13(4): 531–5.

HMICFRS (HM Inspectorate of Constabulary (and) Fire and Rescue Services) (2021) 'Policing in the pandemic: the police response to the coronavirus pandemic during 2020', Available from: https://www.justiceinspectorates.gov. uk/hmicfrs/publication-html/the-police-response-to-the-coronavirus-pande mic-during-2020/ [Accessed 19 July 2021].

Laufs, J. and Waseem, Z. (2020) 'Policing in pandemics: a systematic review and best practices for police response to COVID-19', *International Journal of Disaster Risk Reduction*, 51: 101812, DOI: https://doi.org/10.1016/j.ijdrr.2020.101812.

Local Government Association (2021). 'Public health on the frontline: responding to COVID-19', [online] Available from: https://www.local.gov.uk/our-support/coronavirus-council-information-and-support/covid-19-service-information/covid-19-2 [Accessed 19 July 2021].

Lockey, S., Graham, L., Zheng, Y., Hesketh, I., Plater, M. and Gracey, S. (2021) 'The impact of workplace stressors on exhaustion and work engagement in policing', *The Police Journal*, 95(1), DOI: https://doi:10.1177/0032258X211016532.

Martin, H.C., Rogers, C., Samuel, A.J. and Rowling, M. (2017). 'Serving from the top: police leadership for the twenty-first century', *International Journal of Emergency Services*, 6(3): 209–19, DOI: https://doi.org/10.1108/IJES-04-2017-0023.

Police Research Unit (2021), *National Police Wellbeing Survey 2020: Summary of Evidence and Insights*, Durham: Durham University Policing Research Unit.

Thorstensen-Woll, C. and Fenney, D. (2021) 'Collaboration, respect and humility: directors of public health responding locally to COVID-19', [Blog] 29 April, Available from: https://www.kingsfund.org.uk/blog/2021/01/directors-public-health-responding-locally-covid-19 [Accessed 10 December 2021].

Whelehan, D.F., Algeo, N. and Brown, D.A. (2021) 'Leadership through crisis: fighting the fatigue pandemic in healthcare during COVID-19', *BMJ Leader*, 5: 108–12.

PART IV

Investigation

47

Crime scene investigation

Stephanie Davies

Introduction

No one in policing wants to hear the words 'have we missed something?' Especially when a case has long since been closed and there is no recoverable evidence left. Hard-working professionals who regularly commit to long hours in these times of austerity do a fantastic job bringing offenders to justice. Although rare, however, mistakes can happen, which can start at the crime scene and escalate from there. Crime scene investigation is not just about identifying, seizing and analysing forensic evidence to prove or disprove the culpability of a suspect; it requires a more holistic approach – something additional to incorporating policing experience, background knowledge and the ability to 'read' a scene. The detective or police officer needs to be able to see that what is present at the scene is wholly consistent with the narrative being given to them. They also need to easily spot inconsistencies – those red flags – so that further scrutiny can be exercised where needed. Increasingly, historic closed cases and suspected miscarriages of justice are making their way to the forefront, placing increasing demands on resource-limited police forces on a national and international level. This discussion touches on potential vulnerabilities in policing at crime scenes; there can be disastrous consequences if things are missed. Early errors can start a chain of events going in entirely the wrong direction, which can lead to costly reviews, damage to reputations and fundamentally impair public confidence in the police.

The 'CSI effect'

Forensic awareness is more ubiquitous these days, mainly due to the advances in forensic science and such details being regularly reported in television programmes, magazines and books. The term the 'CSI effect' came about in the media following the emergence of forensic television programmes such as *CSI* and it is theorised that this effect may (positively or negatively) influence some areas of criminal justice (Cole and Dioso-Villa, 2007). One such area includes the amount of forensic knowledge offenders possess and that the CSI effect can increase their overall forensic awareness (Zaikman and Vicary, 2017). Such reporting of forensic techniques in the media can educate would-be-offenders about how 'every contact leaves a trace', and how that is relevant to the commission of (and getting away with) a crime. There is a plethora of material available in the public domain which details the mistakes offenders have made or describes how detectives managed to hunt down a killer. Armed with this knowledge, offenders are arguably more likely to take precautionary acts prior to a crime and successfully clean up afterwards – making it far harder for tangible evidence to be found. Fictional shows can also mislead the public in terms of the speed of investigations and put further pressure on judicial services to quickly solve the crime and bring the offender to justice.

Planned versus ad hoc crimes

For a successful conviction, the judiciary tend to require at least one of the following: forensic evidence, witness testimony or a confession. If a crime occurred on impulse – so without forethought and lack of preparation – there can be a multitude of recoverable evidence left linking the offender to the crime scene. Once faced with this evidence, the perpetrator may then confess and plead guilty. However, if the offender meticulously plans the crime beforehand, they can decide when to carry it out (for example, when there are no witnesses), take precautionary acts (such as wearing gloves), clean up afterwards (such as washing a weapon), and they are unlikely to confess to the crime – especially when there is little forensic evidence linking them. Planned crimes and murders are notoriously difficult to solve, but thankfully they comprise a small percentage of all crime.

Confirmation bias

When attending a crime scene, it is vital the investigator approaches the scene objectively and tries to avoid the negative effects of cognitive bias. Cognitive bias is part of an individual's subjective thoughts, which are borne out of their own perspectives, observations and experiences. One could argue that professional learning derived from experience and knowledge is also a form of cognitive bias (and as such it may never be possible for the investigator to be free from it). Confirmation bias, or tunnel vision, is a form of cognitive bias where the individual seeks out information that supports their belief as to what happened (Klayman, 1995; Rassin et al, 2010). The scope of the investigation essentially becomes narrow in that information that contradicts the preconceived theory tends to be missed or ignored. For example, if a call comes into the police saying there has been a suicide the police may attend the scene fully expecting to see a suicide. They may miss evidence that suggests otherwise. This is especially dangerous if an offender has skilfully 'staged' the scene, where for example a murder has been made to look like a suicide. If the investigator already has the belief the death is a suicide, they will almost certainly miss those ever so subtle red flags at the scene.

These days, police officers and detectives in the UK are taught to treat all deaths as suspicious until the evidence confirms otherwise. It is far preferable to scale down an investigation once the evidence confirms no suspicious circumstances, rather than upgrade one that has already been closed, where the evidence has been irretrievably lost. More and more historic cases are being reopened (or at least debated in the media) due to new information, new evidence, or by looking at the same evidence but in an alternative, more modernised way – so that a whole new scenario then presents itself and the original hypothesis and manner of death are brought into question.

A miscarriage of justice?

Take the Bamber family murders at White House Farm in 1985 as an example. The police were initially given the narrative that the daughter had 'gone berserk' and shot her parents, her two children and then herself. From the outset, the case was treated as murder-suicide and detectives quickly concluded they were not looking for anyone else. Due to this belief, the need to forensically secure the scene and gather evidence was deemed unnecessary. However, later a witness came forward with information which raised serious doubts about the murder-suicide theory. The police then focused on the remaining family member, the son Jeremy Bamber, as having committed the murders, and realised that he must have staged the scene, making it look like his sister was the killer. At the trial, the jury found Bamber guilty of murder, but arguably there was a lack of forensic evidence that conclusively placed Bamber at the scene at the time of the murders. Nearly forty years after the event, it is still being debated whether Bamber is guilty or innocent. It is also being debated if his conviction was 'safe', considering this lack of forensic evidence. This is a situation whereby should Bamber be innocent of this crime, a gross miscarriage of justice would have occurred and he should be released immediately. Had that scene been given the forensic respect and scrutiny it should have, there would have been little room for doubt and there would be assurance that the correct judicial verdict was reached all those years ago.

Equivocal deaths

Another area that can cause issues for policing is that of equivocal death. Equivocal deaths are where the manner of death is ambiguous, so it could be a murder, suicide or an accident. For example, if a victim was found dead with a single stab wound to the chest, it may not clear if it was self-inflicted or committed by a third party. Detectives will treat the case initially as suspicious and it may be that a forensic post-mortem examination (PME) will conclude if the injury was self-inflicted or not. However, sometimes the case is still unexplained following the PME, meaning the police need to continue the investigation to gain further clarity how the deceased came by their death.

For such deaths, it is vital for the investigator to be knowledgeable in suicide investigation and to understand what factors are consistent or inconsistent with suicides. They also need to be familiar with suicide scenes. If there were several inconsistencies present at one scene, this should invite further scrutiny until these inconsistencies can be explained or accounted for. There can still be unusual or complex suicides which may initially raise suspicion and require further analysis, but good-quality investigations should soon rule out third-party involvement.

Staged crime scenes

This is also relevant with staged crime scenes. The offender will present the scene how they expect a *typical* scene to look like – bearing in mind they may never have had experience of genuine crime scenes. The consensus behind Jeremy Bamber's conviction was that he had staged his sister's death to look like a suicide. However, the failure to forensically test if this was indeed the case was lost at the outset. For example, no tests were carried out for gunshot residue on either the deceased sister or Bamber himself. This would have unequivocally demonstrated if the sister or Bamber fired the gun. Even if police are not looking for anyone else in connection with a death, they still should forensically test to be sure *beyond reasonable doubt* (the criminal burden of proof) that no one else was involved and that the assumed murderer indeed took their own life.

The key purpose for an offender to stage a crime scene is to mislead police and to misdirect the investigation, so that they are not considered as a suspect. In almost all staging cases, the victim and the offender will be known to each other and the offender recognises they will likely be the prime suspect if the police establish that a crime has occurred (Hazelwood and Napier, 2004; Schlesinger et al, 2012; Ferguson and Petherick, 2016; Ferguson, 2019). So, the aim is to get the police to think that a different, non-suspicious manner of death occurred – such as suicide or an accident instead of a murder – or that a different person carried out the crime instead. That way the offender has a much better chance of getting away with the crime.

Staging is not always limited to how the scene is visually presented however. It can also manifest in the circumstances and the narrative given (verbal staging can begin as early as the first emergency services call). Forensic linguistics and evidence-based research (such as that conducted by Harpster et al, 2009) has demonstrated that a useful investigative skill is being able to identify innocent or guilty indicators when analysing calls or statements made by a potential suspect.

The case of Graham Backhouse in 1984 depicts circumstantial staging, where Backhouse gave police the narrative that he shot his neighbour in self-defence after his neighbour attacked him with a knife. He had set the scene so his neighbour would be blamed for an earlier attempted murder on Backhouse's wife. However, the crime scene showed that the bloodstain patterns were not consistent with his account and the police soon worked out what had really happened. Backhouse was later convicted for both murdering his neighbour and for the earlier attempted murder of his wife.

Offender behaviour: modus operandi or signature?

The motives to carry out a crime can vary for each offender, but the principal elements tend to centre around financial gain, power/control or sex. Arguably there is nothing to say that there cannot more than one concurrent motive at any one time (for example, where the initial motive is financial but during the commission of the crime fantasy behaviour is also acted upon, thus feeding a psychological need). The method of carrying out the crime and getting away with it (the modus operandi or MO) can evolve and change over time (such as the offender becomes more skilled and learns from each event), or it can devolve (worsening of mental health). For those offenders that also have a psychological need to fulfil (such as turning fantasy into reality or posing the body a certain way), they do this above and beyond what is required to commission the crime itself. The offender is in effect leaving a psychological imprint at each scene. Unlike the MO, the fundamental psychological need is unlikely to change much over time. The unique combination of MO behaviour along with psychological gratification has been referred to as the 'signature' of the offender, which has been documented in some serial murders (Douglas and Munn, 1992; Keppel, 1995). It is this 'signature' that can help detectives to link serial cases together. Looking at the MO in isolation can mean detectives can fail to link some cases – such as happened in the serial murders committed by Peter Sutcliffe.

Another example where case linkage was not immediately realised was the Stephen Port serial murders, where four young men were murdered by Port in 2014–15. The victims were found at different times in (or near to) the same graveyard. They died from drug overdoses and their clothing indicated movement by a third party. Police initially felt all deaths were non-suspicious and they only took a closer look due to the insistence of the families and friends of the victims. Port was eventually convicted for the four murders. In late 2021 an inquest jury determined that the police had missed a series of opportunities that could have prevented the deaths of at least three of the victims.

Is a new breed of investigator needed?

So, what does this mean for the future? Are police officers and detectives in the UK fully equipped and trained to look out for inconsistencies at each crime scene? Do they consider all perspectives, utilising investigative, forensic and psychological tools? No police force ever wants to 'get it wrong' but mistakes can and do happen. An understanding in terms of forensic science, police investigations, forensic psychology, basic pathology and crime scene analysis is improving each day. Police forces should not be afraid to share information with each other. Smart offenders know to target different jurisdictions to avoid being caught and this is where case linkages can be missed. The most vital thing is to take away that essential learning and to ensure such mistakes do not happen again in the future. If the UK is now experiencing a new breed of offender, perhaps it needs a new breed of investigator to ensure it consistently remains ahead?

Summary

To summarise, this chapter discusses some areas where the police can be vulnerable when investigating crime scenes. Thankfully, mistakes are rare, but when they do happen the ramifications can be enormous – an innocent person can be sent to prison, or a murderer is left roaming free and victims' family and friends are denied justice. Misinterpretations and the failure to maintain an open mind can mean offenders literally get away with murder. It is vital for detectives and police officers to be adequately trained and skilled in new and emerging forensic and psychological tools, so that their balanced repertoire enables them to get it right the first time, *every time*.

References

Cole, S.A. and Dioso-Villa, R. (2007) '*CSI* and its effects: media, juries, and the burden of proof', *New England Law Review*, 41: 435–70.

Douglas, J.E. and Munn, C. (1992) 'Violent crime scene analysis: modus operandi, signature and staging', *FBI Law Enforcement Bulletin*, 61: 1–10.

Ferguson, C. (2019) 'Forensically aware offenders and homicide investigations: challenges, opportunities and impacts', *Australian Journal of Forensic Sciences*, 51: 1–4.

Ferguson, C. and Petherick, W. (2016) 'Getting away with murder: an examination of detected homicides staged as suicides', *Homicide Studies*, 20(1): 3–24.

Harpster, T., Adams, S.H. and Jarvis, J.P. (2009) 'Analyzing 911 homicide calls for indicators of guilt or innocence: an exploratory analysis', *Homicide Studies*, 13(1): 69–93.

Hazelwood, R. and Napier, M. (2004) 'Crime scene staging and its detection', *International Journal of Offender Therapy and Comparative Criminology*, 48: 744–59.

Keppel, R.D. (1995) 'Signature murders: a report of several related cases', *Journal of Forensic Sciences*, 40(4): 670–4.

Klayman, J. (1995) 'Varieties of confirmation bias', *Psychology of Learning and Motivation*, 32(1): 385–418.

Rassin, E., Eerland, A. and Kuijpers, I. (2010) 'Let's find the evidence: an analogue study of confirmation bias in criminal investigations', *Journal of Investigative Psychology & Offender Profiling*, 7(3): 231–46.

Schlesinger, L., Gardenier, A., Jarvis, J. and Sheehan-Cook, J. (2012) 'Crime scene staging in homicide', *Journal of Police and Criminal Psychology*, 29(1): 44–51.

Zaikman, Y. and Vicary, A. (2017) 'The CSI effect: an investigation into the relationship between watching crime shows and forensic knowledge', *North American Journal of Psychology*, 19(1): 51–64.

48

Investigative interviewing

Davut Akca

Investigative interviewing is a critical component of criminal investigations. In order to resolve criminal cases thoroughly and to ensure due process in the later stages of the judicial process, the interviewing of witnesses, victims and suspects needs to be accomplished appropriately and effectively. In almost every aspect of their job, police officers talk to people to gather certain types of information. When necessary information cannot be obtained by other means, such as in the case of historical crimes, interviewing people becomes particularly crucial (Milne and Bull, 1999). There are a variety of situations in which the police talk to people, including roadside interactions, helping people on the streets, job interviews with prospective police applicants, suicide attempts, hostage negotiations and controlling rallies. Although all of these interactions are used to gather information from the interviewees for different purposes, only the information-gathering activities within an investigation process are considered as 'investigative interviewing' (Schollum, 2005).

From interrogation to investigative interviewing

Investigative interviewing is a broad term which refers to all forms of formal communications with suspects, victims and witnesses within a criminal investigation. The term 'interrogation' generally refers to the interviews with suspects and connotes police tactics to elicit confession. However, there has been an increasing tendency among practitioners and academics towards using the term 'investigative interview' to refer to all interview types in criminal investigations (for example, suspect, witness and victim; see Griffiths and Rachlew, 2018). The main reason for this transformation is the evolution of the techniques used in suspect interviews, from a persuasion-based approach towards an information-gathering approach. This change has come about in line with evidence from psychological research during the last few decades in favour of the information-gathering approach, and revelations about the miscarriages of justice caused by persuasion-based methods (Eastwood et al, 2020).

The main purpose of investigative interviewing is to elicit reliable, accurate and legally admissible information from suspects, victims and witnesses to find the facts within the context of a crime investigation (Schollum, 2005). The information elicited through investigative interviewing is estimated to constitute 80 per cent of all evidence gathered throughout a typical crime investigation, while the 'real and documentary evidence' (for example, physical evidence such as objects and documents gathered to prove or disprove the guilt in an investigation) constitutes the remaining 20 per cent (Yeschke, 2003, p 47). Therefore, the quality of interviewing directly affects the judicial quality of an investigation file, which is important for the decision-making processes in judiciary.

The UK Home Office developed seven principles of investigative interviewing in 1992 and these principles have been adopted in many countries since then (Schollum, 2005). First of all, the Home Office identified the role of investigative interviewing as obtaining reliable and accurate information from suspects, witnesses and victims to find the facts about a criminal case. To achieve this goal, the interviewer should have an open mind and pay attention to the relationship between the account given by the interviewee and the previous information in the case file. Another principle that an investigative interviewer should take into consideration is that of fair conduct in interviews. The principles of the Home Office do not consider persistent questioning as unfair. It is clearly explained that the interviewer does not have to accept the first answer given by the interviewee, even if the latter prefer to exercise the right to silence. The only restriction on asking the interviewee questions is where the interviews are with child victims of sexual or violent abuse. Finally, the interviewer must treat vulnerable interviewees with care (Milne et al, 2007).

Research on investigative interviewing

What makes an investigative interview successful? The answer has been researched by forensic psychologists for decades. Indeed, one of the main topics in the forensic psychology discipline is the psychology of police investigations, specifically the psychology and behaviours of the actors in investigative interviews, including police officers, suspects, victims and eyewitnesses (Griffiths and Rachlew, 2018). Researchers have measured the outcomes of interviews and the performance of interviewers by using a wide range of variables such as the amount and accuracy of information gathered, questioning style (for example, usage of appropriate questioning techniques such as open-ended, non-leading questions), interviewers' adherence to the interview protocol, a rapport built between the interviewer and interviewee and the amount of true and false confessions elicited (in suspect interviews). Studies conducted in psychology labs and those based on real-life interviews also focused on finding the factors that affect the outcomes of the interview. It is difficult to define the key features of a successful investigative interview because of the complicated nature of interviewing. There are several aspects that might affect the outcomes of interviews, such as the time and place of the interview, the type of crime, the role of the interviewee in the crime, the techniques and protocols used in the interview, and the behaviours and characteristics of the interviewee and the interviewer. For example, the interviewees might not be willing to share information for various reasons and becomes an additional challenge for the interviewer in their efforts to reach the necessary information. Furthermore, the interview is a dynamic process of interaction between the interviewer and the interviewee. Thus, it is almost impossible to predict before the interview what will happen in the interview room (Yeschke, 2003).

Evidence-based interviewing

Thanks to the increasing scholarly interest in investigative interviewing, evidence-based and ethical interview frameworks and models have been developed and widely used by police organisations across the world. For instance, the PEACE framework, which was developed in the UK in 1992 and is based on the evidence from psychological research and input from practitioners, is considered the gold standard in all types of interviews (Milne et al, 2007). The model consists of five stages, and the mnemonic PEACE represents these stages: (1) Planning and Preparation, (2) Engage and Explain, (3) Account (Clarification and Challenge), (4) Closure, and (5) Evaluation. In the Planning and Preparation phase, the interviewer identifies the objectives of the interview, gathers background information on the interviewee and the criminal case, assesses the pieces of evidence in the file, reviews the legislation and guidelines and prepares the logistics and procedures that will be followed in the interview. The Engage and Explain phase refers to the opening part of the interview, which includes the attempts to establish rapport with the interviewee and to explain the reasons for and the procedure of the interview to the interviewee, before questioning them about the criminal case. In the Account phase, the interviewer asks open-ended questions to allow the interviewee to provide their free account on the case being investigated and probes into the main points in the free narrative. The Closure phase is where the interviewer reviews and summarises the account of the interviewee, verifies all of the information provided and explains what will happen next. After the interview is completed, the interviewer examines the information gathered in line with the other evidence in the file; this is called the Evaluation phase.

In addition to its phased method, the PEACE framework incorporates elements of cognitive interview (CI) and conversation management models, depending on the type of interview. The conversation management model helps interviewers to overcome resistance on the part of suspects by revealing the contradictions between their account and what the interviewer already knows about the case. Cognitive interviewing was developed in the 1980s and has been used to enhance the memory of cooperative interviewees through various techniques. The effectiveness of the CI has been demonstrated through lab-based research and field studies on both children and adult interviewees (Meissner, 2021). The initial version of cognitive interviewing included four memory enhancement techniques: report everything, mental reinstatement of the context, recalling of events in different temporal orders and change perspective (Milne and Bull, 1999). During the 'report everything' technique, interviewees are encouraged to report everything that they remember regarding the case through open-ended questions and without interruption. In the 'mental reinstatement' technique, the interviewee is asked to put themselves in the context of the event, reconstruct their memory and create the picture of the case in their mind. Eye closure or looking at a blank wall are side techniques which can be used during the 'mental reinstatement' technique to eliminate any distraction in the interview room. 'Changing the temporal order' technique invites the interviewee to report the event from the end to the beginning. Telling the same story in a reverse order might help eliminate the mundanity of the daily events and cause the interviewee to remember important details that happened between the daily routines. In the 'changing perspective' technique, interviewees are asked to remember the event from the perspective of another person who was also present in the crime scene, which helps the interviewee report more accurate details. The structure of the CI model was developed in the 1990s, through the enhanced CI model. The main contribution made in this structured version is the appropriate sequencing of questioning so as to facilitate memory retrieval. Some new techniques were also added to the model, such as witness-compatible questioning, rapport building, mental imagery and transferral of control of the interview to the witness (Milne and Bull, 1999).

Research has also shed light on appropriate and effective questioning techniques. To elicit accurate, reliable and extensive amount of information, interviewers should use open-ended questions (for example, tell me, explain to me, describe and so on) and probing questions (for example, Why questions or yes/no questions) as needed (Oxburgh et al, 2010). Interviewers need to avoid using leading (suggestive), multiple and complex questions, which can lead to confusion and misleading answers from the interviewee (Snook et al, 2012).

Suspect interviews

Interviewing suspects is an area of concern in the study of police investigations because of the usage of controversial and non-evidence-based techniques in some models that are currently practised. In a broader sense, the interview approaches in suspect interviews are categorised under two groups: (1) persuasion-based/accusatorial approaches; and (2) information-gathering approaches (Eastwood et al, 2020). Persuasion-based/accusatorial approaches, such as the Reid technique, which is the predominant interrogation approach utilised in North America, focus on eliciting confessions from suspects by using psychologically manipulative or coercive tactics. These tactics include direct confrontation (for example, 'We have no doubt that you stole the money'), usage of fabricated evidence to incriminate the suspect, leading questions (for example, 'The runaway car was a blue SUV, right?'), minimisation (such as 'I understand that you might have got the money to help buy food for your family') and maximisation (for example, 'You might get a harsher punishment if you do not tell the whole story'). Conversely, information-gathering approaches, such as the PEACE framework, aim to gather information from suspects by using inquisitorial methods such as open-ended questions and allowing them to provide free narrative without interruptions, coercion or manipulation. For instance, conversation management, which is a component of the PEACE framework, asks the suspects to clarify the inconsistencies between their account and the other evidence in the investigation file instead of using manipulative or coercive techniques.

Studies comparing the persuasion-based approaches (such as the Reid technique) to the information-gathering approaches (for example, PEACE framework) have consistently found that the former leads innocent suspects to confess falsely at significantly higher rates than the latter. False confessions are one of the main reasons behind the wrongful conviction of innocent people and this fact has been proven through DNA evidence that exonerated hundreds of suspects who falsely confessed during police interrogations. Interestingly, research findings indicated that persuasion-based and information-gathering approaches lead guilty suspects to confess their guilt truly at similar rates. For instance, in a lab-based study, Eastwood et al (2020) found that a persuasion-based interview approach generated substantially more false confessions from innocent participants than an information-gathering approach (45 per cent compared with 0 per cent respectively), whereas the two approaches were equally effective in eliciting true confessions (95.24 per cent and 94.74 per cent respectively). Based on these findings, researchers have called for reform in interview practices to eliminate the controversial techniques used in persuasion-based approaches and to adopt more ethical and equally effective information-gathering approaches (Snook et al, 2010).

Interviewing children

Questioning of young people and children is another important aspect of investigative interviewing which has required special attention from psychologists and practitioners due to the developmental differences within these populations. Interviewers should keep in mind that children have limited capacity in terms of memory retrieval ability, communicating their ideas and thoughts and distinguishing truths and lies. Children are also more suggestible to leading questions, social pressure and false information. Cognitive interviewing is one of the methods recommended when interviewing children and young people to overcome these challenges, and research has shown that it has enhanced memory retrieval in child interviews (Milne and Bull, 1999). Also, evidence-based interview protocols specific to child interviews have been created, such as the National Institute of Child Health and Human Development Protocol, developed by a group of researchers led by Michael Lamb, and the Memorandum of Good Practice for Video Recorded Interviews with Child Witnesses for Criminal Proceedings developed by the UK Home Office (Cyr and Lamb, 2009). Some of the best practices in evidence-based child interview protocols include using a step-by-step process to question a child about a past event, employing a developmentally appropriate language, building a rapport with the child, reviewing interview ground rules at the beginning of the interview, relying on open-ended questioning, and using props and cues to aid memory retrieval and communication (Milne et al, 2007).

Conclusions

Forensic psychology has significantly contributed to the development of evidence-based interview frameworks, as well as contributing to interview training courses which have translated this scientific knowledge into practice. The outcomes of the interviews conducted with the guidance of science, and the impact of training, have also been evidenced through lab-based studies and field research during the last few decades (Akca et al, 2021). More research is needed to establish evidence-based interview approaches and to eliminate controversial interview practices that lead to miscarriages of justice. Most importantly, an enhanced collaboration between forensic psychologists and practitioners is needed to assess and understand the needs of the field and to translate research into practice more efficiently.

References

Akca, D., Larivière, C.D. and Eastwood, J. (2021) 'Assessing the efficacy of investigative interviewing training courses: a systematic review', *International Journal of Police Science & Management*, 23(1): 73–84, DOI: https://doi.org/10.1177/14613557211008470.

Cyr, M. and Lamb, M.E. (2009) 'Assessing the effectiveness of the NICHD investigative interview protocol when interviewing French-speaking alleged victims of child sexual abuse in Quebec', *Child Abuse & Neglect*, 33(5): 257–68, DOI: https://doi.org/10.1016/j.chiabu.2008.04.002.

Eastwood, J., Dunk, M. and Akca, D. (2020) 'Assessing the diagnosticity of a persuasion-based and a dialogue-based interrogation approach', *Journal of Police and Criminal Psychology*, 37: 569–75, DOI: https://doi.org/10.1007/s11896-020-09410-1.

Griffiths, A. and Rachlew, A. (2018) 'From interrogation to investigative interviewing: the application of psychology', in A. Griffiths and R. Milne (eds) *The Psychology of Criminal Investigation: From Theory to Practice*, London: Routledge, pp 154–79.

Meissner, C.A. (2021) '"What works?" Systematic reviews and meta-analyses of the investigative interviewing research literature', *Applied Cognitive Psychology*, 35(2): 322–8, DOI: https://doi.org/10.1002/acp.3808.

Milne, B., Shaw, G. and Bull, R. (2007) 'Investigative interviewing: the role of research', in D. Carson, R. Milne, F. Pakes, K. Shalev and A. Shawyer (eds) *Applying Psychology to Criminal Justice*, Chichester: Wiley, pp 65–80.

Milne, R. and Bull, R. (1999) *Investigative Interviewing: Psychology and Practice*, Chichester: Wiley.

Oxburgh, G.E., Myklebust, T. and Grant, T. (2010) 'The question of question types in police interviews: a review of the literature from a psychological and linguistic perspective', *International Journal of Speech Language and the Law*, 17(1): 45–66.

Schollum, M. (2005) 'Investigative interviewing: the literature', New Zealand Police, [online] Available from: https://www.yumpu.com/en/document/view/25413039/investigative-interviewing- the-literature-new-zealand-police [Accessed 7 June 2022].

Snook, B., Luther, K., Quinlan, H. and Milne, R. (2012). 'Let 'em talk! A field study of police questioning practices of suspects and accused persons', *Criminal Justice and Behavior*, 39(10): 1328–39, DOI: https://doi.org/10.1177/0093854812449216.

Snook, B., Eastwood, J., Stinson, M., Tedeschini, J. and House, J.C. (2010) 'Reforming investigative interviewing in Canada', *Canadian Journal of Criminology and Criminal Justice*, 52(2): 215–29, DOI: https://doi.org/10.3138/cjccj.52.2.215.

Yeschke, C.L. (2003) *The Art of Investigative Interviewing: A Human Approach to Testimonial Evidence*, Boston: Butterworth-Heinemann.

49

Detecting deception

Clea Wright

Introduction and key ideas

Deception is the deliberate attempt to mislead another person with a communication that is in some way false. Communication may occur across multiple channels including verbal (such as an account of an event), non-verbal (for example, nodding) and paraverbal (including tone of voice), and any of these channels may include deceptive information. Further, although deception is often thought of as falsification (presenting false information as truthful), it may also involve withholding true information known to be relevant, or diversion, exaggeration and half-truths. The purpose of a deceptive communication is to affect the decision making of the receiver of the communication by controlling information to manipulate their cognitive, psychological or emotional state.

Deception is a ubiquitous behaviour and most people engage in some form of deceptive communication every day (DePaulo et al, 1996). The majority of this deception is low-stake 'white lies', the consequences of which are not serious. However, in the world of crime and policing, not only is there is an increased contextual expectation of deception, but in this type of high-stakes scenario the consequences of deception (whether successful or unsuccessful) are likely to be significant. Detecting deception, therefore, may be important in several areas, including: interrogation, which is an approach used in several countries (including the US) that rests on the idea that it is possible to accurately judge the veracity of a suspect, and then employ a process that results in a confession; intelligence gathering, in which the credibility of information may have to be assessed in order to make decisions; investigative interviewing, the function of which in the UK is information gathering not judging veracity, although it is likely that in practice veracity judgements are made; and jury decision making, which may in part be based on the perceived veracity of defendants, victims and witnesses.

The detection of deception (whether by humans or an automated system), is dependent on the premise that there are behaviours, also known as cues, that differ between truthful and deceptive communications. Furthermore, the cues must be observable in some way (individuals need to be able to perceive them, with or without specialist equipment); the cues should be consistent within and between individuals (the same cues occur for all types of deception for everybody); the cues must be specific to deception (they do not occur for other reasons); and the cues must be sensitive to deception (they always occur in a deceptive communication).

The cues should also be robust to countermeasures (so that they cannot be suppressed or faked), and the cues must be understood by the observer (so that individuals know that the cues indicate deception). The only known cue that satisfies all these criteria is Pinocchio's nose, which has the obvious limitation of being fictional. There is general agreement among researchers that, in reality, an equivalent cue does not exist (van Koppen, 2012). However, there is little else in the deception detection literature upon which there is general agreement. It has been established that there is no strong consensus among deception researchers about which cues or approaches to detecting deception are most valuable, and no agreed-upon dominant and unifying theory. This leaves a body of literature on detecting deception that is rather fragmented and inconsistent.

Key findings and approaches

Two widely cited meta-analytic findings suggest that cues to deception tend to be unreliable and weak, and that generally people's ability to detect deception is barely above the level of chance (including people who regularly encounter deception in their professional lives) (DePaulo and Bond, 2012). These findings clearly seem related, as accuracy in detecting deception necessarily depends on available cues. A meta-analysis exploring the relationship between these findings confirmed that people's intuitive beliefs about cues to deception are rarely incorrect and that what limits accuracy is the weaknesses of the cues (Hartwig and Bond, 2011). The logical implication of this is that accuracy will be increased by maximising the behavioural differences between truthful and deceptive communications. Related to this is the common call among researchers to address issues of ecological validity in the literature: the majority of findings are the result of lab-based experimental studies in which there are no serious consequences for not being believed. This methodology may be analogous to the experience of producing everyday 'white lies', but may not reflect the cognitive, emotional and motivational correlates of lying in a high-stakes context, such as a police interview (Frank and Svetieva, 2012). Furthermore, calls for the consideration of context are increasing among researchers, as not all high-stakes lies will necessarily resemble each other (for example, a person lying about killing a close relative may be expected to experience some differences in emotion compared to a person lying about insurance fraud) and so cues may vary according to context (van Koppen, 2012).

There are four major approaches to detecting deception: observing non-verbal behaviour, measuring physiological responses, measuring neural activity (sometimes called 'brain mapping') and analysing accounts (that is, verbal behaviour). In discussing these, the focus will be directed at approaches which do not require specialist equipment, as they are likely to have greater utility in an applied policing context. It should be noted that, due largely to the substantial threat posed by modern terrorism, the field has developed to include attempts to identify hostile intent. The focus is no longer solely on lying about past actions, but now includes lying about future intentions, with the aim of preventing harmful acts before they occur (Mac Giolla et al, 2015, p 155).

Non-verbal behaviour

An idea often propagated in the media is that people can spot when people are being deceptive by leakage of their true intent via non-verbal behaviours such as facial expressions, face touching, fidgeting and gaze aversion. The common assumption is that behaviours which indicate nervousness are related to deception, but there is very little empirical support that any non-verbal behaviours appear consistently in deceptive communications and the premise that people can identify deception by watching a person's behaviour is not robust (Bond et al, 2015, pp 42–5). Emerging research areas around non-verbal behaviours that may prove more fruitful in the future as they are not based on nervousness but on cognition include ocular responses (Gamer and Pertzov, 2018, pp 169–86) and reaction times (Suchotzki, 2018, pp 243–68), although, as both require specialist equipment, they are not considered here in detail. In the interests of dispelling myths, it should be noted that there is no evidence for the popular proposition related to neurolinguistic programming that people look to their upper right when lying (Gamer and Pertzov, 2018, pp 171–2).

Physiological responses

Measuring physiological responses is typically associated with the polygraph (sometimes incorrectly referred to as a lie detector), which measures cardiovascular, respiratory and electrodermal responses, all of which are indicators of arousal of the autonomic nervous system (part of the nervous system that regulates involuntary processes). Arousal is an involuntary physiological response to, among other things, anxiety, pain, stress and situations that are unusual or threatening. The premise is that when people are lying they may experience increased arousal due to the psychological discomfort associated with lying and this can be measured. The obvious problem with this approach is that arousal is a very generalised response that is not specific to deception and can have innumerable causes (for example, many people may find a police interview stressful whether they are truthful or deceptive). Nevertheless, polygraphs are used in investigations in several countries and occasionally in the monitoring of sex offenders post-conviction. The accuracy of the polygraph has not been robustly established despite decades of research and the results of polygraph exams are generally not admissible as evidence (Ambach and Gamer, 2018, pp 24–5).

Due to the importance of modern transit security, and the large-scale screening required, several automated systems have been developed in an attempt to detect hostile intent in real time. These systems remotely measure physiological and non-verbal responses including facial temperature, heart and respiration rates, eye movements, facial expressions and body movements, and vocal pitch.

Notwithstanding the ethical and privacy concerns around covertly collecting biological data in an attempt to predict people's future intentions, scientists have voiced concerns over the theoretical foundations of these systems, which are based largely on the assumption that those with hostile intent will experience greater arousal than others, a theory for which there is no robust evidence (Weinberger, 2010). In sum, although physiological responses can be measured very sensitively, the major limitation of this approach is specificity (that is, the responses occur for a variety of reasons, not specifically due to deception).

Neural activity

Measuring neural activity to detect deception will be very briefly discussed as research is in its infancy and specialist equipment is required, so the relevance to policing is very limited. Overall, there is some evidence that areas of the brain related to performing complex cognitive tasks tend to be activated during deceptive communication, but those areas are also activated during other cognitive tasks, so the issue again is with specificity (Ganis, 2018, p 152). A promising strand of research is around the P300 response, based on the principle that a measurable response to meaningful information occurs in the brain 300 milliseconds after exposure to the information. Consequently, it can be expected that guilty suspects will produce this response when provided with crime-relevant details, whereas innocent suspects will not. This has the benefit of being outside conscious control and resistant to countermeasures, and some studies have reported very high accuracy, although it is yet to be established whether laboratory findings can be replicated in the field (see Rosenfield et al, 2018). Despite this, the P300 response has recently been used as evidence in the prosecution of a murder case in Dubai (Al Shouk, 2021).

Analysing verbal accounts

The two most well-established approaches to analysing accounts of events to assess credibility are Statement Validity Analysis (SVA) (Kohnken and Steller, 1988) a core component of which is Criteria-Based Content Analysis, and Reality Monitoring (Johnson and Raye, 1981). These approaches share conceptually similar underpinning theories, which are that genuinely experienced events are recalled and described differently to fabricated events, as people fabricating events have less knowledge and experience of what happened. Both approaches have a broad evidence base, and SVA is admissible as evidence in child sexual abuse cases in several countries (SVA was developed for use in this type of case). There is substantial overlap in the cues identified in these approaches, and meta-analytic findings indicate that the majority of those with the strongest evidential support are cues related to detail and specificity, which are predictive of truthful accounts: contextual embedding, reproduction of conversation, quantity of details, and perceptual, temporal and spatial information (Vrij, 2015). Again, in the interests of dispelling myths, Scientific Content Analysis, a method of assessing accounts developed by former policeman Avinoam Sapir that is widely used by practitioners (particularly in the US and Canada), has not been extensively tested and has scant supporting evidence (Oberlader et al, 2021).

Eliciting cues to deception

More recently, several tools have been developed which take a more active approach by eliciting cues to deception, rather than passively observing. A commonly accepted theoretical proposition is that liars experience greater cognitive load than truth tellers, as they have complex and simultaneous cognitive tasks to perform. Simply put, liars need to think harder than truth tellers. Consequently, increasing the cognitive load of interviewees should maximise the differences between liars and truth tellers. Asking unanticipated questions relating to reasonably expected knowledge, and encouraging interviewees to provide more detail are useful in an applied context, and result in truth tellers providing a greater quantity of details and providing more consistent accounts than liars (Mac Giolla and Luke, 2021). Frameworks that have achieved relatively consistent research evidence include the Strategic Use of Evidence (SUE) (Granhag, 2010) and the Verifiability Approach (VA) (Nahari et al, 2014). SUE exploits the strategic differences between liars and truth tellers, insomuch that liars tend to be avoidant and vague in order to avoid detection or to use denials. By not initially disclosing the evidence held, investigators can use evidence-related questions to expose a lack of internal consistency and a lack of consistency with the evidence in deceptive accounts. The VA is based on the premise that liars try to avoid providing details that can be checked by investigators (as this would result in being caught out), but also want to provide a detailed account as this is considered more believable. The resulting strategy adopted by some liars is therefore to provide a quantity of details that cannot be verified. To magnify this effect, investigators can specifically ask interviewees to provide details that can be checked by the investigator, as truth tellers are able to do this to a higher degree than liars.

Controlled Cognitive Engagement (Ormerod and Dando, 2015) is an interview model that as yet has a modest evidence base, but early findings based on rigorous methodology are promising, particularly in the context of aviation security. The model has three phases, which are repeated in cycles around topics. In the first phase the interviewer asks neutral questions, which are non-challenging for both liars and truth tellers to answer truthfully. The purpose of this is to develop rapport and to establish a baseline of how an interviewee responds verbally when being truthful. The second phase is information gathering, in which the interviewee is asked an open question and commits themselves to an account. In the third phase, a question is asked that tests the veracity of the preceding information; these are focused questions, often about verifiable details, that the interviewee should be able to provide if their previous answers were true. The interviewer looks for changes in the quality of the answers provided; liars produce shorter responses and less information than truth tellers as the questions continue, they have more inconsistencies in their responses and more gaps in expected knowledge. Investigative interviewers trained in the PEACE (Preparation and Planning, Engage and Explain, Account and Clarification, Closure and Evaluation) framework will recognise some of the techniques mentioned earlier.

Conclusion

In summary, the search for Pinocchio's nose is unlikely to ever be wholly successful. Rather than focusing on individual cues, it may be more productive to look for clusters of cues; a meta-analysis achieved relatively high accuracy in classifying communications as truthful or deceptive using combinations of cues (Hartwig and Bond, 2014); for example, several indicators that an interviewee is experiencing increased cognitive load in a particular area of an account. Cognitive approaches and active strategies to maximise the verbal differences between deceptive and truthful accounts have solid evidence bases and are probably most useful in an investigative context as they are non-invasive and can be incorporated into existing practices. Cues that are common to these approaches are a lack of detail and consistency in liars' communications and these can be useful evidentially. Future technological approaches may centre around the guilty knowledge indicated by the P300 response, although the P300 is unlikely to be generally admissible as evidence in the near future.

References

Al Shouk, A. (2021) 'Dubai police map brainwaves to solve murder mystery', *Gulf News*, [online] 25 January, Available from: https://gulfnews.com/uae/gov ernment/dubai-police-map-brainwaves-to-solve-murder-mystery-1.76725468 [Accessed 10 June 2022].

Ambach, W. and Gamer, M. (2018) 'Physiological measures in the detection of deception and concealed information' in J.P. Rosenfield (ed) *Detecting Concealed Information and Deception: Recent Developments*, London: Elsevier, pp 21–31.

Bond, C.F., Levine, T.R. and Hartwig, M. (2015) 'New findings in non-verbal lie detection' in P.A. Granhag, A. Vrij and B. Verschuere (eds) *Detecting Deception: Current Challenges and Cognitive Approaches*, Chichester: John Wiley & Sons, pp 37–58.

DePaulo, B.M. and Bond, C.F. (2012) 'Beyond accuracy: bigger, broader ways to think about deceit', *Journal of Applied Research in Memory and Cognition, Special Issue*, 1(2): 120–1.

DePaulo, B.M., Kashy, D.A., Kirkendol, S.E., Wyer, M.M. and Epstein, J.A. (1996) 'Lying in everyday life', *Journal of Personality and Social Psychology*, 70: 979–95.

Frank, M.G. and Svetieva, E. (2012) 'Lies worth catching involve both emotion and cognition', *Journal of Applied Research in Memory and Cognition, Special Issue*, 1(2): 131–3.

Gamer, M. and Pertzov, Y (2018) 'Detecting concealed knowledge from ocular responses' in J.P. Rosenfield (ed) *Detecting Concealed Information and Deception: Recent Developments*, London: Elsevier, pp 169–86.

Ganis. G. (2018) 'Detecting deception and concealed information with neuroimaging', in J.P. Rosenfield (ed) *Detecting Concealed Information and Deception: Recent Developments*, London: Elsevier, pp 145–66.

Granhag, P.A. (2010) 'The Strategic Use of Evidence (SUE) technique: a scientific perspective' High Value Detainee Interrogation Group (HIG; FBI). HIG Research Symposium: Interrogation in the European Union, Washington, DC.

Hartwig, M. and Bond, C.F (2011) 'Why do lie-catchers fail? A lens model meta-analysis of human lie judgments' *Psychological Bulletin*, 137(4), 643–59.

Hartwig, M. and Bond, C.F. (2014) 'Lie detection from multiple cues: a meta-analysis', *Applied Cognitive Psychology*, 28(5): 661–76.

Johnson, M.K. and Raye, C.L. (1981) 'Reality monitoring', *Psychological Review*, 88, 67–85.

Köhnken, G. and Steller, M. (1988) 'The evaluation of the credibility of child witness statements in the German procedural system', *Issues in Criminological & Legal Psychology*, 13: 37–45.

Mac Giolla, E and Luke, T.J. (2021) 'Does the cognitive approach to lie detection improve the accuracy of human observers?' *Applied Cognitive Psychology*, 35(2): 385–92, DOI: https://doi.org/10.1002/acp.3802.

Mac Giolla, E., Granhag, P.A. and Vrij, A. (2015) 'Discriminating between true and false intentions' in P.A. Granhag, A. Vrij and B. Verschuere (eds) *Detecting Deception: Current Challenges and Cognitive Approaches*, Chichester: John Wiley & Sons, pp 155–74.

Nahari, G., Vrij, A. and Fisher, R.P. (2014) 'Exploiting liars' verbal strategies by examining the verifiability of details', *Legal and Criminological Psychology*, 19(2): 227–39.

Oberlader, V.A., Quinten, L., Banse, R., Volbert, R., Schmidt, A.F. and Schönbrodt, F.D. (2021) 'Validity of content-based techniques for credibility assessment: how telling is an extended meta-analysis taking research bias into account?' *Applied Cognitive Psychology*, 35(2): 393–410, https://doi.org/10.1002/acp.3776.

Ormerod, T.C. and Dando, C.J. (2015) 'Finding a needle in a haystack: toward a psychologically informed method for aviation security screening', *Journal of Experimental Psychology: General*, 144(1): 76–84.

Rosenfield, J.P., Ward, A., Wasserman, J., Sitar, E., Davydova, E. and Labkovsky, E. (2018) 'Effects of motivational manipulations on the P300-based complex trial protocol for concealed information detection', in J.P. Rosenfield (ed) *Detecting Concealed Information and Deception: Recent Developments*, London: Elsevier, pp 125–43.

Suchotzki, K. (2018) 'Challenges for the application of reaction time-based deception detection methods', in J.P. Rosenfield (ed) *Detecting Concealed Information and Deception: Recent Developments*, London: Elsevier, pp 243–68.

Van Koppen, P.J. (2012) 'Deception detection in police interrogations: closing in on the context of criminal investigations', *Journal of Applied Research in Memory and Cognition, Special Issue*, 1(2): 124–5.

Vrij, A. (2015) 'Verbal lie detection tools: Statement Validity Analysis, Reality Monitoring and Scientific Content Analysis', in P.A. Granhag, A. Vrij and B. Verschuere (eds) *Detecting Deception: Current Challenges and Cognitive Approaches*, Chichester: John Wiley & Sons, pp 3–36.

Weinberger, S. (2010) 'Airport security: intent to deceive?' *Nature*, 465: 412–15.

50

Criminal false confessions

Ava Green

Introduction

There is a long-standing myth that innocent people do not falsely confess to crimes they did not commit. This myth has, however, been rebutted by prevalent research, which reveals that 367 convicted individuals in the US have been exonerated by DNA evidence since 1989; 28 per cent of these convictions involved false confessions (Lackey, 2020). As this chapter will demonstrate, police-induced or 'confession-driven' false confessions are a leading cause of wrongful convictions. An overview will be provided demonstrating the causes and different types of false confessions, before discussing interrogation techniques and their implications for producing erroneous and misleading testimony. This chapter concludes with recommendations for policing and the judicial system in order to improve the accuracy of confession evidence and to reduce the likelihood of miscarriages of justice.

Causes and types of false confessions

The chapter will now discuss causes and types of false confessions. Kassin and Wrightsman (1985) identified three types, namely 'voluntary', 'coerced-internalised' and 'coerced-compliant' false confessions. Voluntary false confessions are offered by individuals in the absence of external pressure from police interrogation, suggesting that this type of confession is internally driven by the confessor's underlying psychological state. Kassin and Wrightsman (1985) argued that voluntary false confessions occur for a number of reasons: a desire for notoriety, an unconscious need to expiate guilt over previous wrongful acts or an inability to differentiate between reality and fantasy. In addition, people may also provide a false confession due to external pressure; for instance, to protect the real culprit or provide an alibi for an unrelated crime.

Voluntary false confessions

Due to the internal pressure that elicits voluntary false confessions, this type of confession may be more common from individuals with a mental illness. Gudjonsson (2003) suggested that voluntary false confessions originate from different processes of psychopathology, with three interrelated features: a loss of reality testing, an element of depression and a need for notoriety. The first component, a loss of reality testing, is associated with severe psychiatric illnesses such as schizophrenia. Due to the distorted perceptions of reality, schizophrenic individuals develop a false belief that they are guilty of the criminal act, which results in a false confession (see case example 'Miss S' in Gudjonsson, 2003, p 218).

The second component, an element of depression, pertains to severely depressed individuals whose false confession is triggered by intense and deep-seated feelings of guilt. Gudjonsson (2003) theorised that the guilt emerges from past experiences and is, in turn, projected onto current external occurrences. These individuals are likely to be psychotically depressed, which, unlike schizophrenia, is defined as delusional thought processes that are accusatorial in nature. In other words, the delusions stem from actual past experiences, with the resulting long-standing guilt being the primary motive to falsely confess to crimes (for example, 'Mrs H' in Gudjonsson, 2003, p 219).

The last component, a need for notoriety, is characterised by individuals who have a pathological need to enhance their self-esteem and exhibit a morbid desire for recognition. It is assumed that these feelings are generated by marked feelings of inadequacy, which can be compensated by a state of being infamous. The need for notoriety, therefore, can involve falsely confessing to crimes in the desire to gain attention for being a 'criminal', despite being faced with the prospect of punishment. These individuals commonly exhibit severe personality disorders, such as anti-social and narcissistic personality disorders, which interfere with their faulty reality monitoring, resulting in an inability to distinguish reality from fantasy (such as 'Mr. M' in Gudjonsson, 2003, p 220).

Coerced-internalised false confessions

The coerced-internalised false confession is where innocent suspects begin to doubt their memory during the interrogation process and are persuaded that they did, in fact, commit the crime they are accused of (Kassin and Wrightsman, 1985). This type of memory distortion can occur in two contexts: the first context is where the suspects are guilty of committing the crime but have no recollection of committing it, possibly due to amnesia or being intoxicated at the time of the offence. As a result, these suspects come to believe that they must have committed the offence that they are accused of. In the second context, the suspects are confident of their innocence at the beginning of the interrogation process; however, due to the manipulative tactics used by the interrogator, they gradually begin to doubt their assertions of innocence. In other words, due to suspects' memory distortions, they are more likely to become susceptible to suggestions during police interviewing, despite having no actual memory of the alleged offence (see the example of Mr Peter Reilly in Gudjonsson, 2003, p 234).

Coerced-compliant false confessions

The coerced-compliant type of false confession, however, occurs when the suspect succumbs to the coerciveness or pressures of the interrogation process.

Here, the suspect knowingly confesses to gain perceived immediate instrumental benefit, for instance to end an aversive custodial interrogation process, to take advantage of promised leniency or avoid an anticipated punitive sentence. In other words, the suspect considers the benefits of providing a self-incriminating confession due to short-term benefits (such as release from custody, mitigated punishment), which are perceived to outweigh the long-term consequences of denial (for example, apprehension, harsher punishment). Kassin and Wrightsman (1985) conjectured that suspects may naively believe their innocence will, sooner or later, exonerate them. Coerced-compliant confessors are therefore likely to retract their false confession as soon as the immediate pressures associated with the interrogation are over.

While individuals are able to withstand interrogation pressure, certain psychological vulnerabilities generate a greater risk towards confabulatory responding and misleading self-incriminating confessions under pressure (a good example of this is the 'Birmingham Six'; see Gudjonsson, 2003, p 452). These features include individuals who are highly suggestible or compliant, have learning disabilities, high anxiety, low IQ, poor self-esteem, low assertiveness, or are eager to please people, particularly authority figures. To sum up, the causes and implications of false confessions can take several forms; however, the literature has thus far dedicated extensive work towards the prominent cause of wrongful convictions: coercive-compliant false confessions.

Interrogative interview techniques

Although many interrogation manuals have originated from the US, the Reid technique (Inbau et al, 2013) is the most dominant and influential police manual on suspect interviewing. This technique is accusatorial and guilt-presumptive in nature, based on a nine-step model which uses direct confrontation, psychological coercion and theme development to break down a suspect's resistance to provide a self-incriminating confession. Here, interrogators are encouraged to employ a two-stage process; the first stage is called the 'behavioural analysis interview' and is non-accusatory, aims to obtain general background information about the suspect, build trust and rapport, and to determine signs of deception and guilt displayed by the suspect. If the suspect is considered to be dishonest in relation to the alleged offence, the interrogator proceeds to a nine-step accusatory approach, referred to as the 'interrogation' (Inbau et al, 2013).

The first step involves 'direct, positive confrontation'; the interrogator confronts the suspect with 'absolute certainty' regarding his or her involvement in the alleged offence and attempts to convince the suspect of the benefits of confessing. This is used even in cases where there is no tangible evidence to suggest that the suspect is, in fact, guilty. The second step refers to 'theme development'; the interrogator attempts to gain the suspect's trust by displaying signs of sympathy and understanding. The aim here is for the interrogator to minimise the moral implications and seriousness of the alleged offence by, for instance, providing contextual or moral excuses for the commission of the crime. The third step is 'handling denials'; during this phase most suspects deny their guilt. The interrogator is encouraged to, in its crudest form, interrupt the suspect when denial statements are made, as failure to do so would provide the suspect with a psychological advantage over the interrogator. The fourth step is 'overcoming objections'; the interrogator attempts to overcome objections made by the suspect when denying their involvement, and does so through emphasising and maintaining their guilt.

The fifth step includes the 'procurement and retention of the suspect's attention'; the suspect starts to show signs of withdrawal from active participation in the interrogation once the objections for their innocence become ineffective. The interrogator responds to this by, for instance, moving physically closer to the suspect, making physical contact (for example, hand on shoulder) and mentioning the suspect's first name. As a result of this manipulative ploy, the 'guilty' suspect becomes more attentive to the suggestions provided by the interrogator. The sixth step is 'handling the suspect's passive move'; the aim here is for the interrogator to continue breaking down the suspect's remaining resistance by exhibiting signs of sympathy and understanding, and by appealing to their sense of decency, with the ultimate intention to elicit a confession.

The seventh step involves 'presenting an alternative question'; the suspect is presented with two alternatives, both highly incriminating, for the commission of the crime. The rationale underpinning this step is that, if the suspect is presented with two alternatives where one alternative is more 'save-facing' than the other, the suspect is more likely to admit to a lesser offence and thereby more likely to fully confess. The eighth step includes 'having the suspect orally relate various details of the offence'; the suspect has accepted one of the alternatives provided in the previous step and consequently produces a full self-incriminating admission. This includes providing a detailed account of the motive, circumstances and nature of the criminal offence. The ninth and final step is 'converting an oral confession into a written confession', as this is deemed much stronger evidence in court than an oral confession.

Evidently, the guilt-presumptive and psychologically manipulative tactics inherent in the Reid technique have ethical implications for the lives of the innocent and policy implications for police training. Despite these concerns, Inbau et al (2013, p 187) consider this approach to be admissible on the grounds that 'none of the steps is apt to make an innocent person confess and that all the steps are legally as well as morally justified'. The authors also claim that, since its initial implementation in 1962, the technique is 'effective' in eliciting confessions through breaking down suspects' resistance to deny the alleged criminal act. Specifically, the authors assert an 80 per cent (true) confession rate, despite the distinct lack of scientific evidence to support this claim (Gudjonsson, 2003).

Further limitations of this technique concern the psychological inducement of promising the suspect a more lenient punishment upon confessing and threatening a more punitive sentence if the suspect is reluctant to confess. There is a risk that the false confessions obtained by police impropriety and coercion are likely to be ruled inadmissible and therefore have no evidential value in court (Gudjonsson, 2003). A technique that potently aims to elicit a confession, particularly at the expense of thorough and ethical criminal investigation, arguably has legal implications for policing and the criminal justice system. It is important to acknowledge here that the majority of custodial interrogations – guided by the Reid manual or otherwise – are inevitably coercive to an extent, due to the authority and power dynamic of the interrogation (Kassin et al, 2010b). Nevertheless, the limitations associated with the Reid technique have led researchers to recommend alternative interrogation techniques.

Recommendations for future practice

A competing model for future practice, referred to as the PEACE technique, has been developed in the UK. The PEACE model (an acronym for Preparation and Planning, Engage and Explain, Account and Clarification, Closure and Evaluation), is based on prudential principles and non-coercive techniques that align closely with the domains of rapport building and trust (Meissner et al, 2015). This model has been generally regarded as a promising and effective method that predicts robust supervision and specialised training, facilitates true confessions and safeguards the innocent against the risk of false confessions (Meissner et al, 2015). Since its implementation in 1993, the PEACE model has been widely employed in the UK as well as in other countries, including Australia, Norway and Sweden.

Other research-based recommendations include the mandatory electronic recording of police interrogations, improved educational training on false confessions for police officers and the prohibition of coercive interrogation methods, including deceiving suspects to obtain a confession (Kassin et al, 2010a; Meissner et al, 2015). Although the US has made slower progress in incorporating these reforms, a call for enhanced interrogation practices in the last few years has prompted the US government to evaluate and identify productive evidence-based techniques for interviewing suspects. Evidence-based practice has the potential to reduce the incidence of false confessions and prevent wrongful convictions of the innocent.

Conclusions

To conclude, this chapter has outlined the different causes and factors that cause innocent individuals to confess to crimes they did not commit, and it has discussed the ethical and legal implications of psychologically coercive interrogation methods. Alternative interrogation techniques and research-based recommendations to prohibit or reduce false confessions have been reviewed, emphasising the importance of educating both the police and the judicial system in order to protect the innocent from future incidence of wrongful convictions.

References

Gudjonsson, G.H. (2003) *The Psychology of Interrogations and Confessions: A Handbook*, Chichester: Wiley.

Inbau, F.E., Reid, J.E., Buckley, J.P. and Jayne, B.C. (2013) *Essentials of the Reid Technique*, Burlington, MA: Jones & Bartlett.

Kassin, S.M. and Wrightsman, L.S. (1985) *The Psychology of Evidence Trial Procedure*, Beverly Hills, CA: SAGE.

Kassin, S.M., Appleby, S.C. and Perillo, J.T. (2010a) 'Interviewing suspects: practice, science, and future directions', *Legal and Criminological Psychology*, 15(1): 39–55.

Kassin, S.M., Drizin, S.A., Grisso, T., Gudjonsson, G.H., Leo, R.A. and Redlich, A.D. (2010b) 'Police-induced confessions: risk factors and recommendations', *Law and Human Behavior*, 34(1): 3–38.

Lackey, J. (2020) 'False confessions and testimonial injustice', *Journal of Criminal Law and Criminology*, 110: 43–68.

Meissner, C.A., Kelly, C.E. and Woestehoff, S.A. (2015) 'Improving the effectiveness of suspect interrogations', *Annual Review of Law and Social Science*, 11: 211–33.

51

False allegations and wrongful convictions

Greg Stratton and Monique Moffa

Wrongful conviction and false allegations of offending represent significant miscarriages of justice that focus the criminal justice system's (CJS's) attention towards innocent people and away from those who participate in criminal activity. A wrongful conviction occurs when an innocent person is convicted for a crime they did not commit. It is distinguished from other miscarriages of justice in that it tends to refer to the concept of actual, factual innocence rather than examples where a court determines an error of law has been made. High-profile examples of wrongful conviction, such as the Central Park Five (US), the Birmingham Six and the Post Office 39 (UK) and Lindy Chamberlain (Australia), highlight that error is the result of faults and prejudices within the justice system. A similar issue, false allegations, can broadly fall into two categories: firstly, where the alleged incident did not occur, and secondly, where the events in question did occur but were committed by another person. Where false allegations do not result in the conviction and subsequent punishment of an innocent person, they nonetheless see the innocent investigated and potentially implicated in a trial despite their innocence. While acquittals or discontinued charges might be viewed as the CJS functioning as intended, for many, these cases represent 'near misses' for the system and can have a severe impact on the accused and those making the allegation. Both false allegations and wrongful convictions represent the CJS's failure to protect the innocent's freedoms, further traumatises and prevents or delays closure for victims of crime, and potentially exposes society to the threat of continued victimisation by actual offenders.

The innocence movement

The problem of wrongful conviction, while rare, is not insignificant. According to the National Registry of Exonerations (2022), over three thousand people in the US have been exonerated of a crime and cleared of all charges for which they were convicted. Much of the global awareness of wrongful convictions has emerged from the success of the New York-based Innocence Project, which has largely relied on DNA evidence to assist in post-conviction exoneration. In addition to exoneration successes, the Innocence Project has raised awareness through advocacy campaigns, policy reform and the provision of post-release support to exonerees. A subsequent movement of innocence projects in the US and elsewhere has increased wrongful conviction awareness (Norris, 2017). Still, the full extent of the problem is unknown, mainly because of the mechanics within legal systems that limit the types of offences and convictions that these projects can successfully advocate, leaving many misdemeanours or 'lesser' crimes unexplored in terms of these gross errors.

The innocence movement's work has highlighted the traditionally flawed approach by police and the legal profession towards the evidence used to convict the innocent. The revelation of DNA evidence has increased the system's opportunity to prove error through forensic science. The increased recognition of many of these errors has acted as a catalyst to further reform procedures from police investigation through to trial. In what have become known as the causal factors of wrongful conviction, eyewitness misidentification, false confession, police error or corruption, prosecutorial misconduct and forensic science error can contribute to the phenomenon of false allegations and wrongful convictions (Garrett, 2020). Importantly, some of these causes are linked to the evidence provided by members of the public, such as witnesses or victims, while others are related to system actors and representatives. However, while many of these issues have been studied by academics and advocates for years (see Garrett, 2020, for a review), it is only with the certainty provided by DNA evidence to exonerate that flaws in the justice system have been exposed, providing the opportunity for reform in these areas. Of the causal factors, the nexus of wrongful conviction, false allegations, psychology and policing has been primarily focused on eyewitness misidentification and false confessions.

Eyewitness misidentification

A wealth of research has examined the difficulties in attaining reliable witness evidence and has identified the fallibility and malleability of witness memory (Loftus, 2018). The seminal works of Gary Wells (1978), Elizabeth Loftus (1996) and others have influenced the legal perceptions of eyewitness testimony and the acceptance that witness statements are not always reliable sources of fact. The factors affecting the reliability of eyewitness identification are often categorised into system and estimator variables. System variables refer to elements within the control of the CJS used by investigators to enable a witness to recognise a suspect or recall the events concerning a crime. Differences in procedures, including the instructions used by investigators, use and construction of police line-ups, and the use of photographs, among others, are ways that the justice system can contribute to erroneous identification and wrongful conviction. While justice system reform can control for errors caused by system variables, it must also account for estimator variables that include characteristics about the witness (including age, race, memory) or the situation (including lighting, presence of a weapon, duration of the incident) (Wells, 2020).

The National Registry of Exonerations (2022) has found 27 per cent of all exonerations involve unintentional eyewitness misidentification, with an increase to 67 per cent in sexual assault wrongful convictions. Partly explaining the high rates of exoneration in these crimes is that the victim often can provide a witness statement and testify at trial. In most cases, the information provided by the victim is reliable. However, the often-traumatic circumstances of the crimes can result in vulnerabilities in the memory of those involved. When confronted with problematic policing practices such as the improper use of line-ups or suggestive police techniques (such as photos emphasising the primary suspect), victims and other eyewitnesses can make errors (Wells et al, 1998). Where misidentification can be the result of a range of system and estimator variables that contribute to faulty, malleable and erroneous memories, eyewitness procedures around the world are attempting to address the concerns exposed by wrongful convictions. These include improving witness instructions, developing blinding procedures, improved line-up and photo compositions, and the sequential presentation of evidence, all of which have been implemented around the world to increase the accuracy and reliability of a crucial form of evidence in criminal cases (Wells, 2020).

False confessions

Similarly, false confessions are a common feature in wrongful convictions and false allegations supported through years of research (Gudjonsson, 2018, 2021). While many still find the idea that someone would confess to a crime they did not commit implausible, the examples of wrongful conviction involving false confessions provide evidence of the practice. High-profile wrongful convictions, including those of the Central Park Five and the West Memphis Three, which both saw multiple false confessions, help provide public awareness of the issue and its impact. The National Registry of Exonerations (2022) has found 12 per cent of all exonerations involve false confessions, with an increase to 22 per cent in homicide cases. Research by Saul Kassin (2008), Gisli Gudjonsson et al (2016) have demonstrated that a combination of suspect vulnerability and police techniques can lead innocent people to confess.

Personal risk of false confession is increased for young people and/or people with cognitive impairment and/or mental health issues. Gross and Shaffer (2012) analysed the first 873 cases registered in the National Registry of Exonerations, finding an 8 per cent false confession rate among exonerations of adults with no known mental health issue. However, the presence of a false confession among young people wrongfully convicted increased to 42 per cent, and to 75 per cent in cases where the exoneree had an identified mental health issue. The vulnerability of these groups is compounded by the use of particular 'interrogation' and interview techniques, including isolating the suspect, the length of time under arrest and in interviews, minimisation tactics and deception by police officers (Kassin, 2015). In the US, the latter is exacerbated in some jurisdictions where interviewing officers are able to deceive suspects about the presence of incriminating evidence (Gohara, 2005). This vulnerability is combined with the structural and situational aspects of investigations, often involving a guilt-presumptive interaction between an officer with a belief about the suspect's guilt and where the officer's definition of success is securing an admission.

Police questioning surrounding a false allegation may induce suspects to falsely confess. There are three types of false confessions. Voluntary false confessions occur where innocent people make self-incriminating comments without pressure from investigators/police. Coerced-compliant confessions occur when innocent people change their position from denial to admission in order to end the interrogation, or because of a perception that continued denial will result in a harsher outcome. Finally, coerced-internalised confessions involve a suspect who becomes confused by misleading evidence, questions their memory and innocence, and admits to the alleged offence(s) (Kassin, 2014). Wrongful convictions have exposed the fallibility of some interview and interrogation techniques, in particular the Reid technique, providing an impetus for interview reform in the US and around the world. From the standardisation of video-recording suspect interviews to the implementation of the PEACE model of interviewing (which attempts to elicit accurate information rather than a confession, see Clarke and Milne, 2001; Gudjonsson and Pearse, 2011), many reforms in investigative interviewing have been pre-empted by the wrongful convictions caused by problematic interviews and interrogations.

Systemic responses

The discovery of investigative bias in false allegations and wrongful convictions has highlighted the need for systemic responses to limit the cognitive and contextual biases police experience from crime scenes to interviews. In the United States, the growing recognition of wrongful convictions has led to great accountability within police departments and evidence-based reform of investigative procedures. (Garrett, 2020). While such attempts are being made to prevent false allegations and wrongful convictions occurring in the first place, there still exists a need for post-conviction review mechanisms. Aside from innocence projects, the introduction of Conviction Integrity Units and other appeal mechanisms have allowed for issues like false confession and eyewitness error to be considered in an environment where their causes are understood. Similarly, Criminal Case Review Commissions (CCRCs) in the UK and New Zealand have provided an avenue for the innocent to have their cases reinvestigated. However, the impacts of these post-review mechanisms are often limited (Hoyle and Sato, 2019). The UK CCRC is often criticised for its low referral rate, with an average 3 per cent of cases referred to the appeal courts per year, and even lower success rate (CCRC, 2021).

The experience of enduring a false allegation and wrongful conviction can be strenuous, particularly when imprisoned. This can include challenges to an innocent person's identity and sense of self, and it can impact negatively on a person's mental health. Commonly referred to as the 'innocent prisoner's dilemma', the wrongfully convicted must choose between maintaining their innocence or performing guilt (Weisman, 2004). Maintaining innocence, while often employed as a coping mechanism to survive incarceration, can add further disadvantages. The stigma of denial can often result in adverse treatment by correctional staff and bodies, including parole boards (Ruyters et al, 2020). Denial of offending and lack of acknowledgement of wrongdoing can be interpreted as a lack of remorse, can impact eligibility to participate in rehabilitative programmes and is often viewed by staff as a risk factor for further offending, all of which can elongate the sentence if parole is denied. Alternatively, if the wrongfully convicted person does admit guilt, any admissions may impact possible investigations into the convictions later by post-conviction review mechanisms such as CCRCs, innocence projects and government-sanctioned pardons.

References

CCRC (Criminal Cases Review Commission) (2021) 'Annual report and accounts 2020/21', [online] Available from: https://ccrc.gov.uk/corporate-info rmation-and-publications/ [Accessed 6 June 2022].

Clarke, C. and Milne, R. (2001) *National Evaluation of the PEACE Investigative Interviewing Course. Police Research Award Scheme*, London: Home Office.

Garrett, B.L. (2020) 'Wrongful convictions', *Annual Review of Criminology*, 3: 245–59.

Gohara, M.S. (2005) 'Lie for a lie: false confessions and the case for reconsidering the legality of deceptive interrogation techniques', *Fordham Urban Law Journal*, 33(3): 791–843.

Gross, S.R. and Shaffer, M. (2012) 'Exonerations in the United States, 1989–2012', Report by the National Registry of Exonerations. University of Michigan Law School. Available from: https://www.law.umich.edu/special/exoneration/ Documents/exonerations_us_1989_2012_full_report.pdf [Accessed 4 January 2023].

Gudjonsson, G.H. (2018) *The Psychology of False Confessions: Forty Years of Science and Practice*, Chichester: Wiley Blackwell.

Gudjonsson, G.H. (2021) 'The science-based pathways to understanding false confessions and wrongful convictions', *Frontiers in Psychology*, 12: 308–23.

Gudjonsson, G.H. and Pearse (2011) 'Suspect interviews and false confessions', *Current Directions in Psychological Science*, 20(1): 33–7.

Hoyle, C. and Sato, M. (2019) *Reasons to Doubt: Wrongful Convictions and the Criminal Cases Review Commission*, Oxford: Oxford University Press.

Kassin, S.M. (2008) 'False confessions: causes, consequences, and implications for reform', *Current Directions in Psychological Science*, 17(4): 249–53.

Kassin, S.M. (2015) 'The social psychology of false confessions', *Social Issues and Policy Review*, 9(1): 25–51.

Loftus, E.F. (1996) *Eyewitness Testimony*, Cambridge, MA: Harvard University Press.

Loftus, E.F. (2018) 'Eyewitness science and the legal system', *Annual Review of Law and Social Science*, 14(1): 1–10.

National Registry of Exonerations (2022) 'The National Registry of Exonerations', [online] Available from: https://www.law.umich.edu/special/exoneration/Pages/about.aspx [Accessed 6 June 2022].

Norris, R.J. (2017) *Exonerated: A History of the Innocence Movement*, New York: New York University Press.

Ruyters, M., Stratton, G. and Moffa, M. (2020). 'Wrongful convictions and the implications for corrective services', in P. Birch and L. Sicard (eds) *Prisons and Community Corrections: Critical Issues and Emerging Controversies*, London: Routledge, pp 29–42.

Weisman, R. (2004) 'Showing remorse: reflections on the gap between expression and attribution in cases of wrongful conviction', *Canadian Journal of Criminology and Criminal Justice*, 46(2): 121–38.

Wells, G.L. (1978) 'Applied eyewitness-testimony research: system variables and estimator variables', *Journal of Personality and Social Psychology*, 36(12): 1546.

Wells, G.L. (2020) 'Psychological science on eyewitness identification and its impact on police practices and policies', *American Psychologist*, 75(9): 1316–29.

Wells, G.L., Small, M., Penrod, S., Malpass, R.S., Fulero, S.M. and Brimacombe, C. A. E. (1998) 'Eyewitness identification procedures: Recommendations for lineups and photospreads', *Law and Human Behavior*, 22(6): 603–47.

52

Witness testimony

Victoria Blinkhorn

Introduction

Witness testimony is the account a bystander or victim provides to the police or court, describing what they observed during the specific incident in question. This account is used as evidence to present what occurred from a witness's perspective, and of course, the more detailed the account, the more helpful it is to the court. Historically, memory recall was seen as very reliable; however, forensic evidence now supports psychological research, demonstrating that memories and individual perceptions can be unreliable, manipulated and biased. This chapter will discuss some of the ways in which witness testimony can be flawed by focusing on two of the three stages of memory: encoding and storage. The third stage, retrieval, relates to the way the police interview witnesses and this has been discussed in Chapters 50 and 51.

There are two types of factors that can affect witness accuracy: estimator and system variables. Estimator variables cannot be controlled by the legal justice system and are mainly related to the encoding and storage stages of memory. Examples of estimator variables are the amount of stress the victim was under, what the lighting was like in their environment and whether their memory was later contaminated by conflicting accounts from other sources. In contrast, system variables can be controlled by the legal justice system and are mainly related to the retrieval stage of memory. Examples of system variables would be the kind of questions asked of witnesses by the police and particular interview techniques to encourage memory recall.

Encoding factors

The first stage of memory, encoding, refers to the initial creation of a memory and depends on the extent to which an individual is paying attention to their environment. There are a number of factors relating to this stage of memory that can affect witness accuracy. Firstly, high levels of stress can have a negative effect on memory recall accuracy. Many laboratory studies have been conducted to investigate this and all report that the more stress an individual experiences, the more incorrect information they recall (see Morgan et al, 2013). However, it is important to note that in real life the witnesses under greater stress actually recall events more accurately (Yuille and Cutshell, 1986). The reason behind this is because outside a laboratory environment it is much harder to control for other variables; for example, the witnesses under greater stress during an incident are usually closer to the perpetrator. This relates to another factor, 'weapon focus', in which witnesses tend to dedicate all their attention to the weapon during an incident and, as a result, fail to notice other details around them. This occurs due to the threat or fear associated with the weapon in question and also due to the witness being very unlikely to have ever encountered one before. Weapon focus, however, does reduce the longer the witness is exposed to the weapon, and after a short while they will shift their attention from the weapon to the perpetrator (Hope and Wright, 2007).

Change blindness is another issue that can occur during a witness observing a crime. At any moment, the witness may shift their attention, looking in one direction then the other. If a change within the environment occurs in that brief moment the witness is looking away, they may not notice and this is what is called change blindness. A famous piece of research undertaken in this area, coined the 'Door' Study (Simons and Levin, 1998), had an experimenter initiate a conversation with a pedestrian; during the interaction, he was surreptitiously replaced by a different experimenter (the original filmed footage can be found online). Only half of the pedestrians noticed the change. More recently, much research has shown that witnesses are more likely to not notice a key change, for example, 61 per cent of individuals reported they did not notice the identity of a burglar had changed after the camera angle altered halfway through the crime video (Davies and Hine, 2007). It is also well known that individuals who are assumed to be skilled observers of crimes, such as police personnel, are just as susceptible to change blindness as laypeople. However, despite the quantity of research on this factor, there has been little investigation in an actual forensic setting and more is needed to establish when witnesses are most likely to make these errors.

Just like many topics within the social psychology field, stereotyping can have a significant effect on the reliability of witness testimony. Crime events can be highly complex, resulting in a high cognitive load at the encoding level or, in other words, lots of information to attend to and process. Information from the crime may be confusing, so therefore, in order to create a more coherent memory, witnesses can unconsciously use their pre-existing stereotypes. Older adults are known to be more susceptible to stereotype processing of crime information, and encoded information that fits within a particular stereotype is preserved well (Overman et al, 2013). In fact, age itself is known to be a factor that can affect the reliability of witnesses. Young adults are known to have the most reliable memories and older adults may be less accurate due to age-related declines in encoding quality. As such, they are likely to remember fewer details about events, or at least, less accurate details (Li and Lindenburger, 2005). In addition, children also make less reliable witnesses and this is mainly due to lacking the life experience needed to employ useful scripts and schemas that help all individuals make sense of an event and recall information accurately (Baker-Ward et al, 1993).

Not surprisingly, when witnesses are intoxicated, whether it is due to alcohol or other substances, their recollection of an event is less accurate. This is because intoxication affects the attention and encoding of information and narrows the visual focus to more central details at the expense of other peripheral ones. It is widely accepted that witnesses who are intoxicated generally report less information; however, the accuracy of their account does not change over time (Flowe et al, 2015). One of the problematic issues concerning intoxicated witnesses is that for particular types of crimes, such as sexual or violent assaults, it is rather common for both the victims and witnesses to be intoxicated, simply due to these crimes occurring more often at night. As such, this makes it much more difficult for the police and the wider criminal justice system to obtain a reliable conviction.

Storage factors

Now to move on to the second stage of memory: storage. At this stage, the memory of a specific event is vulnerable to external influences and can also alter over time. The first is the issue relating to post-event information. Separating witnesses while others testify has long been relied on to preserve the independent character of witness testimony. However, individuals often witness crimes in the presence of others and discuss what they saw with them. As a result, witnesses can pay attention to, remember and misremember different aspects of the crime. Through later discussion, witnesses may learn information about the event that they did not observe themselves, and if then combined with their own account, this can cause problem (Skagerberg and Wright, 2008). A typical case study to demonstrate this is the Jill Dando case from 1999. Jill Wendy Dando was an English journalist, television presenter and newsreader for the BBC. On the morning of 26 April 1999 she was shot dead outside her home in London. It prompted the biggest murder inquiry conducted by the Metropolitan Police and the country's largest criminal investigation since the hunt for Peter Sutcliffe. A local man, Barry George, was convicted and imprisoned for the murder, but was later, after eight years in prison, acquitted after an appeal and retrial. The case remains unsolved. At the time, only one out of 16 witnesses identified the police suspect, George, from the original line-up. The witness who made the positive identification seemed to have influenced the other witnesses. After some had shared a taxi home together, one of the witnesses, who had previously failed to make a positive identification, changed her mind. She then claimed she was 95 per cent sure that the man she had seen was in the line-up (see Wright and Goodwin, 2009, for more detail on the case).

So, when are individuals more likely to be influenced by other witnesses? There are a number of hypothesises as to why this is. Firstly, the Updateable Memory Hypothesis (Braun and Loftus, 1998) suggests that stored memories are overwritten with the misinformation individuals' encounter. Memory is a product of reconstruction and individuals continually reinterpret events they see. An alternative perspective is known as 'strategic effects', which suggests that memory is not impaired by misinformation, but rather witnesses' memory reports are affected by task demands and test-talking strategies. Finally, 'blocked memory access' (Chandler, 1991) is another perspective that argues that memory traces for the original event and the misleading information coexist in memory. As such, this creates response competition between the two and whichever is stronger blocks the other out. In addition to the hypotheses mentioned earlier, there are a number of other explanations. For some individuals, when the source of the post-event information seems to have a better memory they will choose to take on that version to replace their own account (Gabbert et al, 2007). Sometimes, dependant on the social situation, the cost of disagreeing with others is significant, and therefore the witness feel obliged to take the perspective of others rather than keep their own (Wright et al, 2009). Lastly, if the witness sees the other individual in question to be a credible expert or someone in a position of authority, again, they will be more likely to allow that person's views to influence, or replace, their own (Williamson et al, 2013).

The length of time between the crime occurring and the witness providing testimony can vary from a few minutes to several years depending on the individual event in question. Understandably, information is more likely to be forgotten if there are longer delays. Memory reports may be especially accurate when witnesses are interviewed immediately after the crime because memory traces are strong. Memory initially decays rapidly, followed by a much slower decline. Repeated interviews have complex effects on memory reports. For example, studies have found evidence of hyperamnesia (Scrivner and Safer, 1988), reminiscence (Howe, 1991) and increased inconsistencies (Warren et al, 1991). Information is also more likely to be accurately reported across interviews when it is consistent with a crime schema, for example, stereotypical details of a crime that an individual may have a preconception about based on media sources (Tuckey and Brewer, 2003).

As with many types of behaviours, emotion can explain a lot. Emotional memories are often recalled with a high degree of vividness and evidence shows that emotional memories may be more accurately remembered due to the additional cognitive stimuli they create (Terr, 1979). However, individuals' memories for significant emotional events may not always be especially accurate, even when the memory appears to be vivid. Much research has shown that these memories are sometimes influenced by reconstructive processes, and are altered over time as the event becomes more personally important and emotionally impactful (Wright and Conrad, 2008). Although individuals do not forget the event, the decline in accuracy of their memory reports is similar to that of other autobiographical memories. Studies have showed that memory vividity declines over the first year and external influences, for example, the media, shapes what is remembered. For example, Hirst et al (2015) conducted over twenty studies to demonstrate this, based on the 9/11 attacks and witnesses' testimonies. So, perhaps, this means that emotional or traumatic memories are not remembered any better than everyday memories after all.

Conclusion

In summary, forensic evidence now supports ongoing psychological research demonstrating that memories and individual perceptions can be unreliable, manipulated and biased. This chapter has discussed some of the ways in which witness testimony can be flawed by focusing two of the three stages of memory: encoding and storage. Within the encoding stage, the factors that can affect witness accuracy are stress, weapon focus, change blindness, stereotyping, age and intoxication. Within the storage stage, post-event information, delay and emotional and traumatic memories can all affect the reliability of witness testimony. False memories can also be a problematic factor with regard to the storage of information.

References

Baker-Ward, L., Gordon, B.N., Ornstein, P.A., Larus, D.M. and Clubb, P.A. (1993) 'Young children's long-term retention of a paediatric examination', *Child Development*, 64: 1519–33.

Braun, K.A. and Loftus, E.F. (1998) 'Advertising's misinformation effect', *Applied Cognitive Psychology: The Official Journal of the Society for Applied Research in Memory and Cognition*, 12: 569–91.

Chandler, C.C. (1991) 'How memory for an event is influenced by related events: interference in modified recognition tests', *Journal of Experimental Psychology: Learning, Memory, and Cognition*, 17: 115.

Davies, G. and Hine, S. (2007) 'Change blindness and eyewitness testimony', *Journal of Psychology*, 141: 423–34.

Flowe, H.D., Takarangi, M.K., Humphries, J.E. and Wright, D.S. (2015) 'Alcohol and remembering a hypothetical sexual assault: can people who are under the influence of alcohol during the even provide accurate testimony?' *Memory*, 24: 1042–61.

Gabbert, F., Memon, A. and Wright, D.B. (2007) 'I saw it for longer than you: the relationship between perceived encoding duration and memory conformity', *Acta Psychologica*, 124: 319–31.

Hirst, W., Phelps, E.A., Meksin, R., Vaidya, C.J., Johnson, M.K., Mitchell, K.J. and Olsson, A. (2015) 'A ten-year follow-up of a study of memory for the attack of September 11, 2001: flashbulb memories and memories for flashbulb events', *Journal of Experimental Psychology: General*, 144: 604–23.

Hope, L. and Wright, D. (2007) 'Beyond unusual? Examining the role of attention in the weapon focus effect', *Applied Cognitive Psychology*, 21: 951–61.

Howe, M.L. (1991) 'Misleading children's story recall: forgetting and reminiscence of the facts', *Developmental Psychology*, 27: 746–62.

Li, S.C., Naveh-Benjamin, M. and Lindenberger, U. (2005) 'Aging neuromodulation impairs associative binding neurocomputational account', *Psychological Science*, 16: 445–50.

Morgan, C.A., Southwick, S., Steffian, G., Hazlett, G.A. and Loftus, E.F. (2013) 'Misinformation can influence memory for recently experienced, highly, stressful events', *International Journal of Law and Psychiatry*, 36: 11–17.

Overman, A.A., Wiseman, K.D., Allison, M. and Stephens, J.D. (2013) 'Age differences and schema effects in memory for crime information', *Experimental Aging Research*, 39: 215–34.

Scrivner, E. and Safer, M.A. (1988) 'Eyewitnesses show hypermnesia for details about a violent event', *Journal of Applied Psychology*, 73: 371–7.

Simons, D.J. and Levin, D.T. (1998) 'Failure to detect changes to people during a real-world interaction', *Psychonomic Bulletin & Review*, 5: 644–9.

Skagerberg, E.M. and Wright, D.B. (2008). 'The prevalence of co-witnesses and co-witness discussions in real eyewitnesses', *Psychology, Crime & Law*, 14: 513–21.

Terr, L.C. (1979) 'Children of Chowchilla: a study of psychic trauma', *The Psychoanalytic Study of the Child*, 34: 547–623.

Tuckey, M.R. and Brewer, N. (2003) 'The influence of schemas, stimulus ambiguity, and interview schedule on eyewitness memory over time', *Journal of Experimental Psychology: Applied*, 9: 101–18.

Warren, A., Hulse-Trotter, K. and Tubbs, E.C. (1991) 'Inducing resistance to suggestibility in children', *Law and Human Behavior*, 15: 273–85.

Williamson, P., Weber, N. and Robertson, M.T. (2013) 'The effect of expertise on memory conformity: a test of informational influence', *Behavioral Sciences and the Law*, 31: 607–23.

Wright, D., London, K. and Waechter, M. (2009) 'Social anxiety moderates memory conformity in adolescents', *Applied Cognitive Psychology*, 24: 1034–45.

Wright, G. and Goodwin, P. (2009) 'Decision making and planning under low levels of predictability: enhancing the scenario method', *International Journal of Forecasting*, 25: 813–25.

Wright, R.L. and Conrad, C.D. (2008) 'Enriched environment prevents chronic stress-induced spatial learning and memory deficits', *Behavioural Brain Research*', 187: 41–7.

Yuille, J.C. and Cutshall, J.L. (1986) 'A case study of eyewitness memory of a crime', *Journal of Applied Psychology*, 75: 268–73.

53

False memories

Sue Palmer-Conn

Introduction

What is a false memory? It is a recollection that seems real in one's mind but is fabricated in part or in whole. Most people have examples of false memories, for example a child may believe they had been grounded for the first time for not washing the dishes at the age of 12, but is later told by their mother it was due to rudeness, and that they had been grounded before. Most false memories are not malicious or even intentionally hurtful. They are shifts or reconstructions of memory that do not align with the true events. However, some false memories can have significant consequences, including in legal, forensic or police settings where a false memory may convict someone wrongfully.

False memory

Memories are complex, subject to change, are malleable and often unreliable. Human memory is an imperfect archive of an individual's experience and thus it is important to distinguish *false memory* from *memory fallibility*. Examples of memory fallibility are so commonplace that juries are instructed on how to interpret sworn testimony.

Although witnesses are told 'to tell the truth, the whole truth and nothing but the truth', they can only testify to the best of their recollections. Juries are instructed to decide what truth probability to assign to testimony in reaching a verdict, known as *credibility determination*. The law, as well as researchers, understands memory fallibility in terms of erosion of memory through forgetting, as, without using notes or recordings, individuals can only retrieve a fraction of their experiences as time passes. In contrast, *false memory* refers to circumstances in which individuals are possessed of positive, definite memories of events that did not actually happen to them; for example, a witness may 'recall' seeing a defendant standing behind a victim just before a stabbing when in fact the witness saw them on separate occasions, or testifies they saw a knife in the defendant's hand when it was a hairbrush. This form of false memory is one of errors of commission rather than omission.

Creation of false memories

False memories are created in several ways. Each affects what is changed about the memory or how it is stored. It may be hard to know which of these issues caused a false memory, but knowing the cause can ultimately help psychologists understand why false memories are so common. *Inference, or suggestion*, is a powerful force. For example, an individual may create new false memories through someone else's prompting or by the questions they are asked, for example, someone may ask a witness if the bank robber was wearing a red mask. The witness may agree, then quickly change their mind to say it was black. In truth, the robber wasn't wearing a mask, but the suggestion they were wearing one planted a memory that was not real in the mind of the witness. Police questioning techniques have frequently, in the past, been responsible for creating false memories by asking leading questions. If a witness cannot remember information, they are more likely to respond as though they do rather than say they cannot remember (Lamb and Fauchier, 2001).

It is possible to be fed improper or *false information* about an event and be convinced that it actually did occur. A new memory could be created, or the false information could combine with real memories to produce artificial ones which are very convincing. A witness presented with physical evidence that they may have not previously encountered can make the evidence seem (falsely) familiar when they are subsequently questioned about it. In a way, the brain is like a computer, storing what it is given. If bad information is given, it stores bad information. The gaps left in a memory may be filled in later with the individual's own *created recollections*. For example, if the light at the scene of a crime was not good, but there was only one witness, the witness may unwittingly fill in the gaps from what they would have expected to happen. In a memory, it is possible to *combine elements* of different events into a singular one. When the memory is subsequently recalled, while the events actually happened, the timeline is jumbled with an assortment of events that now form a singular memory in the mind.

The emotions of the moment may have a significant impact on how and what is stored as a memory. *Negative emotions*, such as fear or anger, lead to more false memories than positive or neutral emotions. An example of this, is if there was a weapon, or at least the witness *thought* there was a weapon at the robbery, the witness may only remember the negative facts and could create the rest unintentionally (Storebeck and Clore, 2005). *False memory* is a matter of serious concern for applied domains such as law, policing and forensic psychology as misled subjects do not often change their answers to misleading questions when given the opportunity to do so. This is due to their confidence that their answers were right and conviction of the correctness of their answer actually increases with time, known as the *false-memory sleeper effect*. This suggests that the nature of an interviewer's language and the form of the questions posed can powerfully distort memory reports in both children and adults.

Assessing memories

A major problem for forensic research is that it is difficult to assess the falsifiability of witnesses' memories in actual legal cases as it is not normally possible to know the precise events that happened and, therefore, researchers are dependent on witnesses' memory reports for a record of the events. This means it is almost impossible to accurately say which memory reports are true or false unless the reports can be confirmed by unimpeachable physical evidence. Asking a witness to recall information in different temporal orders is a key feature of investigative interviewing in an attempt to get a more complete picture of an event. However, the suggestibility of memory is easily affected by police interviewing techniques if leading questions are involved.

Despite the availability of forensic evidence, this does not always guarantee a conviction. Imagine if a set of fingerprints were lifted off the counter after a bank robbery. Although this might appear to be compelling evidence, what if the suspect claims they were at the bank earlier in the day to change some money? Even if the teller does not remember this, it is no proof that the suspect is lying. The suspect would have to also be identified by the bank teller as being the robber. Identification is easier if there is some distinguishing mark or if the suspect is well known to the teller. Other than this, an investigation is reliant on a teller's memory, which may be impacted by false memory, and indeed the teller might remember the suspect from earlier in the day but because of the emotional aspect of being held up have transferred their memory across two time slots.

Potential consequences of false memory

During the course of criminal investigations, witnesses or victims who report events that did not happen, or people or objects that were not present, can steer investigations in wrong directions or cause other evidence to be misinterpreted. In the worst-case scenario, it can cause innocent people to be treated as suspects and can even lead to their prosecution and conviction. The process of trying to establish guilt can mean the truly guilty go free and incriminating evidence can be lost. With adult witnesses, there are two areas of criminal investigation in which false memory phenomena are most pertinent: witness interviews and eyewitness identification of suspects via photographic spreads or multi-person line-ups. False memory events have a high probability in both cases. In some instances, this has resulted in convicting defendants who were certainly innocent because they were later exonerated on the basis of DNA evidence. A particular type of false memory report, false confession, has been shown to be responsible for implicating defendants in 14 per cent of cases while false identification due to false memory occurs in 55 per cent of cases (Johnson, 2006).

The misinformation paradigm shows that post-event memory suggestions can impair the contents of a witness's memory report in two basic ways: by lowering their ability to recognise or recall actual events; or by elevating their tendency to recognise or recall misinformation as if it was an actual experience. Suppose, however, that the person was a suspect, not a witness. In the same way, post-event suggestions can create a false memory leading to a false confession, especially if the memory leads to self-incrimination. This is even more serious than false identification by a witness which might lead to a conviction of an innocent person. Self-incriminating false memory reports leading to false confessions are seen as guilty pleas. Such implanting of false memories through police interviewing has led to an overhaul of interviewing techniques in an attempt to stamp this out (Inbau et al, 2001). This is particularly important as jurors place such a high weight on the importance of confessions, a weighting which far exceeds the reliability of such evidence.

Eyewitness identifications are central to the prosecution of some of the most serious types of crime – armed robbery, drug sales, rape, shootings – and without confessions such cases often cannot be prosecuted without positive identification of suspects by victims or witnesses. However, even under the most favourable conditions, high false-positive identification is common in 57 per cent of cases, even when the actual culprit was absent from the identification task, and 27 per cent of the time when the actual culprit was present when the suspect was unknown to the witness (Scoboria et al, 2017). If a witness believes that the suspect is present in the identification event, they will pick someone out who most closely matches the memory of the person they think committed the crime. Putting witnesses under such pressure is bound to affect their ability to recognise a suspect.

False memories may be an element of one or more factors involved in normal memory: storage, retrieval, forgetting. Storage factors would include exposure time, weapon focus, stress and the influence of drugs or alcohol. Any of these factors can interfere with accurate storage, making post-event interference more likely. There are other biases which might also affect storage, such as cross-race and gender bias where individuals are more likely to remember people of the same race and gender to themselves. Retrieval factors are variables that may be present at the time of the identification event, including level of confidence. If a witness feels confident in their memory of events, especially if their memory fits in with the gist of their experience, they are more likely to feel their recall is accurate. However, research shows a low correlation between confidence and accuracy. This has led to an overhaul in the way identification events are run. All line-ups must be fair, so that the foils are similar in appearance to the suspect; the general descriptions given by witnesses should be used to select foils, rather than a random method.

Forgetting is a common factor in memory research. Memory fades fastest in the time immediately following an event. Therefore, a high premium should be placed on the golden hour, the first hour following the event, to gather as much witness information as possible. A few hours can make a bigger difference than a few days and therefore it is important to obtain accurate identifications as quickly as possible after the event, especially if the suspect has been retained in custody at the crime scene.

False memory and childhood sexual abuse

A chapter on false memory would not be complete without reference to some of the highly contentious false memories of children pertaining to childhood sexual abuse cases. Child sexual abuse rarely leaves physical evidence and therefore the burden of proof falls on the child's retrieval of memories from a time in their life which they believe was traumatic. Interviewing techniques for vulnerable witnesses have been adapted to interviewing child witnesses. Child witnesses are more susceptible to suggestion, especially if the person they are talking to is a trusted adult like a parent or teacher, who may suspect abuse for other reasons. Storage, retrieval and forgetting factors in children's memory interact with age, with younger children being more susceptible to suggestion effects. A major problem with younger children is if they are asked the same question more than once they assume they have given a wrong answer first time. Victims of abuse are also often told 'not to tell' or threatened with retribution if they do tell, making them more vulnerable to suggestive questioning at interview. Using a cognitive interview approach, adapted for children, is the best protocol to achieve the most accurate outcomes.

Summary

In summary, normal memory is subject to fallibility of retrieval. Under circumstances of stressful situations for both adults and children, this fallibility may result in false memory formation due to inappropriate questioning in interviews. Achieving best evidence is done by using a cognitive interviewing approach which will aid memory retrieval rather than implant false information.

References

Inbau, F., Reid, J. and Buckley, J. (2001) *Criminal Interrogations and Confessions* (5th edn), New York: Jones & Bartlett Learning.

Johnson, M.K. (2006) 'Memory and reality', *American Psychologist*, 61: 760–71.

Lamb, M. and Fauchier, A. (2001) 'The effects of question type on self-contradictions by children in the course of forensic interviews', *Applied Cognitive Psychology*, 5(1), 483–49, DOI: https://doi.org/10.1002/acp.726.

Scoboria, A. Wade, K.A., Lindsay, D.S., Azad, T., Strange, D., Ost, J. and Hyman, I.E. (2017) 'A meta-analysis of memory reports from eight peer-reviewed false memory implantation studies', *Memory*, 25(2): 146–63, DOI: https://doi.org/10.1080/09658211.2016.1260747.

Storebeck, J. and Clore, G. (2005) 'With sadness comes accuracy; with happiness, false memory: mood and the false memory effect', *Psychological Science*, 16(10): 785–91, DOI: https://doi.org/10.1111/j.1467-9280.2005.01615.x.

54

Expert evidence

Gary Macpherson

Introduction: wh~ ~rt evidence?

Expert e~ ~lly opinion evidence from an expert witness who, via training ~. ~e, assists the court or quasi-judicial body in reaching a decision by pro~ ~g independent evidence-based knowledge in the form of a report or opinion in court, or after trial but before sentencing, or acts as advisor to opposing legal counsel. Expert evidence differs from ordinary witness testimony by allowing the expression of opinion rather than evidence of witness to the fact. For expert evidence to be allowed in legal proceedings it has to be both relevant and admissible to the specific case. Relevance is determined by the value of the evidence in any given case. Admissibility is whether the evidence can be heard by the court.

The recent ruling by the UK's Supreme Court in *Kennedy* v *Cordia* recognised the wish of the courts to regulate expert evidence and offered guidance regarding the admissibility of expert evidence and the responsibilities of the court in relation to such evidence (Supreme Court, 2016). The ruling set out four considerations governing the admissibility of expert evidence in the UK. An expert should be able to answer yes to all four of these questions:

- Will the expert evidence assist the court in its task?
- Does the expert have the necessary knowledge and experience?
- Is the expert impartial in presentation and assessment of the evidence?
- Is there a reliable body of knowledge or experience to underpin the expert's evidence?

The ruling emphasised that an expert must be able to provide impartial, unbiased, objective evidence, properly researched and supported by literature and professional guidelines, on matters within their field of expertise, and matters outwith the knowledge and experience to be expected of the ordinary person.

Experts should not simply select important papers to justify an opinion but should bring to the attention of the court *all* relevant material. The expert should also assist the court by explaining any technical terms, and literature referenced in a report should support the opinion advanced by the expert. The UK government also developed standards to improve the quality of expert evidence by setting minimum criteria that an expert must meet in order to be appointed by the court. These practice directions or Criminal Procedure Rules

(2019) focus on the duties of an expert to the court and are available in similar guises for experts in civil and family proceedings.

Who is an expert?

There is no set of rules or guidelines that defines an expert. A common misperception is that a professional 'becomes' an expert via a professional qualification or by attending a specific training course. However, the court, rather than a professional body, determines whether an individual is an expert, and the judge is the gatekeeper of whether or not expert testimony is allowable.

The legal guidance from the Crown Prosecution Service (CPS, 2019) defines an expert as an individual 'able furnish the court with information which is likely to be outside the experience and the knowledge of a judge or jury' (Criminal Practice Direction V Evidence 19A Expert Evidence). The British Psychological Society (BPS) Expert Witness Advisory Group guidance offers useful suggestions on the practical, ethical and legal issues than can arise while serving as an expert in the UK (BPS, 2021). The BPS guidance defines an expert witness as 'a person who through special training, study or experience, is able to furnish the court, tribunal, or oral hearing with scientific or technical information which is likely to be outside the experience and knowledge of a judge, magistrate, convenor or jury'. That is to say, an expert is an individual who has the relevant skills or knowledge, achieved through research, experience or professional application, to allow them to give independent and impartial opinion that may assist the court.

The main difference between an expert witness and an ordinary witness or 'witness to the fact' is that the expert witness is able to provide an opinion, whereas the ordinary witnesses can only give factual evidence based on what they have witnessed. The duty of an expert is to help the court by giving an opinion which is objective and unbiased in relation to matters within their expertise. This duty overrides any obligation to the party from whom the expert is receiving instructions. The general rule for expert evidence to be admissible is that the issues concern matters outside the experience and knowledge of the court but also evidence which gives the court assistance in forming its conclusions. The court is not bound to accept the evidence of an expert and can exclude the expert's evidence in certain circumstances, for example, when evidence deals with matters that are for a judge to decide on or if, from the facts of the case, the judge can form his or her own conclusion without the assistance of an expert. The court also has the power to reject evidence that is otherwise admissible, for example, if it decides that an expert has not established independence or has not complied with the overriding duty to the court, or that the evidence is not beyond the understanding of the layperson. That is to say, if the expert is seeking to advance an opinion which is not relevant to the issue in the case or which might be deemed common sense and on which the jury could reach its own conclusions, then the opinion of an expert would be inadmissible.

The latest survey of members of the BPS conducted by the Expert Witness Advisory Group (2021) noted that less than two thirds of experts surveyed reported receiving specific training in working as an expert witness. This is surprising given the challenging environment and complexity of this role in the adversarial setting. The survey found that 90 per cent of those who responded would have liked to have received training. The survey also highlighted that almost all respondents identified the most important factor in achieving best evidence was a high-quality report, answering the instruction, an objective assessment and referring to a scientific evidence base when forming an opinion.

There is also a type of witness referred to as a professional witness, whose remit can cross the boundary of both fact and opinion. Professional witnesses are generally formal employees of one party, for example, an National Health Service psychologist giving evidence about progress of a patient to a tribunal or a psychologist employed by HM Prison Service giving evidence on a prisoner at a hearing. Professional witnesses owe a duty to the court in the same way as expert witnesses.

One further issue is whether police officers can give expert opinions. In *R v Hodges* (2003) EWCA Crim 290, the evidence of a police officer with years of experience in the investigation of drugs offences and using knowledge acquired from informants and arrested suspects was admissible as expert evidence in relation to the issue of the normal manner of supply of an illicit substance and the street value and quantity of the substance for personal usage. The evidence from the police officer was deemed relevant and admissible by the judge as expert evidence based on the probative value of the evidence in the specific case.

Expert evidence in the courtroom

Courtrooms are formal settings with their own rules and procedures, and an outsider may be surprised to discover that establishing truth is not the primary function of the court. An effective expert has to become familiar with these rules. Remote hearings conducted via live remote web links follow exactly the same processes. Within Europe, courts employ an inquisitorial method of trial in the absence of a jury. The courts in the nations of the UK are adversarial, that is to say, two sides opposed to each other, and the expert must understand that they will be a participant in a process in which their credentials, objectivity and expertise will be scrutinised by legal counsel less concerned with establishing the truth than with asserting the position of their client.

One issue that experts in psychology find challenging is the court's duty to deal in absolutes. Psychologists undertaking comprehensive assessments in complex cases commonly produce psychological formulations. Firstly, there may be tensions between the extent to which the formulation of the issues is focused on assisting the client versus an objective analysis for the court as the client. Secondly, difficulties arise with the professional preference for formulations rather than the courts' wish for an absolute in the form of a diagnosis. Thirdly, the courts use their own terminology and an expert cannot assume that 'abnormality of mind' or 'fitness to plead' have the same meaning in psychology as in law. Finally, legal concepts differ within the courts of the nations comprising the UK and so an expert must become familiar not only with the jargon but with the legal jurisdiction where such concepts are applied.

Three phases of oral expert evidence

As far as evidence giving in an adversarial court is concerned, there are three main phases. Firstly, there is examination-in-chief or direct examination of the expert witness. This is usually conducted by the party for whom the witness is appearing. This can be straightforward and usually based on the content of an expert's written report. The legal counsel will use the information from the report which supports the case in as clear, concise and convincing a manner as possible, and elicit from the expert agreement with the report in oral evidence for the benefit of the court. Examination-in-chief is made easier by a high-quality report and familiarity with the scientific evidence base contained in the report and the conclusions of the report.

The second phase is cross-examination, which follows immediately after examination-in-chief and is conducted by the opposing counsel. Cross-examination is the legal means of evaluating the merits of the evidence on a continuum from polite probing to full-frontal critique of an expert's methods and opinions. Cross-examination is designed to reveal inconsistencies, weaknesses and misinterpretations. Cross-examination may also aim at reducing an expert's credibility, and by extension, the credibility of the expert's evidence.

Finally, and only if necessary, the third phase is a re-examination of the main points of evidence. This stage is designed to reinforce or to correct any issues arising from cross-examination. Re-examination is carried out by the legal counsel who called the expert. The aim is to emphasise the central points of evidence and the features important for the court and correct any errors or misperceptions which may have emerged during cross-examination. Judges can and do interrupt any phase in order to clarify testimony to assist themselves or the jury in understanding the expert's evidence. In some cases, the process may be repeated, for example, an examination of the facts or voir dire in the absence of a jury followed by a trial with a jury.

Psychologists are not normally permitted to give evidence about how an ordinary person is likely to react to stressful situations. Expert psychological evidence is generally only accepted when the issue to be determined goes beyond the experience of members of the jury. For example, where the defence in a criminal trial raises the defence of diminished responsibility to a charge of murder, an expert in clinical psychology may offer an opinion on whether an accused person suffers from a mental disorder or qualifying condition, and on whether the mental disorder was present at the relevant time. The jury then determine the relative contribution of the abnormality and whether the condition substantially impaired the behaviour of the accused or reduces responsibility for the crime. That is to say, the expert offers opinion evidence of mental disorder, but the ultimate issue of whether the mental disorder is the basis of a substantial impairment of ability to determine or control the acts of the accused is for the jury to decide. Similarly, psychologists are not normally permitted to give evidence on a witness's memory as matters of credibility and reliability are for the court and the jury. However, when matters of memory fall outside the knowledge and experience to be expected of the jury, as in for example childhood amnesia and 'recovered' memories, then evidence may be accepted by the court if the evidence is a highly specialist nature and there is a recognised body of science underpinning the evidence. There is also increasing recognition by the courts of the importance and evidential value of psychologists' expert opinions of an accused person's competence to stand trial, once solely the preserve of psychiatrists and the ubiquitous 'fitness to plead' court report.

Conclusions

Expert evidence can be beneficial to the courts but must follow the basic principles and rules for expert witnesses. This chapter provides an outline of what constitutes expert evidence, who is an expert, and the importance of providing expert testimony in an honest, trustworthy, objective and impartial manner in the adversarial settings of the UK courts. There are many evidential rules governing the admissibility use and scope of expert evidence in both criminal and civil trials. Some recent procedural developments include 'hot-tubbing' or corralling expert witnesses together to reach a decision, or 'court-appointed experts', approved by both parties to assist the court in helping determine the parties' dispute. Regardless of the relative merits and flaws of these developments, expert witnesses should continue to provide impartial, unbiased, objective evidence, properly researched and supported by literature and professional guidelines, on the matters within their field of expertise, as a duty owed to the courts.

References

BPS (British Psychological Society) (2021) *Psychologists as expert witnesses: Guidelines and procedure* (5th edn), [online] Available from: https://www.bps.org.uk/guideline/psychologists-expert-witnesses [Accessed 22 April 2021].

CPS (Crown Prosecution Service) (2019) 'Expert evidence', [online] Available from: https://www.cps.gov.uk/legal-guidance/expert-evidence#:~:text=Expert%20evidence%20is%20admissible%20to,V%20Evidence%2019A%20Expert%20Evidence [Accessed 22 April 2021].

Craig, L.A. and the Expert Witness Advisory Group (EWAG) (2021) 'Psychologists as expert witnesses: survey results from the Expert Witness Advisory Group WAG)', *Journal of Forensic Practice*, 23(2): 77–89.

Criminal Procedure Rules (2019) 'Part 19: expert evidence', [online] Available from: https://www.cps.gov.uk/legal-guidance/expert-evidence [Accessed 22 April 2021].

Supreme Court (2016) *Kennedy (Appellant)* v *Cordia (Services) LLP (Respondent)* (Scotland), UKSC 6, [online] Available from: https://www.supremecourt.uk/cases/uksc-2014-0247.html [Accessed 22 April 2021].

PART V

Conclusion

55

Contemporary and future concepts and debates in forensic psychology, crime and policing

Karen Corteen, Rachael Steele, Noel Cross and Michelle McManus

Introduction

This edited collection was put together during unprecedented times – COVID-19, a global life-threatening and life-taking pandemic. Therefore, it is fitting to conclude this edited collection with a reflection of the impact of COVID-19 on the areas explored in this text, namely forensic psychology, crime, criminal justice and policing. With regard to all these areas in the UK and globally, COVID-19 has forced upon people continuous, often life-altering changes, with little or no time to discuss, plan and agree how to live our day-to-day lives in this current world. It has impacted research inside and outside of academia, and the development of policies and delivery of services for forensic psychologists and criminal justice practitioners, including the police. It has also impacted the manner in which students studying in these areas are taught and trained, with much debate as to the advantages and disadvantages of remote learning. What is certain is that forensic psychology and the criminal justice system (CJS), including the police, are under more pressure than ever before. With those in these key services having worked tirelessly throughout the pandemic, with no signs of the intense demand decreasing any time soon or resources returning to 'normal' levels, there is a concern about the quality and sustainability of these services which are responsible for protecting the most vulnerable. The crises felt within all strands of the CJS, including the police, preceded the pandemic. They have just been further exacerbated by it (CJJI, 2021; Robins and Newman, 2021).

The CJS during and prior to the pandemic

The report by the Criminal Justice Joint Inspection (CJJI, 2021), published in January 2021, looked across the CJS, examining how it responded in the immediate aftermath of the first lockdown and how it has managed since then. The first national lockdown in England and Wales lasted from 23 March to 10 May 2020. Each criminal justice inspectorate, namely HM Inspectorate of Constabulary and Fire and Rescue Services, HM Crown Prosecution

Service Inspectorate, HM Inspectorate of Prisons and HM Inspectorate of Probation, conducted inspections of the response to COVID-19 in their respective agencies. The report discussed innovative practices across the CJS and the greatest risks 'facing the CJS as it continues to respond to and recover from the pandemic' (CJJI, 2021, p 6). The joint inspectorate found that regarding the CJS, all branches of it were affected by COVID-19. However, this did not mean that criminal justice paused, or stopped; as the CJJI (2021, p 5) report acknowledges, 'it could not', as crimes continued to be committed, individuals continued to be processed within the criminal justice and youth justice systems, and in both systems detainees remained in custody. Within the police, the Crown Prosecution Service, the courts, prisons and probation, a number of changes, both small and large, were necessary as a result of the pandemic. The impact of these changes was noted as 'clear and profound [and] not yet fully felt' (CJJI, 2021, p 5), with the subsequent backlog of cases in the Crown Court having 'ripple effects [...] on all parts of the system' (CJJI, 2021, p 5).

It is important to acknowledge that prior to the pandemic the CJS in England and Wales was already frail and 'suffering already from the best part of a decade of austerity' (Robin and Newburn, 2021, p 183). The CJJI (2021, pp 5–6) also recognised that the CJS 'was already excessively fragmented and under-resourced' and, subsequently, 'without considerable resourcing, planning and joint work' it would not be able to manage the significant challenges wrought by COVID-19. The CJJI (2021, p 6) report called 'on all agencies to work together to ensure the CJS can recover from the extreme pressures caused by COVID-19'. However, it also acknowledged that the government has a fundamental role to play by providing 'funding, time and access to expertise to allow the system to recover' (CJJI, 2021, p 6). This was echoed later in the March 2021 House of Lords Committee report on the impact of the coronavirus on courts and tribunals in England and Wales (UK Parliament, 2021).

Despite being hindered by previous challenges and failings on the part of government (such as a lack of funding for the CJS and legal aid, court closures, backlog of cases and prison overcrowding), the CJJI found that at the outset of the pandemic there was evidence of 'swift and sensible decision-making' across the system (CJJI, 2021, p 8). Also, across the system there was an acceleration of digital working and information sharing. One positive outcome was to ensure multi-agency child safeguarding arrangements continued through the use of virtual meetings. However, the positives of digital, remote working seem to be outweighed by the limitations, including an unequal digital playing field across society (digital poverty). This exacerbated issues of visibility in relation to children, young people and families, especially those living in poverty, who were effectively excluded in this move towards digital communication. Furthermore, the prison system was extremely slow in rolling out secure video-calling facilities to allow prisoners to remain in contact with families and friends (CJJI, 2021). The report notes that in prisoner surveys carried out from July to December

2020, 82 per cent of prisoners said that they had not engaged in a video call in the previous month.

The impact of the pandemic on prisons, prisoners and prison staff in England and Wales

Prior to the COVID-19 pandemic, it was already well established that prisoners suffer much higher rates of illness that the general population, with very poor access to healthcare. When the COVID-19 pandemic was declared in March 2020, overnight 'prisons became a key public health concern for governments' (DLA Piper, 2020, p 3). This was especially so for prisons that were overcrowded and/or had poor ventilation, hygiene and sanitation, as they are 'known to act as a source of infection, amplification and spread of infectious diseases' (DLA Piper, 2020, p 4). In response to this, within England and Wales it was deemed necessary in order to 'keep prisoners safe from COVID-19, prisoners are being locked in their cells for 90% of the day'. This subsequently led to 'a decline in their mental and physical health and a rise in drug taking and self-harm' (Portal, 2021). As one inmate told inspectors, 'it's being imprisoned while you're in prison'. Other prisoners conveyed to inspectors that they felt like 'caged animals' (Portal, 2021). Furthermore, in response to the pandemic, gyms were closed and family visits, education classes and intervention work were all suspended. During the short periods that prisoners were allowed out of their cells, they had to 'cram [in] daily tasks, such as showers and exercise' (Portal, 2021).

The effects of being locked up for an average of 22.5 hours a day are worsened when prisoners are 'doubled up' – this means a cell designed for one person is occupied by two people (Portal, 2021). Lockdown also meant that prisoners were required to eat their meals in their cells, where there are sometimes unscreened or uncovered toilets (though this was the case in some prisons before the pandemic). Prisons are 'at a point of absolute crisis' (governor of an adult men's jail, cited in Portal, 2021). Increasing numbers of positive COVID cases among prisoners and staff, and a sizable number of staff self-isolating, meant that it became more and more difficult to fulfil even the basic tasks. Prison officers were having to work long hours to fill the basic gaps and needs in provision. Thus, it was not only prisoners who were suffering mentally and physically, so too were prison staff. Prisoner and prison officer resilience was being eroded as the restrictions continued far beyond the beginning of the pandemic and the first lockdown. This is an inhumane situation that cannot continue. Prison reductionism, prison abolitionism or reserving imprisonment for the most serious and violent offending in practice, not in theory, are potential solutions. Such solutions will not be easy or quick to achieve, and they will need political, economic and social will, as well as changes in cultural attitudes towards prisoners and imprisonment in order to be achieved. Such changes will also entail envisioning radical transformative 'non-penal alternatives' (see Malloch, 2017, p 152). Although this may seem utopian, 'real' utopias can be 'a way of imagining things "other-wise"' (Malloch, 2017, p 154).

Another potential solution – that was implemented fairly promptly to reduce the overcrowded and unsafe prison population – is the early release of prisoners. In April 2020, two early release schemes were introduced in England and Wales. However, the scheme had very little impact. Although many prisoners were assessed as suitable for release and referred to HM Prison and Probation Service for consideration, only 316 prisoners were released. Also, England and Wales (together with Italy, Poland, Washington (US) and Guatemala) imposed the most restrictive conditions on released prisoners in the world, in that released prisoners had to submit to electronic monitoring 'for the duration of their release' (DLA Piper, 2020, p 31). This was a 'fundamental condition in the COVID-19 release schemes' in the jurisdictions mentioned above, including England and Wales (DLA Piper, 2020, p 31). The global research conducted by global law firm DLA Piper also found that England and Wales imposed a further condition which 'appear[s] unreasonable and unjustified', as under 'the terms of those COVID-19 release schemes, released prisoners were prohibited from contacting media or using social media to upload and download any material. This measure raises concerns with respect to freedom of expression and other civil rights' (DLA Piper, 2020, p 32). DLA Piper (2020) explain, the End of Custody Temporary Release Scheme in England was criticised for being too complex and so difficult to explain and understand that it was almost impossible to implement. Finally, in respect of prisons in England and Wales, prisoners struggled with their mental health and lack of support during COVID-19 upon release. This happened because support was provided only over the phone, with many prisoners struggling with this style of communication (Portal, 2021). Released individuals also had to prebook appointments with their probation officer, which reduced the frequency of appointments and opportunities to check in.

The impact of the pandemic on the courts in England and Wales

On 30 March 2021 the House of Lords Committee published a report on the impact of the coronavirus on courts and tribunals in England and Wales. A key finding was that reduced funding for the CJS left 'courts and tribunals in a vulnerable condition' when entering the pandemic crisis (UK Parliament, 2021). In the decade before the pandemic, court buildings began to be closed and there was a radical reduction in the budgets for legal aid: '[the] legal aid scheme has been cut to the bone' (Robins and Newman, 2021, p 4). In 2010 the Conservative and Liberal Democratic coalition government initiated a programme of austerity, and between 2010 and 2013 they drastically cut public spending. The resultant pains and struggles are still being felt inside and outside of the CJS. It is noted that these 'pre-existing challenges exacerbated the devastating impact of the pandemic on courts and tribunals in England and

Wales' (UK Parliament, 2021). The CJS is experiencing court backlogs, and the future survival of criminal legal aid firms are hanging in the balance as legal aid payments have not been increased for 20 years. Robins and Newton (2021, p 5) comment that '[d]efence lawyers have not had a pay rise for over two decades and had an 8.75 percent fee cut foisted on them in 2014'. The Criminal Bar Association states that barristers have suffered an average decrease of 28 per cent in earnings since 2006, with juniors recording a median income below the minimum wage (Boon, 2022).

As a result of court backlogs, defendants, complainants and witnesses are being denied timely justice. Adaptions have had to be made in practice. Technology has enabled remote hearings, but the impact across the court services has not been equally felt. Also, consideration has to be given to vulnerable people who may not have the ability to use such technology and/or who may not have access to it. Another key finding was that the 'human cost of the backlog can be measured in part by defendants being held on remand in prison for longer, litigants and victims waiting longer justice, and a greater likelihood of evidence being lost or forgotten during the lengthier waits for a hearing' (UK Parliament, 2021). In order to address the problems preceding the pandemic, and as a result of the pandemic, investment on the part of the government is called for; there is much work to be done to address the constitutional consequences of the pandemic for the courts. The government needs to renew its vision and increase the funding to achieve it. For justice to be done, and be seen to be done, considerable new effort and investment is required (Baroness Taylor, Chair of the Constitution Committee, cited in UK Parliament, 2021).

The impact of the pandemic on crime and policing

The research strongly suggests that the COVID-19 pandemic played an important part in changes to police-recorded crime rates in England and Wales in the first few months of 2020. Crimes such as theft and burglary showed sharp declines in incidence that have only partially been reversed in the time since then, since people spent much more time at home and non-essential shops closed, meaning that access to, and opportunities for, criminal behaviour were significantly reduced. All offence types apart from drugs offences and anti-social behaviour fell below expected levels in terms of police recording during this period. It would be wrong, however (as Langton et al, 2021, admit themselves), to accept these data as being an entirely accurate picture of crime in the COVID-19 era. Increases in drugs offences, for example, could have been caused by proactive police action made possible by having to spend less time on other, property-related offences, or by such offences simply being more visible in public spaces which were far more sparsely populated than they would normally be. Also, although Langton et al (2021) report a decline in police-recorded violence during the pandemic, the number of calls to and contacts with the

National Domestic Abuse Helpline increased by 34 per cent between April and December, calls to the LGBTQIA+ Helpline run by Galop increased by 36 per cent over the same time period, and domestic abuse killings in the first 21 days of the first lockdown were double the total of an average period in the past decade (Oppenheim, 2021). Nonetheless, changes in individual opportunities to commit crime, shaped by social factors such as lockdowns, are clearly visible in recent crime statistics. Another example of this is the rise in public order offences in summer 2020, as the night-time economy reopened and opportunities for alcohol consumption increased, with people seemingly making up for time not spent with family and friends.

It also seems clear that the current government Conservative government of the time, under Boris Johnson, had taken the opportunity of the changing social landscape under COVID-19 to increase police powers to limit public gatherings, for the purposes of protest or otherwise. A series of regulations (the most recent at the time of writing, comprised the Health Protection (Coronavirus, Restrictions) (Steps) (England Regulations 2021) give police powers to disperse public gatherings believed to be in contravention of COVID-19 restrictions, to order those present to go home, to use 'reasonable' force to remove anyone from the scene or to issue fixed penalty notices of up to £10,000, which can lead to prosecution if not paid. The stated principle of policing by consent throughout the pandemic using the 4Es: 'educate, explain, encourage, and enforce' (Newiss and Charman, 2021) seem to contradict the policy around COVID-19 restrictions. Police powers were extended even further by the 2022 Police, Crime Sentencing and Courts Act, which was enacted on 28 April. This wide-ranging piece of legislation includes police powers to place conditions on protests (even protests involving only one person) as a response to 'the noise generated by persons taking part' as well as to impose penalties on those breaching these conditions if they 'ought to have known' the conditions were in place. The Act also includes a new offence of 'intentionally or recklessly causing public nuisance' where someone causes 'serious annoyance', 'serious inconvenience' or simply creates a risk of such behaviours occurring. The maximum penalty for this offence, which largely duplicates other offences of this type in criminal law, is ten years' imprisonment if the case is heard in the Crown Court. Another offence involves causing damage to statues or memorials, which again has a maximum penalty of ten years' imprisonment – twice as long as the maximum penalty for grievous bodily harm without intent under section 20 of the Offences against the Person Act 1861. The link between this offence, which targets behaviour normally dealt with as criminal damage, and the media-sensationalised incident of the statue of the slave trader Edward Colston being pulled down in Bristol by Black Lives Matter protestors in June 2020 is obvious. Such legislation is deliberately repressive and overtly targeted at politically informed protests against the state, which uses the COVID pandemic as a rationale for reducing civil liberties, peaceful protest and human rights.

The impact of the pandemic on the most vulnerable members of society

One of the biggest concerns of the COVID-19 pandemic has been the significant immediate and long-term effects on the most vulnerable sections of society: children, domestic abuse victims, those being exploited by peers, and those suffering extreme poverty and isolation. What the most vulnerable individuals in England and Wales, and indeed globally, have been exposed to throughout the pandemic is unimaginable. Most will know the name of Arthur Labinjo-Hughes. His dreadful experience of lockdown shockingly highlighted the worst fears of many criminal justice, policing and safeguarding practitioners. Arthur was six years old. During the start of the pandemic (March 2020) he moved in with his father and his girlfriend. Within the home, they began to beat him, starve him and deprive him of water, often making him stand in the hallway for 14 hours a day. Despite concerns raised about bruises on Arthur's body by his grandmother, and visits from social workers and police in April 2020, no further action was taken, and Arthur was killed by his father's girlfriend in June 2020. Reflective of the horror after the deaths of Victoria Climbié in 2000, Baby P in 2007 and Daniel Pelka in 2021, both public inquires and serious case reviews have been undertaken and recommendations made with likely similar recommendations around better information sharing among police, social work teams and health practitioners. There are likely to be specific comments relating to COVID-19 restrictions, to the effect that this enabled the most severe forms of crime to escalate behind closed doors, while the invisibility of children in public spaces, at schools, clubs, activities, parks and shops, provided increased opportunities for these perpetrators. This is of further concern when the National Society for the Prevention of Cruelty to Children helpline in 2020/21 reported a 23 per cent increase in contacts from adults concerned about the well-being of a child – around 85,000 contacts.

As discussed by McManus and Ball (2020) within their article on adverse childhood experiences (ACEs) and COVID-19, while the ACEs framework (see Bellis et al, 2016) has been utilised in a move towards a trauma-informed approach within policing and the CJS by asking 'what has happened to you?', a similar individualised approach of trauma experience needs to be taken with COVID-19. Quite simply, there was not an equal playing field prior to COVID-19, with many adults and children becoming imprisoned within cycles of poverty, neglect and abuse, witnessing circumstances such as domestic abuse, substance misuse and mental health deterioration. Consequently, by enforcing home lockdowns, these adverse experiences are inadvertently intensified, with cases like Arthur Labinjo-Hughes and Star Hobson resulting in the most appalling murders. The most important lesson to be learned within the COVID-19 pandemic is visibility in protecting the most vulnerable from unspeakable crimes – visibility of frontline workers such as teachers able to monitor and flag concerns, as well as visibility of children out in the world, engaging with others. Furthermore, while the statement 'safeguarding is everyone's responsibility' is an agreed policy across all key safeguarding sectors, there is work to be done to buffer against the diffusion of responsibility currently visible, which is leaving a glaring gap in terms of which agency and whom within that agency owns safeguarding actions and responsibility. With a 16.7 vacancy rate for social workers (BASW, 2022), and the rise of additional issues such as county lines and child criminal exploitation through local drug running, the need to invest in consistent (permanent), joined-up multi-agency safeguarding teams has never been greater.

The pandemic and forensic psychology

The final area to be examined in this concluding chapter is forensic psychology. As a result of COVID-19, forensic psychologists have had to adapt their service delivery in order to maintain their core business as much as they can, and in order to deliver essential psychology services (PBNI, 2020). In Northern Ireland, within the Probation Board for Northern Ireland, the Psychology Department is a specialist forensic service whose main role is 'to provide psychologically informed opinion or advise with regard to a service user's offending behaviour' (PBNI, 2020). Working collaboratively with staff from across the organisation, the department consults on factors relating to individual users, such as mental health, risk or brain injury, to name a few. As with many practitioners and staff across a range of occupations, the forensic psychologists (and other staff within the service) were required to work from home. Thus, they had to consult with staff and complete initial assessments with service users via phone calls and video contact. Also, to continue to manage an individual's risk successfully via a multidisciplinary viewpoint, multi-agency meetings with partner agencies were conducted through tele- and video-conferencing. Due to the impact of the pandemic on individuals in relation to their mental health and issues relating to addiction, forensic psychologists, together with other services, teams and specialists, have provided additional support (PBNI, 2020).

Conclusions

To conclude, prior to the pandemic, forensic psychologists and criminal justice practitioners, including the police, were under pressure and in demand. This situation was exacerbated by COVID-19. In response, individuals working in forensic psychology and criminal justice showed great commitment, innovation and adaptation in order to continue to provide their vital services. This is to be commended. Despite such dedication and efforts, the pandemic has been hard-hitting and will have detrimental impacts for a long time to come. This is especially true for the families and friends who have lost loved ones inside and outside of the CJS as a result of COVID-19.

It is important to acknowledge that the 'same people who bear the brunt of the pandemic suffer disproportionately from austerity and a broken justice system'

(Robins and Newton, 2021, p 184). It is also a myth that COVID-19 is a 'great leveller' as its consequences are not the same for everyone. The discussions around the concept of 'build back better' also need to be approached with caution. So should the temptation to treat the pandemic as 'an opportunity to reset the justice debate' (Robins and Newton, 2021, p 184) and to fix the crisis in the CJS through interventions such as more police powers, bigger Nightingale courts (temporary courts in England and Wales introduced in response to COVID-19), digital and virtual working, remote justice, tele- and video-conferencing, limiting trial by jury, and telephone assessments and support. This is because to do so is to mystify or minimise the 'intractable structural problems that beset the justice system' (Robins and Newton, 2021, p 184). A more radical and courageous vision and approach is required regarding forensic psychology, crime and policing. For all its positives, negatives and even failures, the rapid response, flexibility and adaption to the pandemic on the part of practitioners, educators, trainers, 'service users', students and the public show that with the political, economic, cultural and social will this can be done.

References

BASW (British Association of Social Workers) (2022) 'Raising vacancy rate among children's social workers shows toll of COVID working, say BASW', [online] 22 February, Available from: https://www.basw.co.uk/resources/psw-magaz ine/psw-online/rising-vacancy-rate-among-childrens-social-workers-shows-toll [Accessed 11 July 2022].

Bellis, M.A., Ashton, K., Hughes, K., Ford, K., Bishop, J. and Paranjothy, S. (2016) 'Adverse childhood experiences (ACEs) in Wales and their impact on health in the adult population: Mariana Dyakova', *European Journal of Public Health*, 26(1), DOI: https://doi.org/10.1093/eurpub/ckw167.009.

Boon, A. (2022) 'Barristers on strike: why criminal lawyers are walking out – and what they really get paid', *The Conversation*, [online] 1 July, Available from: https://theconversation.com/barristers-on-strike-why-criminal-lawy ers-are-walking-out-and-what-they-really-get-paid-186008 [Accessed 11 July 2022].

CJJI (Criminal Justice Joint Inspection) (2021) 'Impact of the pandemic on the criminal justice system', [online] Available from: https://www.justiceinspec torates.gov.uk/cjji/wp-content/uploads/sites/2/2021/01/2021-01-13-State-of-nation_AccessibleVersion.pdf [Accessed 23 June 2021].

DLA Piper (2020) *A Global Analysis of Prisoner Release in Response to COVID-19*, December, [online] Available from: https://globcci.org/wp-content/ uploads/2021/06/Global-Analysis-of-Prisoner-Release-Due-to-COVID-19. pdf [Accessed 6 December 2022].

Langton, S., Dixon, A. and Farrell, G. (2021) 'Six months in: pandemic crime trends in England and Wales', *Crime Science*, 10(6): 1–16, [online] Available from: https://crimesciencejournal.biomedcentral.com/track/pdf/10.1186/s40 163-021-00142-z.pdf [Accessed 30 June 2021].

Malloch, M. (2017) 'Justice for women: a penal utopia', *Justice, Power and Resistance*, Foundation Volume (September 2016): 151–69, [online] Available from: https://dspace.stir.ac.uk/retrieve/f4e56fa1-6a2b-4bf3-948b-a0ebab79f716/Malloch%20%282016%29%20Justice%20for%20Women%20-%20A%20Penal%20Utopia.pdf [Accessed 20 December 2021].

McManus, M.A. and Ball, E. (2020) 'COVID-19 should be considered an adverse childhood experience (ACE)', *Journal of Community Safety and Well-Being*, 5(4), 164–7, DOI: https://doi.org/10.35502/jcswb.166.

Newiss, G. and Charman, S. (2021) 'Damned if they do, damned if they don't? Public sentiment towards the police during the first lock down', [online] Available from: https://blogs.lse.ac.uk/covid19/2021/02/16/damned-if-they-do-damned-if-they-dont-public-sentiment-towards-the-police-during-the-first-lockdown/ [Accessed 10 June 2022].

Oppenheim, M. (2021) '"Home became a prison": calls to national domestic abuse helpline soar by more than third in pandemic', *The Independent*, [online] 3 February, Available from: https://www.independent.co.uk/news/uk/home-news/domestic-abuse-rise-helpline-police-b1796937.html [Accessed 30 June 2021].

PBNI (Probation Board for Northern Ireland) (2020) 'Probation during COVID: forensic psychologist on delivering essential psychology services', [online] 7 July, Available from: https://www.pbni.org.uk/probation-during-covid-forensic-psychologist-on-delivering-essential-psychology-services/ [Accessed 22 June 2021].

Portal, G. (2021) 'COVID: prisoners like "caged animals" in lockdown jails', BBC News, [online] 11 February, Available from: https://www.bbc.co.uk/news/uk-55957048 [Accessed 23 June 2021].

Robins, J. and Newman, D. (2021) *Justice in a Time of Austerity: Stories from as System in Crisis*, Bristol: Bristol University Press.

UK Parliament (2021) 'Report published on the impact of COVID-19 on courts and tribunals in England and Wales', [online] 30 March, Available from: https://committees.parliament.uk/committee/172/constitution-committee/news/153596/report-published-on-the-impact-of-covid19-on-courts-and-tribunals-in-england-and-wales/ [Accessed 23 June 2021].

Index

Index

FCAMHS (Forensic Child and Adolescent Mental Health Service) 116–17
female genital mutilation 69, 91, 142
feminism
    feminist criminologies 100
    perspectives on sexual violence 143–4
Fielding, Henry 176
Finland 170, 172
Fisher, Sir Henry 215
Flanagan, Sir Ronnie 186
Floyd, George 99, 235, 269, 277
FMHS (Forensic Mental Health Services) 59, 60, 62–3
forced marriage 69, 91
Ford, K. 221
forensic psychology 3
    definition 17, 21
    future directions 83–7
    as multidisciplinary field 3, 4–6, 34
    new types of crime 84
    research and knowledge 7, 13–14
    routes to qualification 83–4
    studying and working in 6–7
    wide remit 3, 5, 7, 11, 17, 20, 21, 83
forensic science 103, 291, 319
    Forensic Science Regulation Bill 103
Foucault, M. 95, 135–6
Francis, Peter 265
Francis, Simeon 272
Freud, Sigmund 98
FSS (Forensic Science Service) 102, 103
Fyfe, N. 183

G

G and R (2003, UK) 110
Garland, D. 95
Garrow, William 93
gender-related issues
    1919 Sex Disqualification (Removal) Act 95
    CJS 164
    court system: gender inequality 164–5
    crime, criminal justice and 94–5
    criminal justice professions 95
    gender equality 95
    gender inequality 143, 144, 164
    gendered violence 143, 242, 243
    homicide 76–7, 242
    patriarchy 94, 143, 144
    police macho culture 278, 280
    reading NVC 257
    women in the police force 95, 278

    see also women
genocide 122
George, Barry 326
Germany 115, 122, 169
Giordano, P.C. 56
global crime 85–6
globalisation 181, 183
    globalisation crimes 123–4
Goldin-Meadow, S. and Alibali, M.W. 258
Green, Ava 46, 312–17
green crime see environmental crime
Greenall, Paul V. 59–64, 73–7
Grubb, A.R. and Harrower, J. 36
Gudjonsson, G.H. 312–13, 320

H

Hadfield, James 59
Halford, Eric 147–53, 241–50
Hall, J.A. 258
Hamby, S. 141, 142–3, 144
Hare, R. 65, 66, 67
Harrison, Michael 277
Hart, S.D. 158
hate crime 7, 13–14, 189
HCPC (Health and Care Professions Council) 6–7, 21
Hesketh, Robert 65–8, 78–82
Hester, M. 143
Hewitt, Sir Martin 266
hijacking 85, 86
Hillsborough inquiry 198
Hirst, W. 327–8
HM Inspectorate of Constabulary 80
HM Prison and Probation Service 80, 344
    forensic psychologist and 6, 12, 83
    nationalisation 126, 130
    privatisation 106, 126, 130
    probation officer's role 106
    risk assessment 6, 12
HMICFRS (HM Inspectorate of Constabulary and Fire and Rescue Services) 246, 247, 248, 343–4
    'Policing and mental health: picking up the pieces' 252, 254
Hobson, Star 349
Holdaway, Simon 198
Home Office (UK) 165, 200, 214, 244
    2003 Sexual Offences Act 80
    investigative interviewing 298
    MASHs (Multi-Agency Safeguarding Hubs) 222